STAR TREK®

THE ORIGINAL MOTION PICTURE ADAPTATION

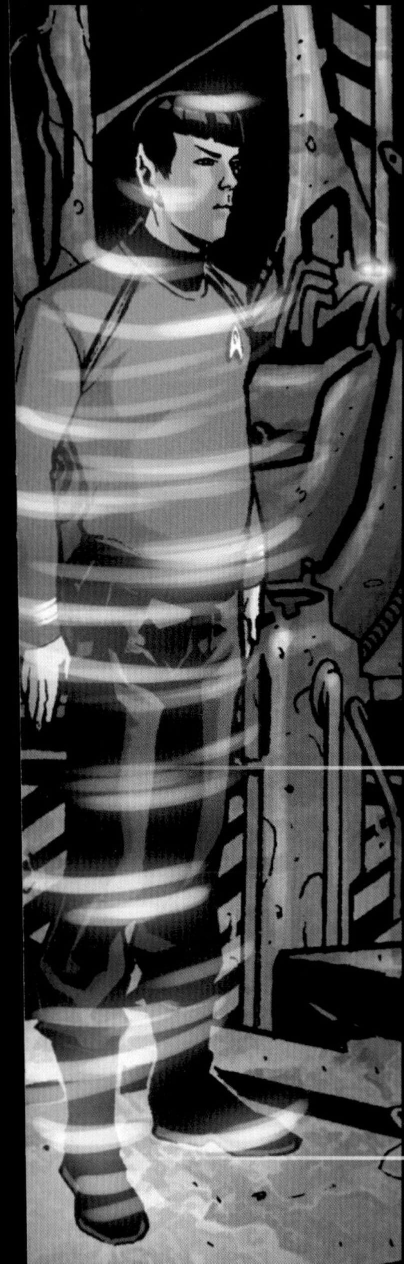

Based on the screenplay by
ROBERTO ORCI, ALEX KURTZMAN

Adaptation by
MIKE JOHNSON, TIM JONES

Pencils by
DAVID MESSINA, CLAUDIA BALBONI

Inks by
GAETANO CARLUCCI

Colors by
GIOVANNA NIRO, NEIL UYETAKE

Edited by
JUSTIN EISINGER

GOLD KEY: THE VOODOO PLANET

Writer
DICK WOOD

Artist
ALBERTO GIOLITTI

INTRODUCING...

STAR TREK®

THE 2009 MOTION PICTURE ADAPTATION

After over forty years of feature films, television episodes, comic books, novels and videogames, the 2009 *STAR TREK* movie was the science fiction saga's most radical reinvention to date.

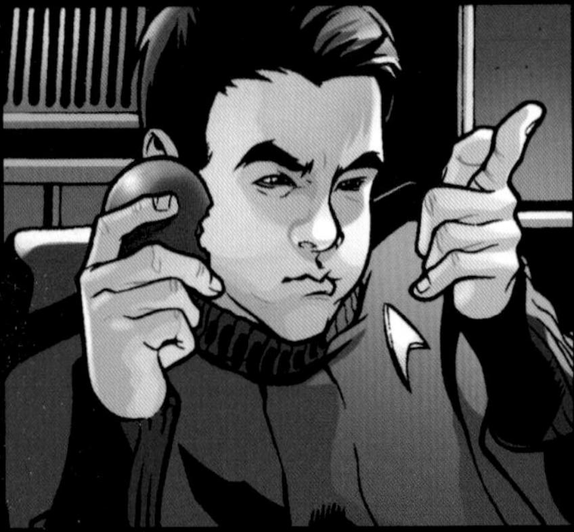

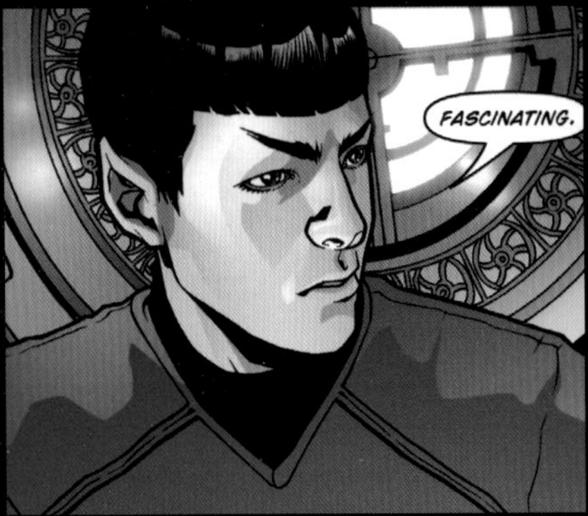
FASCINATING.

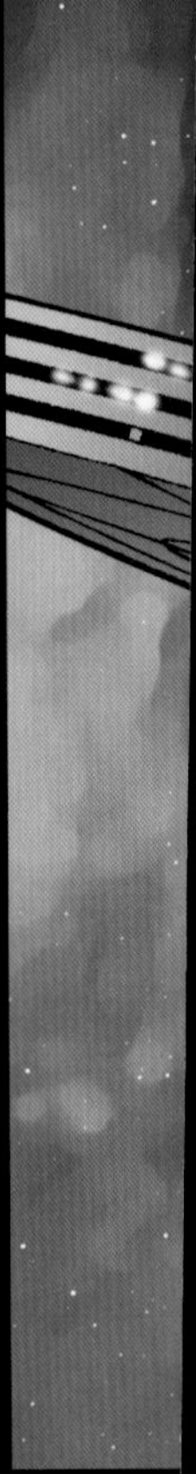

AFTER TRAVELLING ON TV to the future with *STAR TREK: THE NEXT GENERATION*, *STAR TREK: DEEP SPACE NINE* and *STAR TREK: VOYAGER*, and latterly to its past with *STAR TREK: ENTERPRISE*, JJ Abrams's vision of *STAR TREK* would revisit the original 1966 show's core cast of characters and its iconic elements with a new, reinvigorated approach, designed to appeal not only to long-time fans, but to a new audience for the 21st century. The roles of Kirk, Spock, and McCoy et al were reforged with a younger cast on board a new *U.S.S Enterprise*, in a fictional universe that seemed familiar, but that also had the freedom to find fresh takes on classic *STAR TREK* stories.

Based on the script by Roberto Orci and Alex Kurtzman, this six-issue miniseries

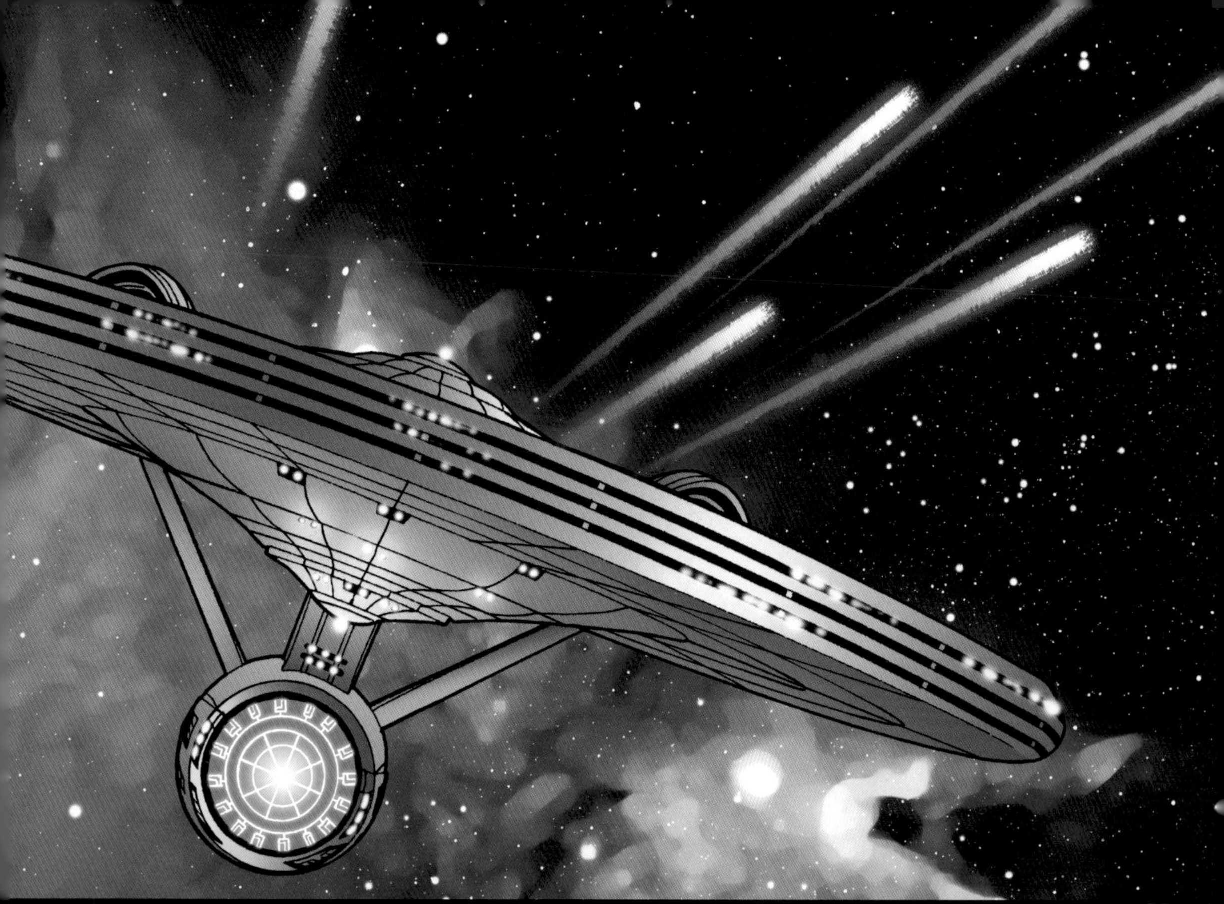

written by Tim Jones and Mike Johnson, with art by David Messina, Claudia Balboni and Gaetano Carlucci, adapted the events of the film to the page in a striking style that captures the energy of the movie – and also includes dialogues and scenes that were cut from the final version of the cinematic release.

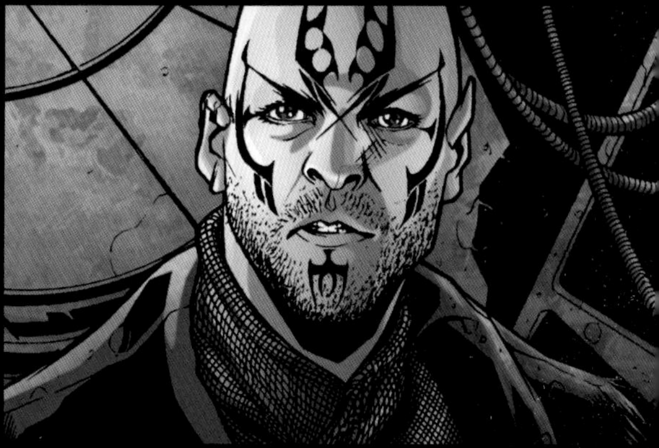

IDW Comics would also expand further upon the events of the 2009 feature film beyond this adaptation; firstly, with the prequel limited series *STAR TREK: Countdown*, which charts the first meeting between the elder Spock and Nero, and the origins of the deadly Hobus supernova. This would be followed by the four-issue *STAR TREK: Nero* miniseries, detailing the untold story of Nero's missing years in the past as a prisoner of the Klingon Empire; and the adventures of Kirk and the *Enterprise* crew continue to unfold in an ongoing *STAR TREK* monthly series that has already passed its 50th issue.

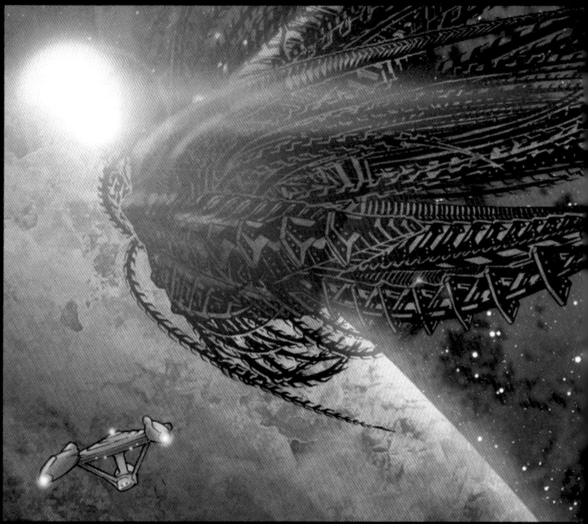

THE STORY SO FAR...

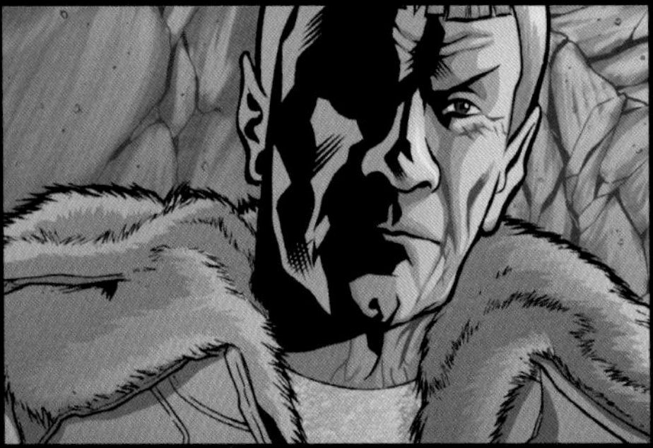

In the 23rd century, with the help of former members of the crew of the *U.S.S. Enterprise* NCC-1701-E, the ageing Ambassador Spock of Vulcan braves certain death to stop a deadly subspace supernova from engulfing the Galaxy, utilizing the unstable compound known as Red Matter to collapse it into a black hole. But Spock's plans are interrupted by the Romulan Nero, whose homeworld and family were destroyed by the nova.

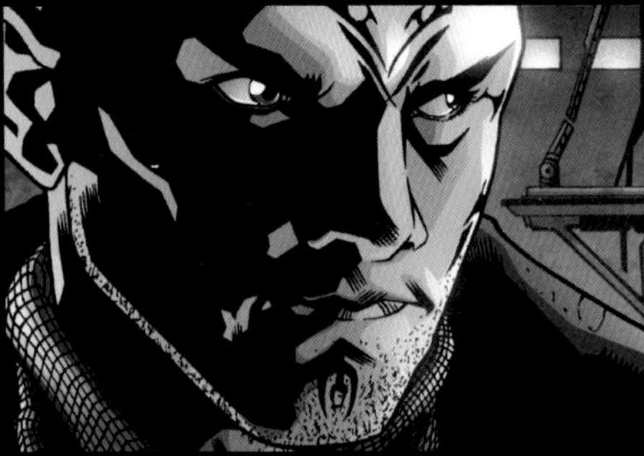

Nero blames Spock and his people for waiting too long to stop the deadly phenomenon, and has sworn to take his revenge on them – but before he is able to kill the Vulcan, Nero's ship, the *Narada*, is dragged into the black hole along with Spock's vessel... and both craft are catapulted over a century into the past through a time warp, altering history forever.

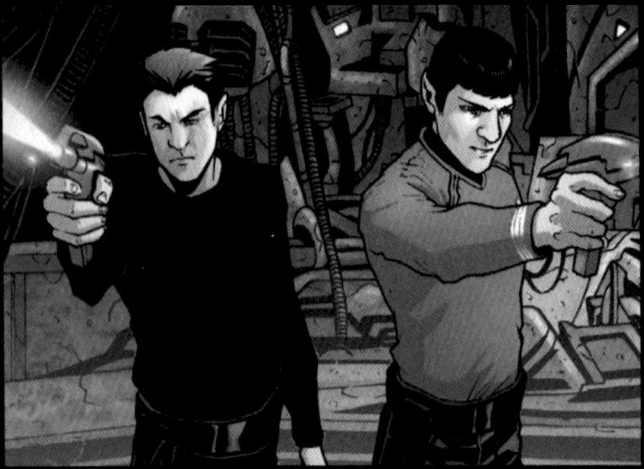

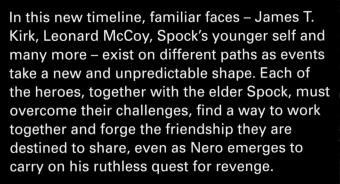

In this new timeline, familiar faces – James T. Kirk, Leonard McCoy, Spock's younger self and many more – exist on different paths as events take a new and unpredictable shape. Each of the heroes, together with the elder Spock, must overcome their challenges, find a way to work together and forge the friendship they are destined to share, even as Nero emerges to carry on his ruthless quest for revenge.

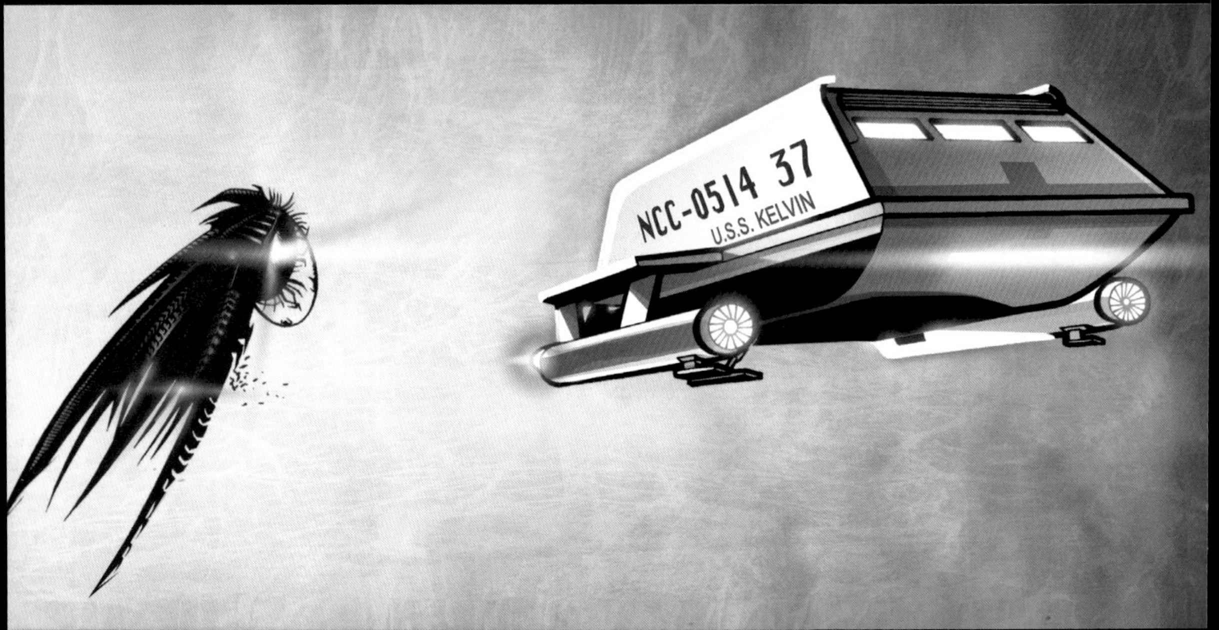
NCC-0514 37
U.S.S. KELVIN

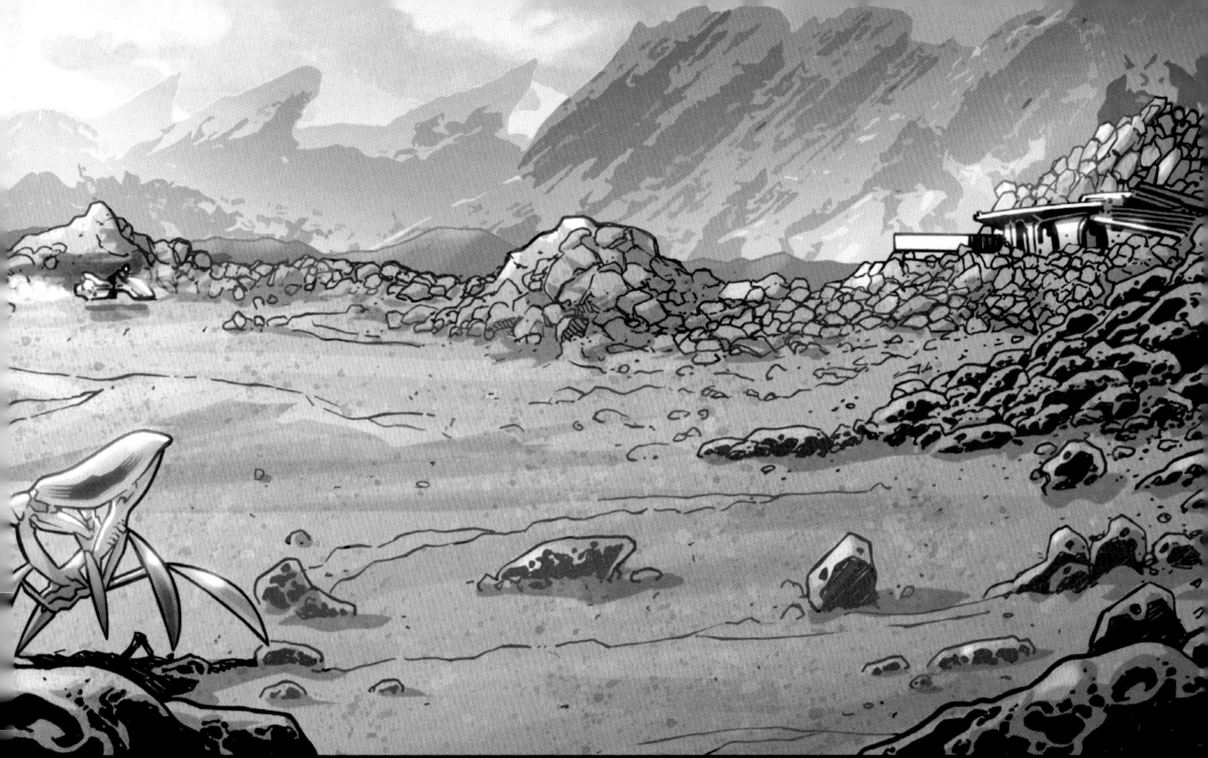

STAR TREK®

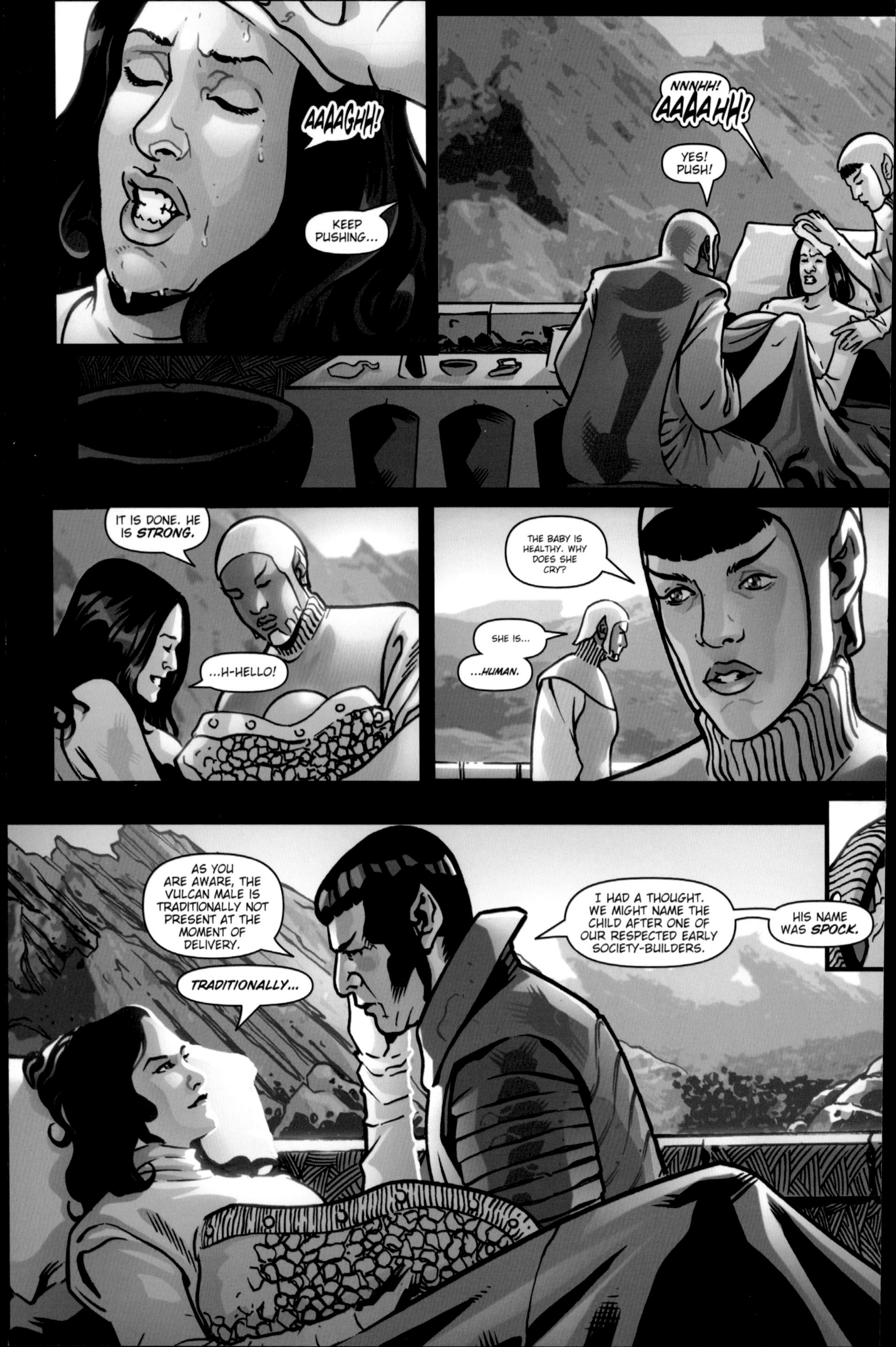
AAAAGHH!
KEEP PUSHING...
NNNHH! AAAAHH!
YES! PUSH!
IT IS DONE. HE IS STRONG.
...H-HELLO!
THE BABY IS HEALTHY. WHY DOES SHE CRY?
SHE IS...
...HUMAN.
AS YOU ARE AWARE, THE VULCAN MALE IS TRADITIONALLY NOT PRESENT AT THE MOMENT OF DELIVERY.
TRADITIONALLY...
I HAD A THOUGHT. WE MIGHT NAME THE CHILD AFTER ONE OF OUR RESPECTED EARLY SOCIETY-BUILDERS.
HIS NAME WAS SPOCK.

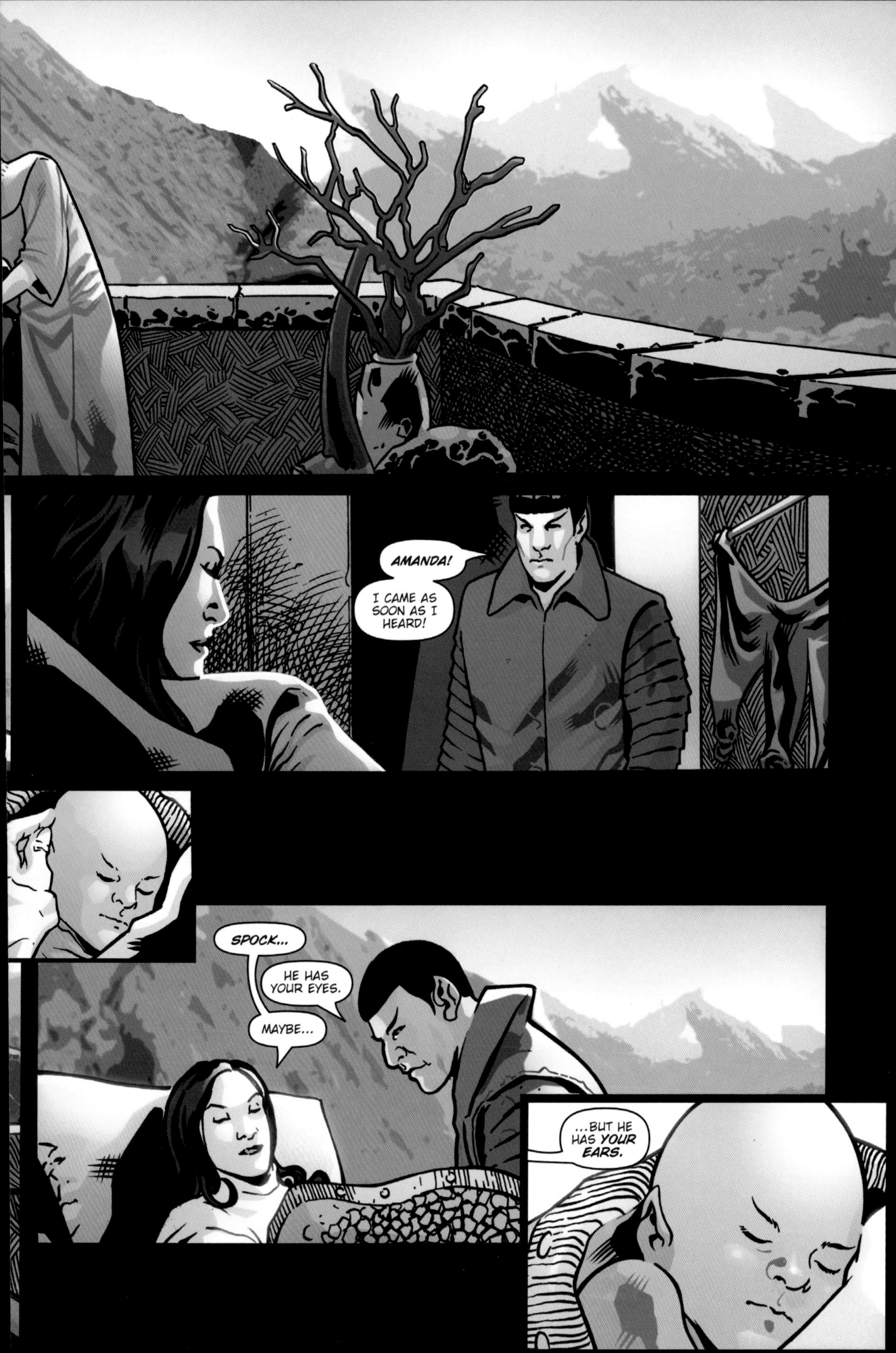
AMANDA!
I CAME AS SOON AS I HEARD!
SPOCK...
HE HAS YOUR EYES.
MAYBE...
...BUT HE HAS YOUR EARS.

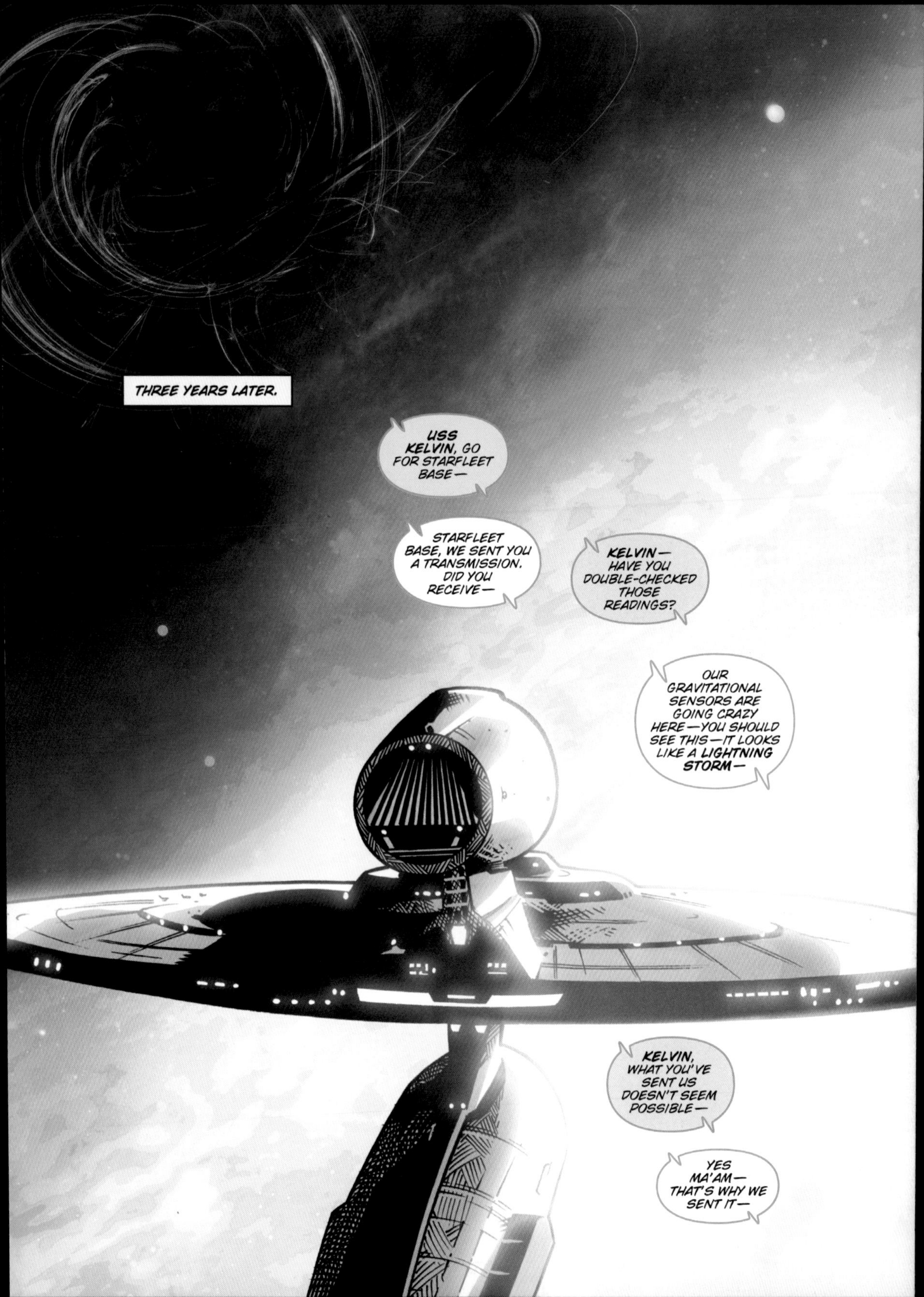
THREE YEARS LATER.
USS KELVIN, GO FOR STARFLEET BASE—
STARFLEET BASE, WE SENT YOU A TRANSMISSION. DID YOU RECEIVE—
KELVIN— HAVE YOU DOUBLE-CHECKED THOSE READINGS?
OUR GRAVITATIONAL SENSORS ARE GOING CRAZY HERE—YOU SHOULD SEE THIS—IT LOOKS LIKE A LIGHTNING STORM—
KELVIN, WHAT YOU'VE SENT US DOESN'T SEEM POSSIBLE—
YES MA'AM— THAT'S WHY WE SENT IT—

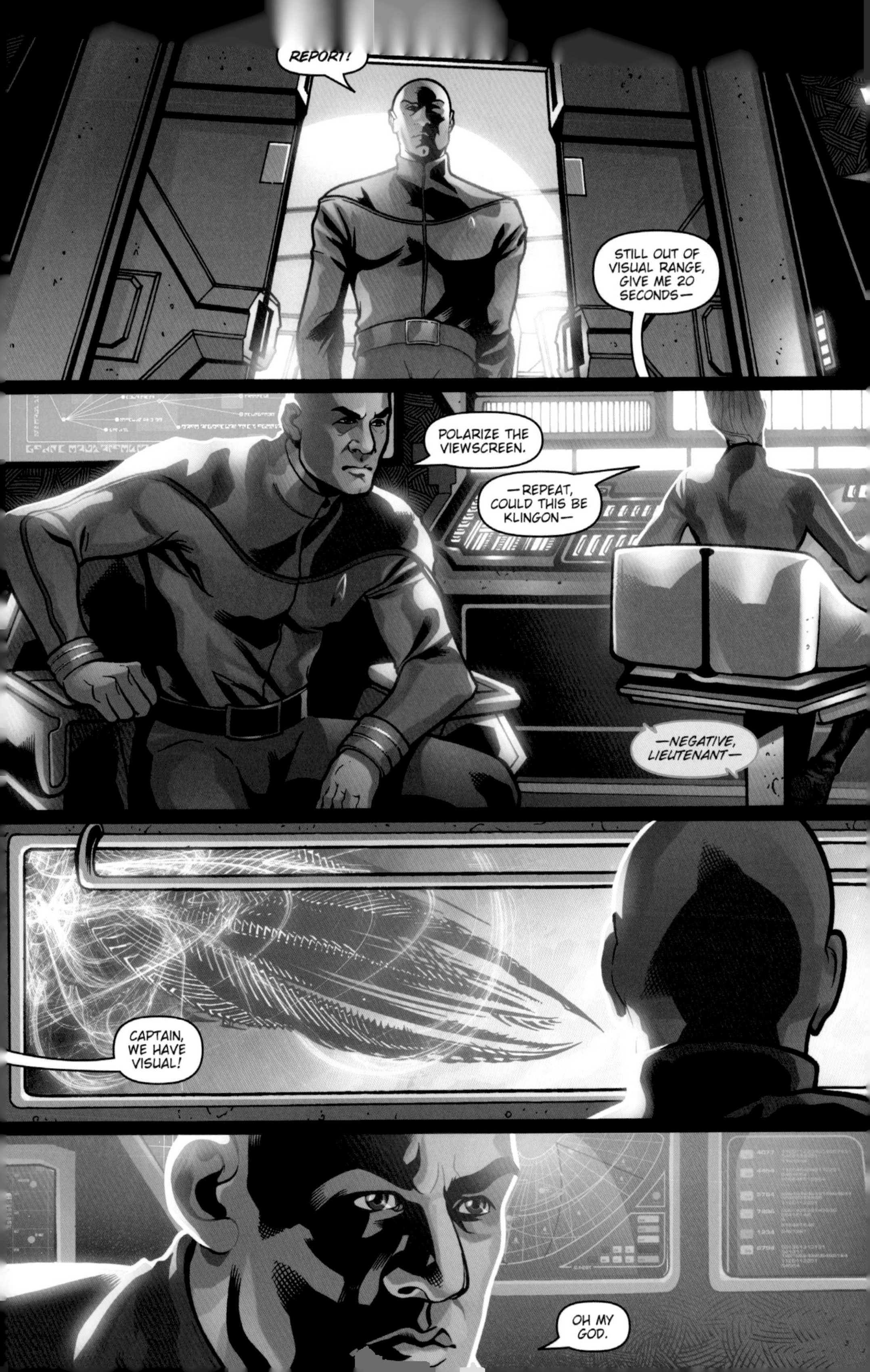
REPORT!
STILL OUT OF VISUAL RANGE, GIVE ME 20 SECONDS—
POLARIZE THE VIEWSCREEN.
—REPEAT, COULD THIS BE KLINGON—
—NEGATIVE, LIEUTENANT—
CAPTAIN, WE HAVE VISUAL!
OH MY GOD.

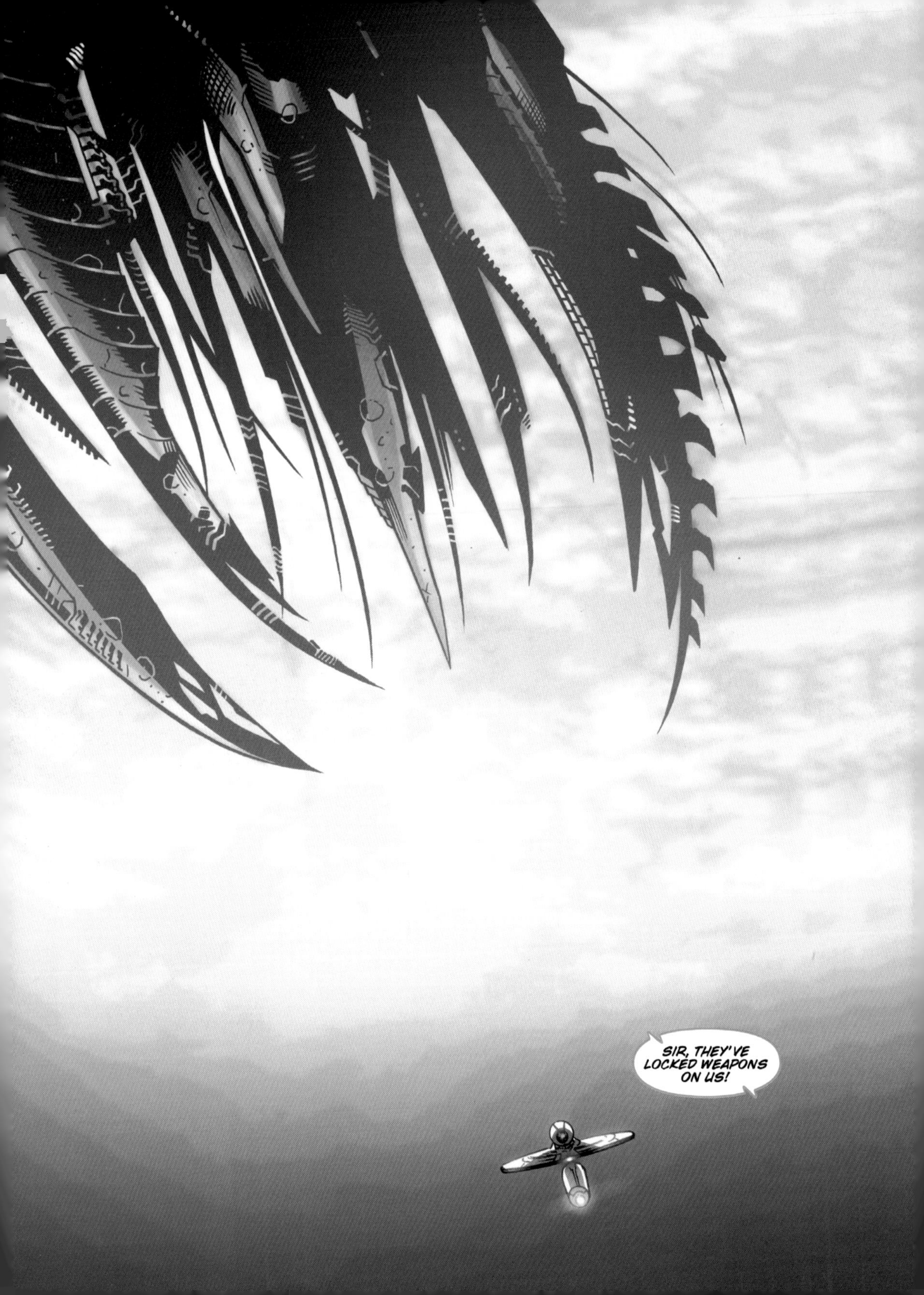
SIR, THEY'VE LOCKED WEAPONS ON US!

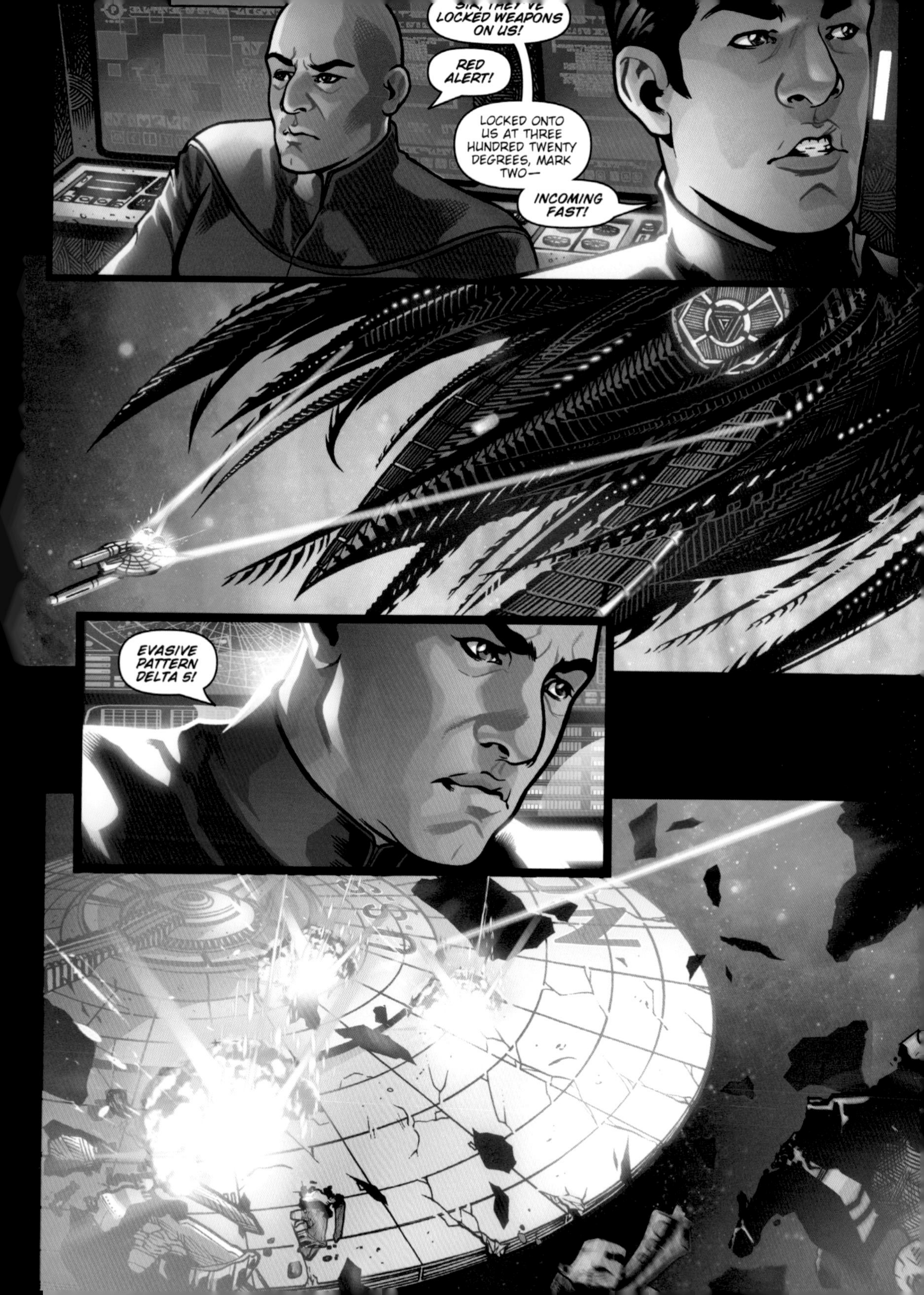
SIR, THEY'VE LOCKED WEAPONS ON US!
RED ALERT!
LOCKED ONTO US AT THREE HUNDRED TWENTY DEGREES, MARK TWO—
INCOMING FAST!
EVASIVE PATTERN DELTA 5!

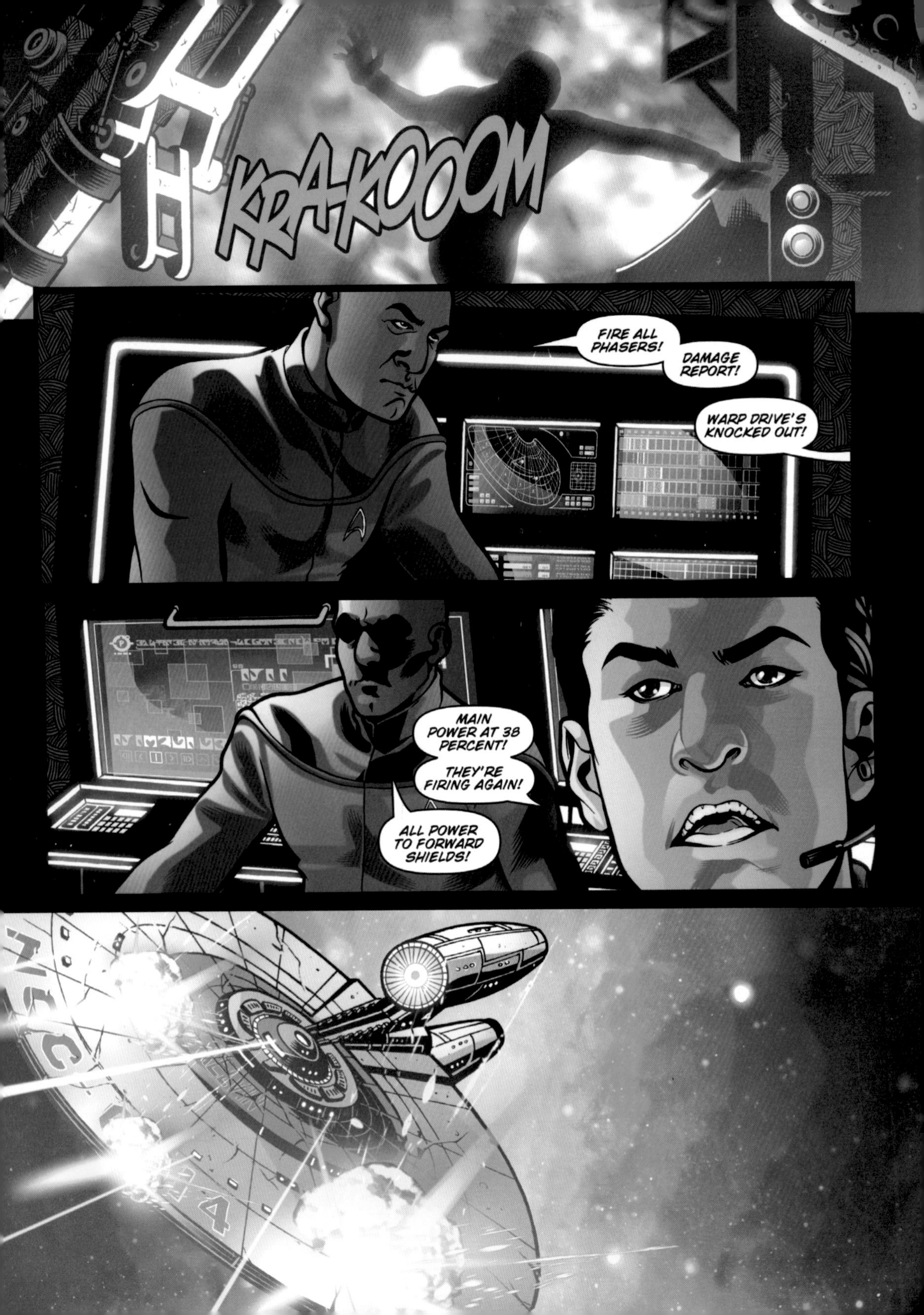
KRA-KOOOM
FIRE ALL PHASERS!
DAMAGE REPORT!
WARP DRIVE'S KNOCKED OUT!
MAIN POWER AT 38 PERCENT!
THEY'RE FIRING AGAIN!
ALL POWER TO FORWARD SHIELDS!

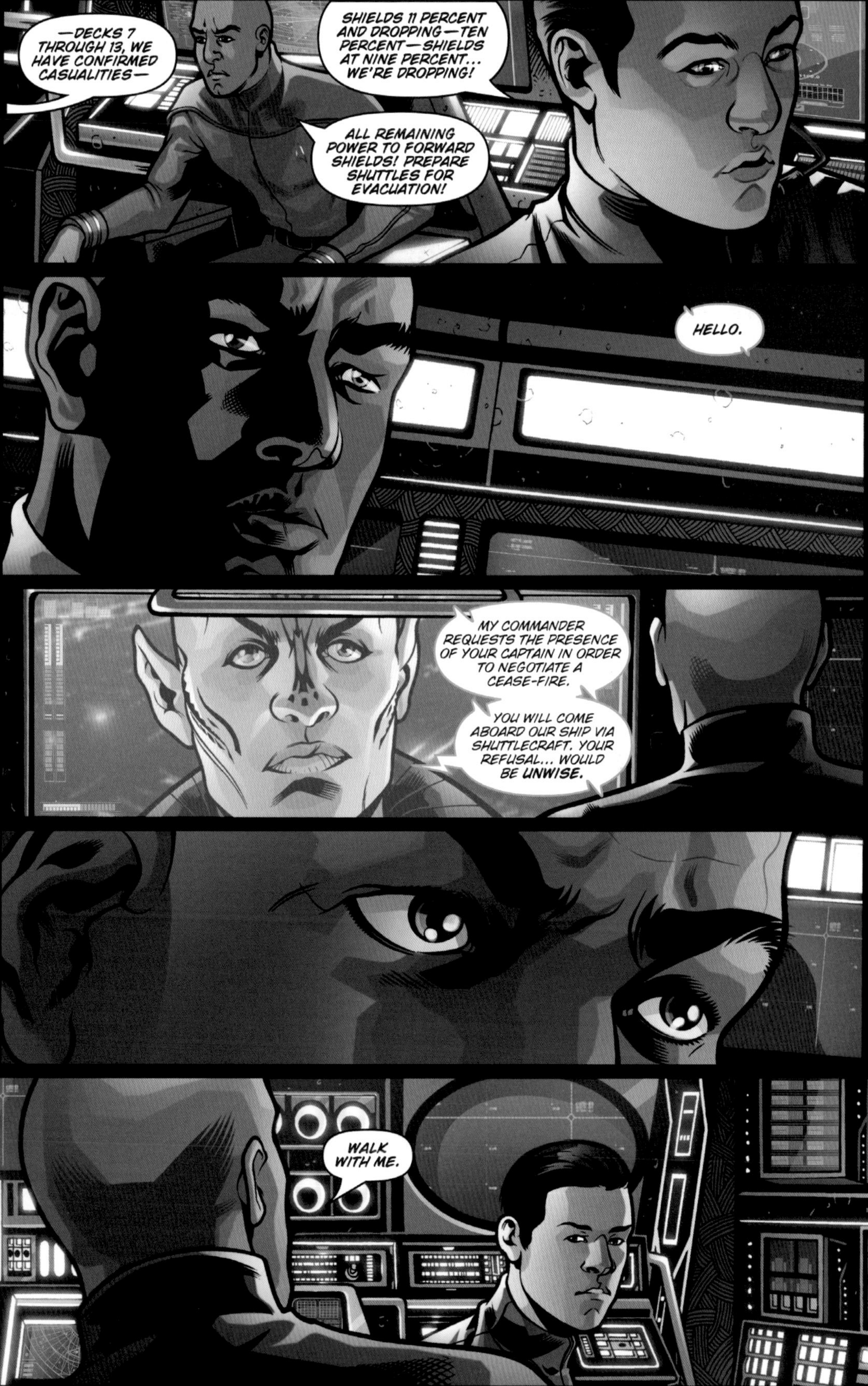
—DECKS 7 THROUGH 13, WE HAVE CONFIRMED CASUALITIES—
SHIELDS 11 PERCENT AND DROPPING—TEN PERCENT—SHIELDS AT NINE PERCENT... WE'RE DROPPING!
ALL REMAINING POWER TO FORWARD SHIELDS! PREPARE SHUTTLES FOR EVACUATION!
HELLO.
MY COMMANDER REQUESTS THE PRESENCE OF YOUR CAPTAIN IN ORDER TO NEGOTIATE A CEASE-FIRE.
YOU WILL COME ABOARD OUR SHIP VIA SHUTTLECRAFT. YOUR REFUSAL... WOULD BE UNWISE.
WALK WITH ME.

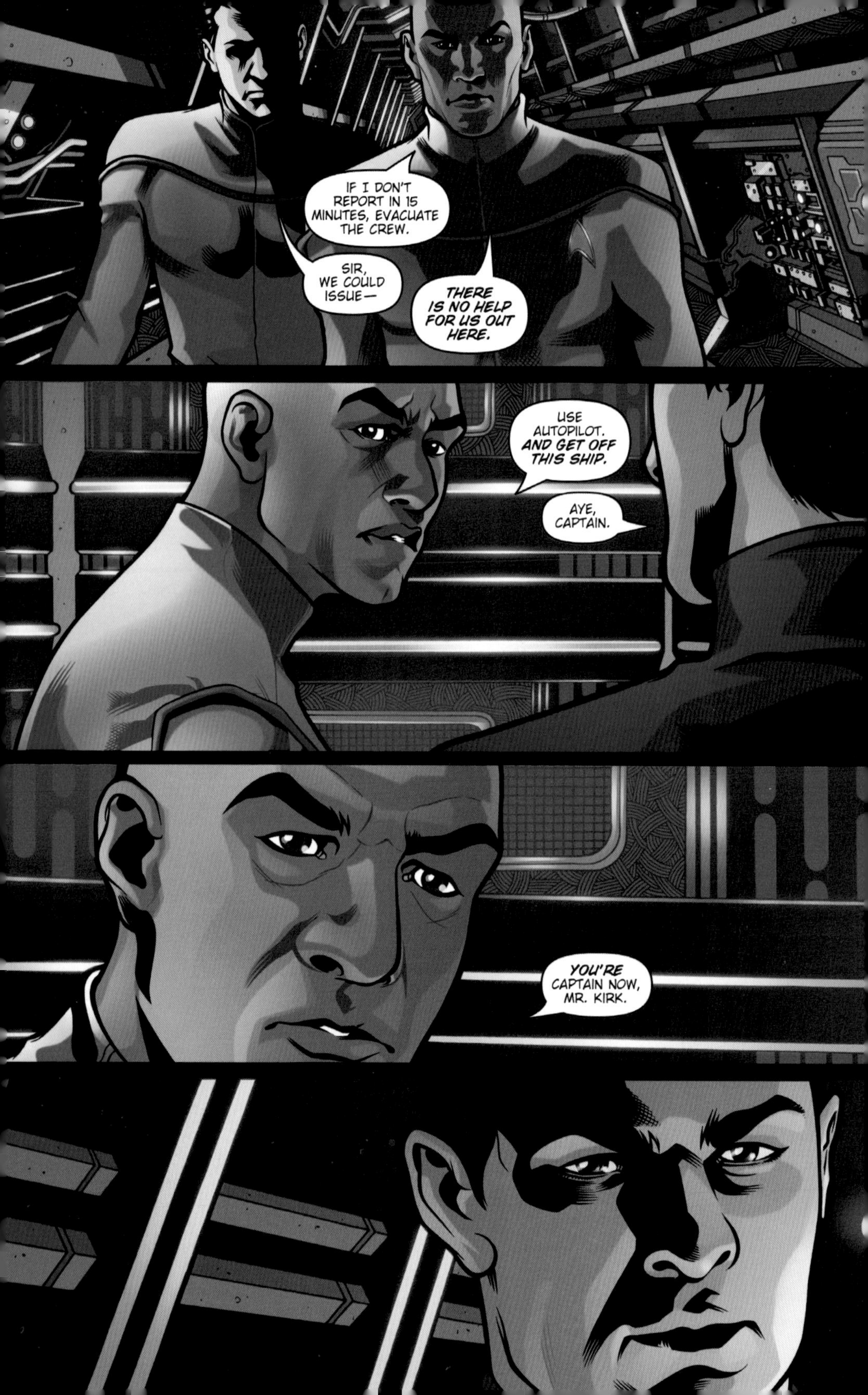
IF I DON'T REPORT IN 15 MINUTES, EVACUATE THE CREW.
SIR, WE COULD ISSUE—
THERE IS NO HELP FOR US OUT HERE.
USE AUTOPILOT. AND GET OFF THIS SHIP.
AYE, CAPTAIN.
YOU'RE CAPTAIN NOW, MR. KIRK.

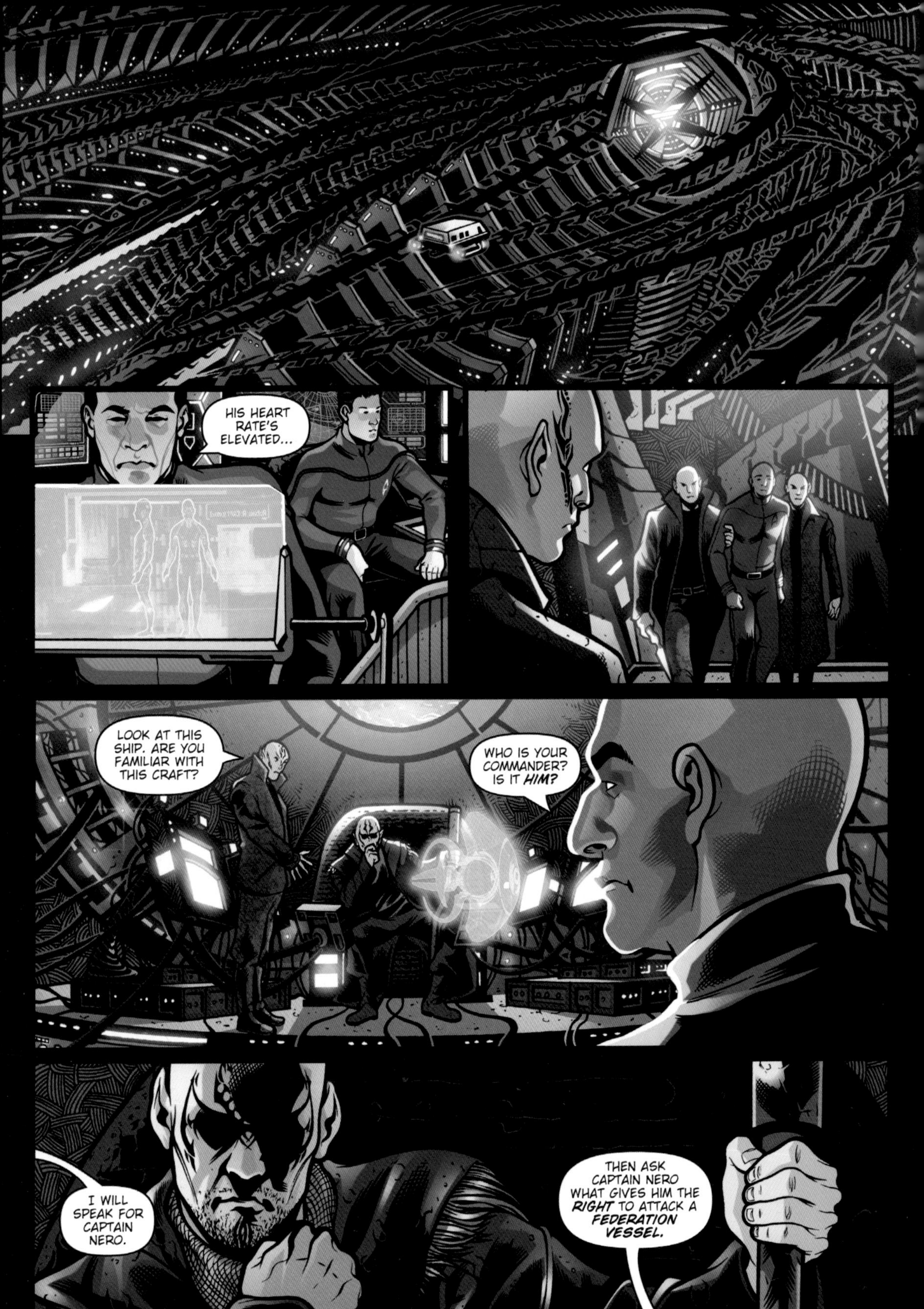
HIS HEART RATE'S ELEVATED...
LOOK AT THIS SHIP. ARE YOU FAMILIAR WITH THIS CRAFT?
WHO IS YOUR COMMANDER? IS IT HIM?
I WILL SPEAK FOR CAPTAIN NERO.
THEN ASK CAPTAIN NERO WHAT GIVES HIM THE RIGHT TO ATTACK A FEDERATION VESSEL.

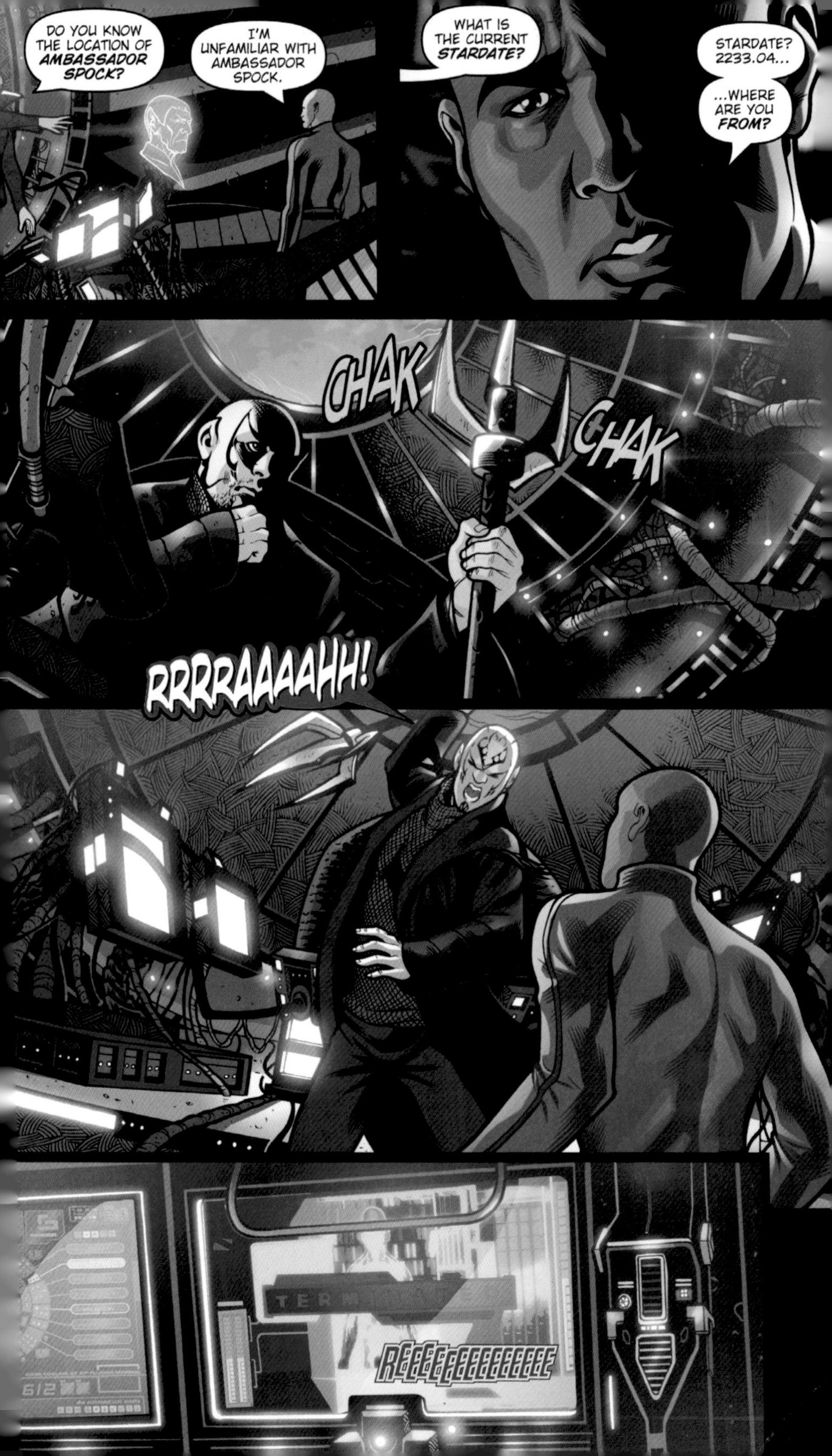
DO YOU KNOW THE LOCATION OF AMBASSADOR SPOCK?
I'M UNFAMILIAR WITH AMBASSADOR SPOCK.
WHAT IS THE CURRENT STARDATE?
STARDATE? 2233.04...
...WHERE ARE YOU FROM?
CHAK
CHAK
RRRRAAAAHH!
REEEEEEEEEEEEEE

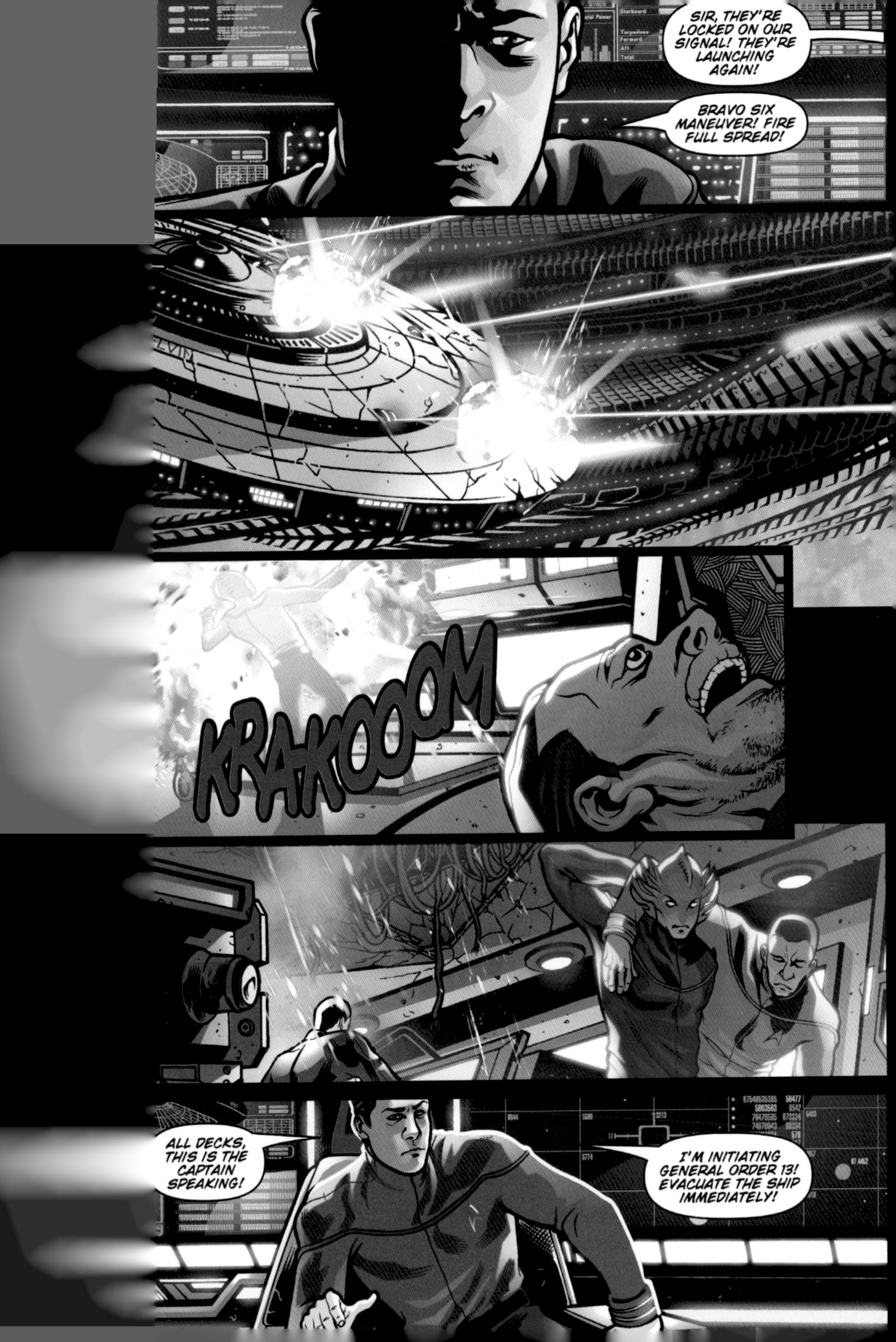
SIR, THEY'RE LOCKED ON OUR SIGNAL! THEY'RE LAUNCHING AGAIN!
BRAVO SIX MANEUVER! FIRE FULL SPREAD!
KRAKOOOM
ALL DECKS, THIS IS THE CAPTAIN SPEAKING!
I'M INITIATING GENERAL ORDER 13! EVACUATE THE SHIP IMMEDIATELY!

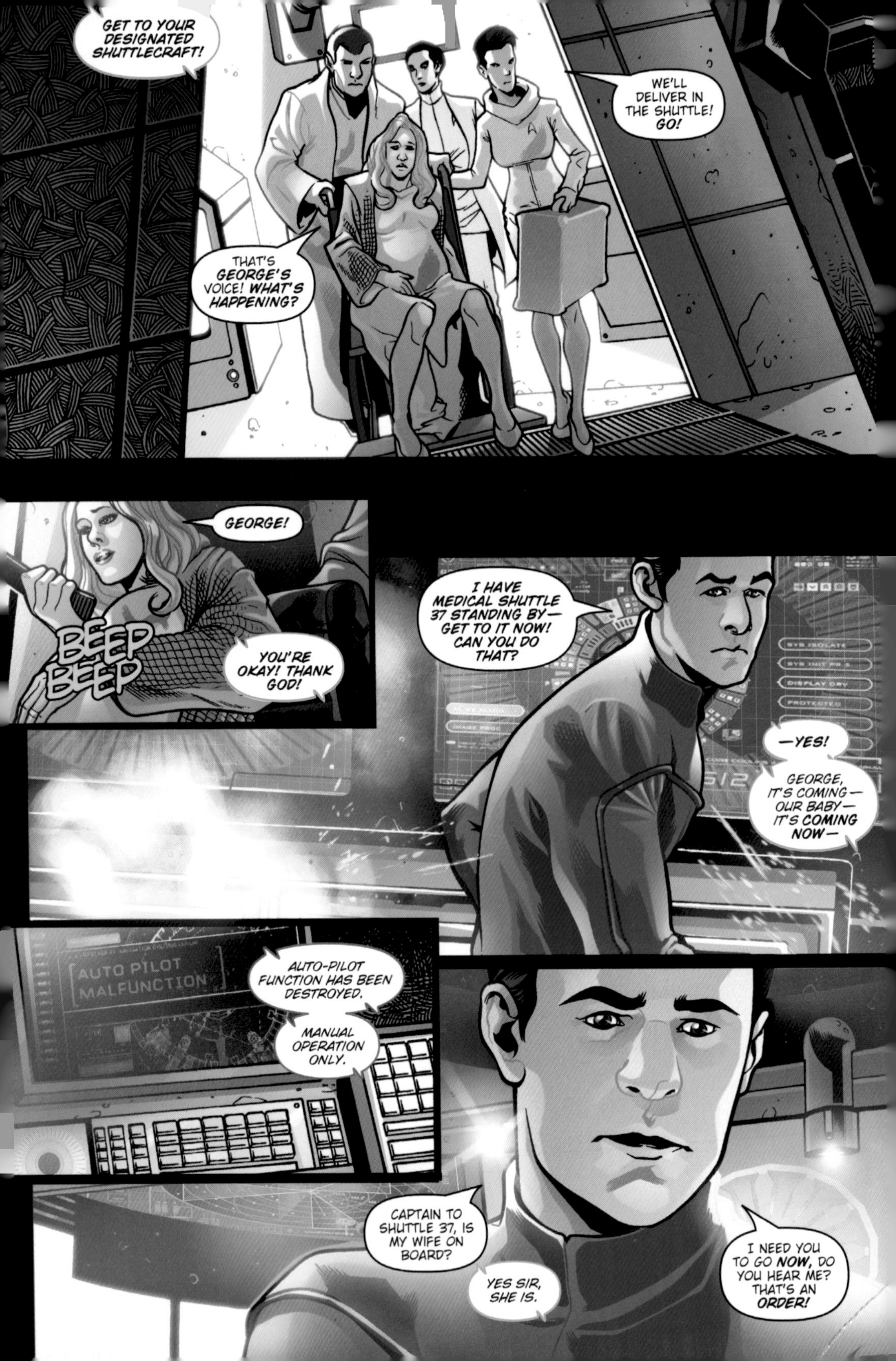
GET TO YOUR DESIGNATED SHUTTLECRAFT!
WE'LL DELIVER IN THE SHUTTLE! GO!
THAT'S GEORGE'S VOICE! WHAT'S HAPPENING?
GEORGE!
BEEP BEEP
YOU'RE OKAY! THANK GOD!
I HAVE MEDICAL SHUTTLE 37 STANDING BY— GET TO IT NOW! CAN YOU DO THAT?
—YES!
GEORGE, IT'S COMING— OUR BABY— IT'S COMING NOW—
AUTO PILOT MALFUNCTION
AUTO-PILOT FUNCTION HAS BEEN DESTROYED.
MANUAL OPERATION ONLY.
CAPTAIN TO SHUTTLE 37, IS MY WIFE ON BOARD?
YES SIR, SHE IS.
I NEED YOU TO GO NOW, DO YOU HEAR ME? THAT'S AN ORDER!

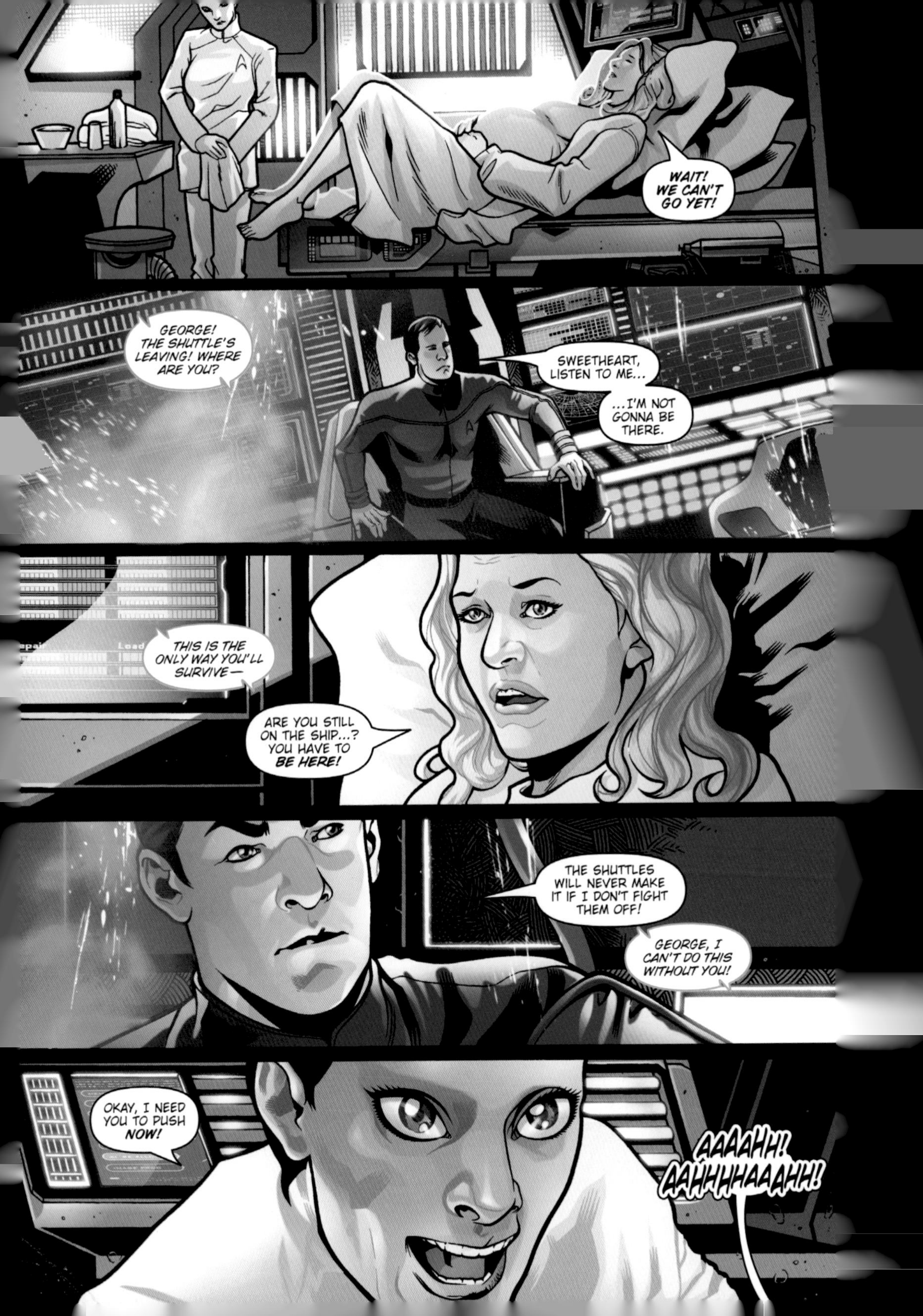
WAIT! WE CAN'T GO YET!
GEORGE! THE SHUTTLE'S LEAVING! WHERE ARE YOU?
SWEETHEART, LISTEN TO ME...
...I'M NOT GONNA BE THERE.
THIS IS THE ONLY WAY YOU'LL SURVIVE—
ARE YOU STILL ON THE SHIP...? YOU HAVE TO BE HERE!
THE SHUTTLES WILL NEVER MAKE IT IF I DON'T FIGHT THEM OFF!
GEORGE, I CAN'T DO THIS WITHOUT YOU!
OKAY, I NEED YOU TO PUSH NOW!
AAAAHH! AAHHHHAAAHH!

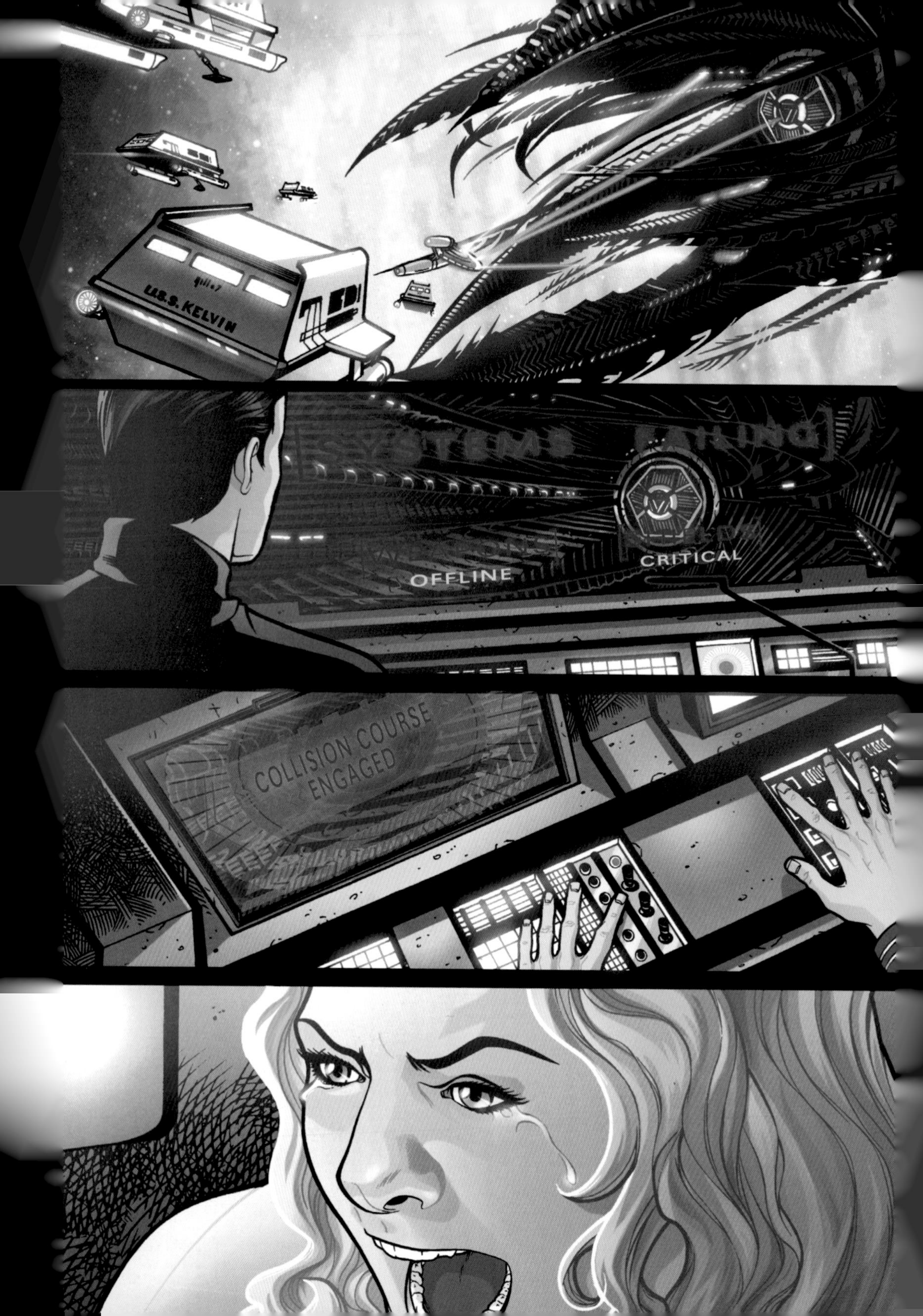
U.S.S. KELVIN
SYSTEMS FAILING
OFFLINE
CRITICAL
COLLISION COURSE
ENGAGED

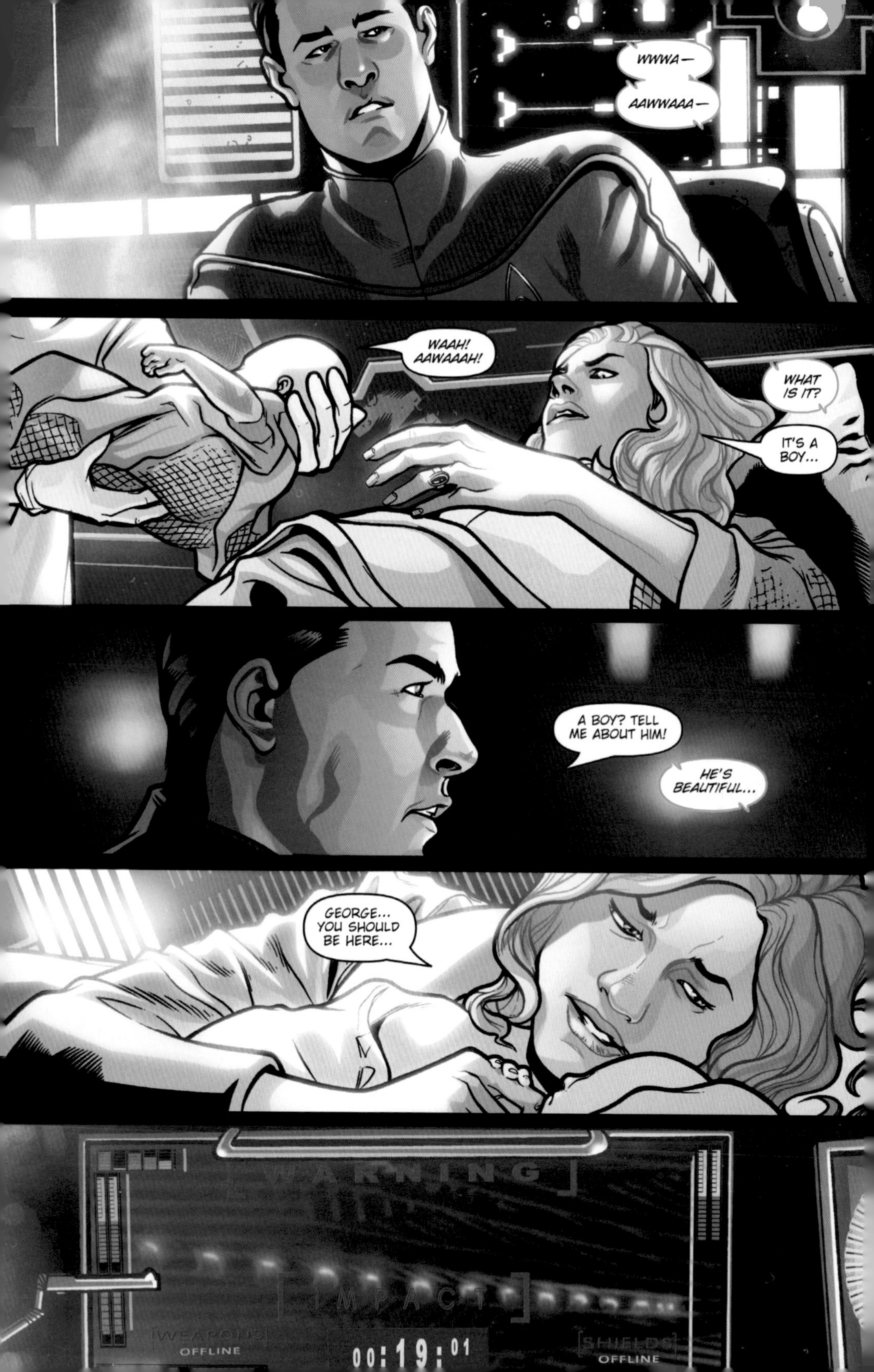
WWWA—
AAWWAAA—
WAAH! AAWAAAH!
WHAT IS IT?
IT'S A BOY...
A BOY? TELL ME ABOUT HIM!
HE'S BEAUTIFUL...
GEORGE... YOU SHOULD BE HERE...
WARNING
IMPACT
WEAPONS OFFLINE
00:19:01
SHIELDS OFFLINE

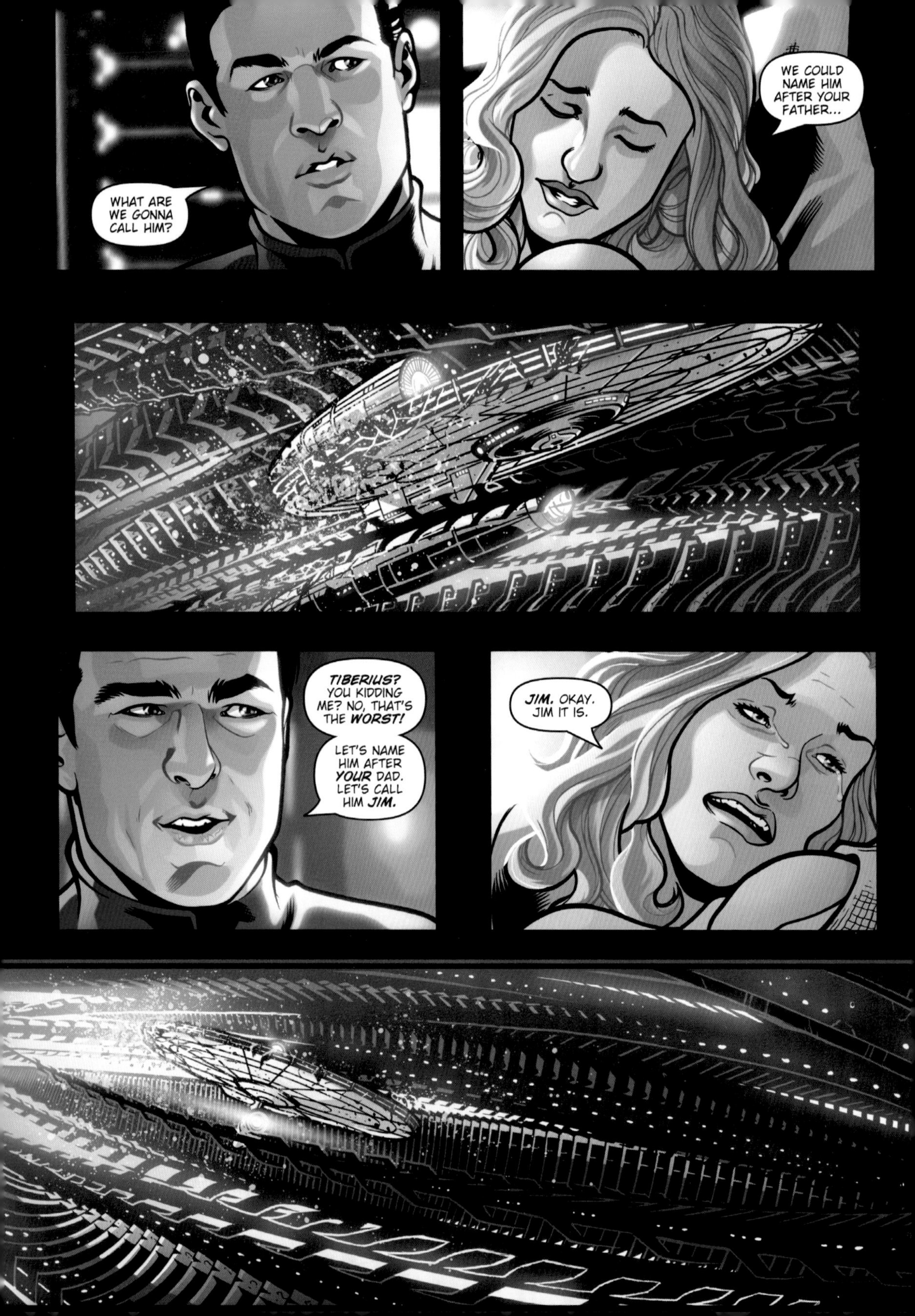
WHAT ARE WE GONNA CALL HIM?
WE COULD NAME HIM AFTER YOUR FATHER...
TIBERIUS? YOU KIDDING ME? NO, THAT'S THE WORST!
LET'S NAME HIM AFTER YOUR DAD. LET'S CALL HIM JIM.
JIM. OKAY. JIM IT IS.

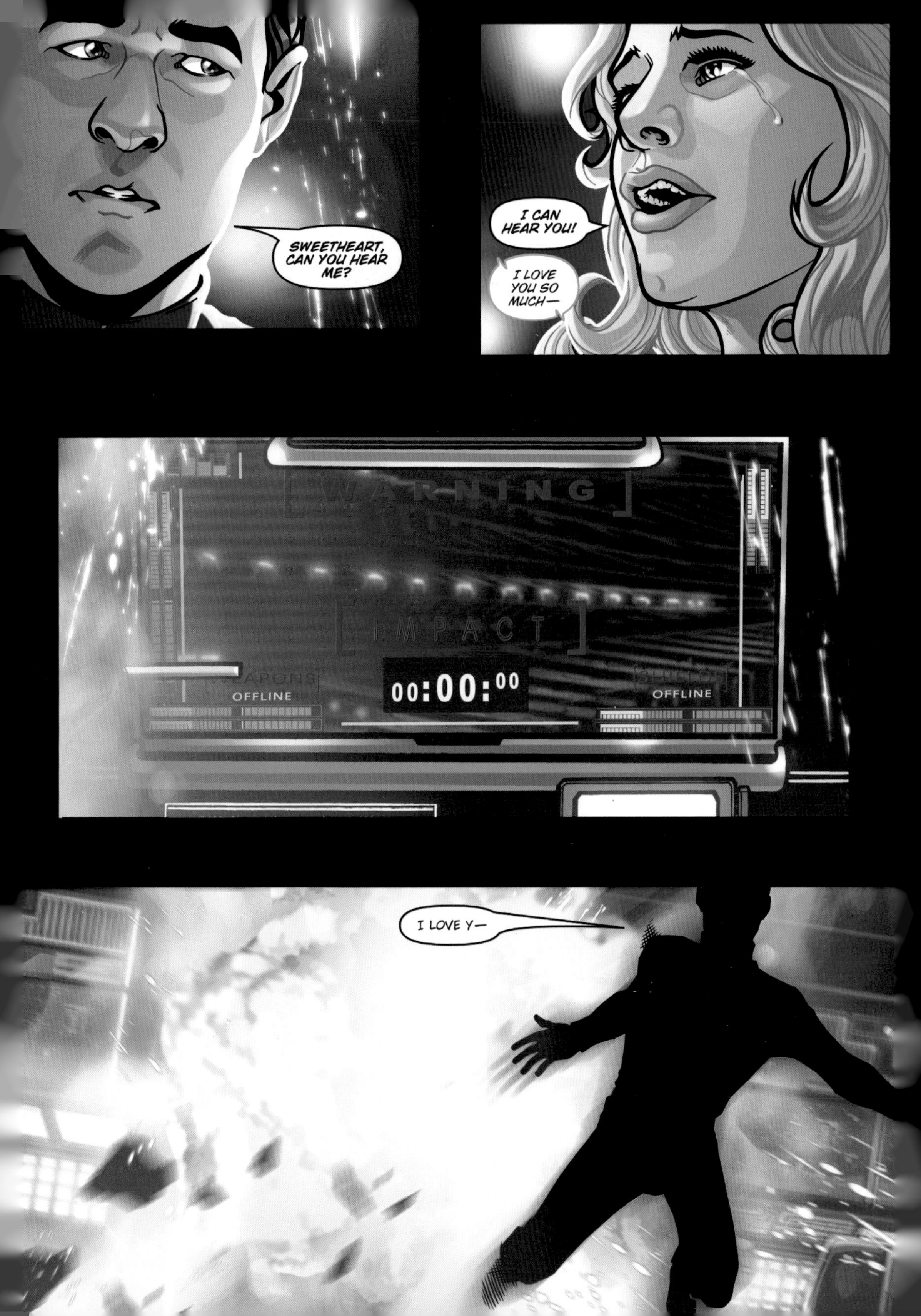
SWEETHEART, CAN YOU HEAR ME?
I CAN HEAR YOU!
I LOVE YOU SO MUCH—
WARNING
IMPACT
WEAPONS OFFLINE
00:00:00
OFFLINE
I LOVE Y—

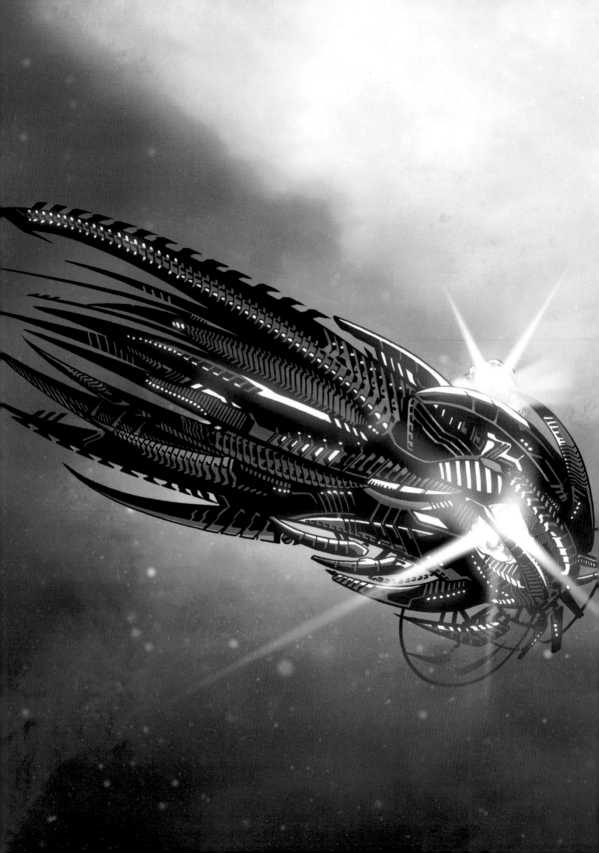

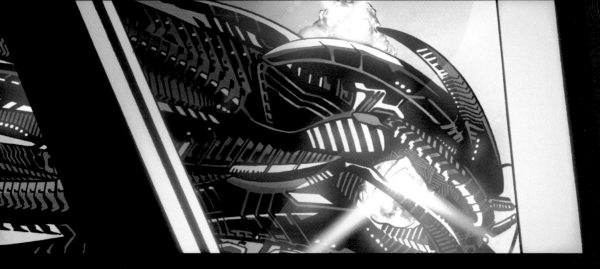

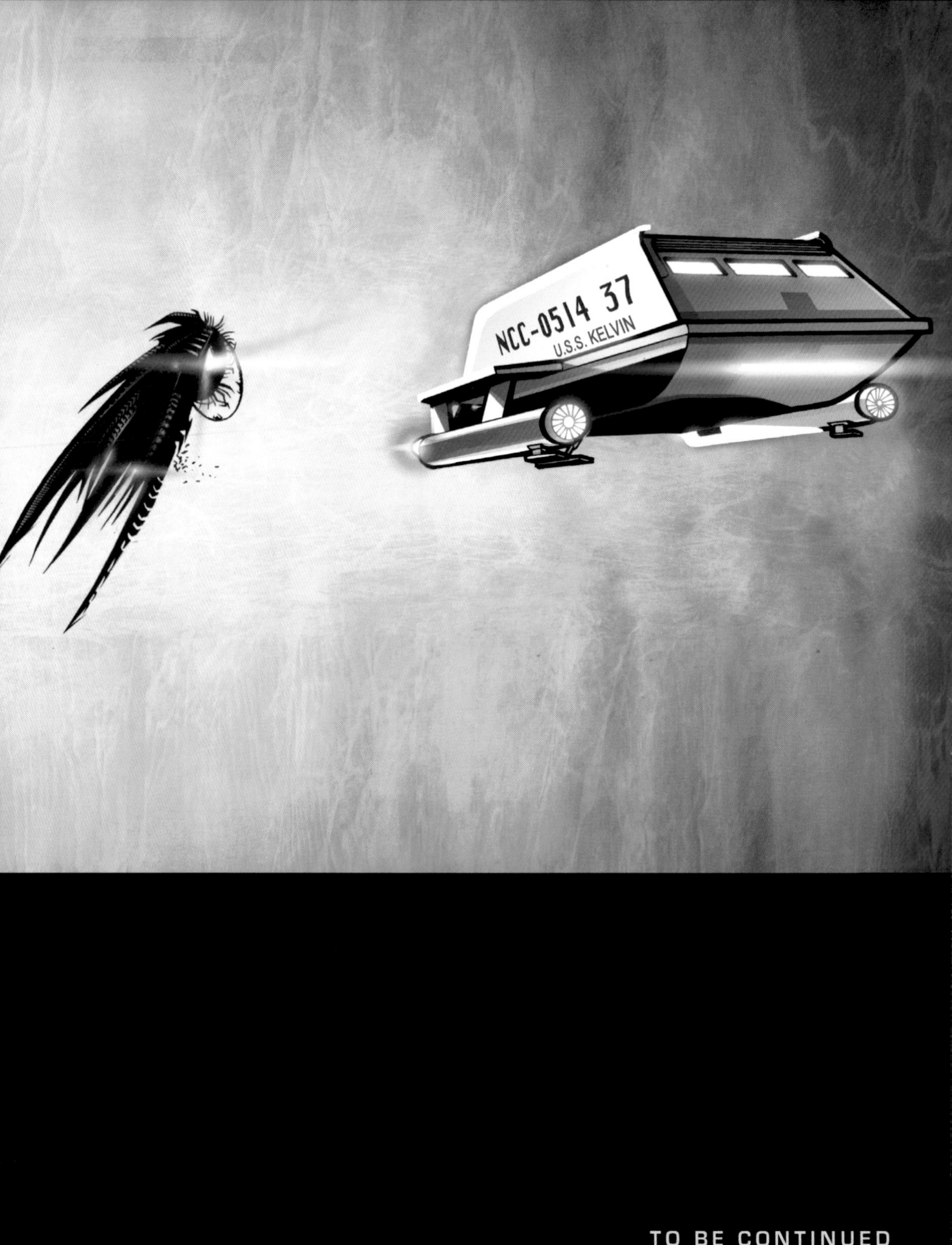
NCC-0514 37
U.S.S. KELVIN

TO BE CONTINUED

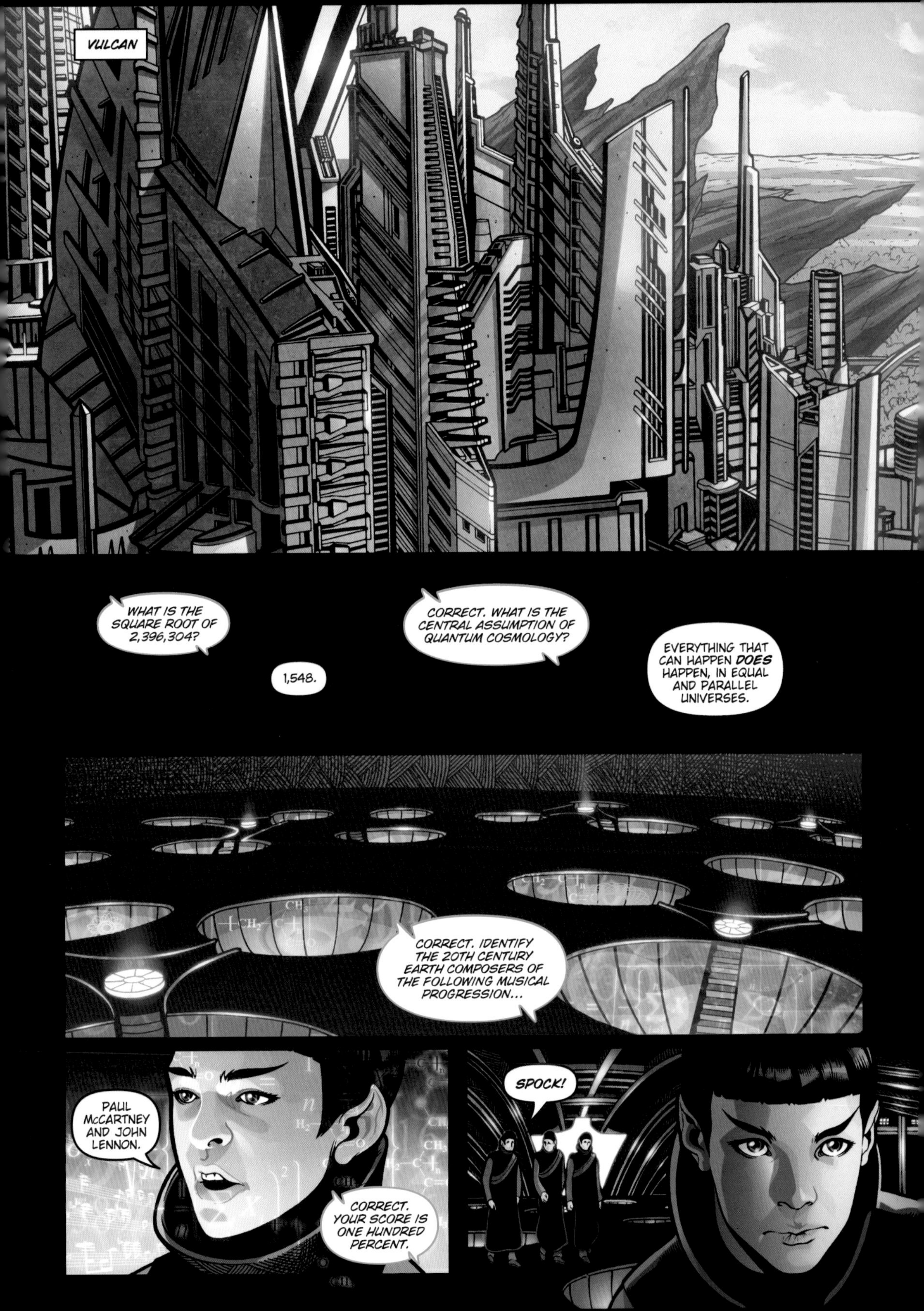
VULCAN
WHAT IS THE SQUARE ROOT OF 2,396,304?
1,548.
CORRECT. WHAT IS THE CENTRAL ASSUMPTION OF QUANTUM COSMOLOGY?
EVERYTHING THAT CAN HAPPEN DOES HAPPEN, IN EQUAL AND PARALLEL UNIVERSES.
CORRECT. IDENTIFY THE 20TH CENTURY EARTH COMPOSERS OF THE FOLLOWING MUSICAL PROGRESSION...
PAUL McCARTNEY AND JOHN LENNON.
CORRECT. YOUR SCORE IS ONE HUNDRED PERCENT.
SPOCK!

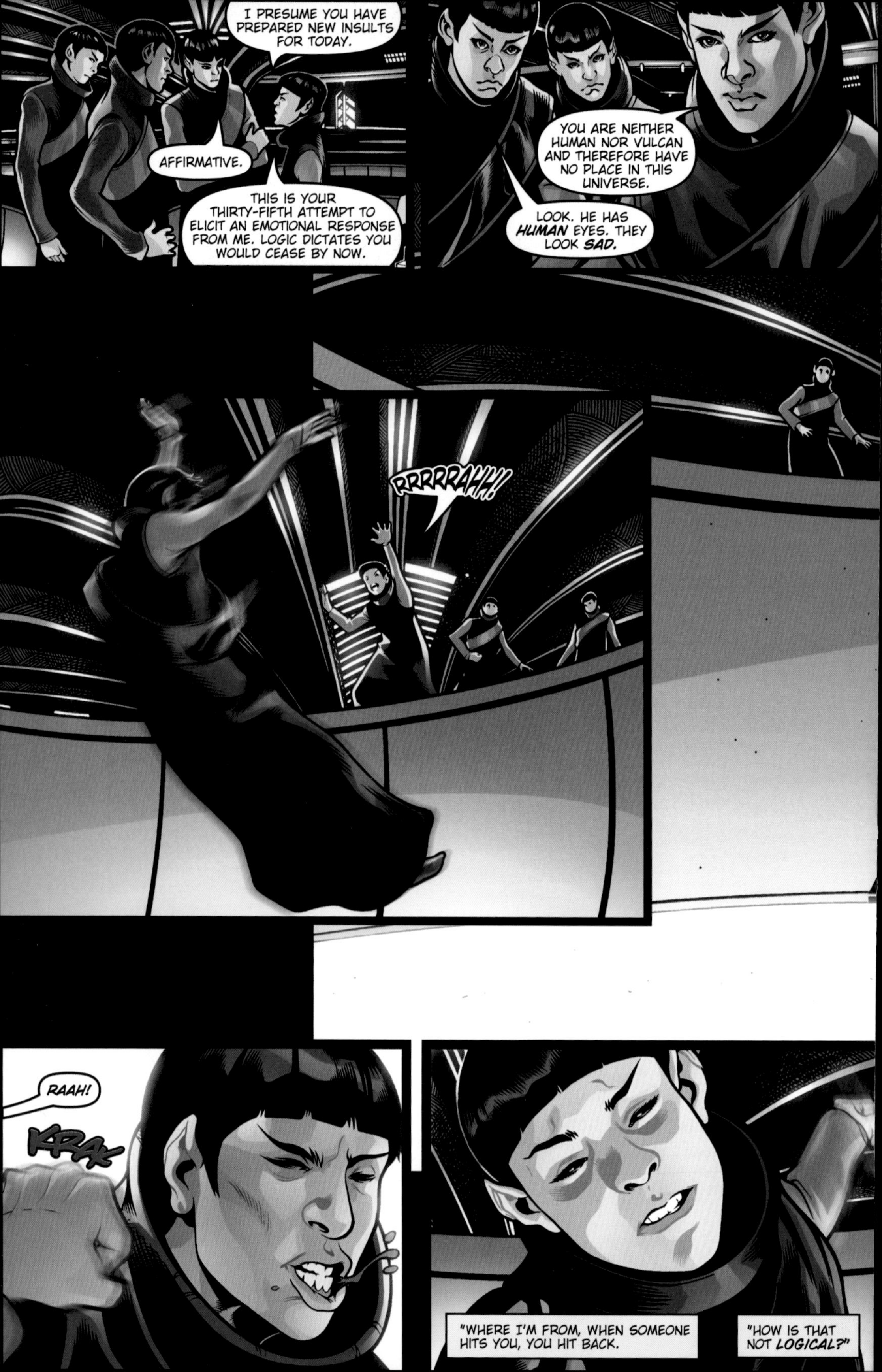

I PRESUME YOU HAVE PREPARED NEW INSULTS FOR TODAY.
AFFIRMATIVE.
THIS IS YOUR THIRTY-FIFTH ATTEMPT TO ELICIT AN EMOTIONAL RESPONSE FROM ME. LOGIC DICTATES YOU WOULD CEASE BY NOW.
YOU ARE NEITHER HUMAN NOR VULCAN AND THEREFORE HAVE NO PLACE IN THIS UNIVERSE.
LOOK. HE HAS *HUMAN* EYES. THEY LOOK *SAD.*
RRRRRAHH!
RAAH!
KRAK
"WHERE I'M FROM, WHEN SOMEONE HITS YOU, YOU HIT BACK.
"HOW IS THAT NOT *LOGICAL?"*

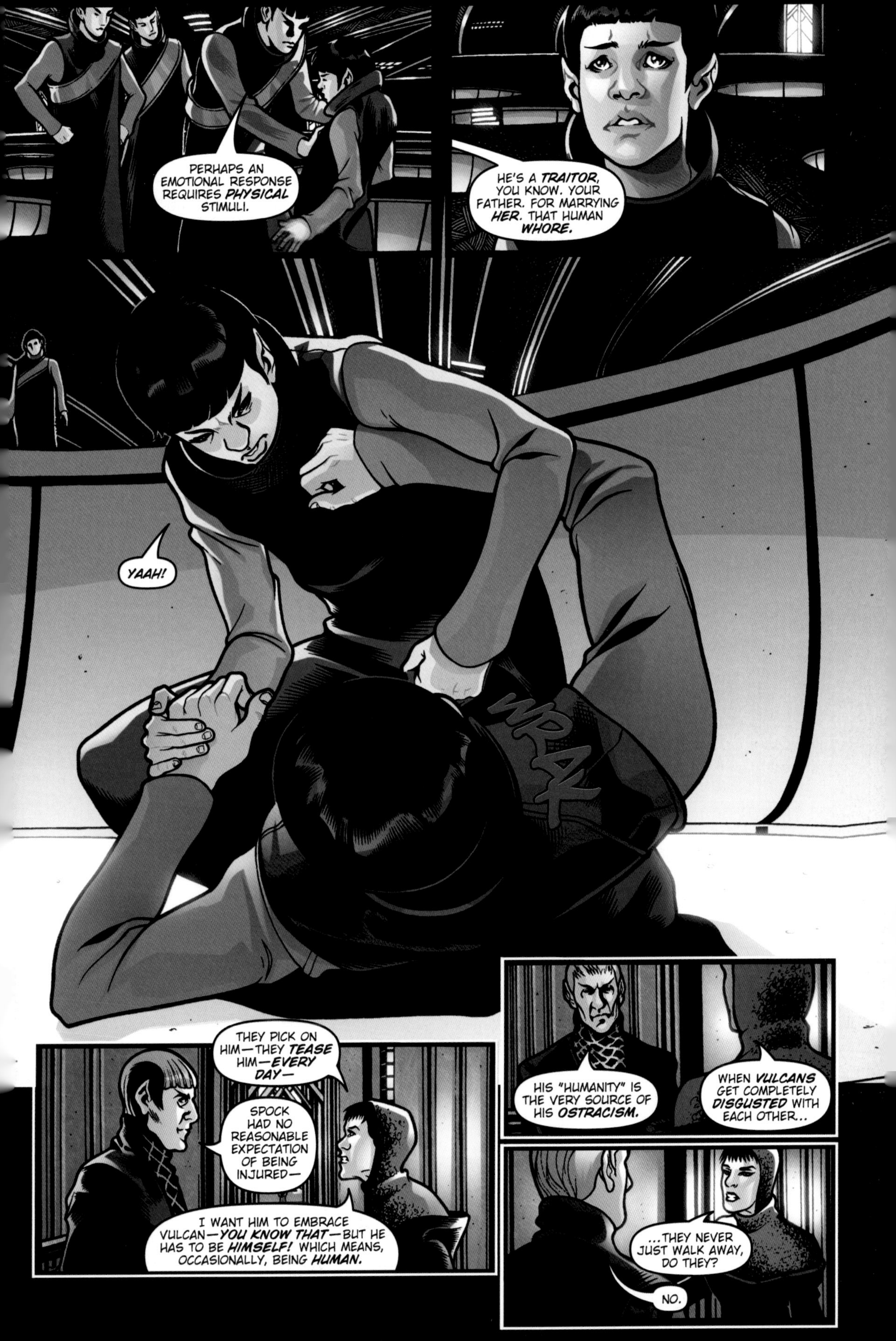
PERHAPS AN EMOTIONAL RESPONSE REQUIRES PHYSICAL STIMULI.
HE'S A TRAITOR, YOU KNOW. YOUR FATHER. FOR MARRYING HER. THAT HUMAN WHORE.
YAAH!
WRAK
THEY PICK ON HIM—THEY TEASE HIM—EVERY DAY—
SPOCK HAD NO REASONABLE EXPECTATION OF BEING INJURED—
I WANT HIM TO EMBRACE VULCAN—YOU KNOW THAT—BUT HE HAS TO BE HIMSELF! WHICH MEANS, OCCASIONALLY, BEING HUMAN.
HIS "HUMANITY" IS THE VERY SOURCE OF HIS OSTRACISM.
WHEN VULCANS GET COMPLETELY DISGUSTED WITH EACH OTHER...
...THEY NEVER JUST WALK AWAY, DO THEY?
NO.

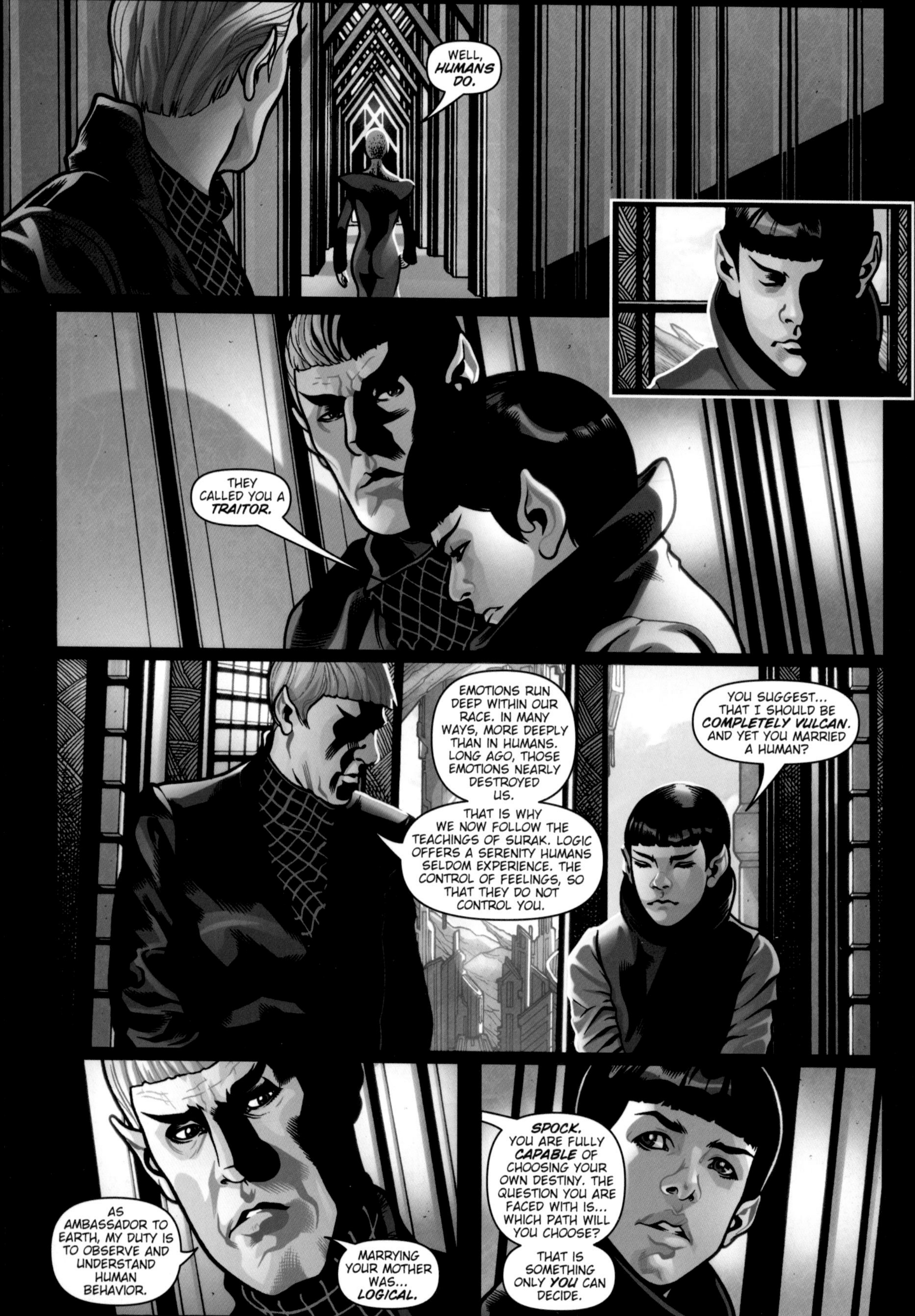

WELL, HUMANS DO.
THEY CALLED YOU A TRAITOR.
EMOTIONS RUN DEEP WITHIN OUR RACE. IN MANY WAYS, MORE DEEPLY THAN IN HUMANS. LONG AGO, THOSE EMOTIONS NEARLY DESTROYED US.
THAT IS WHY WE NOW FOLLOW THE TEACHINGS OF SURAK. LOGIC OFFERS A SERENITY HUMANS SELDOM EXPERIENCE. THE CONTROL OF FEELINGS, SO THAT THEY DO NOT CONTROL YOU.
YOU SUGGEST... THAT I SHOULD BE COMPLETELY VULCAN. AND YET YOU MARRIED A HUMAN?
AS AMBASSADOR TO EARTH, MY DUTY IS TO OBSERVE AND UNDERSTAND HUMAN BEHAVIOR.
MARRYING YOUR MOTHER WAS... LOGICAL.
SPOCK. YOU ARE FULLY CAPABLE OF CHOOSING YOUR OWN DESTINY. THE QUESTION YOU ARE FACED WITH IS... WHICH PATH WILL YOU CHOOSE?
THAT IS SOMETHING ONLY YOU CAN DECIDE.

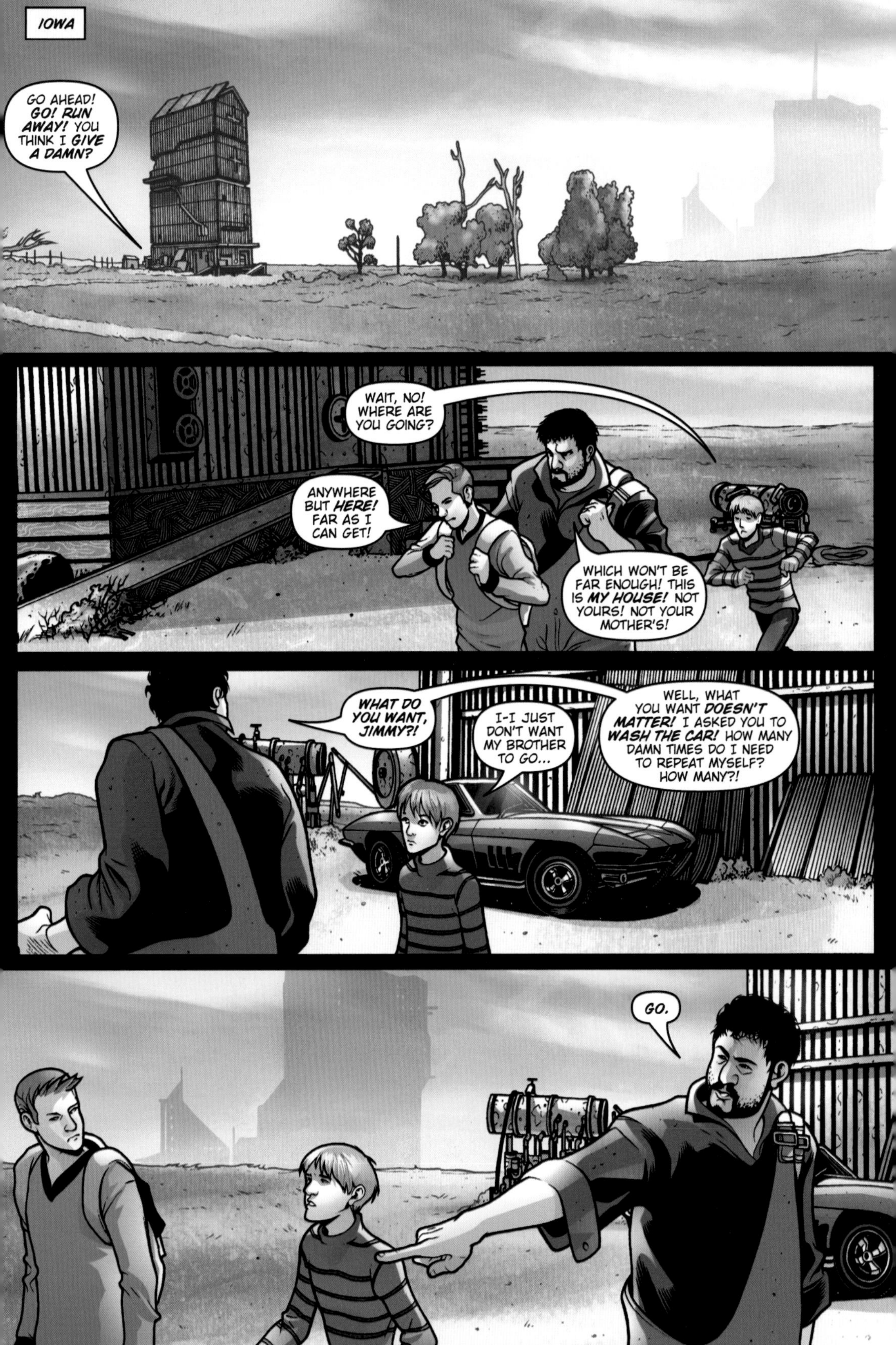
IOWA
GO AHEAD! GO! RUN AWAY! YOU THINK I GIVE A DAMN?
WAIT, NO! WHERE ARE YOU GOING?
ANYWHERE BUT HERE! FAR AS I CAN GET!
WHICH WON'T BE FAR ENOUGH! THIS IS MY HOUSE! NOT YOURS! NOT YOUR MOTHER'S!
WHAT DO YOU WANT, JIMMY?!
I-I JUST DON'T WANT MY BROTHER TO GO...
WELL, WHAT YOU WANT DOESN'T MATTER! I ASKED YOU TO WASH THE CAR! HOW MANY DAMN TIMES DO I NEED TO REPEAT MYSELF? HOW MANY?!
GO.

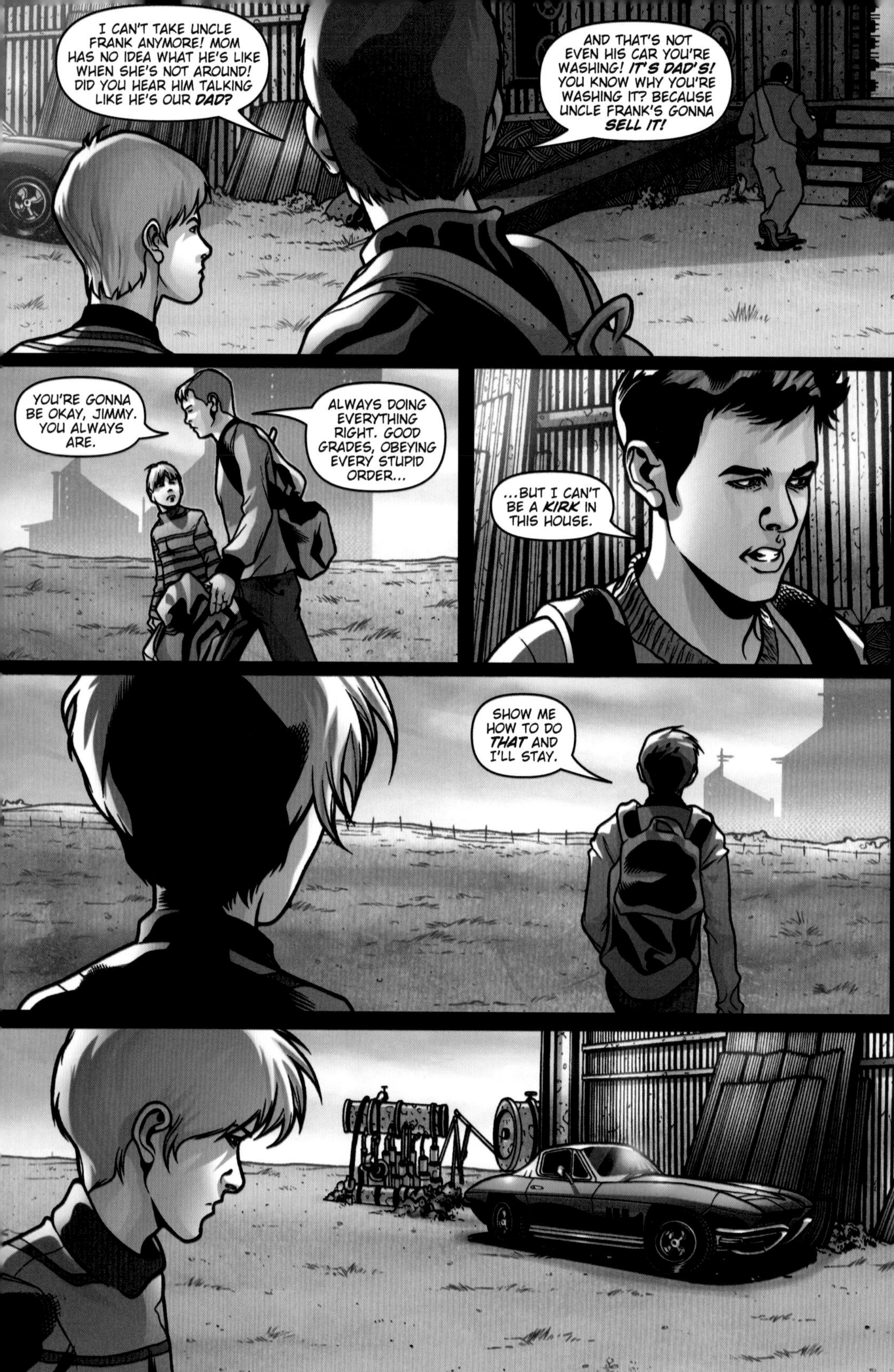
I CAN'T TAKE UNCLE FRANK ANYMORE! MOM HAS NO IDEA WHAT HE'S LIKE WHEN SHE'S NOT AROUND! DID YOU HEAR HIM TALKING LIKE HE'S OUR *DAD?*
AND THAT'S NOT EVEN HIS CAR YOU'RE WASHING! *IT'S DAD'S!* YOU KNOW WHY YOU'RE WASHING IT? BECAUSE UNCLE FRANK'S GONNA *SELL IT!*
YOU'RE GONNA BE OKAY, JIMMY. YOU ALWAYS ARE.
ALWAYS DOING EVERYTHING RIGHT. GOOD GRADES, OBEYING EVERY STUPID ORDER...
...BUT I CAN'T BE A *KIRK* IN THIS HOUSE.
SHOW ME HOW TO DO *THAT* AND I'LL STAY.

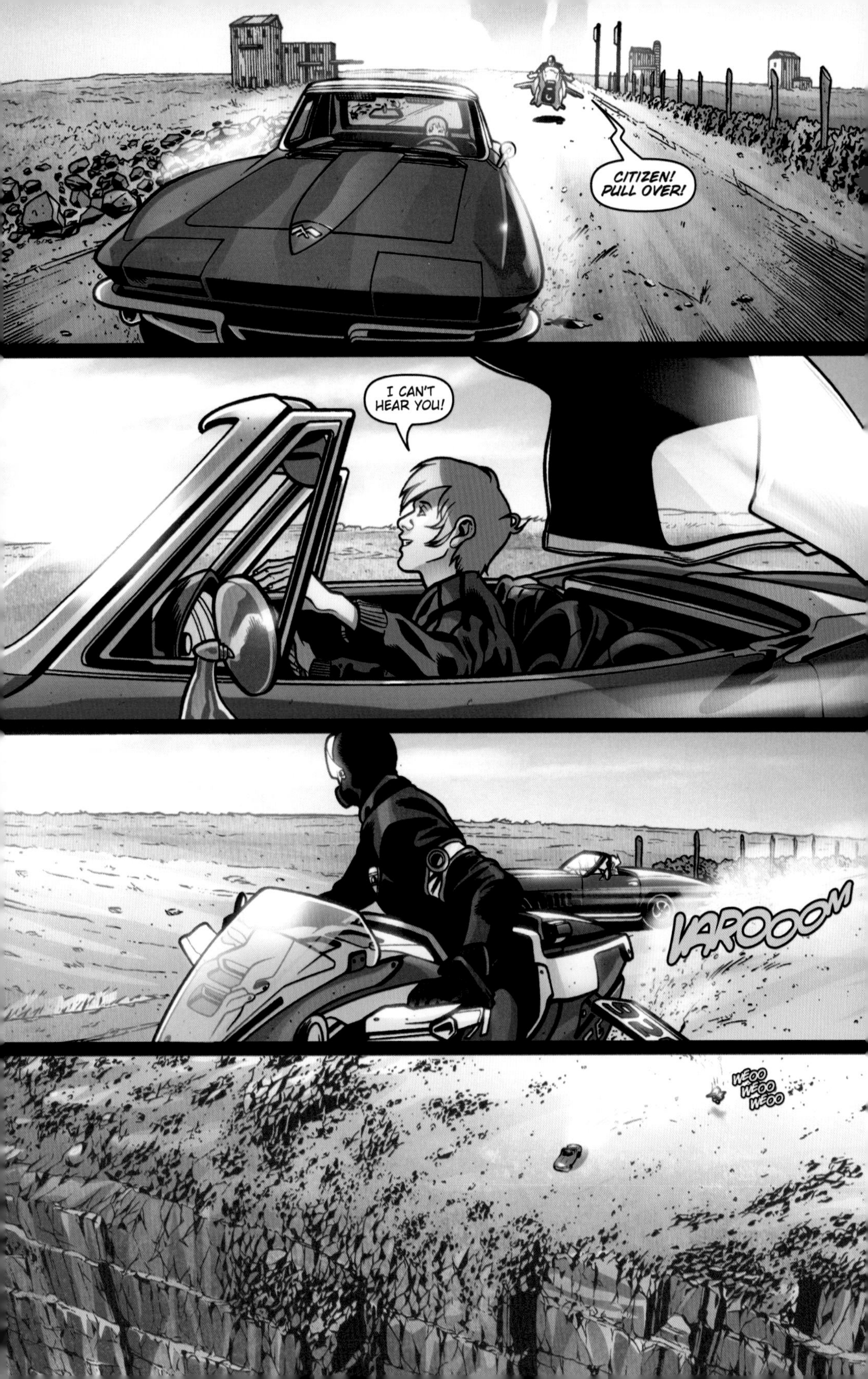
CITIZEN! PULL OVER!
I CAN'T HEAR YOU!
VAROOOM
WEOO WEOO WEOO

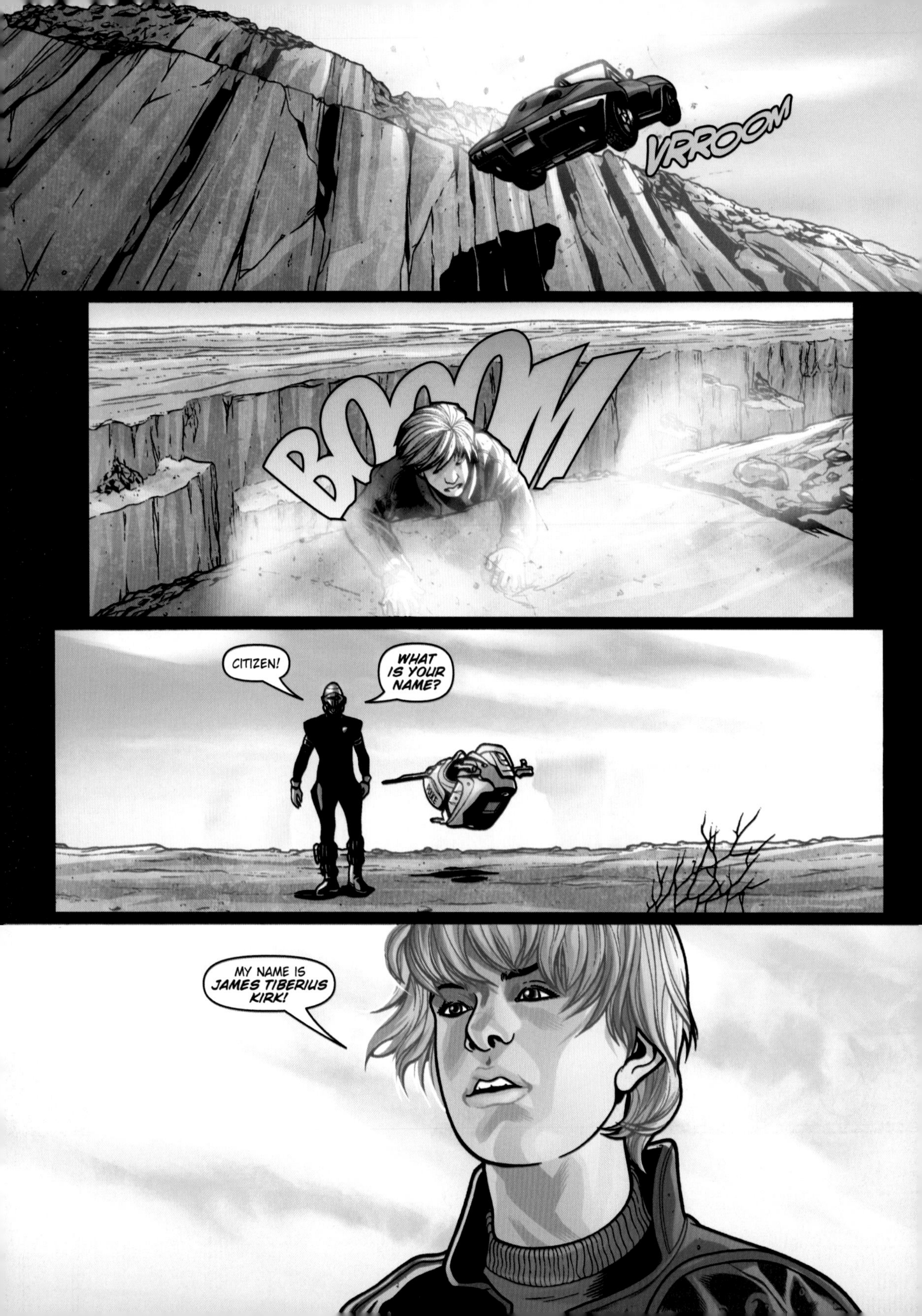
VRROOM
BOOOM
CITIZEN!
WHAT IS YOUR NAME?
MY NAME IS JAMES TIBERIUS KIRK!

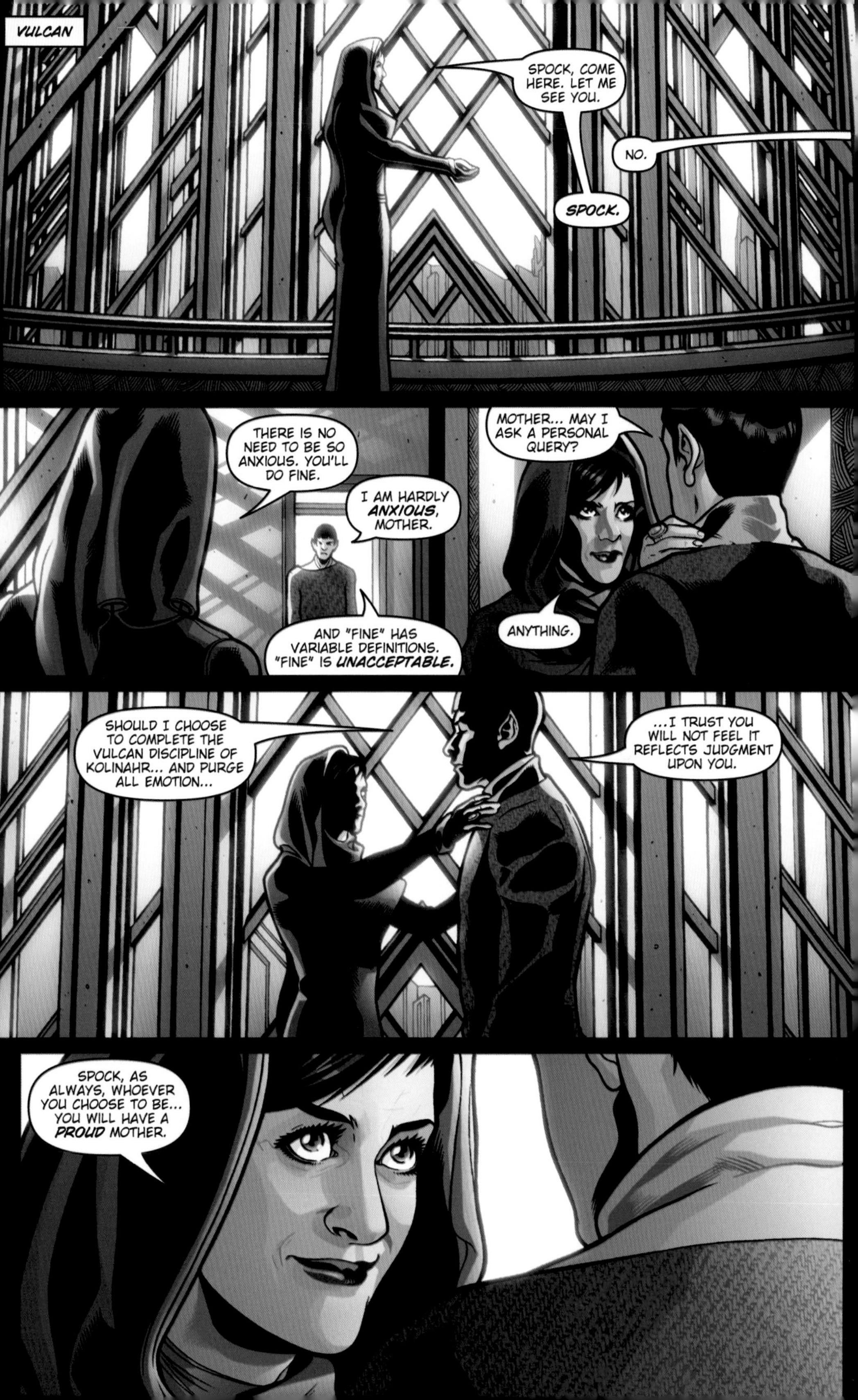
VULCAN
SPOCK, COME HERE. LET ME SEE YOU.
NO.
SPOCK.
THERE IS NO NEED TO BE SO ANXIOUS. YOU'LL DO FINE.
I AM HARDLY ANXIOUS, MOTHER.
AND "FINE" HAS VARIABLE DEFINITIONS. "FINE" IS UNACCEPTABLE.
MOTHER... MAY I ASK A PERSONAL QUERY?
ANYTHING.
SHOULD I CHOOSE TO COMPLETE THE VULCAN DISCIPLINE OF KOLINAHR... AND PURGE ALL EMOTION...
...I TRUST YOU WILL NOT FEEL IT REFLECTS JUDGMENT UPON YOU.
SPOCK, AS ALWAYS, WHOEVER YOU CHOOSE TO BE... YOU WILL HAVE A PROUD MOTHER.

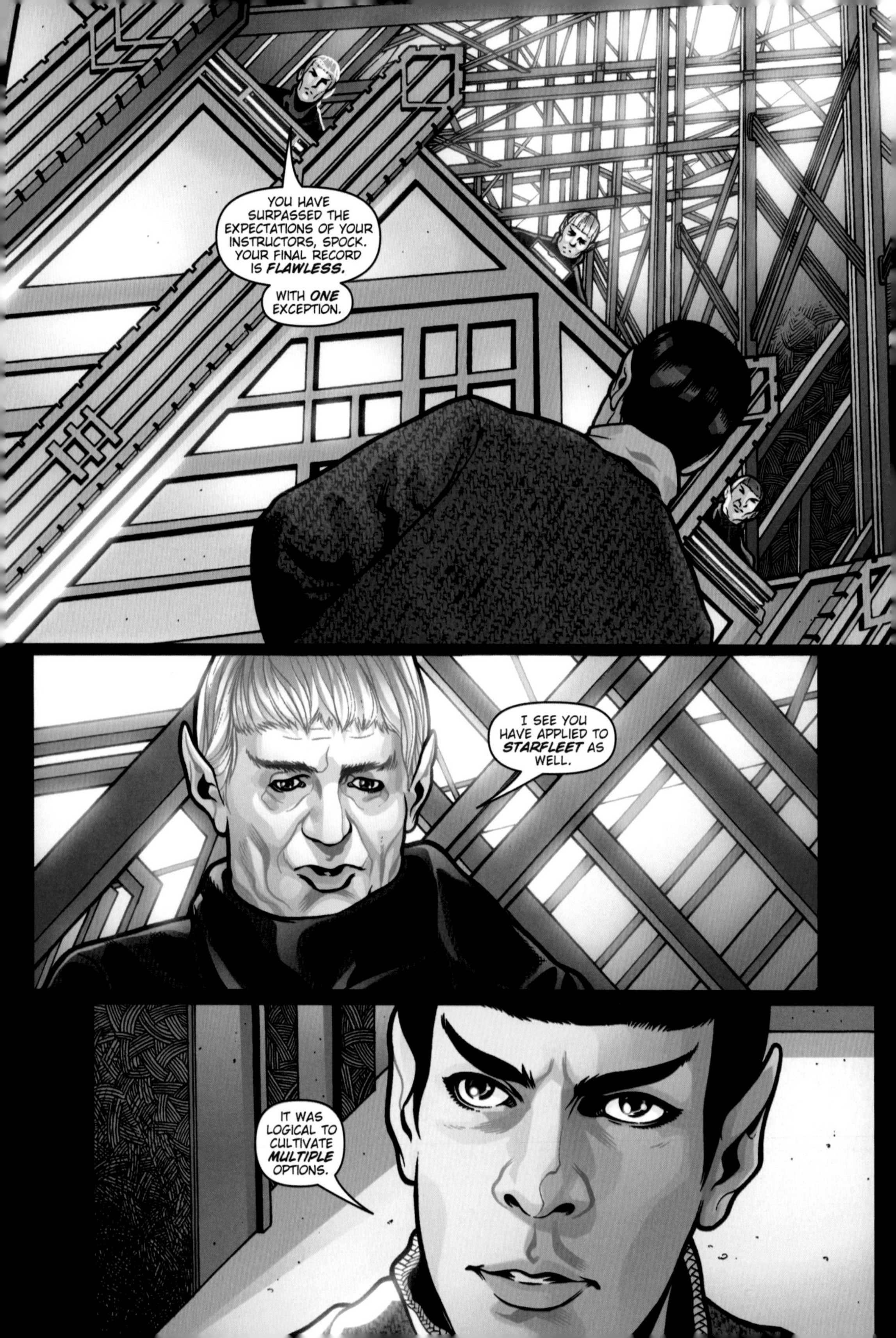
YOU HAVE SURPASSED THE EXPECTATIONS OF YOUR INSTRUCTORS, SPOCK. YOUR FINAL RECORD IS FLAWLESS.
WITH ONE EXCEPTION.
I SEE YOU HAVE APPLIED TO STARFLEET AS WELL.
IT WAS LOGICAL TO CULTIVATE MULTIPLE OPTIONS.

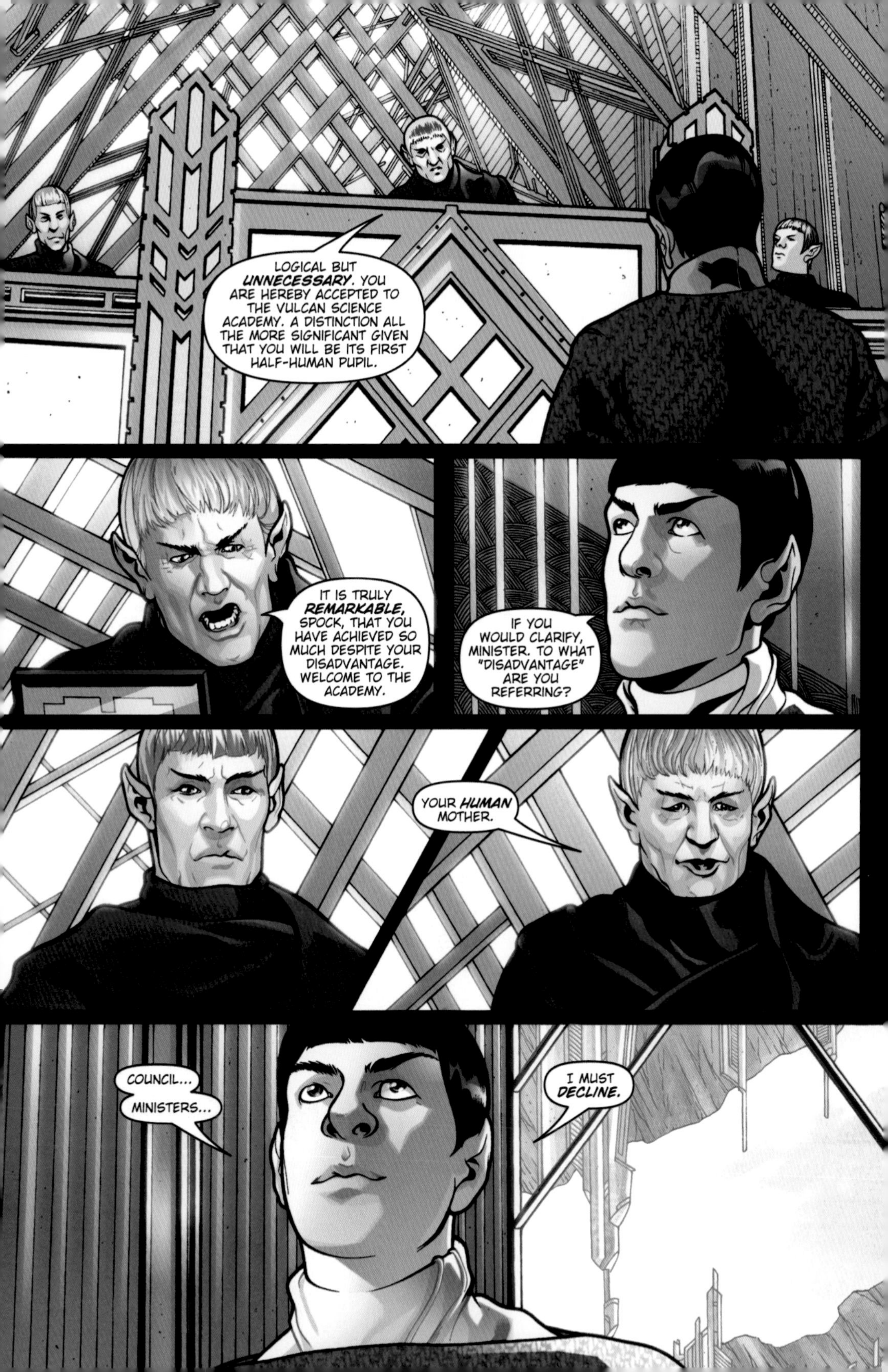
LOGICAL BUT ***UNNECESSARY***. YOU ARE HEREBY ACCEPTED TO THE VULCAN SCIENCE ACADEMY. A DISTINCTION ALL THE MORE SIGNIFICANT GIVEN THAT YOU WILL BE ITS FIRST HALF-HUMAN PUPIL.
IT IS TRULY ***REMARKABLE,*** SPOCK, THAT YOU HAVE ACHIEVED SO MUCH DESPITE YOUR DISADVANTAGE. WELCOME TO THE ACADEMY.
IF YOU WOULD CLARIFY, MINISTER. TO WHAT "DISADVANTAGE" ARE YOU REFERRING?
YOUR ***HUMAN*** MOTHER.
COUNCIL...
MINISTERS...
I MUST ***DECLINE.***

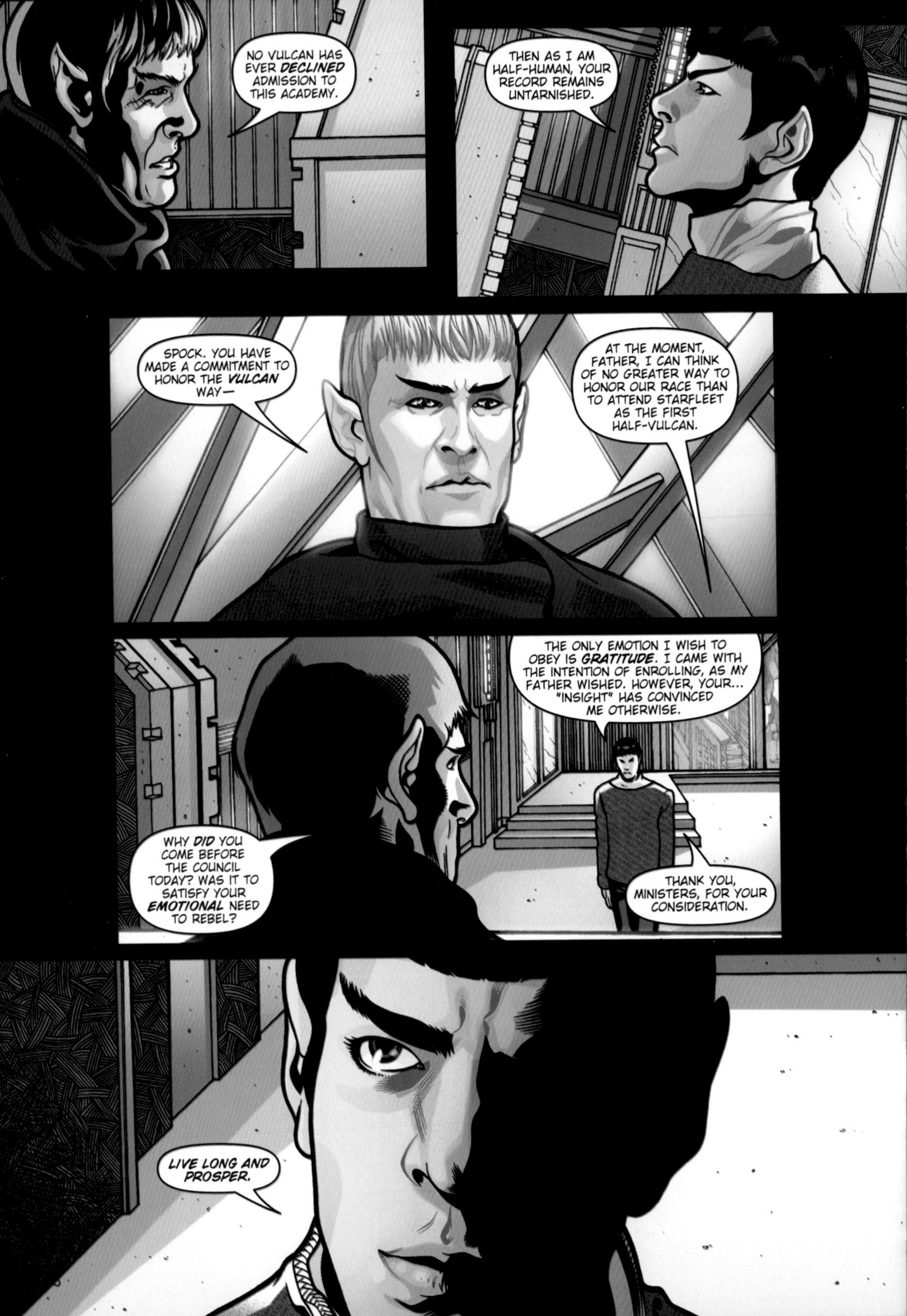
NO VULCAN HAS EVER *DECLINED* ADMISSION TO THIS ACADEMY.
THEN AS I AM HALF-HUMAN, YOUR RECORD REMAINS UNTARNISHED.
SPOCK. YOU HAVE MADE A COMMITMENT TO HONOR THE *VULCAN* WAY—
AT THE MOMENT, FATHER, I CAN THINK OF NO GREATER WAY TO HONOR OUR RACE THAN TO ATTEND STARFLEET AS THE FIRST HALF-VULCAN.
WHY *DID* YOU COME BEFORE THE COUNCIL TODAY? WAS IT TO SATISFY YOUR *EMOTIONAL* NEED TO REBEL?
THE ONLY EMOTION I WISH TO OBEY IS *GRATITUDE*. I CAME WITH THE INTENTION OF ENROLLING, AS MY FATHER WISHED. HOWEVER, YOUR... "INSIGHT" HAS CONVINCED ME OTHERWISE.
THANK YOU, MINISTERS, FOR YOUR CONSIDERATION.
LIVE LONG AND PROSPER.

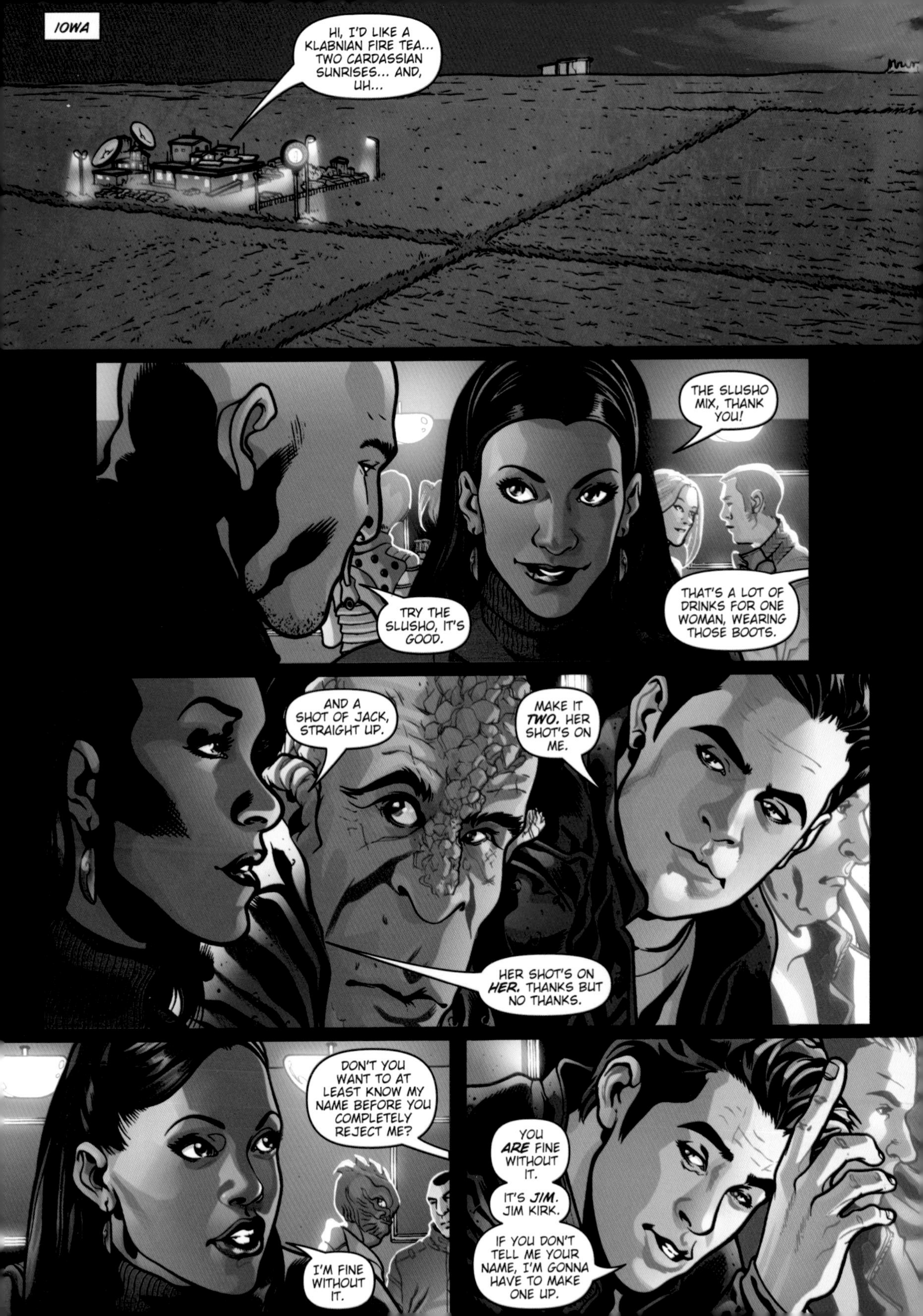
IOWA
HI, I'D LIKE A KLABNIAN FIRE TEA... TWO CARDASSIAN SUNRISES... AND, UH...
THE SLUSHO MIX, THANK YOU!
TRY THE SLUSHO, IT'S GOOD.
THAT'S A LOT OF DRINKS FOR ONE WOMAN, WEARING THOSE BOOTS.
AND A SHOT OF JACK, STRAIGHT UP.
MAKE IT TWO. HER SHOT'S ON ME.
HER SHOT'S ON HER. THANKS BUT NO THANKS.
DON'T YOU WANT TO AT LEAST KNOW MY NAME BEFORE YOU COMPLETELY REJECT ME?
I'M FINE WITHOUT IT.
YOU ARE FINE WITHOUT IT.
IT'S JIM. JIM KIRK.
IF YOU DON'T TELL ME YOUR NAME, I'M GONNA HAVE TO MAKE ONE UP.

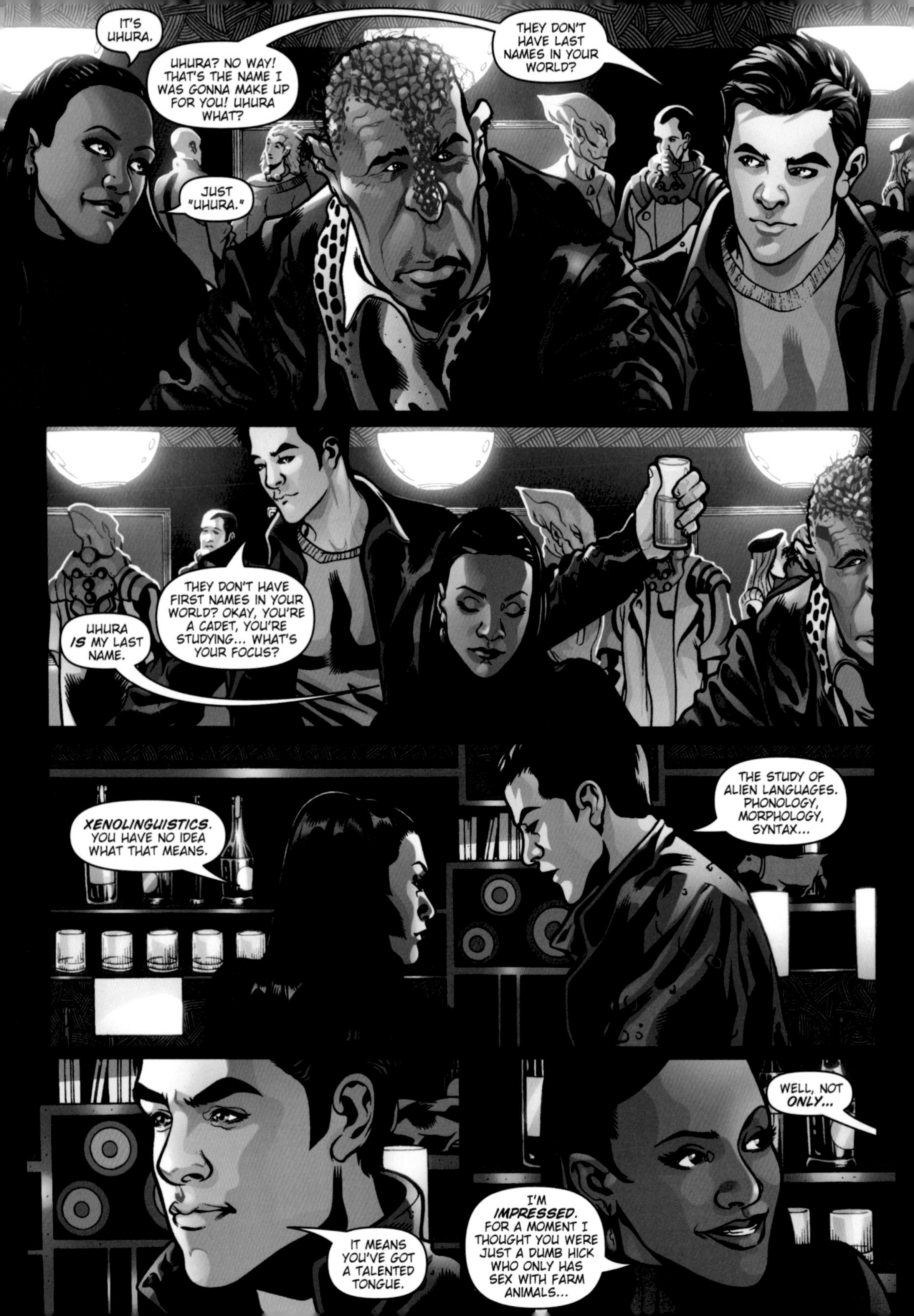
IT'S UHURA.
UHURA? NO WAY! THAT'S THE NAME I WAS GONNA MAKE UP FOR YOU! UHURA WHAT?
THEY DON'T HAVE LAST NAMES IN YOUR WORLD?
JUST "UHURA."
THEY DON'T HAVE FIRST NAMES IN YOUR WORLD? OKAY, YOU'RE A CADET, YOU'RE STUDYING... WHAT'S YOUR FOCUS?
UHURA *IS* MY LAST NAME.
XENOLINGUISTICS. YOU HAVE NO IDEA WHAT THAT MEANS.
THE STUDY OF ALIEN LANGUAGES. PHONOLOGY, MORPHOLOGY, SYNTAX...
IT MEANS YOU'VE GOT A TALENTED TONGUE.
WELL, NOT *ONLY*...
I'M *IMPRESSED*. FOR A MOMENT I THOUGHT YOU WERE JUST A DUMB HICK WHO ONLY HAS SEX WITH FARM ANIMALS...

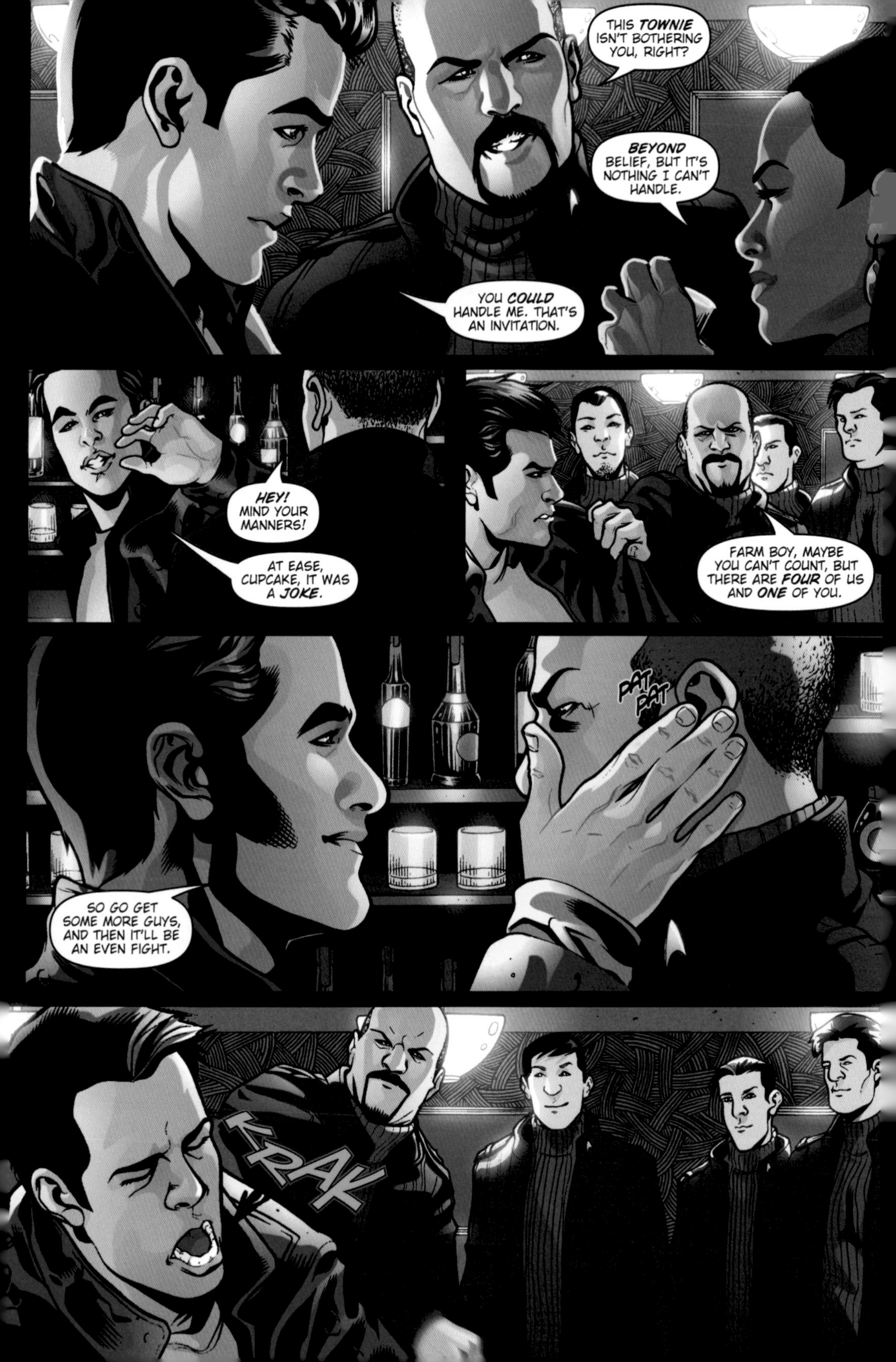
THIS TOWNIE ISN'T BOTHERING YOU, RIGHT?
BEYOND BELIEF, BUT IT'S NOTHING I CAN'T HANDLE.
YOU COULD HANDLE ME. THAT'S AN INVITATION.
HEY! MIND YOUR MANNERS!
AT EASE, CUPCAKE, IT WAS A JOKE.
FARM BOY, MAYBE YOU CAN'T COUNT, BUT THERE ARE FOUR OF US AND ONE OF YOU.
PAT PAT
SO GO GET SOME MORE GUYS, AND THEN IT'LL BE AN EVEN FIGHT.
K-RAK

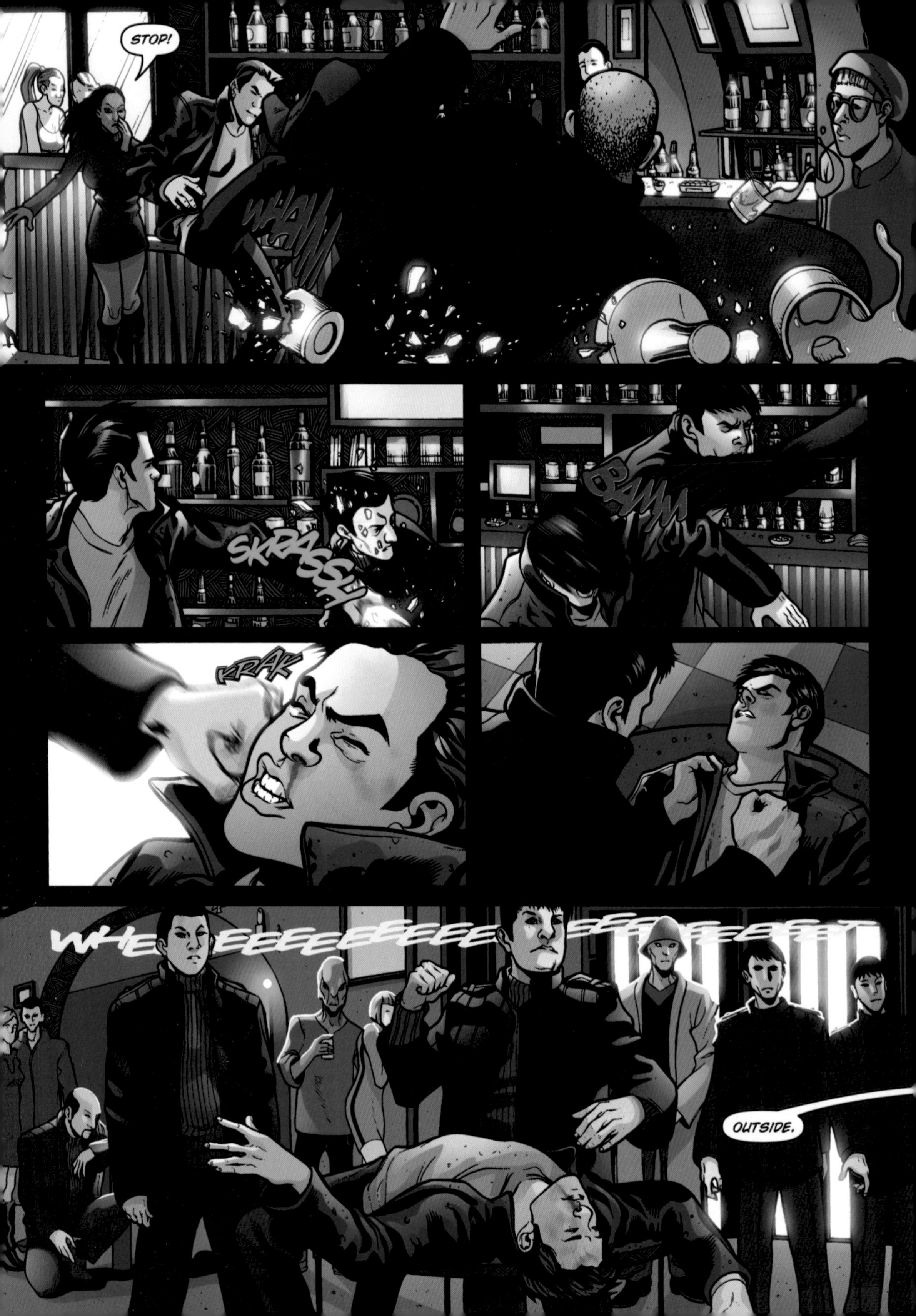
STOP!
WHAM
SKRASSH
BAMM
KRAK
WHEEEEEEEEEEEEEEEEEEEEEEEET
OUTSIDE.

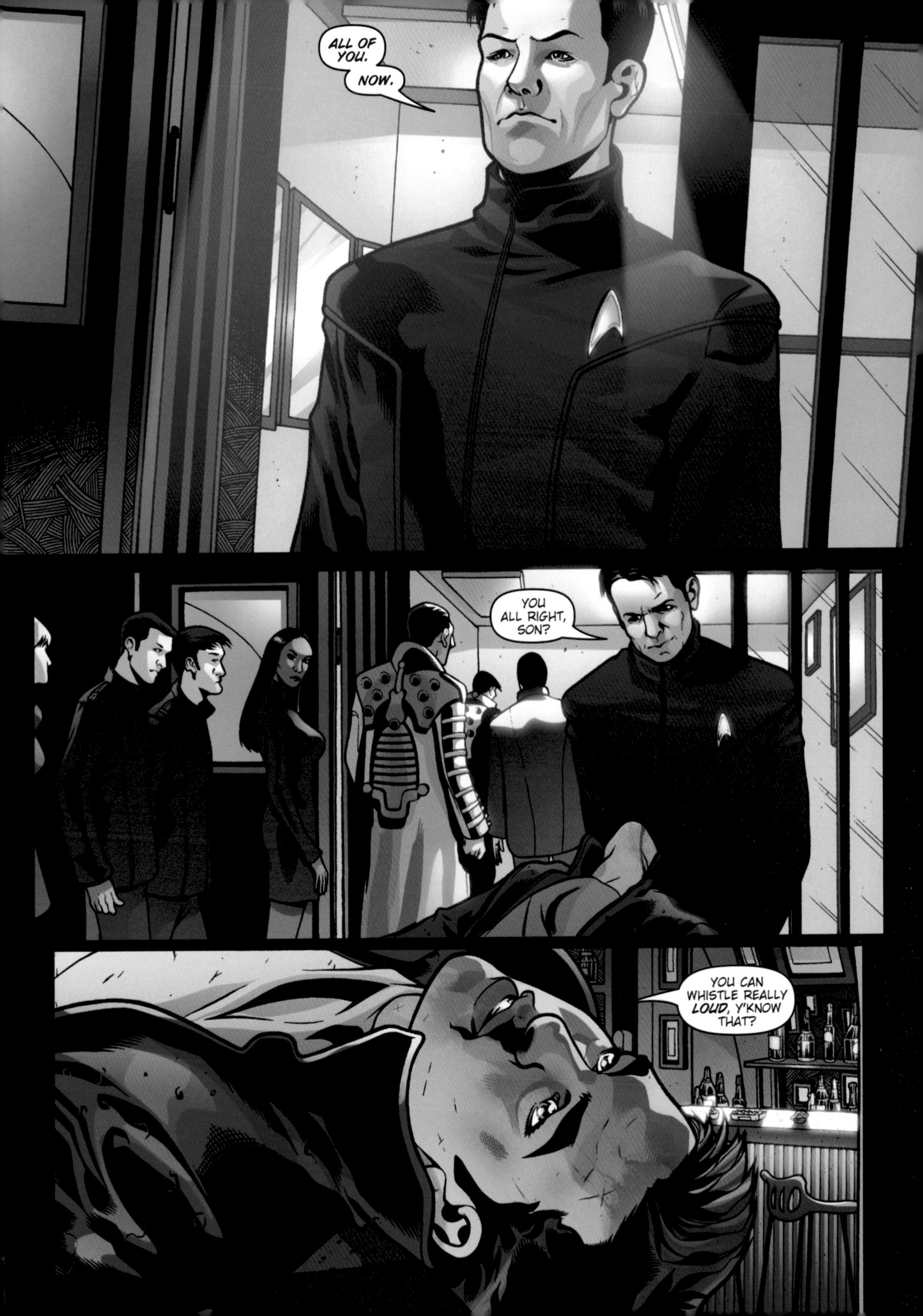
ALL OF YOU.
NOW.
YOU ALL RIGHT, SON?
YOU CAN WHISTLE REALLY LOUD, Y'KNOW THAT?

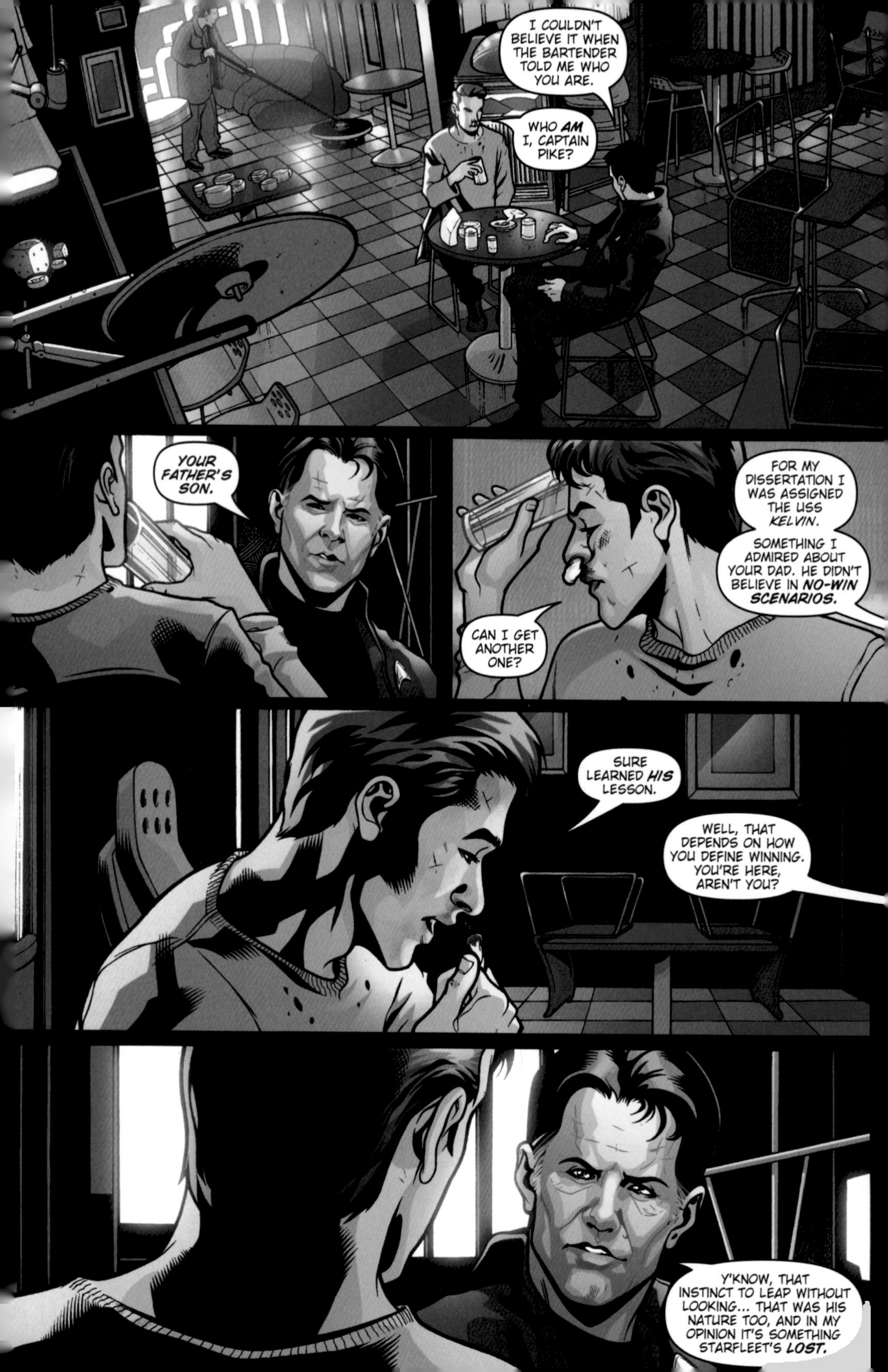
I COULDN'T BELIEVE IT WHEN THE BARTENDER TOLD ME WHO YOU ARE.
WHO AM I, CAPTAIN PIKE?
YOUR FATHER'S SON.
FOR MY DISSERTATION I WAS ASSIGNED THE USS KELVIN.
SOMETHING I ADMIRED ABOUT YOUR DAD. HE DIDN'T BELIEVE IN NO-WIN SCENARIOS.
CAN I GET ANOTHER ONE?
SURE LEARNED HIS LESSON.
WELL, THAT DEPENDS ON HOW YOU DEFINE WINNING. YOU'RE HERE, AREN'T YOU?
Y'KNOW, THAT INSTINCT TO LEAP WITHOUT LOOKING... THAT WAS HIS NATURE TOO, AND IN MY OPINION IT'S SOMETHING STARFLEET'S LOST.

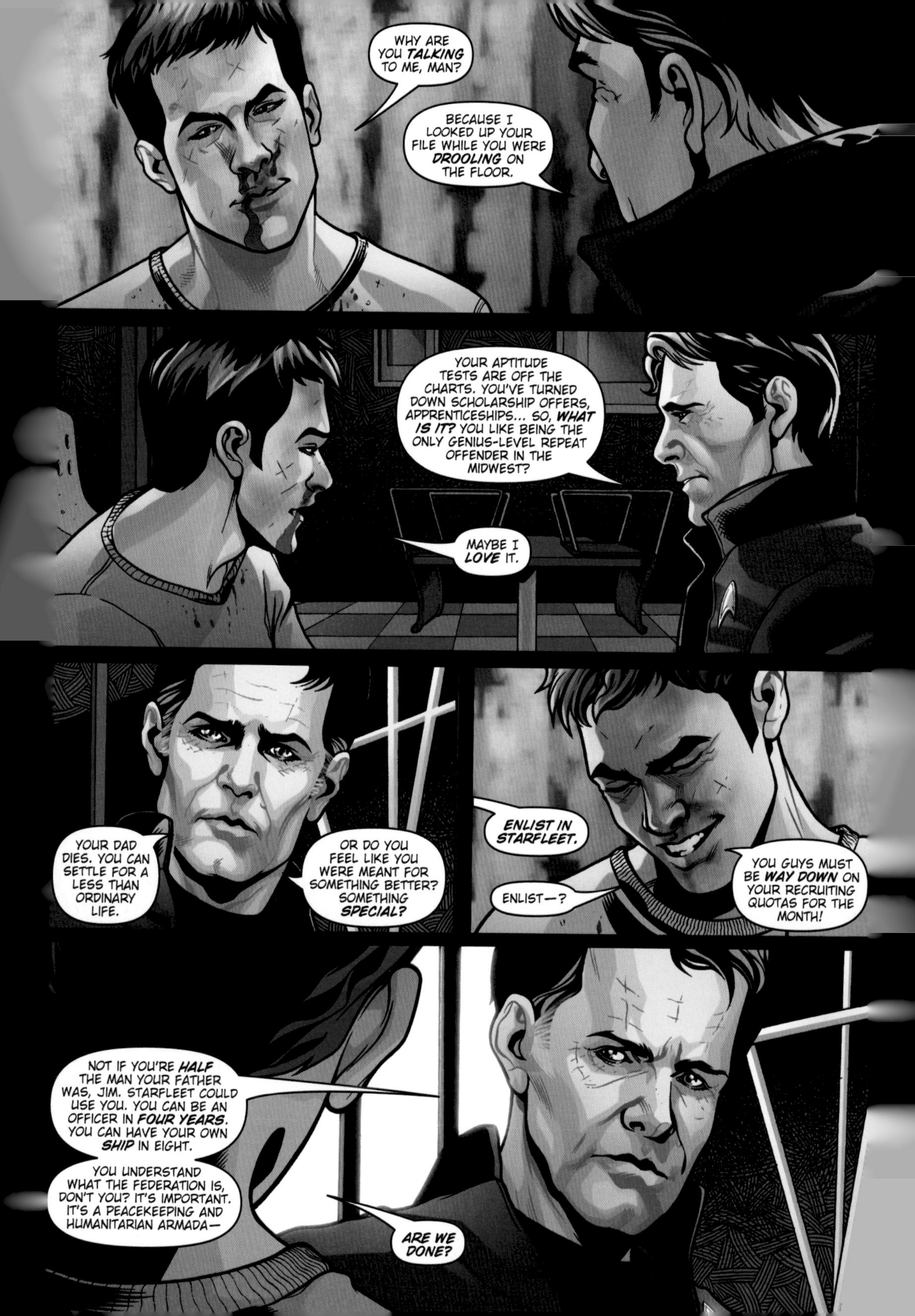
WHY ARE YOU TALKING TO ME, MAN?
BECAUSE I LOOKED UP YOUR FILE WHILE YOU WERE DROOLING ON THE FLOOR.
YOUR APTITUDE TESTS ARE OFF THE CHARTS. YOU'VE TURNED DOWN SCHOLARSHIP OFFERS, APPRENTICESHIPS... SO, WHAT IS IT? YOU LIKE BEING THE ONLY GENIUS-LEVEL REPEAT OFFENDER IN THE MIDWEST?
MAYBE I LOVE IT.
YOUR DAD DIES. YOU CAN SETTLE FOR A LESS THAN ORDINARY LIFE.
OR DO YOU FEEL LIKE YOU WERE MEANT FOR SOMETHING BETTER? SOMETHING SPECIAL?
ENLIST IN STARFLEET.
ENLIST—?
YOU GUYS MUST BE WAY DOWN ON YOUR RECRUITING QUOTAS FOR THE MONTH!
NOT IF YOU'RE HALF THE MAN YOUR FATHER WAS, JIM. STARFLEET COULD USE YOU. YOU CAN BE AN OFFICER IN FOUR YEARS. YOU CAN HAVE YOUR OWN SHIP IN EIGHT.
YOU UNDERSTAND WHAT THE FEDERATION IS, DON'T YOU? IT'S IMPORTANT. IT'S A PEACEKEEPING AND HUMANITARIAN ARMADA—
ARE WE DONE?

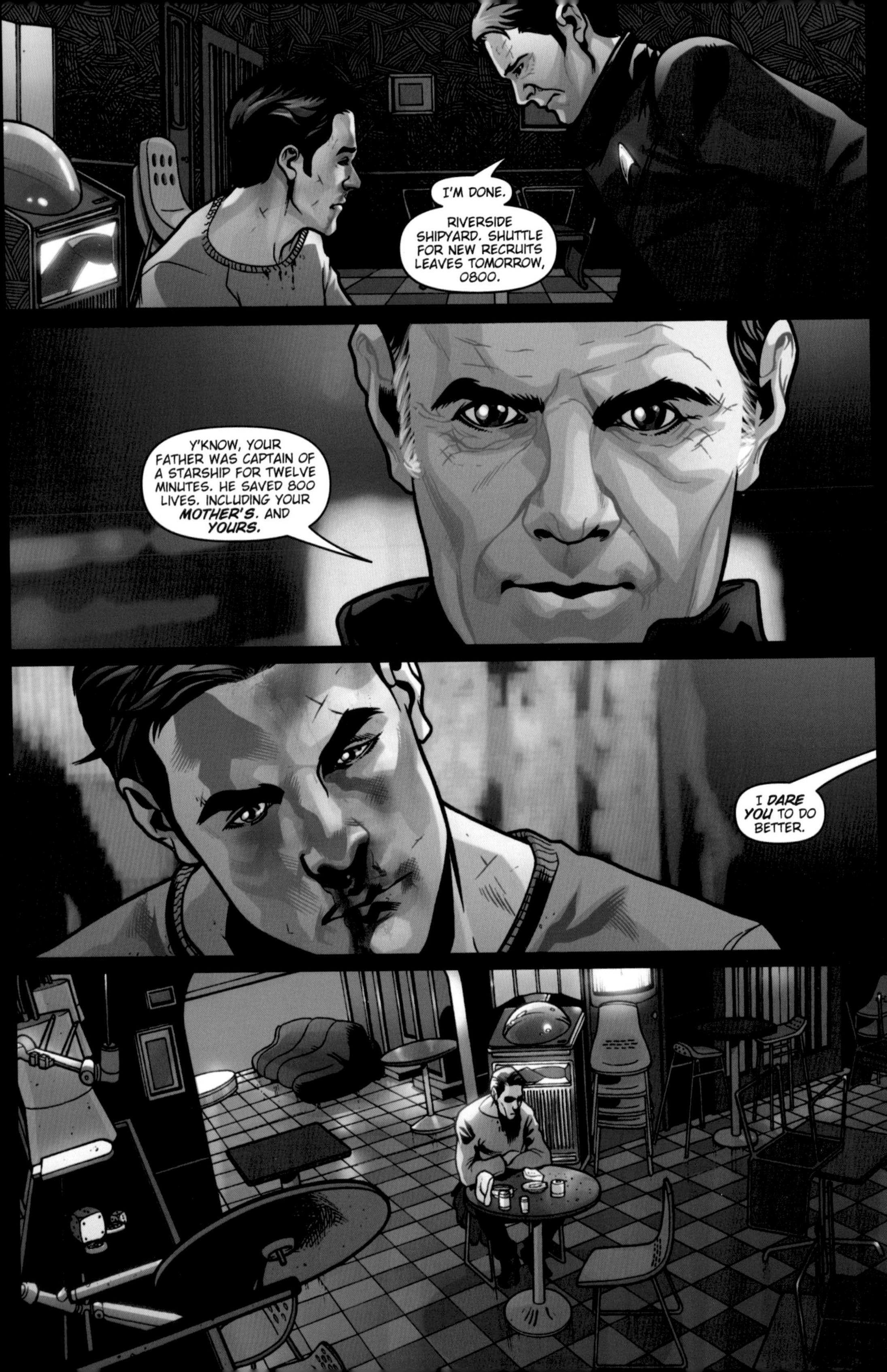
I'M DONE.
RIVERSIDE SHIPYARD. SHUTTLE FOR NEW RECRUITS LEAVES TOMORROW, 0800.
Y'KNOW, YOUR FATHER WAS CAPTAIN OF A STARSHIP FOR TWELVE MINUTES. HE SAVED 800 LIVES. INCLUDING YOUR *MOTHER'S*. AND *YOURS.*
I *DARE YOU* TO DO BETTER.

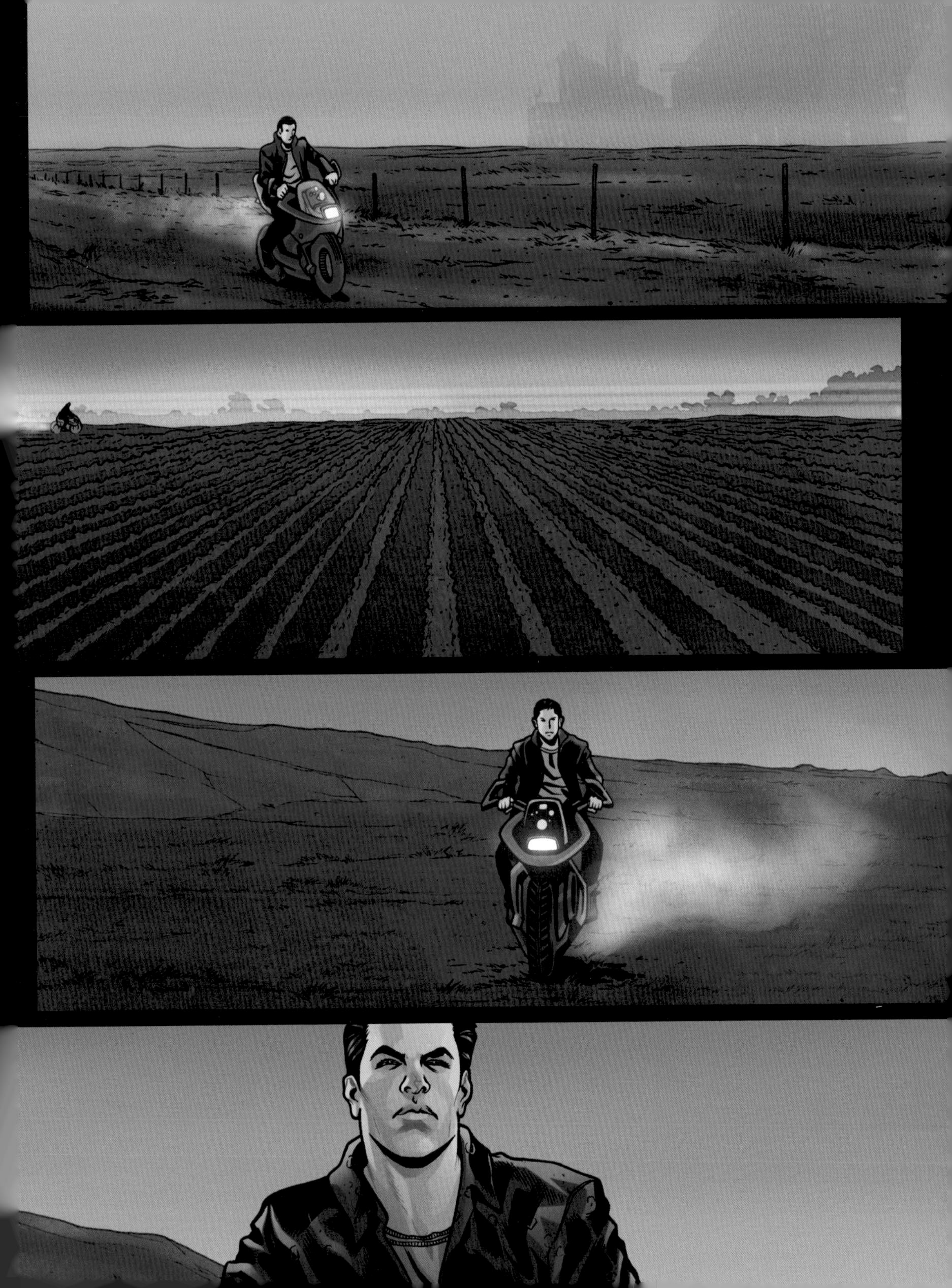

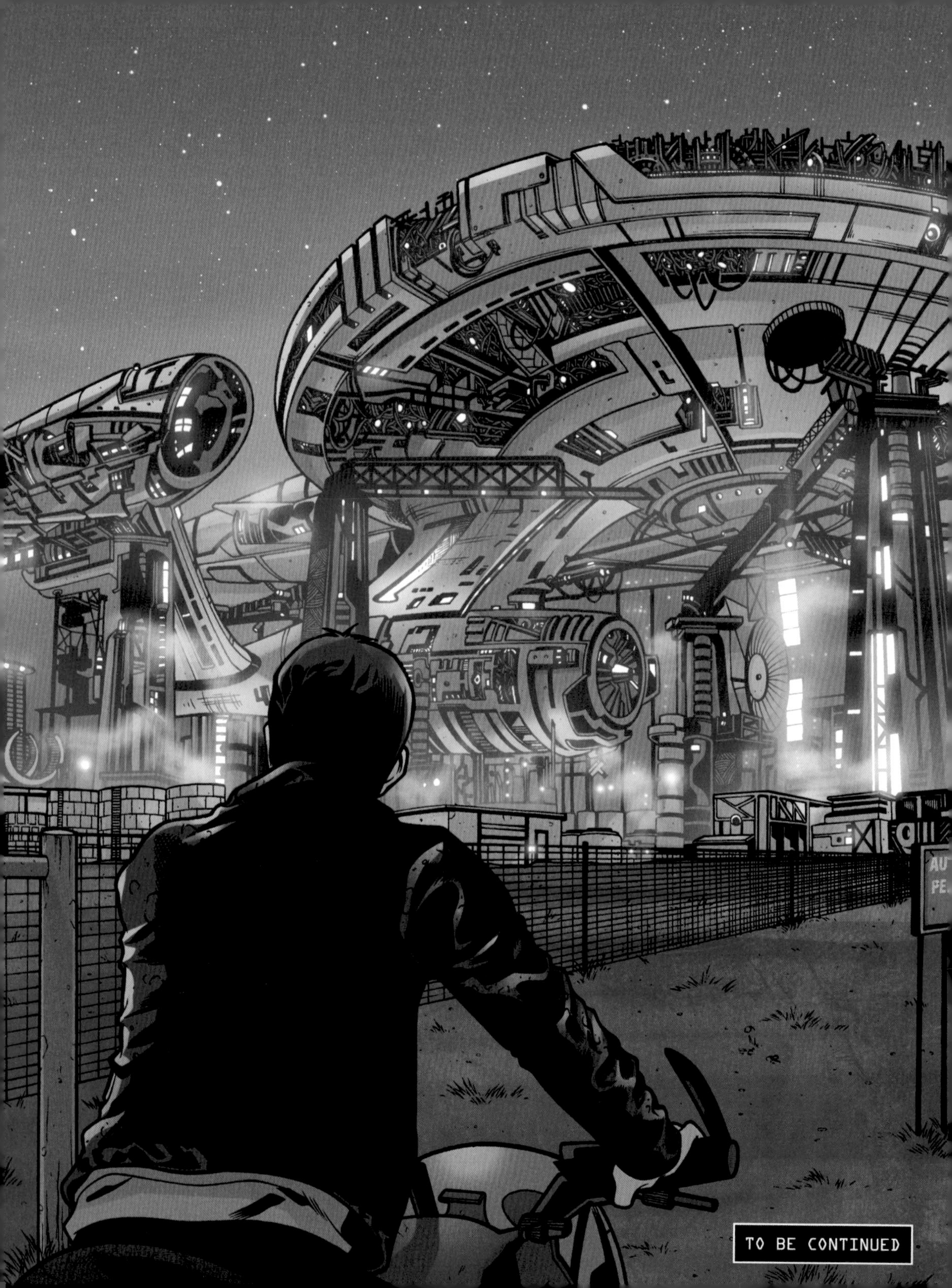
TO BE CONTINUED

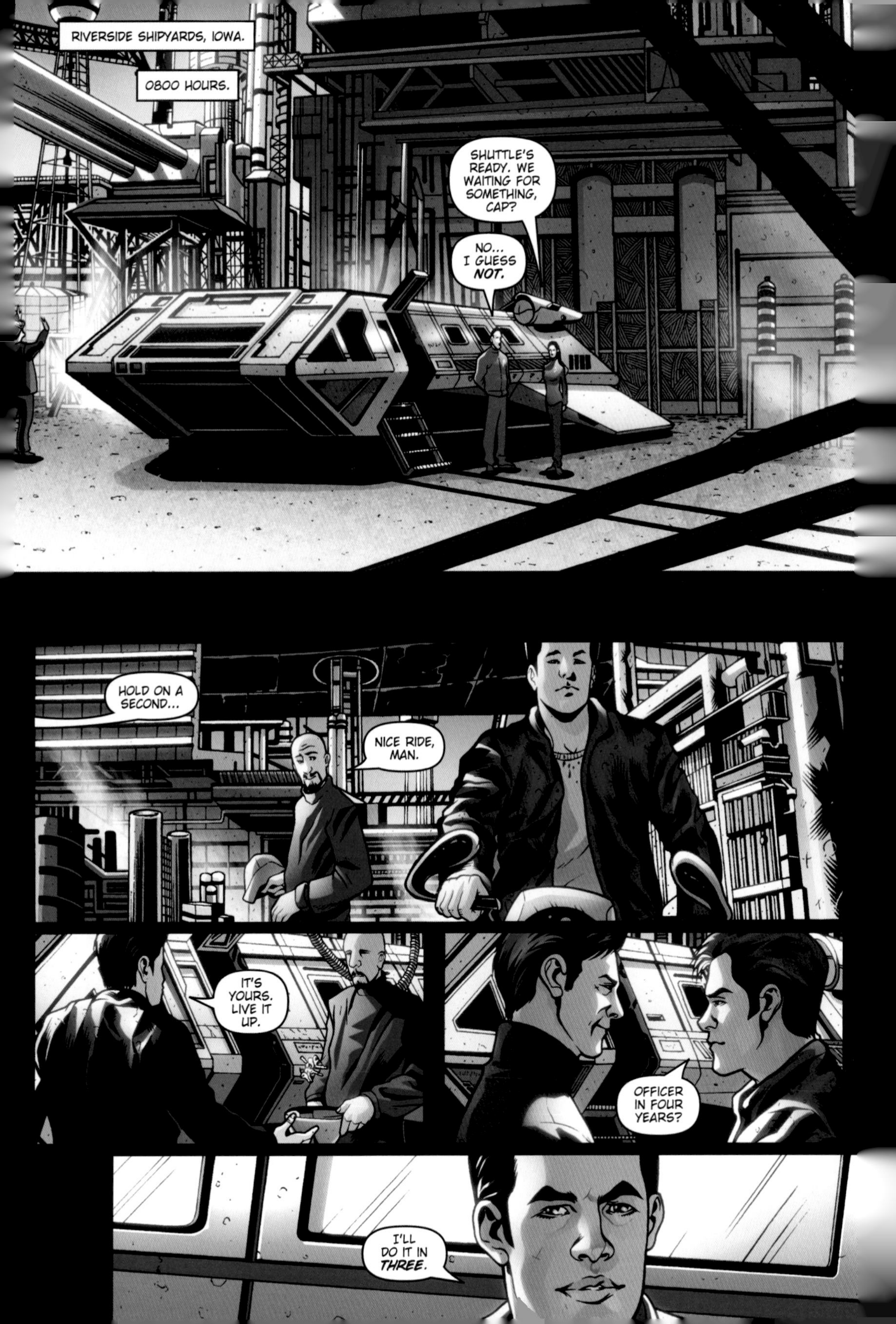

RIVERSIDE SHIPYARDS, IOWA.
0800 HOURS.
SHUTTLE'S READY. WE WAITING FOR SOMETHING, CAP?
NO... I GUESS **NOT.**
HOLD ON A SECOND...
NICE RIDE, MAN.
IT'S YOURS. LIVE IT UP.
OFFICER IN FOUR YEARS?
I'LL DO IT IN ***THREE***.

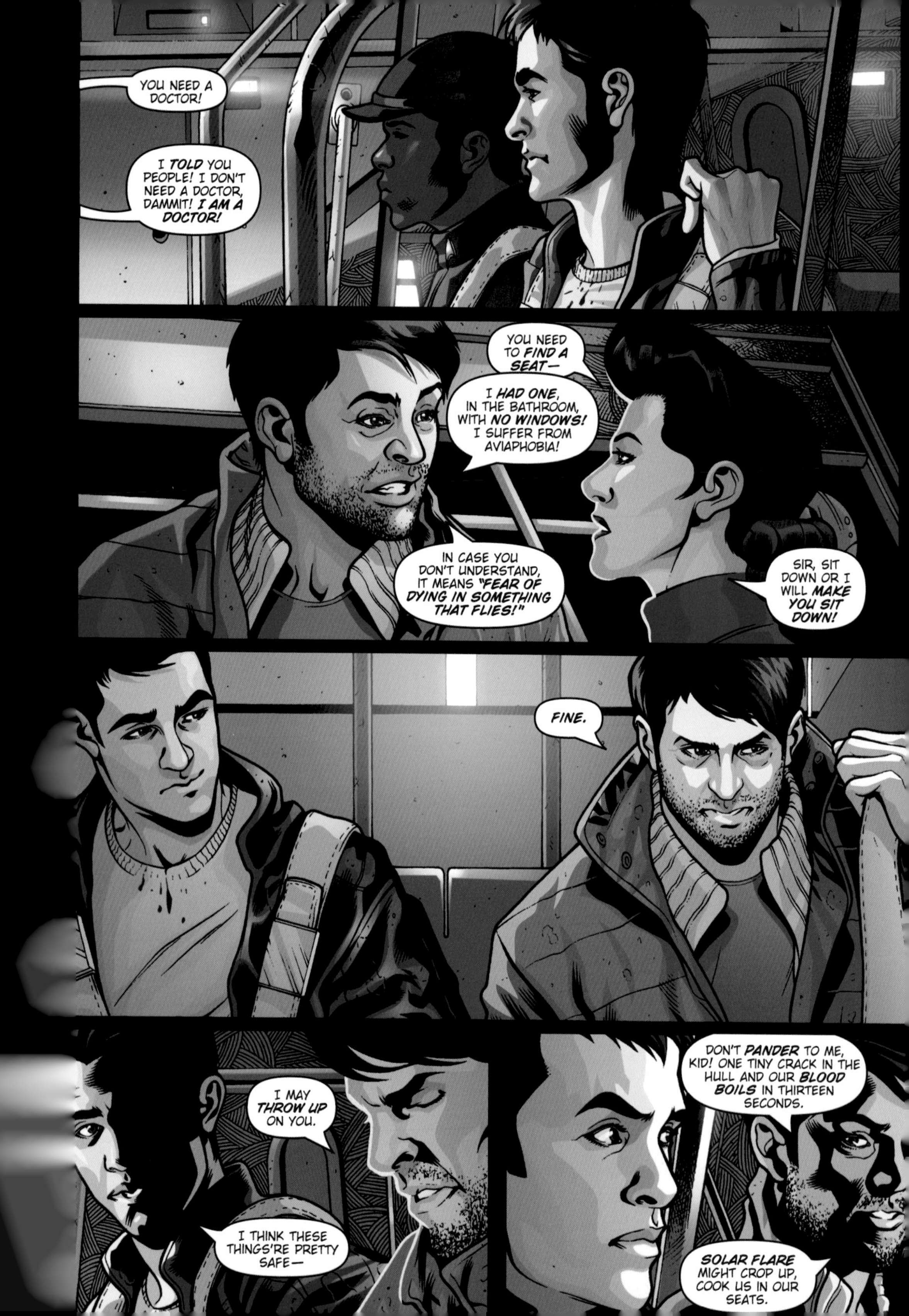

YOU NEED A DOCTOR!
I *TOLD* YOU PEOPLE! I DON'T NEED A DOCTOR, DAMMIT! *I AM A DOCTOR!*
YOU NEED TO *FIND A SEAT*—
I *HAD ONE*, IN THE BATHROOM, WITH *NO WINDOWS!* I SUFFER FROM AVIAPHOBIA!
IN CASE YOU DON'T UNDERSTAND, IT MEANS *"FEAR OF DYING IN SOMETHING THAT FLIES!"*
SIR, SIT DOWN OR I WILL *MAKE YOU SIT DOWN!*
FINE.
I MAY *THROW UP* ON YOU.
I THINK THESE THINGS'RE PRETTY SAFE—
DON'T *PANDER* TO ME, KID! ONE TINY CRACK IN THE HULL AND OUR *BLOOD BOILS* IN THIRTEEN SECONDS.
SOLAR FLARE MIGHT CROP UP, COOK US IN OUR SEATS.

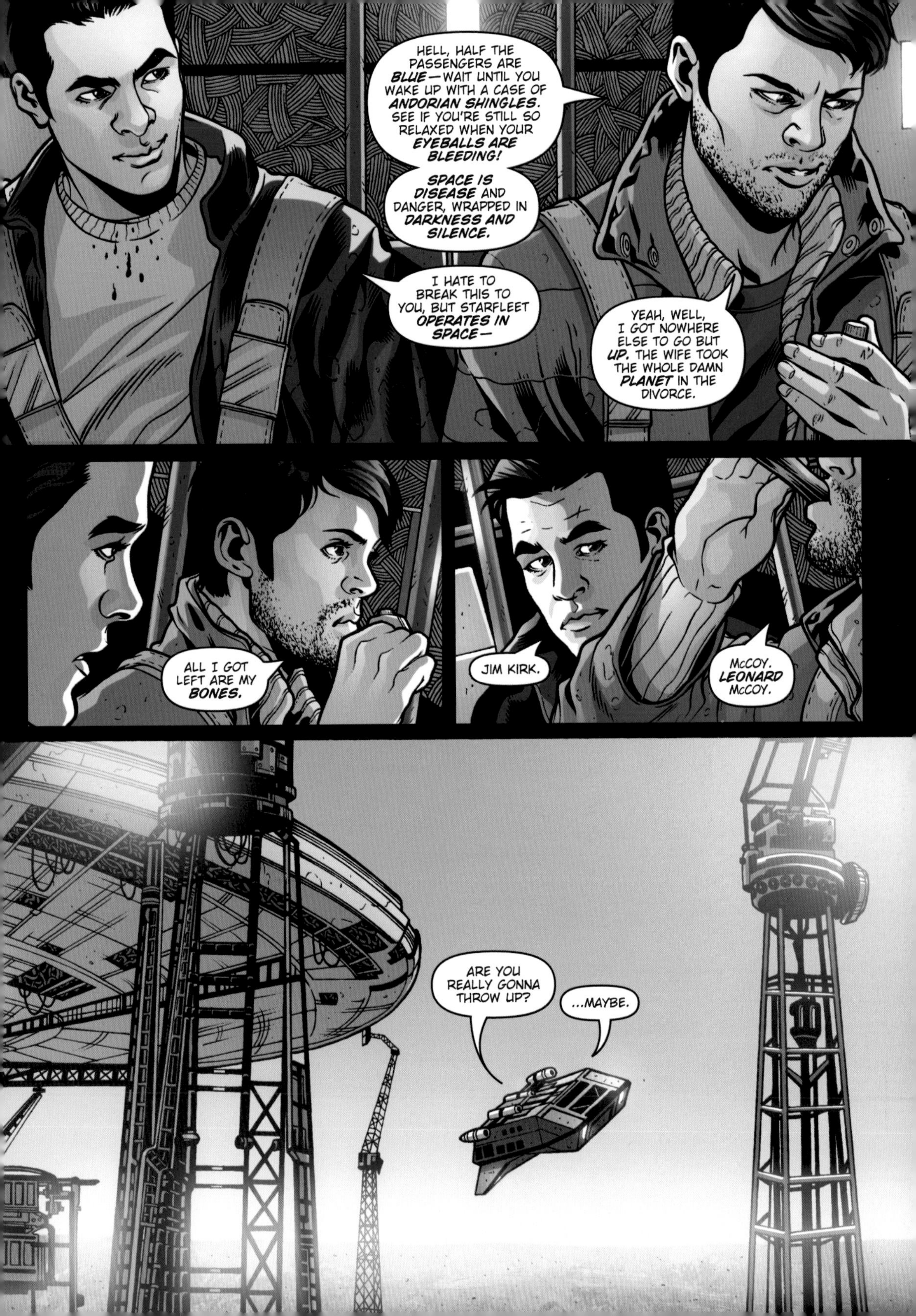
HELL, HALF THE PASSENGERS ARE BLUE—WAIT UNTIL YOU WAKE UP WITH A CASE OF ANDORIAN SHINGLES. SEE IF YOU'RE STILL SO RELAXED WHEN YOUR EYEBALLS ARE BLEEDING!
SPACE IS DISEASE AND DANGER, WRAPPED IN DARKNESS AND SILENCE.
I HATE TO BREAK THIS TO YOU, BUT STARFLEET OPERATES IN SPACE—
YEAH, WELL, I GOT NOWHERE ELSE TO GO BUT UP. THE WIFE TOOK THE WHOLE DAMN PLANET IN THE DIVORCE.
ALL I GOT LEFT ARE MY BONES.
JIM KIRK.
McCOY. LEONARD McCOY.
ARE YOU REALLY GONNA THROW UP?
...MAYBE.

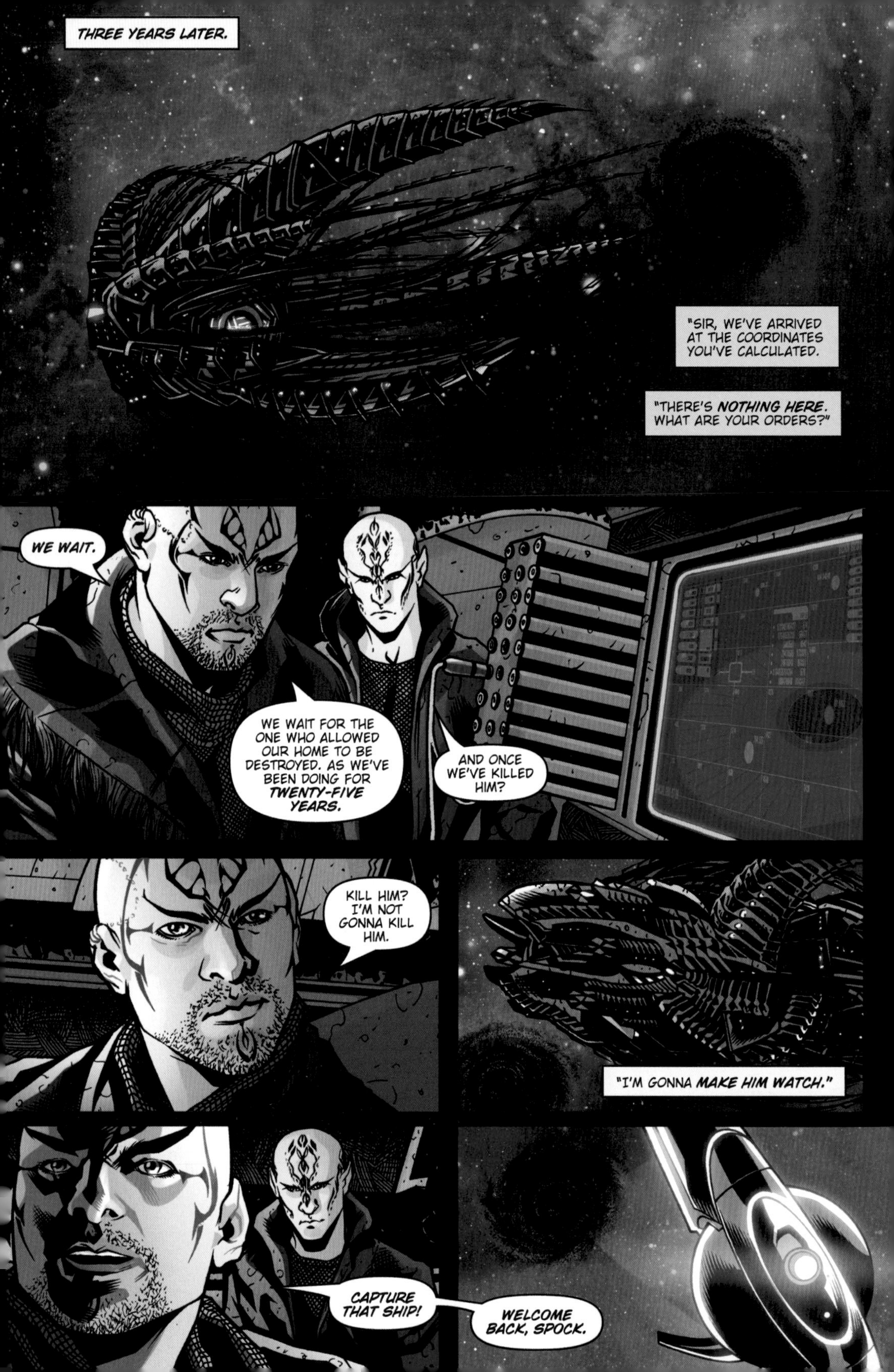
THREE YEARS LATER.
"SIR, WE'VE ARRIVED AT THE COORDINATES YOU'VE CALCULATED.
"THERE'S NOTHING HERE. WHAT ARE YOUR ORDERS?"
WE WAIT.
WE WAIT FOR THE ONE WHO ALLOWED OUR HOME TO BE DESTROYED. AS WE'VE BEEN DOING FOR TWENTY-FIVE YEARS.
AND ONCE WE'VE KILLED HIM?
KILL HIM? I'M NOT GONNA KILL HIM.
"I'M GONNA MAKE HIM WATCH."
CAPTURE THAT SHIP!
WELCOME BACK, SPOCK.

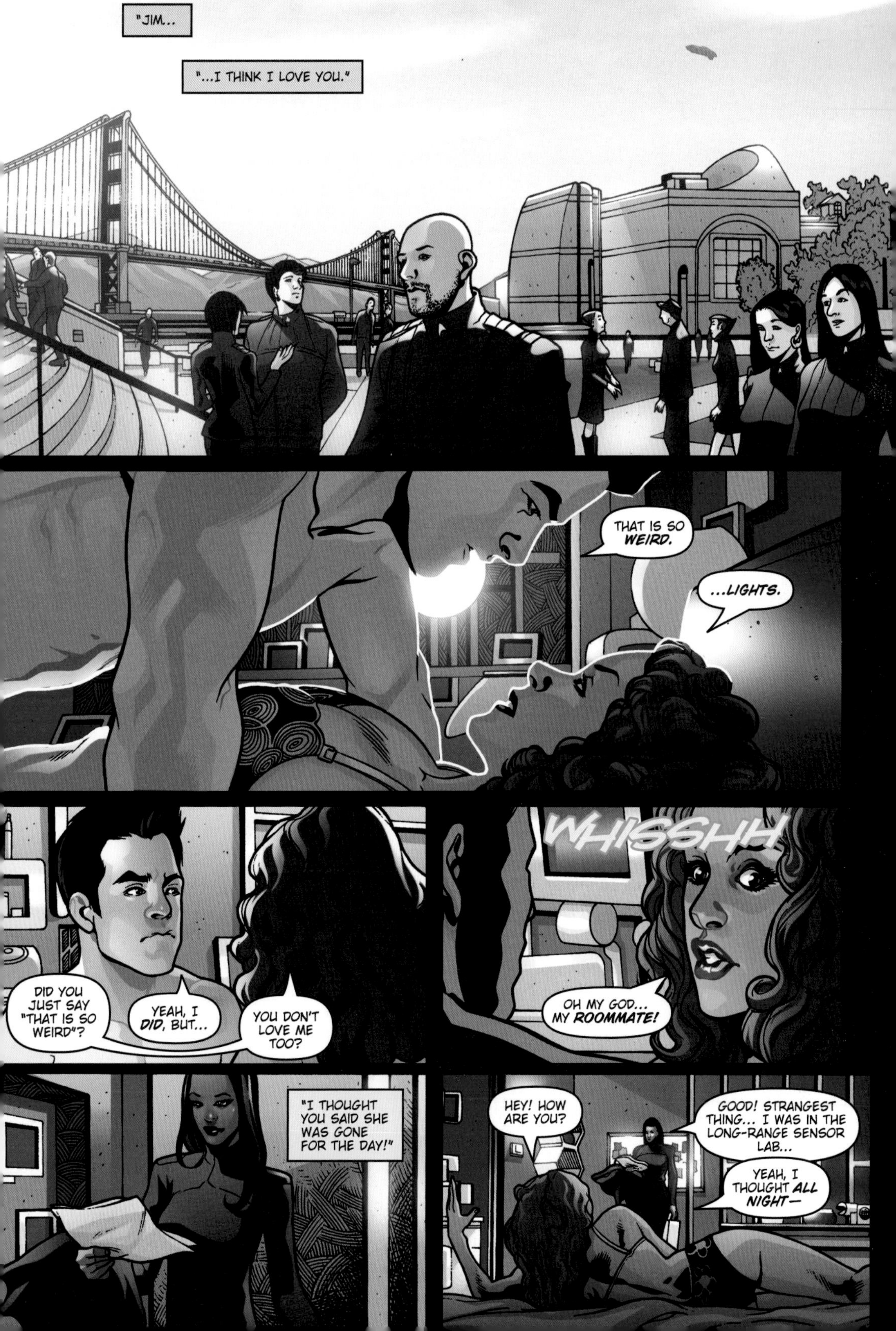
"JIM...
"...I THINK I LOVE YOU."
THAT IS SO WEIRD.
...LIGHTS.
DID YOU JUST SAY "THAT IS SO WEIRD"?
YEAH, I DID, BUT...
YOU DON'T LOVE ME TOO?
WHISSHH
OH MY GOD... MY ROOMMATE!
"I THOUGHT YOU SAID SHE WAS GONE FOR THE DAY!"
HEY! HOW ARE YOU?
GOOD! STRANGEST THING... I WAS IN THE LONG-RANGE SENSOR LAB...
YEAH, I THOUGHT ALL NIGHT—

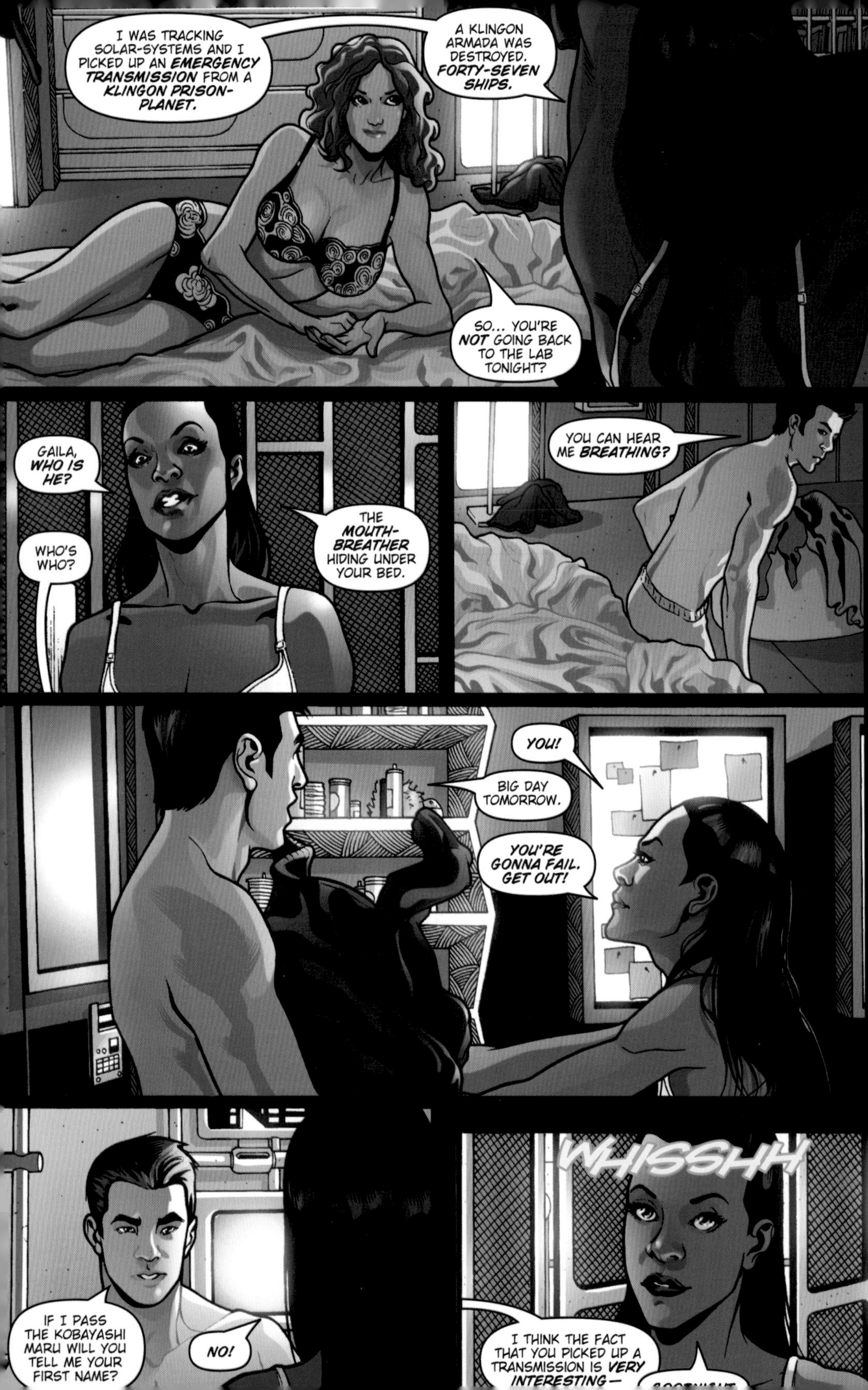
I WAS TRACKING SOLAR-SYSTEMS AND I PICKED UP AN **EMERGENCY TRANSMISSION** FROM A **KLINGON PRISON-PLANET.**
A KLINGON ARMADA WAS DESTROYED. **FORTY-SEVEN SHIPS.**
SO... YOU'RE **NOT** GOING BACK TO THE LAB TONIGHT?
GAILA, **WHO IS HE?**
WHO'S WHO?
THE **MOUTH-BREATHER** HIDING UNDER YOUR BED.
YOU CAN HEAR ME **BREATHING?**
YOU!
BIG DAY TOMORROW.
YOU'RE GONNA FAIL. GET OUT!
IF I PASS THE KOBAYASHI MARU WILL YOU TELL ME YOUR FIRST NAME?
NO!
WHISSHH
I THINK THE FACT THAT YOU PICKED UP A TRANSMISSION IS **VERY INTERESTING—**

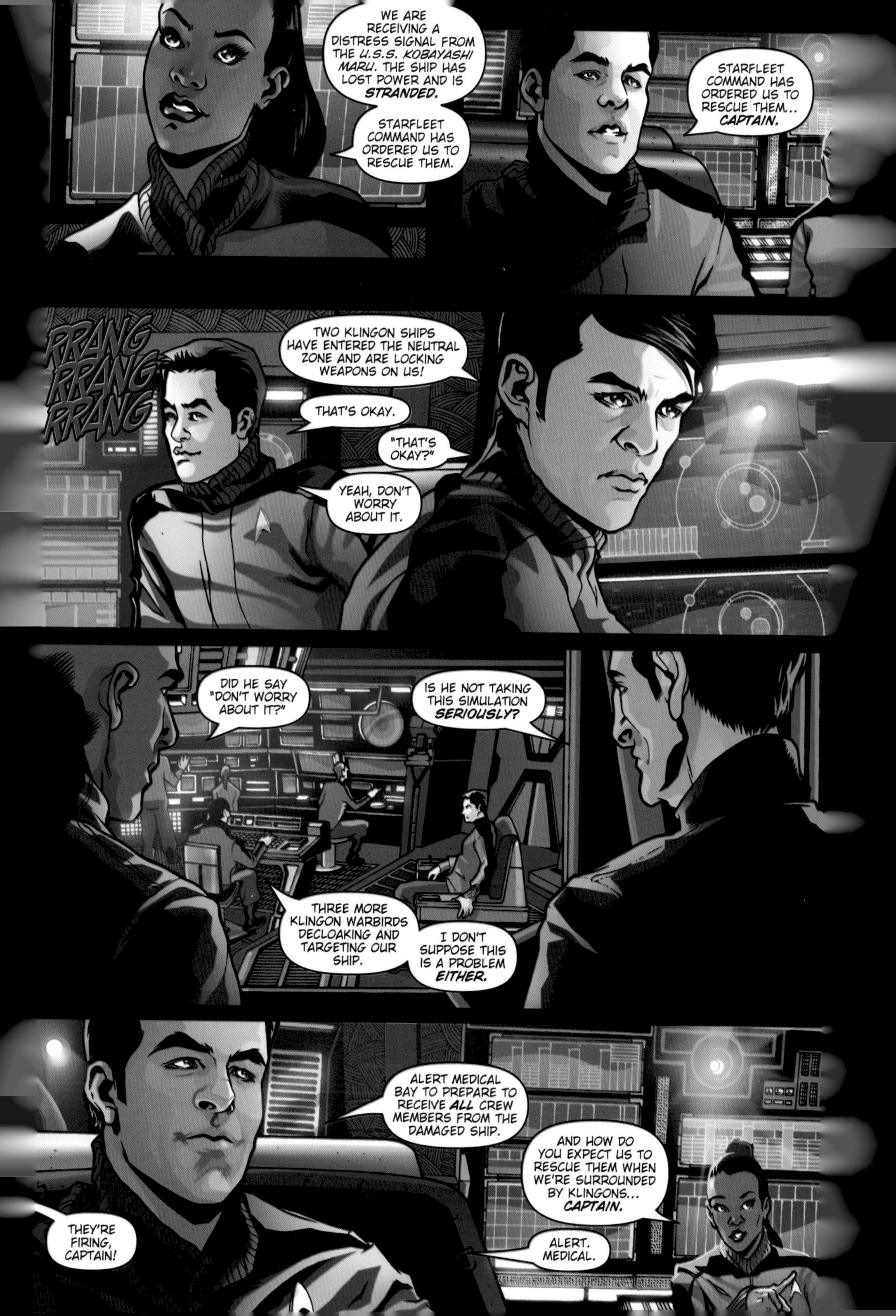

WE ARE RECEIVING A DISTRESS SIGNAL FROM THE U.S.S. KOBAYASHI MARU. THE SHIP HAS LOST POWER AND IS STRANDED.
STARFLEET COMMAND HAS ORDERED US TO RESCUE THEM.
STARFLEET COMMAND HAS ORDERED US TO RESCUE THEM... CAPTAIN.
RRANG RRANG RRANG
TWO KLINGON SHIPS HAVE ENTERED THE NEUTRAL ZONE AND ARE LOCKING WEAPONS ON US!
THAT'S OKAY.
"THAT'S OKAY?"
YEAH, DON'T WORRY ABOUT IT.
DID HE SAY "DON'T WORRY ABOUT IT?"
IS HE NOT TAKING THIS SIMULATION SERIOUSLY?
THREE MORE KLINGON WARBIRDS DECLOAKING AND TARGETING OUR SHIP.
I DON'T SUPPOSE THIS IS A PROBLEM EITHER.
ALERT MEDICAL BAY TO PREPARE TO RECEIVE ALL CREW MEMBERS FROM THE DAMAGED SHIP.
AND HOW DO YOU EXPECT US TO RESCUE THEM WHEN WE'RE SURROUNDED BY KLINGONS... CAPTAIN.
THEY'RE FIRING, CAPTAIN!
ALERT. MEDICAL.

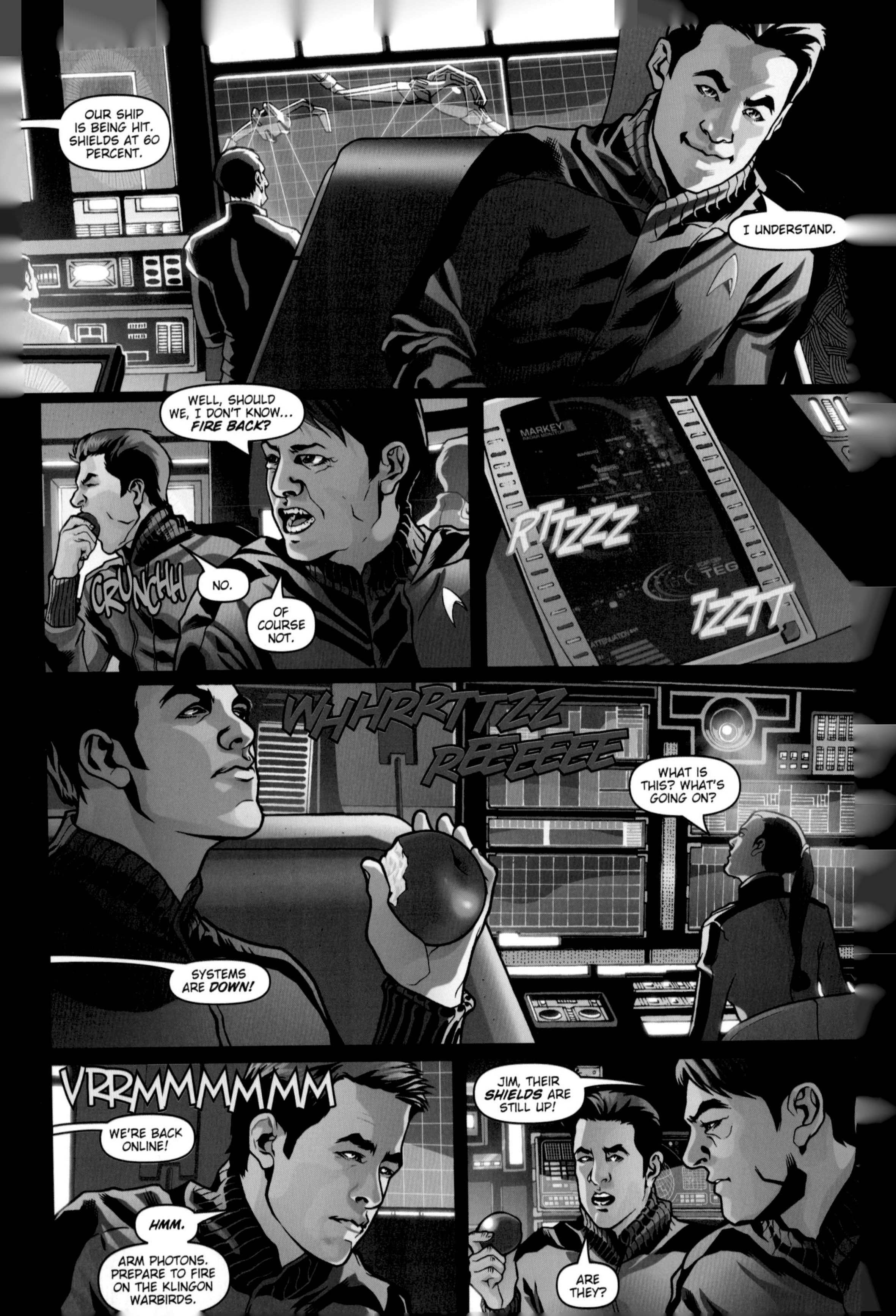
OUR SHIP IS BEING HIT. SHIELDS AT 60 PERCENT.
I UNDERSTAND.
WELL, SHOULD WE, I DON'T KNOW... FIRE BACK?
CRUNCHH
NO.
OF COURSE NOT.
MARKEY
RTTZZZ
TZZTT
WHHRRTTZZ
REEEEEE
WHAT IS THIS? WHAT'S GOING ON?
SYSTEMS ARE DOWN!
VRRMMMMMM
WE'RE BACK ONLINE!
HMM.
ARM PHOTONS. PREPARE TO FIRE ON THE KLINGON WARBIRDS.
JIM, THEIR SHIELDS ARE STILL UP!
ARE THEY?

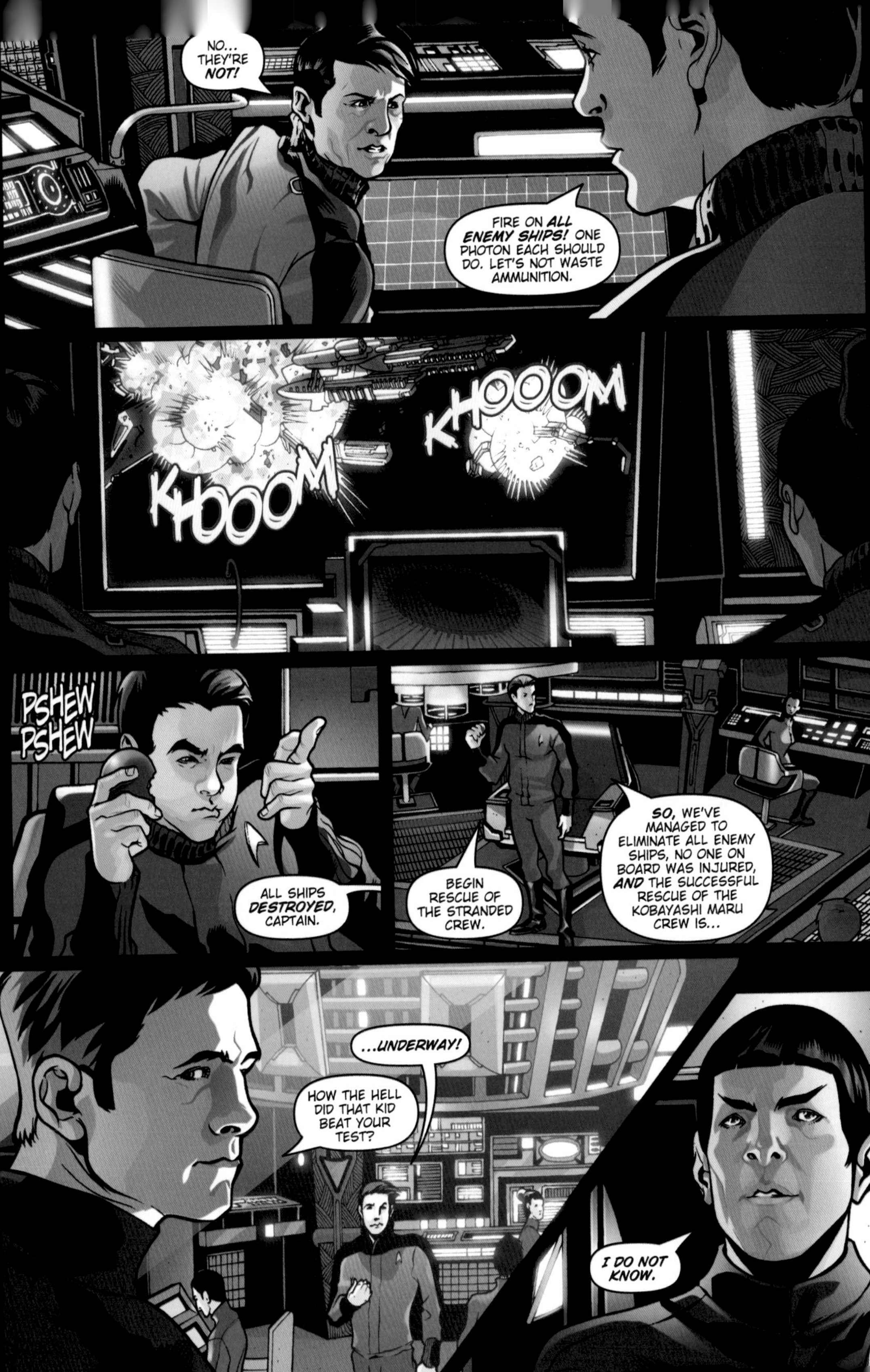
NO... THEY'RE NOT!
FIRE ON ALL ENEMY SHIPS! ONE PHOTON EACH SHOULD DO. LET'S NOT WASTE AMMUNITION.
KHOOOM
KHOOOM
PSHEW PSHEW
ALL SHIPS DESTROYED, CAPTAIN.
BEGIN RESCUE OF THE STRANDED CREW.
SO, WE'VE MANAGED TO ELIMINATE ALL ENEMY SHIPS, NO ONE ON BOARD WAS INJURED, AND THE SUCCESSFUL RESCUE OF THE KOBAYASHI MARU CREW IS...
...UNDERWAY!
HOW THE HELL DID THAT KID BEAT YOUR TEST?
I DO NOT KNOW.

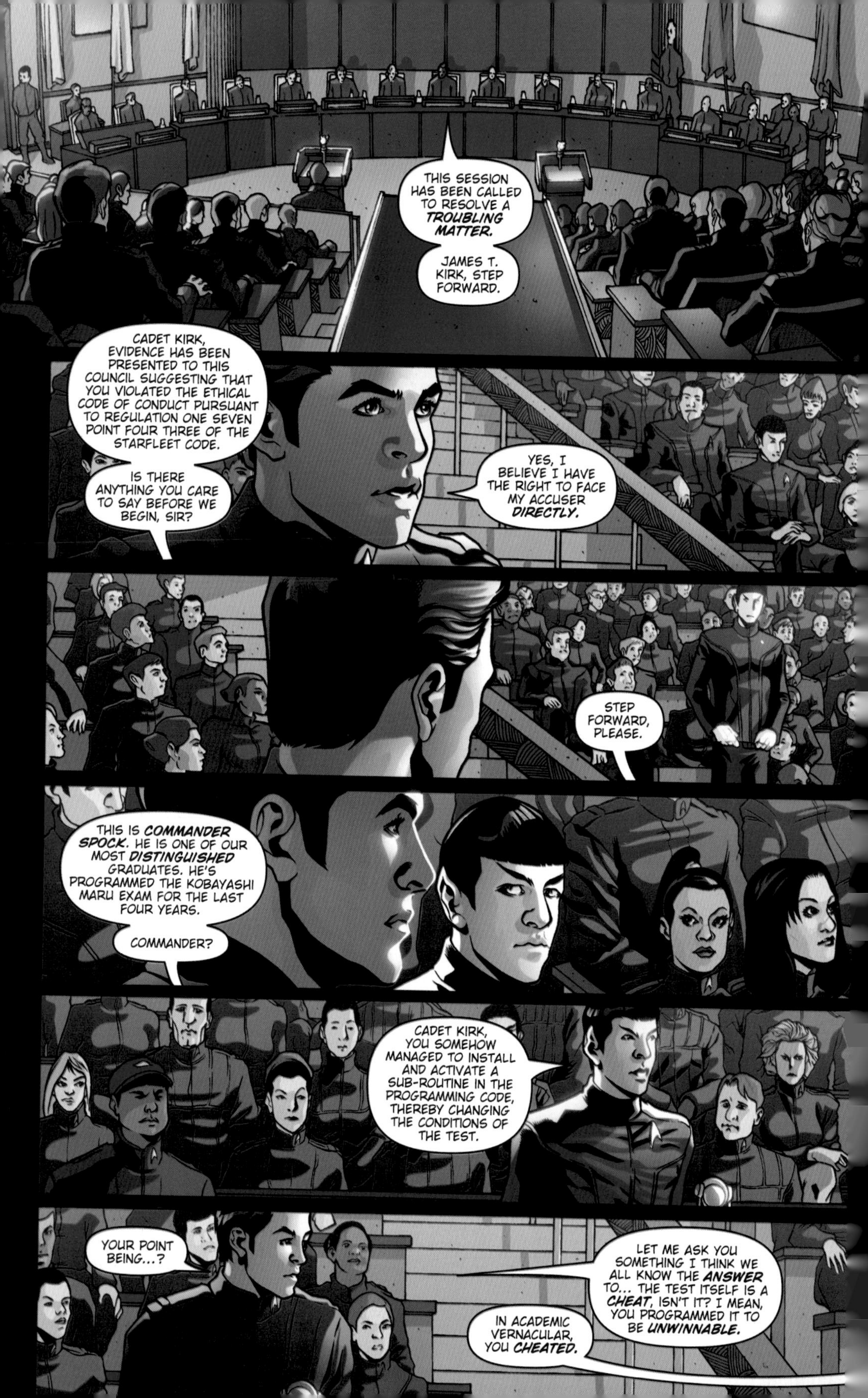
THIS SESSION HAS BEEN CALLED TO RESOLVE A *TROUBLING MATTER.*
JAMES T. KIRK, STEP FORWARD.
CADET KIRK, EVIDENCE HAS BEEN PRESENTED TO THIS COUNCIL SUGGESTING THAT YOU VIOLATED THE ETHICAL CODE OF CONDUCT PURSUANT TO REGULATION ONE SEVEN POINT FOUR THREE OF THE STARFLEET CODE.
IS THERE ANYTHING YOU CARE TO SAY BEFORE WE BEGIN, SIR?
YES, I BELIEVE I HAVE THE RIGHT TO FACE MY ACCUSER *DIRECTLY.*
STEP FORWARD, PLEASE.
THIS IS *COMMANDER SPOCK*. HE IS ONE OF OUR MOST *DISTINGUISHED* GRADUATES. HE'S PROGRAMMED THE KOBAYASHI MARU EXAM FOR THE LAST FOUR YEARS.
COMMANDER?
CADET KIRK, YOU SOMEHOW MANAGED TO INSTALL AND ACTIVATE A SUB-ROUTINE IN THE PROGRAMMING CODE, THEREBY CHANGING THE CONDITIONS OF THE TEST.
IN ACADEMIC VERNACULAR, YOU *CHEATED.*
YOUR POINT BEING...?
LET ME ASK YOU SOMETHING I THINK WE ALL KNOW THE *ANSWER* TO... THE TEST ITSELF IS A *CHEAT*, ISN'T IT? I MEAN, YOU PROGRAMMED IT TO BE *UNWINNABLE.*

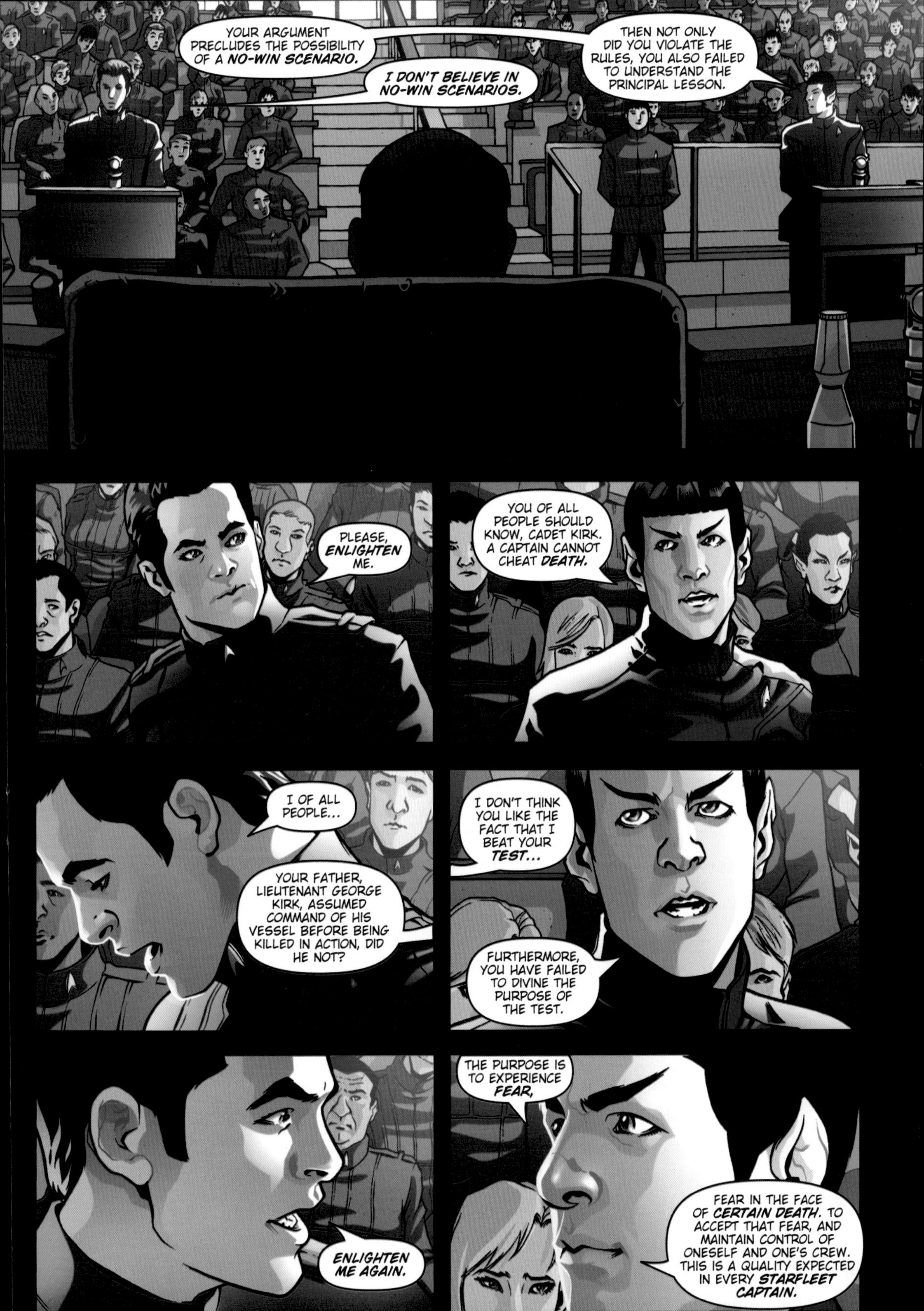
YOUR ARGUMENT PRECLUDES THE POSSIBILITY OF A NO-WIN SCENARIO.
I DON'T BELIEVE IN NO-WIN SCENARIOS.
THEN NOT ONLY DID YOU VIOLATE THE RULES, YOU ALSO FAILED TO UNDERSTAND THE PRINCIPAL LESSON.
PLEASE, ENLIGHTEN ME.
YOU OF ALL PEOPLE SHOULD KNOW, CADET KIRK. A CAPTAIN CANNOT CHEAT DEATH.
I OF ALL PEOPLE...
YOUR FATHER, LIEUTENANT GEORGE KIRK, ASSUMED COMMAND OF HIS VESSEL BEFORE BEING KILLED IN ACTION, DID HE NOT?
I DON'T THINK YOU LIKE THE FACT THAT I BEAT YOUR TEST...
FURTHERMORE, YOU HAVE FAILED TO DIVINE THE PURPOSE OF THE TEST.
ENLIGHTEN ME AGAIN.
THE PURPOSE IS TO EXPERIENCE FEAR,
FEAR IN THE FACE OF CERTAIN DEATH. TO ACCEPT THAT FEAR, AND MAINTAIN CONTROL OF ONESELF AND ONE'S CREW. THIS IS A QUALITY EXPECTED IN EVERY STARFLEET CAPTAIN.

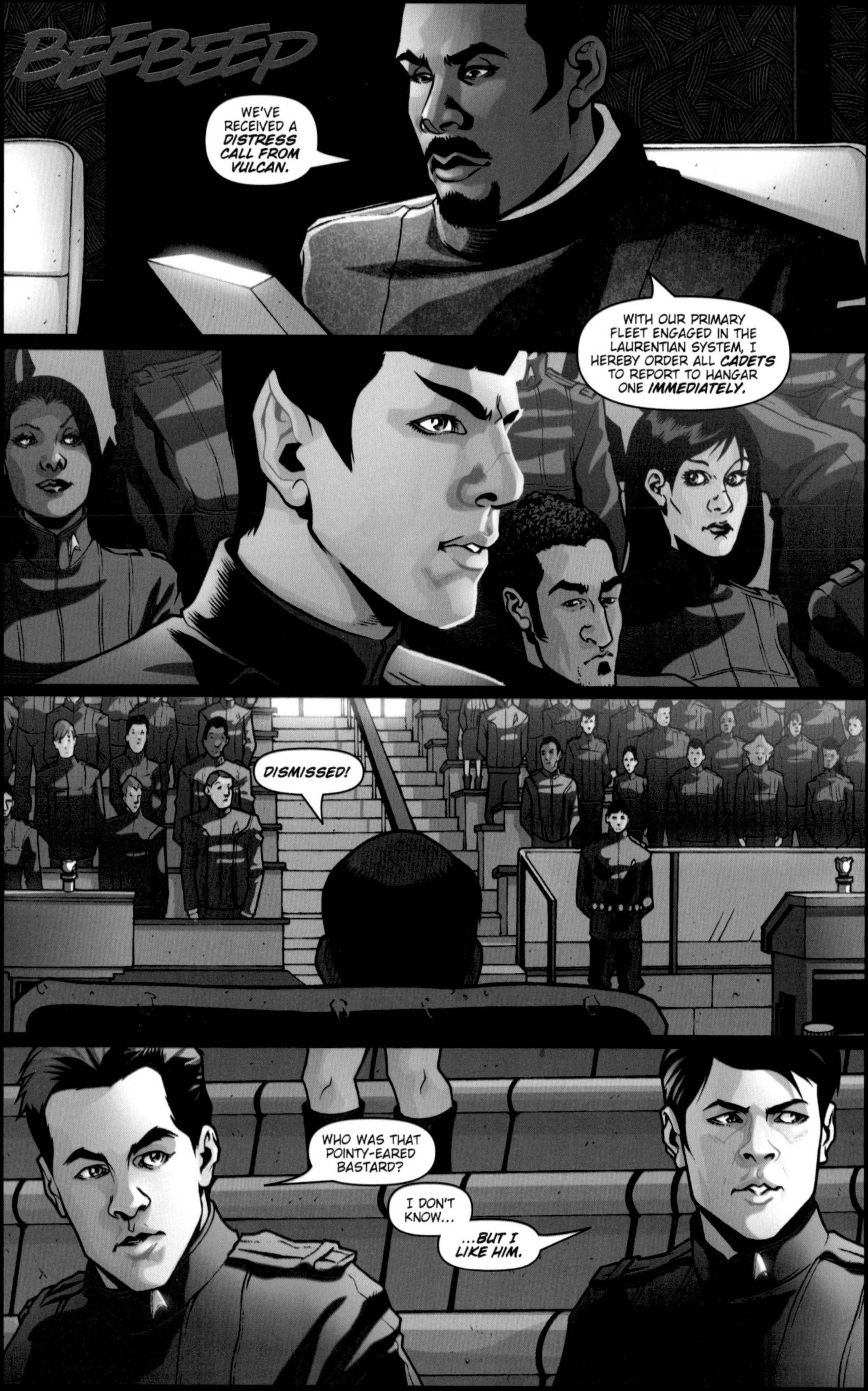
BEEBEEP
WE'VE RECEIVED A DISTRESS CALL FROM VULCAN.
WITH OUR PRIMARY FLEET ENGAGED IN THE LAURENTIAN SYSTEM, I HEREBY ORDER ALL CADETS TO REPORT TO HANGAR ONE IMMEDIATELY.
DISMISSED!
WHO WAS THAT POINTY-EARED BASTARD?
I DON'T KNOW...
...BUT I LIKE HIM.

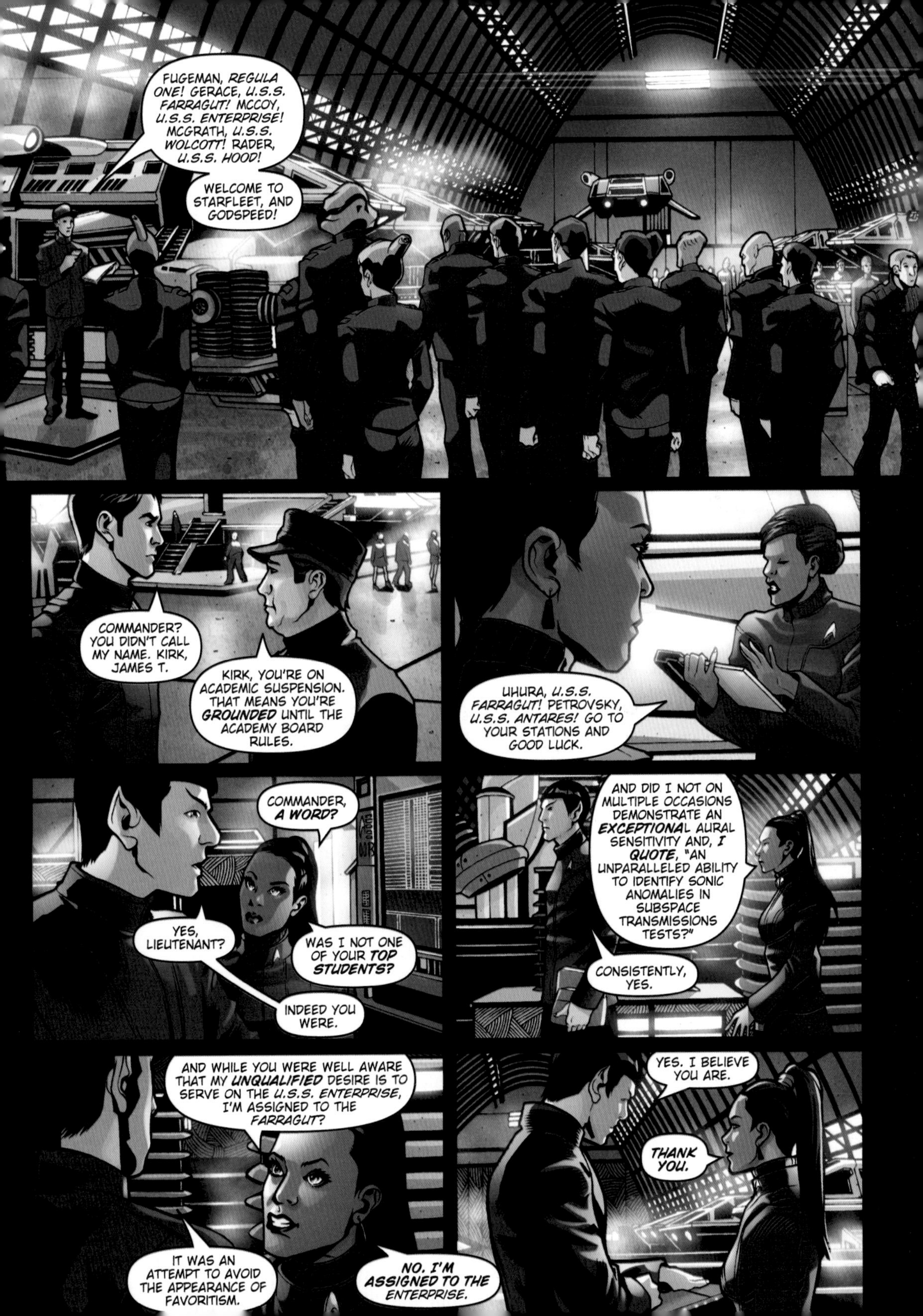
FUGEMAN, REGULA ONE! GERACE, U.S.S. FARRAGUT! MCCOY, U.S.S. ENTERPRISE! MCGRATH, U.S.S. WOLCOTT! RADER, U.S.S. HOOD!
WELCOME TO STARFLEET, AND GODSPEED!
COMMANDER? YOU DIDN'T CALL MY NAME. KIRK, JAMES T.
KIRK, YOU'RE ON ACADEMIC SUSPENSION. THAT MEANS YOU'RE GROUNDED UNTIL THE ACADEMY BOARD RULES.
UHURA, U.S.S. FARRAGUT! PETROVSKY, U.S.S. ANTARES! GO TO YOUR STATIONS AND GOOD LUCK.
COMMANDER, A WORD?
YES, LIEUTENANT?
WAS I NOT ONE OF YOUR TOP STUDENTS?
INDEED YOU WERE.
AND DID I NOT ON MULTIPLE OCCASIONS DEMONSTRATE AN EXCEPTIONAL AURAL SENSITIVITY AND, I QUOTE, "AN UNPARALLELED ABILITY TO IDENTIFY SONIC ANOMALIES IN SUBSPACE TRANSMISSIONS TESTS?"
CONSISTENTLY, YES.
AND WHILE YOU WERE WELL AWARE THAT MY UNQUALIFIED DESIRE IS TO SERVE ON THE U.S.S. ENTERPRISE, I'M ASSIGNED TO THE FARRAGUT?
IT WAS AN ATTEMPT TO AVOID THE APPEARANCE OF FAVORITISM.
NO. I'M ASSIGNED TO THE ENTERPRISE.
YES. I BELIEVE YOU ARE.
THANK YOU.

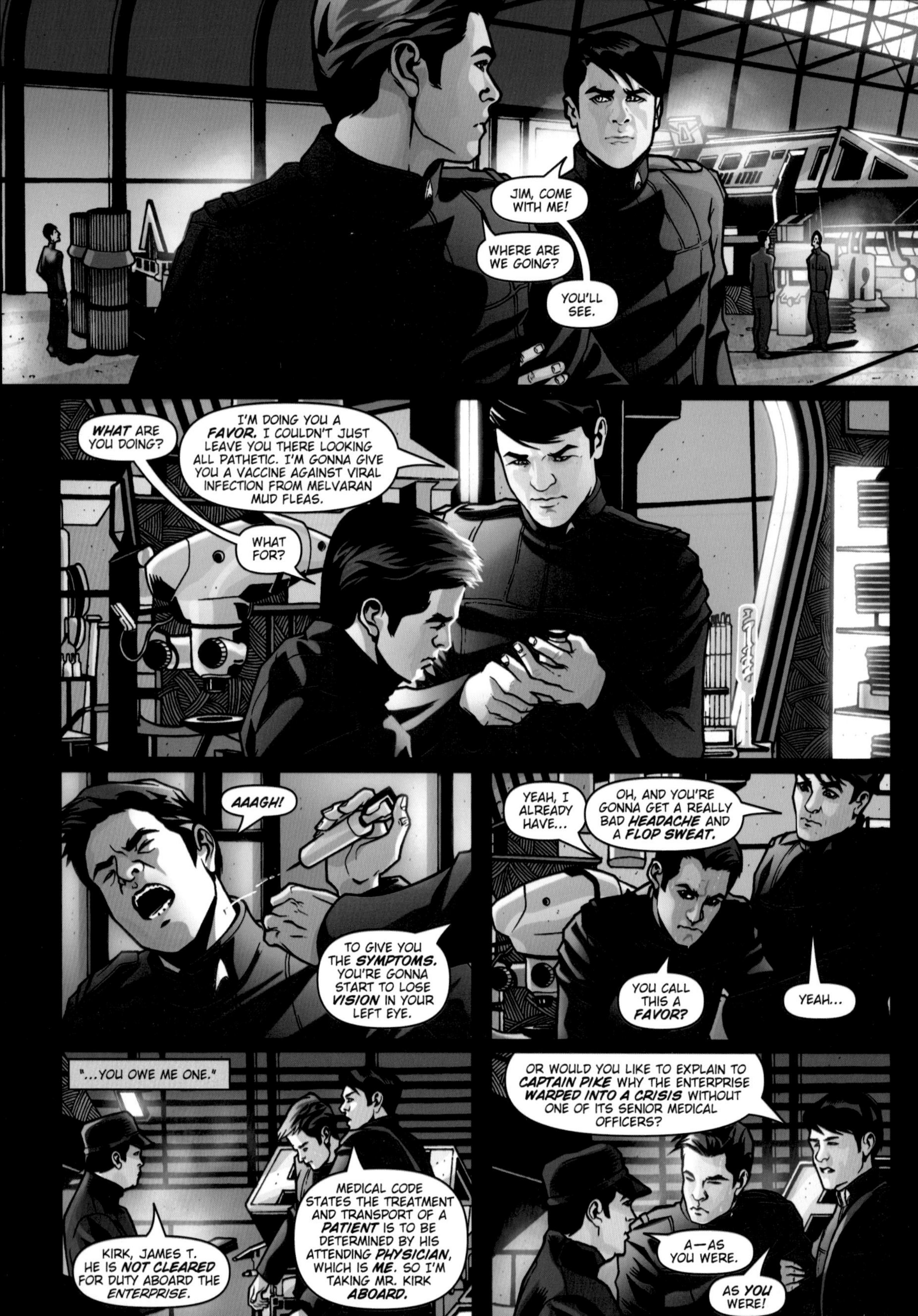
JIM, COME WITH ME!
WHERE ARE WE GOING?
YOU'LL SEE.
WHAT ARE YOU DOING?
I'M DOING YOU A *FAVOR.* I COULDN'T JUST LEAVE YOU THERE LOOKING ALL PATHETIC. I'M GONNA GIVE YOU A VACCINE AGAINST VIRAL INFECTION FROM MELVARAN MUD FLEAS.
WHAT FOR?
AAAGH!
TO GIVE YOU THE *SYMPTOMS.* YOU'RE GONNA START TO LOSE *VISION* IN YOUR LEFT EYE.
YEAH, I ALREADY HAVE...
OH, AND YOU'RE GONNA GET A REALLY BAD *HEADACHE* AND A *FLOP SWEAT.*
YOU CALL THIS A *FAVOR?*
YEAH...
"...YOU OWE ME ONE."
KIRK, JAMES T. HE IS *NOT CLEARED* FOR DUTY ABOARD THE *ENTERPRISE*.
MEDICAL CODE STATES THE TREATMENT AND TRANSPORT OF A *PATIENT* IS TO BE DETERMINED BY HIS ATTENDING *PHYSICIAN*, WHICH IS *ME*. SO I'M TAKING MR. KIRK *ABOARD.*
OR WOULD YOU LIKE TO EXPLAIN TO *CAPTAIN PIKE* WHY THE ENTERPRISE *WARPED INTO A CRISIS* WITHOUT ONE OF ITS SENIOR MEDICAL OFFICERS?
A—AS YOU WERE.
AS *YOU* WERE!

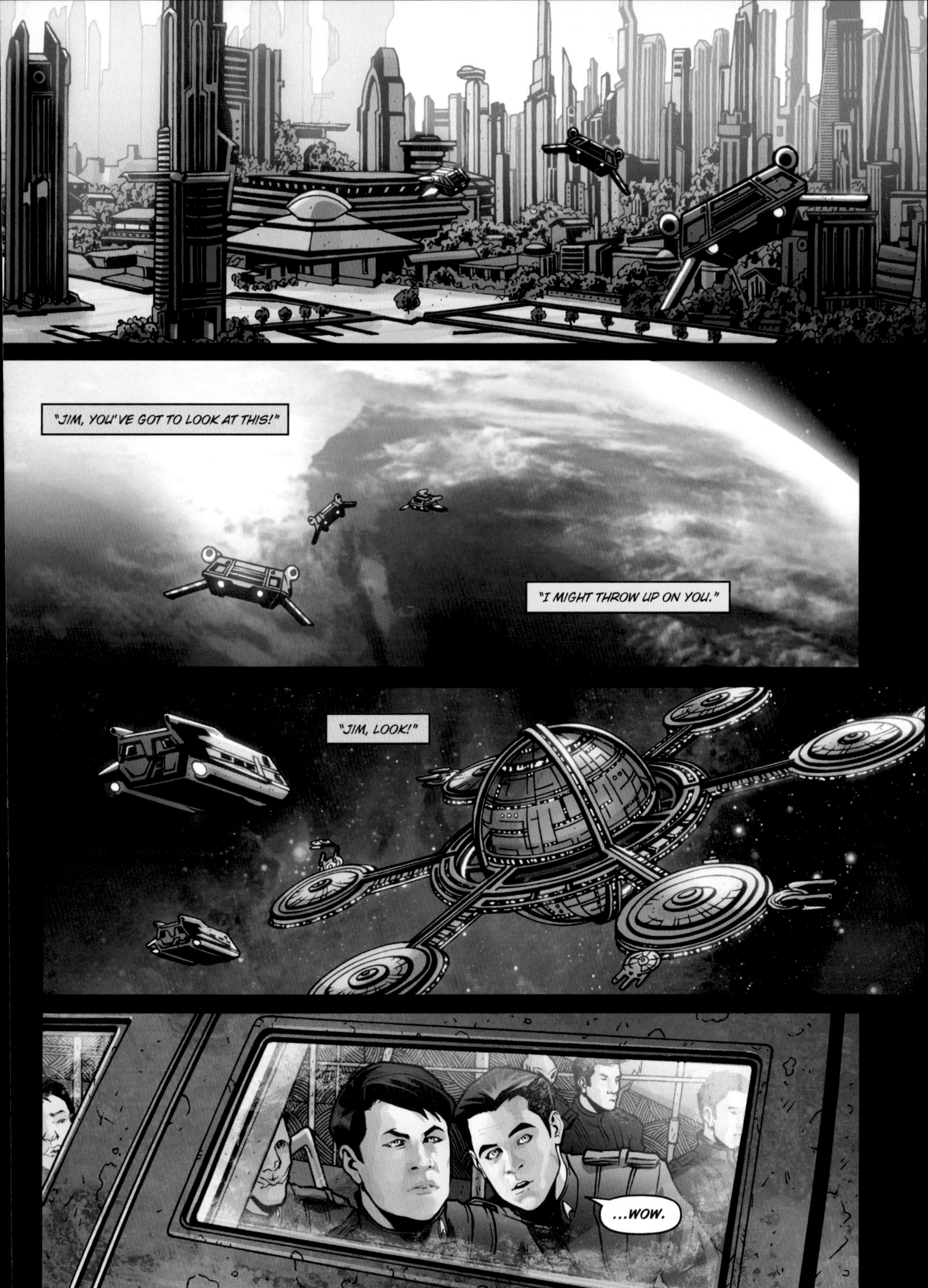
"JIM, YOU'VE GOT TO LOOK AT THIS!"
"I MIGHT THROW UP ON YOU."
"JIM, LOOK!"
...WOW.

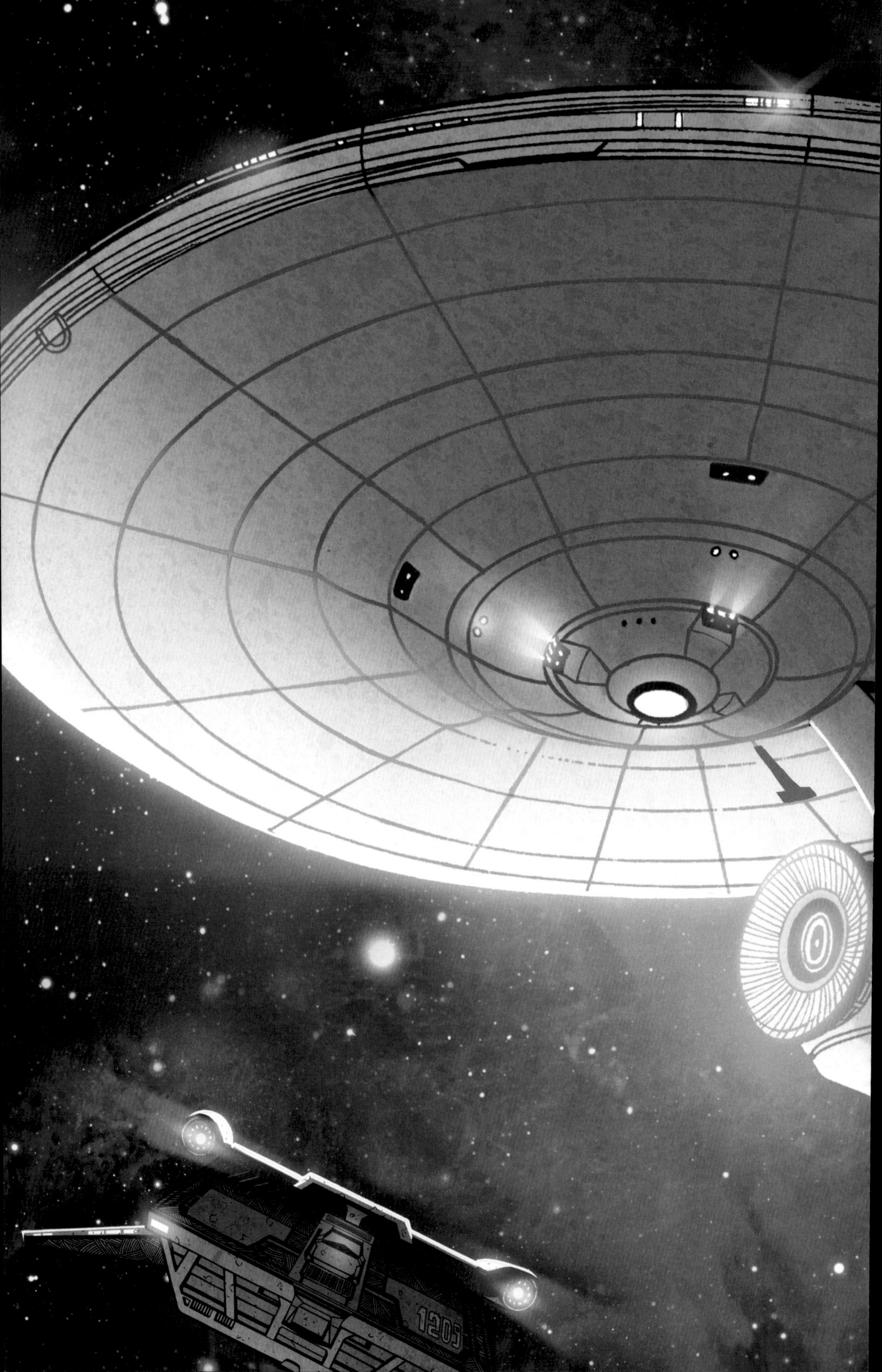
1205

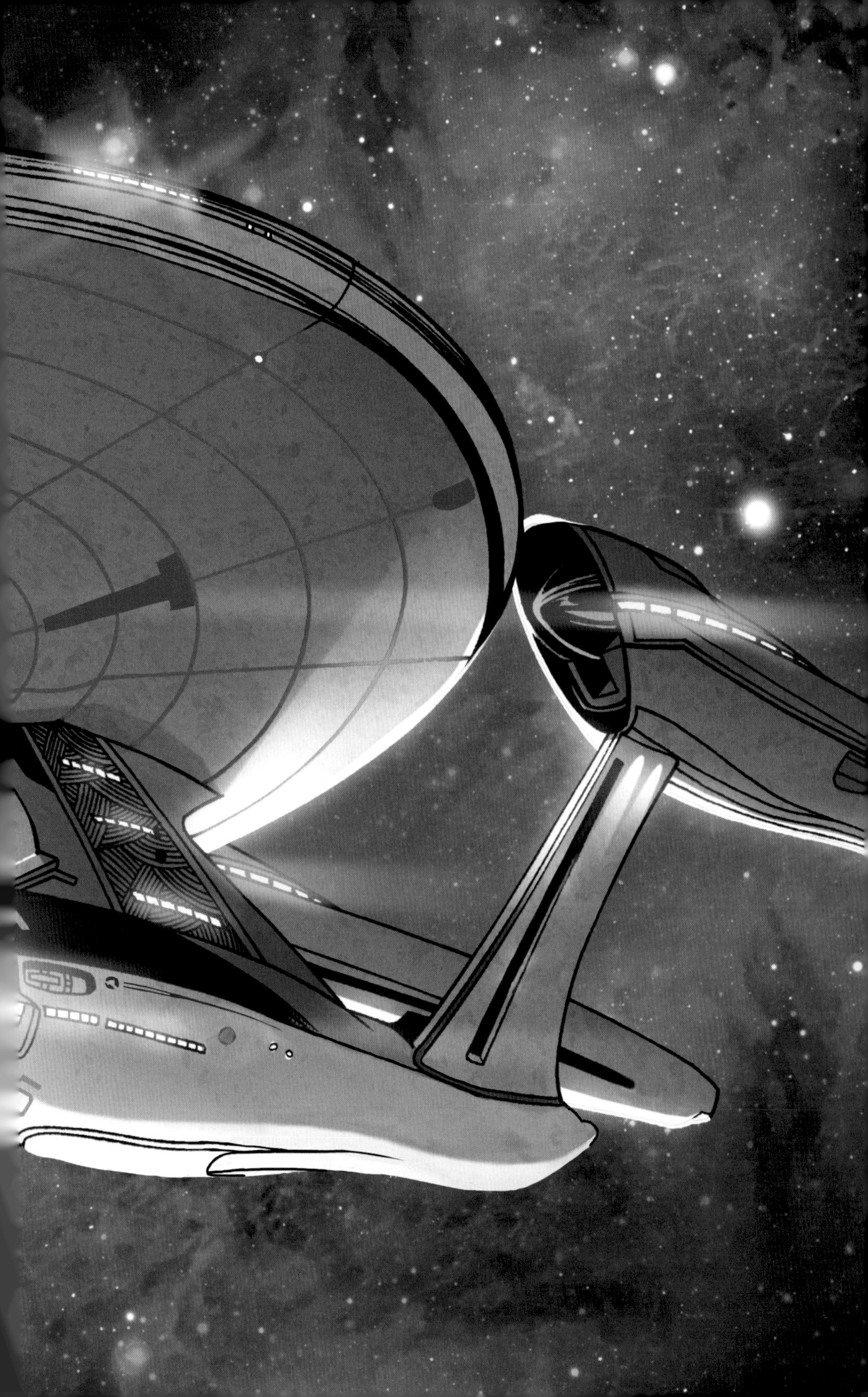

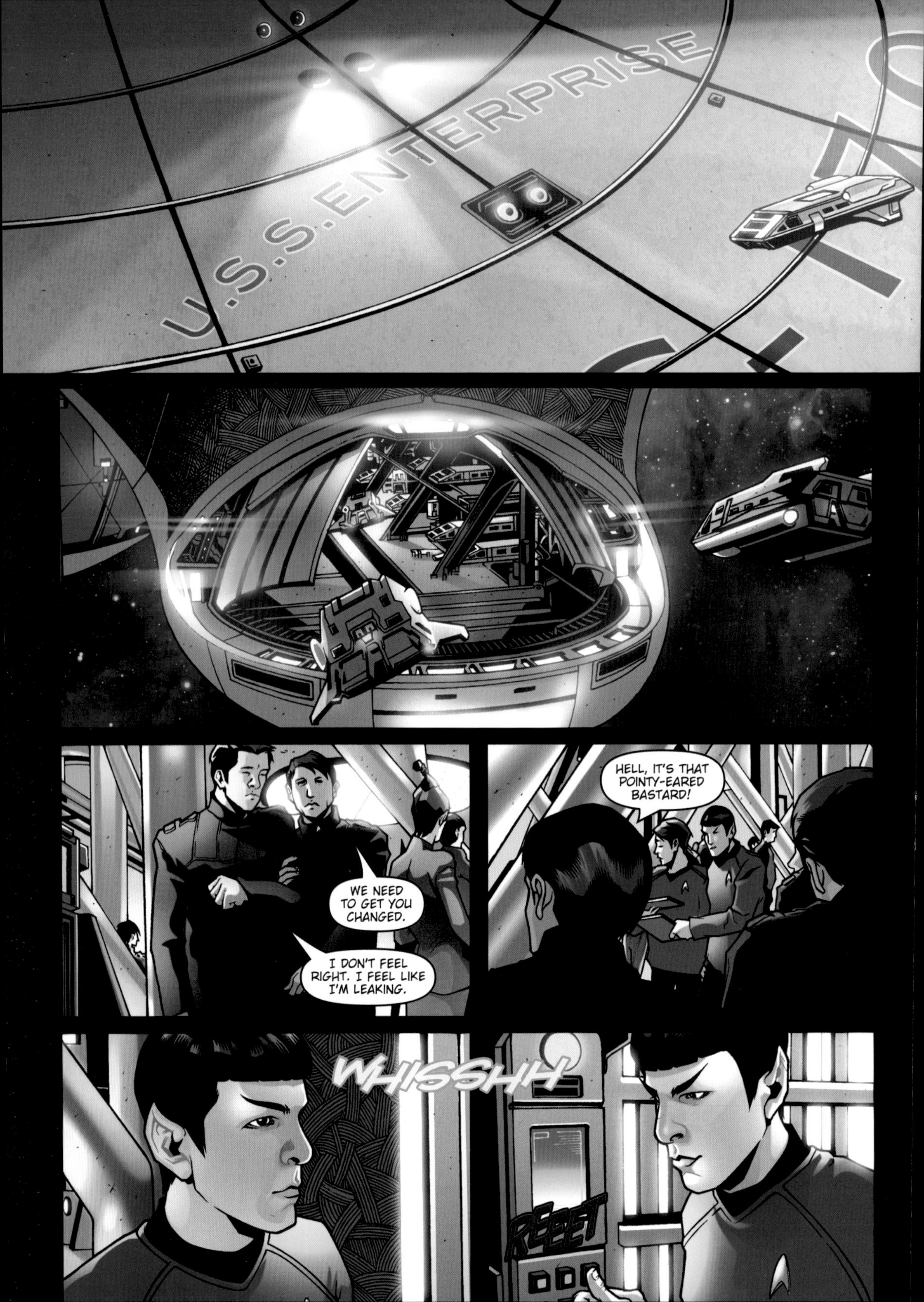
U.S.S. ENTERPRISE
WE NEED TO GET YOU CHANGED.
I DON'T FEEL RIGHT. I FEEL LIKE I'M LEAKING.
HELL, IT'S THAT POINTY-EARED BASTARD!
WHISSHH
REEET

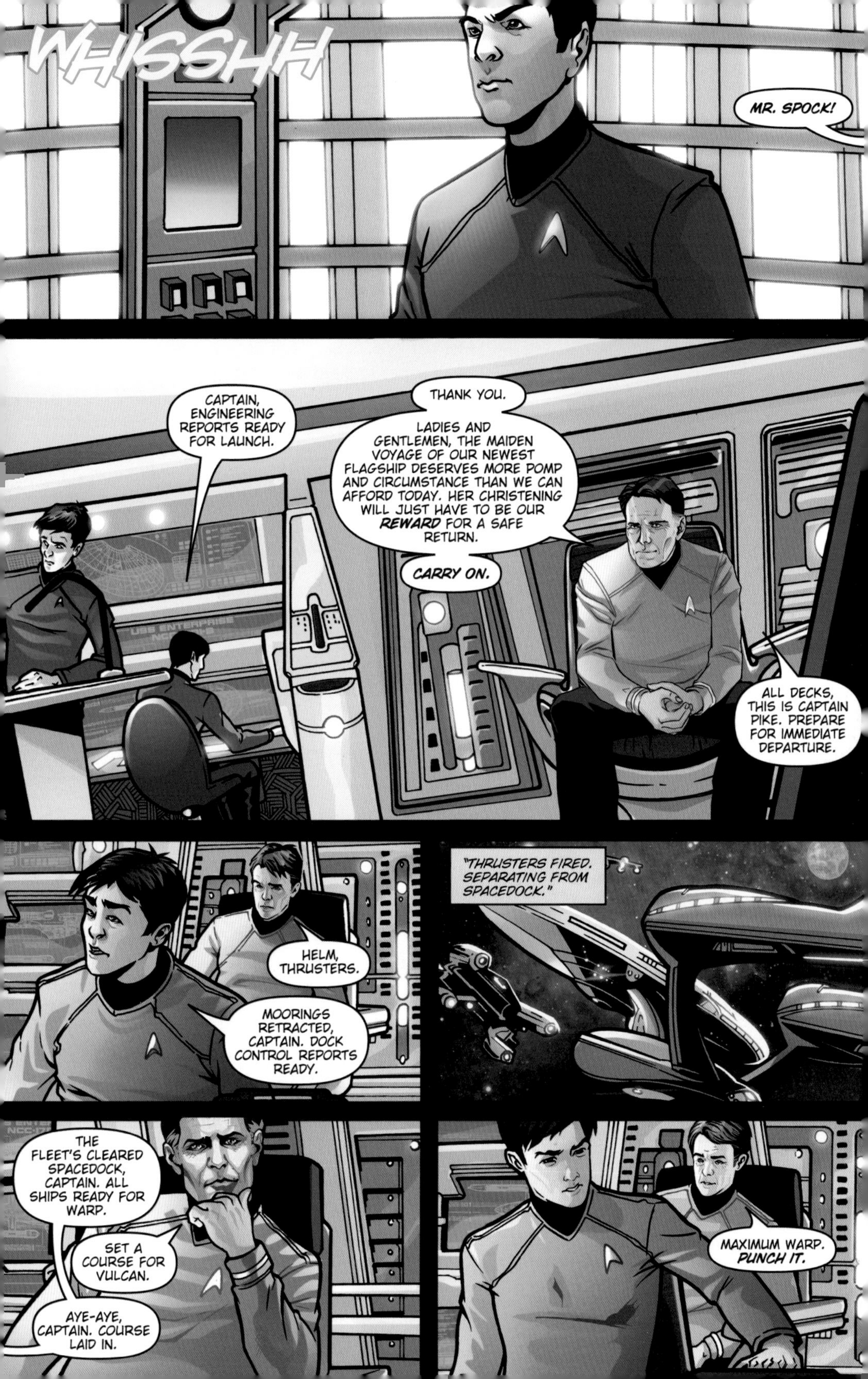
WHISSHH
MR. SPOCK!
CAPTAIN, ENGINEERING REPORTS READY FOR LAUNCH.
THANK YOU.
LADIES AND GENTLEMEN, THE MAIDEN VOYAGE OF OUR NEWEST FLAGSHIP DESERVES MORE POMP AND CIRCUMSTANCE THAN WE CAN AFFORD TODAY. HER CHRISTENING WILL JUST HAVE TO BE OUR REWARD FOR A SAFE RETURN.
CARRY ON.
ALL DECKS, THIS IS CAPTAIN PIKE. PREPARE FOR IMMEDIATE DEPARTURE.
HELM, THRUSTERS.
MOORINGS RETRACTED, CAPTAIN. DOCK CONTROL REPORTS READY.
"THRUSTERS FIRED. SEPARATING FROM SPACEDOCK."
THE FLEET'S CLEARED SPACEDOCK, CAPTAIN. ALL SHIPS READY FOR WARP.
SET A COURSE FOR VULCAN.
AYE-AYE, CAPTAIN. COURSE LAID IN.
MAXIMUM WARP. PUNCH IT.

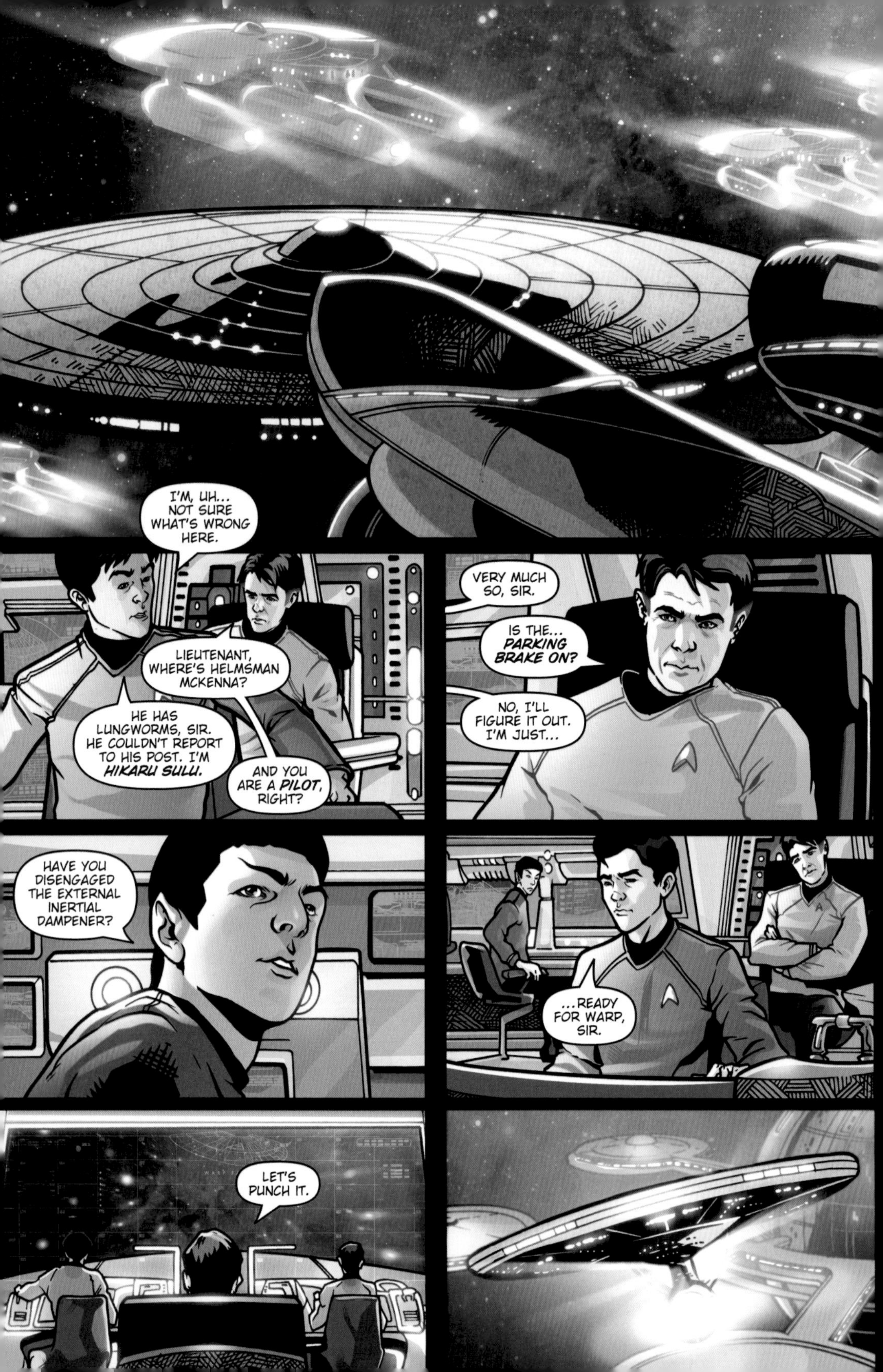
I'M, UH... NOT SURE WHAT'S WRONG HERE.
LIEUTENANT, WHERE'S HELMSMAN MCKENNA?
HE HAS LUNGWORMS, SIR. HE COULDN'T REPORT TO HIS POST. I'M HIKARU SULU.
AND YOU ARE A PILOT, RIGHT?
VERY MUCH SO, SIR.
IS THE... PARKING BRAKE ON?
NO, I'LL FIGURE IT OUT. I'M JUST...
HAVE YOU DISENGAGED THE EXTERNAL INERTIAL DAMPENER?
...READY FOR WARP, SIR.
LET'S PUNCH IT.

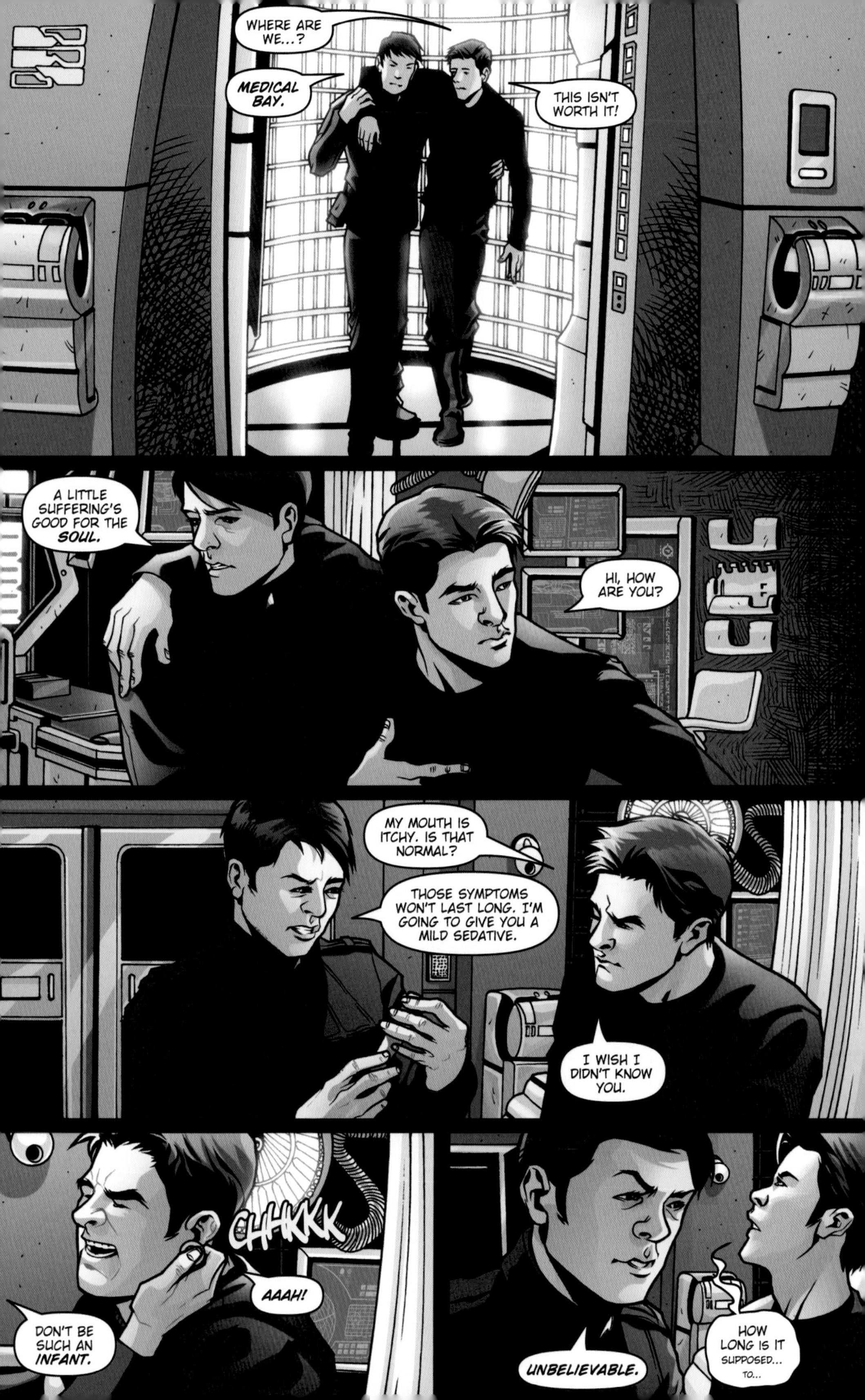
WHERE ARE WE...?
MEDICAL BAY.
THIS ISN'T WORTH IT!
A LITTLE SUFFERING'S GOOD FOR THE SOUL.
HI, HOW ARE YOU?
MY MOUTH IS ITCHY. IS THAT NORMAL?
THOSE SYMPTOMS WON'T LAST LONG. I'M GOING TO GIVE YOU A MILD SEDATIVE.
I WISH I DIDN'T KNOW YOU.
CHHKKK
AAAH!
DON'T BE SUCH AN INFANT.
UNBELIEVABLE.
HOW LONG IS IT SUPPOSED... TO...

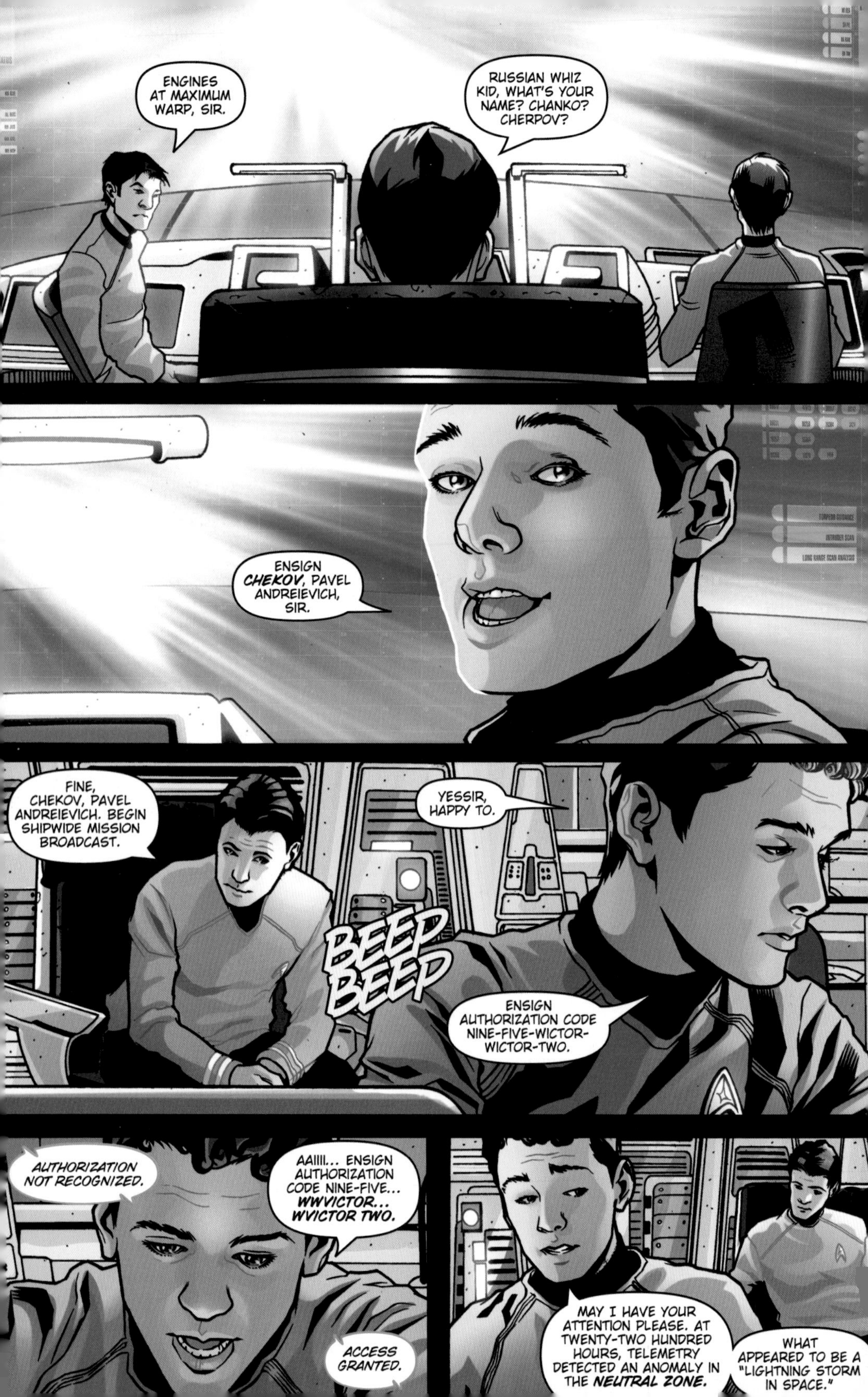
ENGINES AT MAXIMUM WARP, SIR.
RUSSIAN WHIZ KID, WHAT'S YOUR NAME? CHANKO? CHERPOV?
ENSIGN CHEKOV, PAVEL ANDREIEVICH, SIR.
FINE, CHEKOV, PAVEL ANDREIEVICH. BEGIN SHIPWIDE MISSION BROADCAST.
YESSIR, HAPPY TO.
BEEP BEEP
ENSIGN AUTHORIZATION CODE NINE-FIVE-WICTOR-WICTOR-TWO.
AUTHORIZATION NOT RECOGNIZED.
AAIIII... ENSIGN AUTHORIZATION CODE NINE-FIVE... WWVICTOR... WVICTOR TWO.
ACCESS GRANTED.
MAY I HAVE YOUR ATTENTION PLEASE. AT TWENTY-TWO HUNDRED HOURS, TELEMETRY DETECTED AN ANOMALY IN THE NEUTRAL ZONE.
WHAT APPEARED TO BE A "LIGHTNING STORM IN SPACE."
TORPEDO GUIDANCE
INTRUDER SCAN
LONG RANGE SCAN ANALYSIS

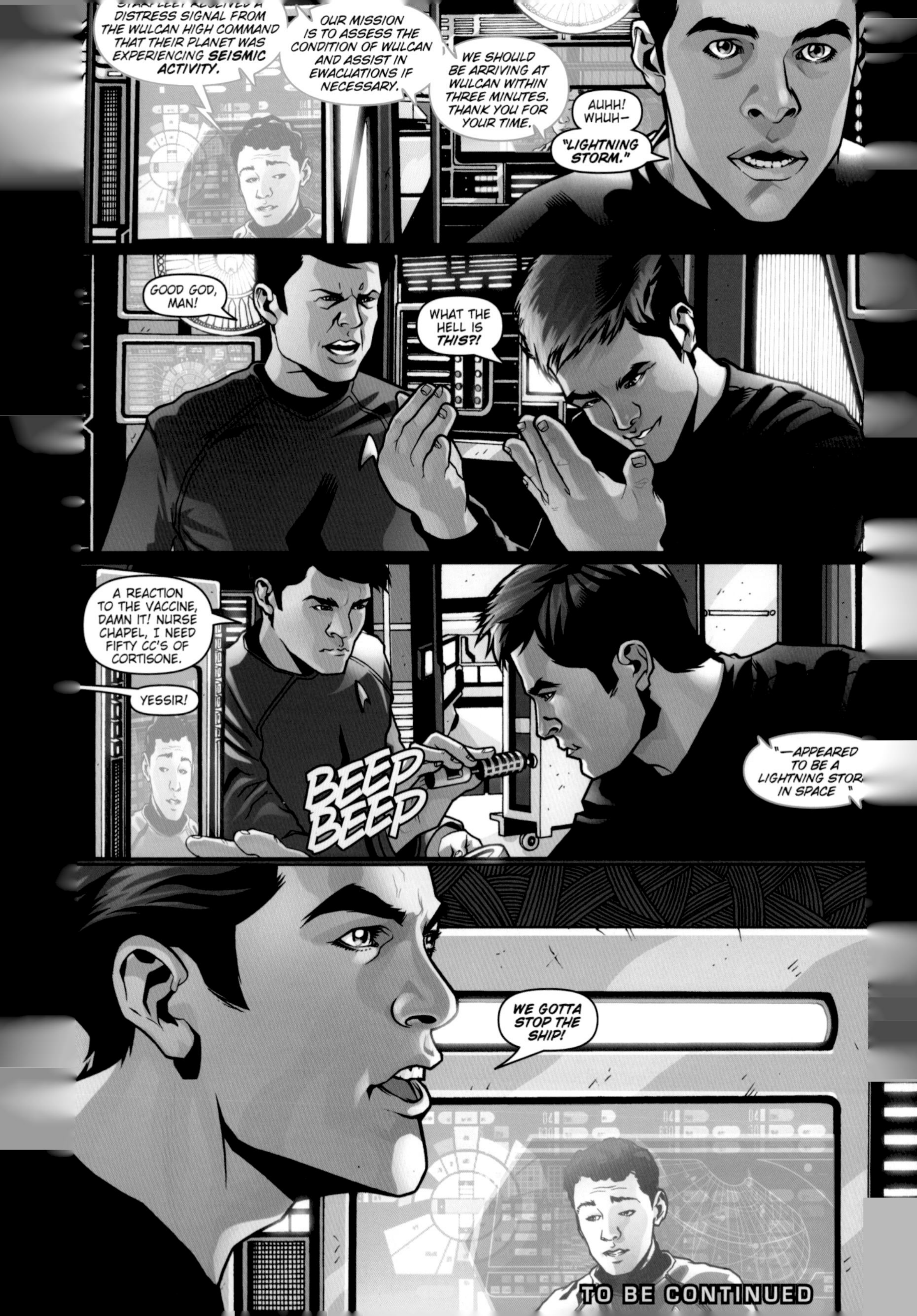
DISTRESS SIGNAL FROM THE WULCAN HIGH COMMAND THAT THEIR PLANET WAS EXPERIENCING **SEISMIC ACTIVITY.**
OUR MISSION IS TO ASSESS THE CONDITION OF WULCAN AND ASSIST IN EWACUATIONS IF NECESSARY.
WE SHOULD BE ARRIVING AT WULCAN WITHIN THREE MINUTES. THANK YOU FOR YOUR TIME.
AUHH! WHUH—
"LIGHTNING STORM."
GOOD GOD, MAN!
WHAT THE HELL IS *THIS?!*
A REACTION TO THE VACCINE, DAMN IT! NURSE CHAPEL, I NEED FIFTY CC'S OF CORTISONE.
YESSIR!
BEEP BEEP
"—APPEARED TO BE A LIGHTNING STOR IN SPACE"
WE GOTTA STOP THE SHIP!
TO BE CONTINUED

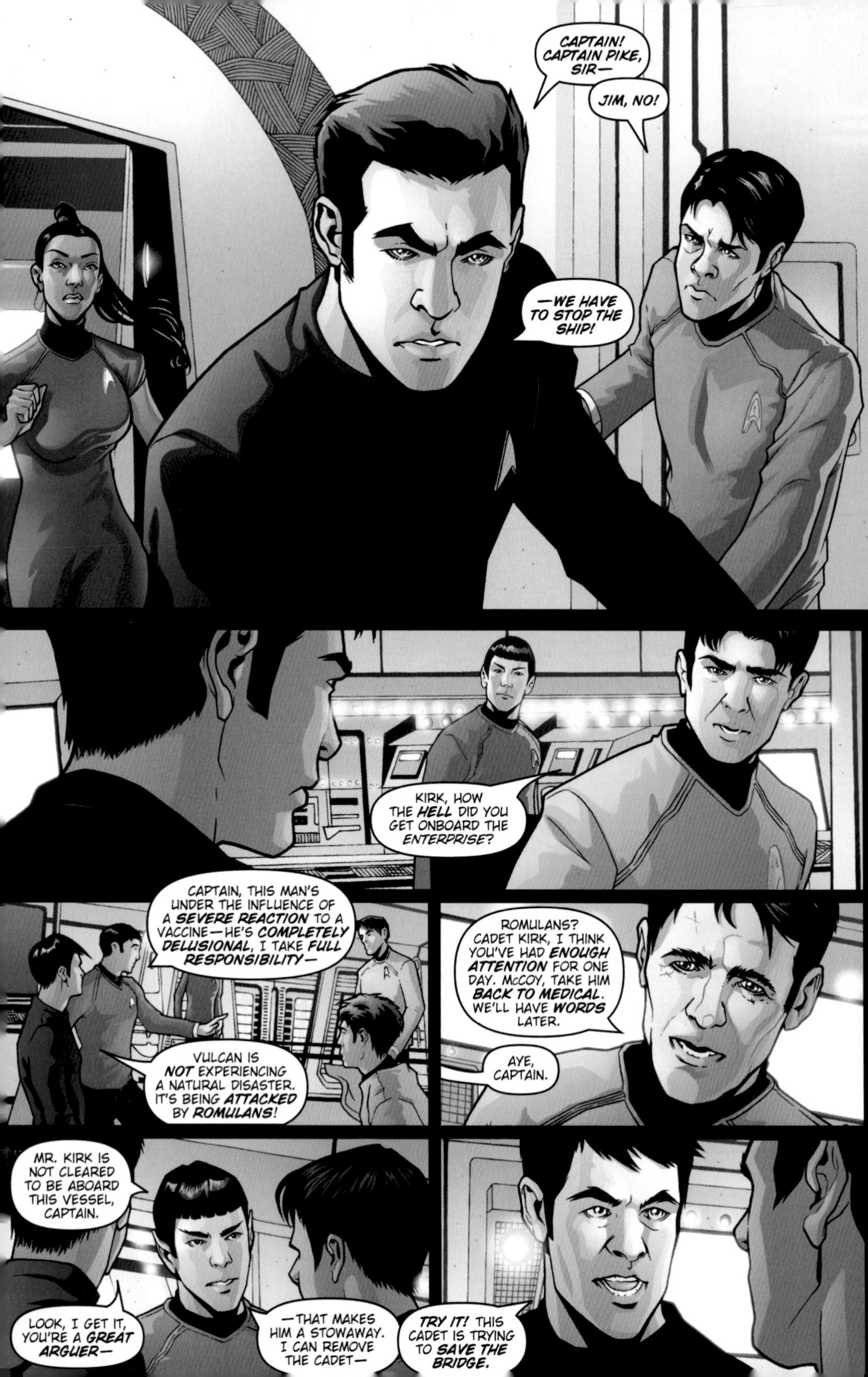
CAPTAIN! CAPTAIN PIKE, SIR—
JIM, NO!
—WE HAVE TO STOP THE SHIP!
KIRK, HOW THE HELL DID YOU GET ONBOARD THE ENTERPRISE?
CAPTAIN, THIS MAN'S UNDER THE INFLUENCE OF A SEVERE REACTION TO A VACCINE—HE'S COMPLETELY DELUSIONAL, I TAKE FULL RESPONSIBILITY—
VULCAN IS NOT EXPERIENCING A NATURAL DISASTER. IT'S BEING ATTACKED BY ROMULANS!
ROMULANS? CADET KIRK, I THINK YOU'VE HAD ENOUGH ATTENTION FOR ONE DAY. McCOY, TAKE HIM BACK TO MEDICAL. WE'LL HAVE WORDS LATER.
AYE, CAPTAIN.
MR. KIRK IS NOT CLEARED TO BE ABOARD THIS VESSEL, CAPTAIN.
LOOK, I GET IT, YOU'RE A GREAT ARGUER—
—THAT MAKES HIM A STOWAWAY. I CAN REMOVE THE CADET—
TRY IT! THIS CADET IS TRYING TO SAVE THE BRIDGE.

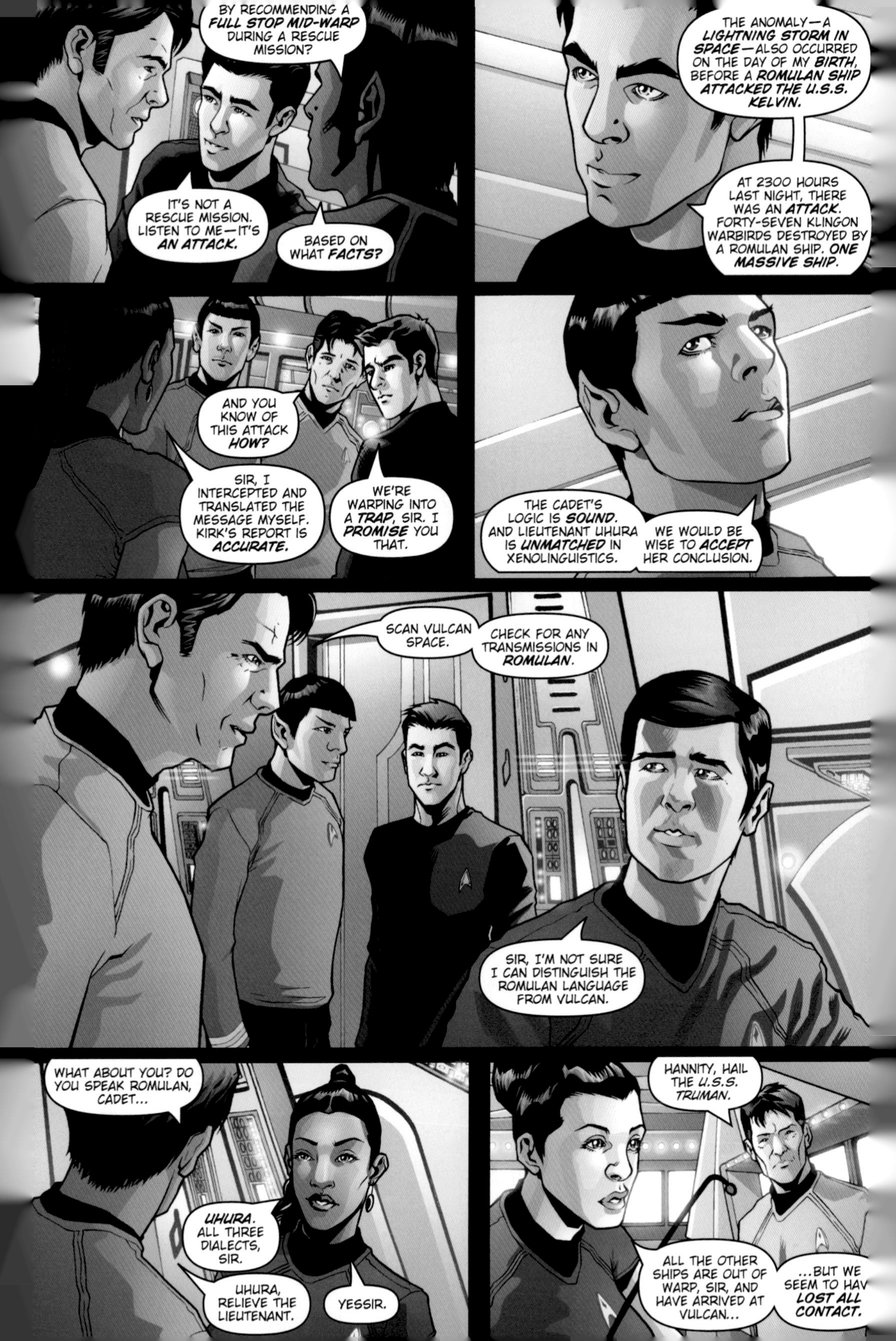
BY RECOMMENDING A FULL STOP MID-WARP DURING A RESCUE MISSION?
IT'S NOT A RESCUE MISSION. LISTEN TO ME—IT'S AN ATTACK.
BASED ON WHAT FACTS?
THE ANOMALY—A LIGHTNING STORM IN SPACE—ALSO OCCURRED ON THE DAY OF MY BIRTH, BEFORE A ROMULAN SHIP ATTACKED THE U.S.S. KELVIN.
AT 2300 HOURS LAST NIGHT, THERE WAS AN ATTACK. FORTY-SEVEN KLINGON WARBIRDS DESTROYED BY A ROMULAN SHIP. ONE MASSIVE SHIP.
AND YOU KNOW OF THIS ATTACK HOW?
SIR, I INTERCEPTED AND TRANSLATED THE MESSAGE MYSELF. KIRK'S REPORT IS ACCURATE.
WE'RE WARPING INTO A TRAP, SIR. I PROMISE YOU THAT.
THE CADET'S LOGIC IS SOUND. AND LIEUTENANT UHURA IS UNMATCHED IN XENOLINGUISTICS.
WE WOULD BE WISE TO ACCEPT HER CONCLUSION.
SCAN VULCAN SPACE.
CHECK FOR ANY TRANSMISSIONS IN ROMULAN.
SIR, I'M NOT SURE I CAN DISTINGUISH THE ROMULAN LANGUAGE FROM VULCAN.
WHAT ABOUT YOU? DO YOU SPEAK ROMULAN, CADET...
UHURA. ALL THREE DIALECTS, SIR.
UHURA, RELIEVE THE LIEUTENANT.
YESSIR.
HANNITY, HAIL THE U.S.S. TRUMAN.
ALL THE OTHER SHIPS ARE OUT OF WARP, SIR, AND HAVE ARRIVED AT VULCAN...
...BUT WE SEEM TO HAV LOST ALL CONTACT.

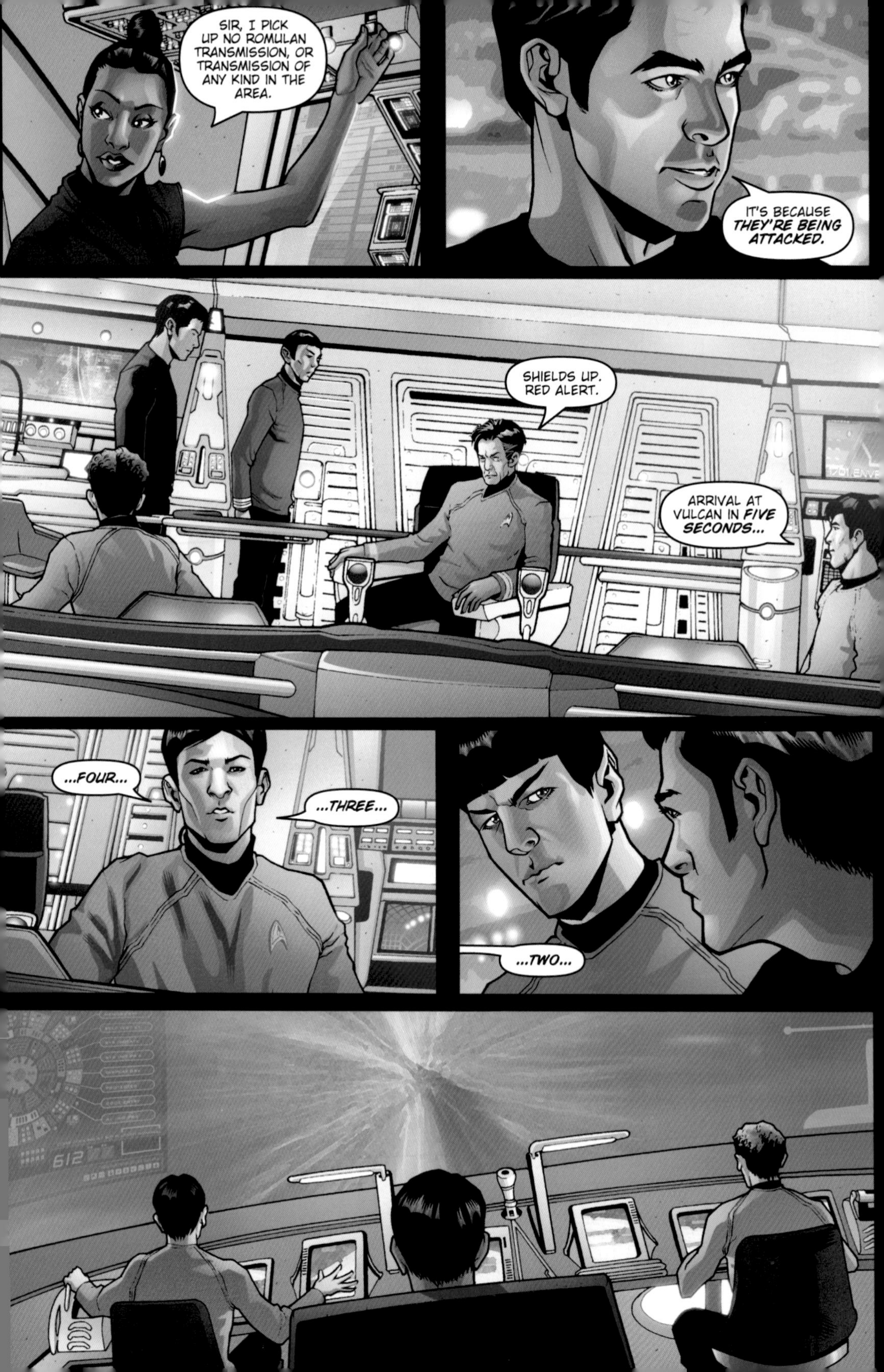
SIR, I PICK UP NO ROMULAN TRANSMISSION, OR TRANSMISSION OF ANY KIND IN THE AREA.
IT'S BECAUSE *THEY'RE BEING ATTACKED.*
SHIELDS UP. RED ALERT.
ARRIVAL AT VULCAN IN *FIVE SECONDS...*
...FOUR...
...THREE...
...TWO...

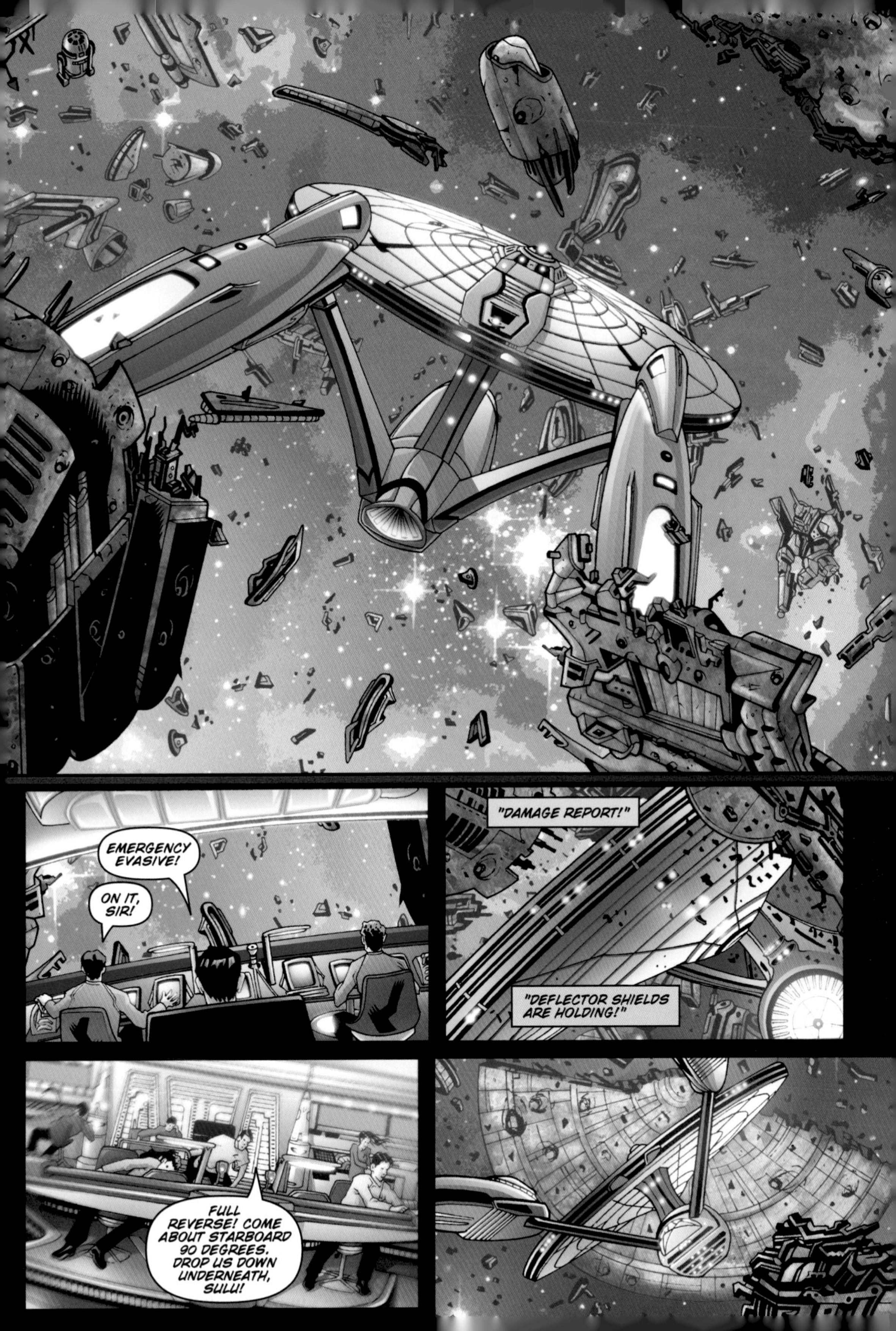
EMERGENCY EVASIVE!
ON IT, SIR!
"DAMAGE REPORT!"
"DEFLECTOR SHIELDS ARE HOLDING!"
FULL REVERSE! COME ABOUT STARBOARD 90 DEGREES. DROP US DOWN UNDERNEATH, SULU!

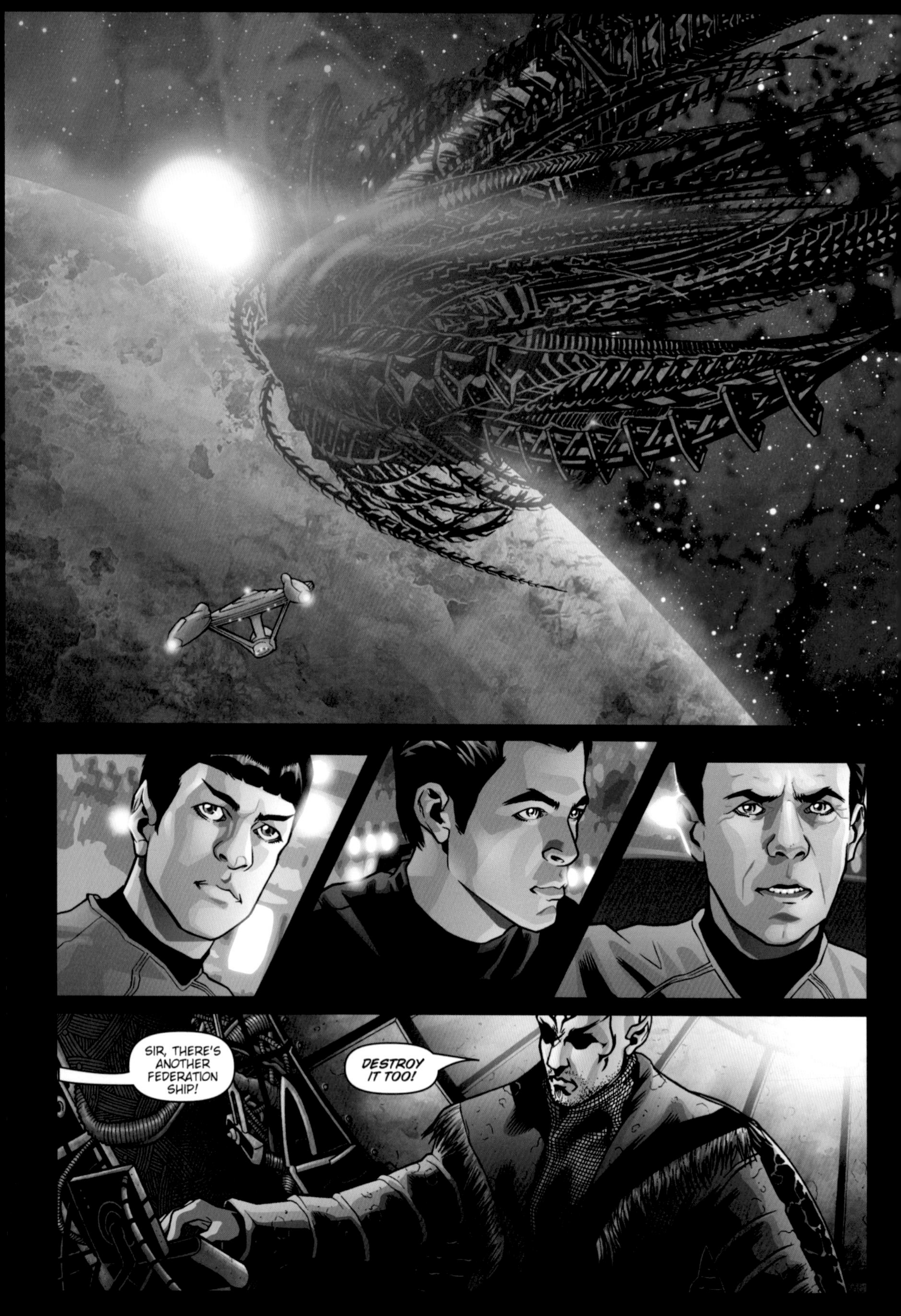
SIR, THERE'S ANOTHER FEDERATION SHIP!
DESTROY IT TOO!

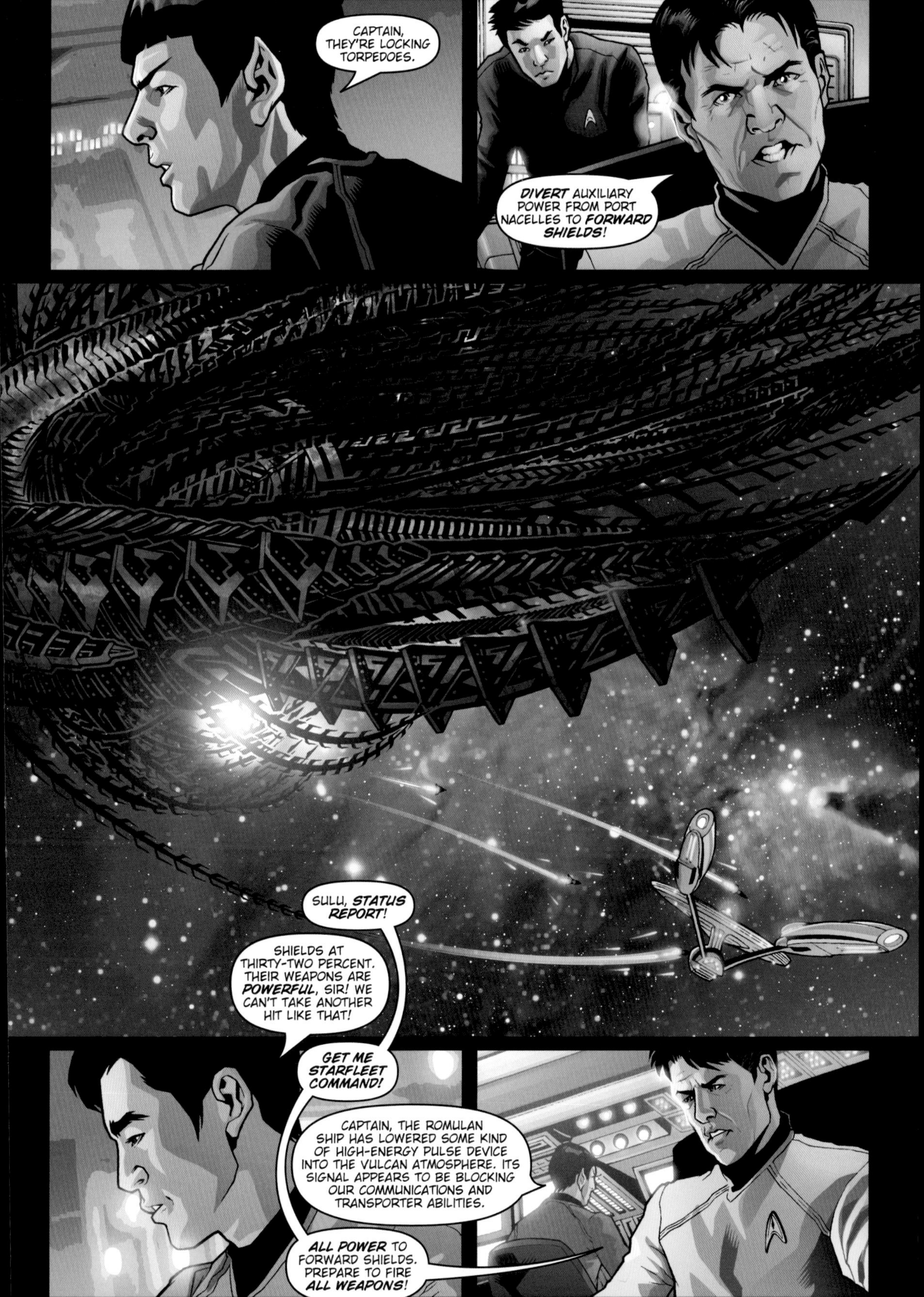
CAPTAIN, THEY'RE LOCKING TORPEDOES.
DIVERT AUXILIARY POWER FROM PORT NACELLES TO FORWARD SHIELDS!
SULU, STATUS REPORT!
SHIELDS AT THIRTY-TWO PERCENT. THEIR WEAPONS ARE POWERFUL, SIR! WE CAN'T TAKE ANOTHER HIT LIKE THAT!
GET ME STARFLEET COMMAND!
CAPTAIN, THE ROMULAN SHIP HAS LOWERED SOME KIND OF HIGH-ENERGY PULSE DEVICE INTO THE VULCAN ATMOSPHERE. ITS SIGNAL APPEARS TO BE BLOCKING OUR COMMUNICATIONS AND TRANSPORTER ABILITIES.
ALL POWER TO FORWARD SHIELDS. PREPARE TO FIRE ALL WEAPONS!

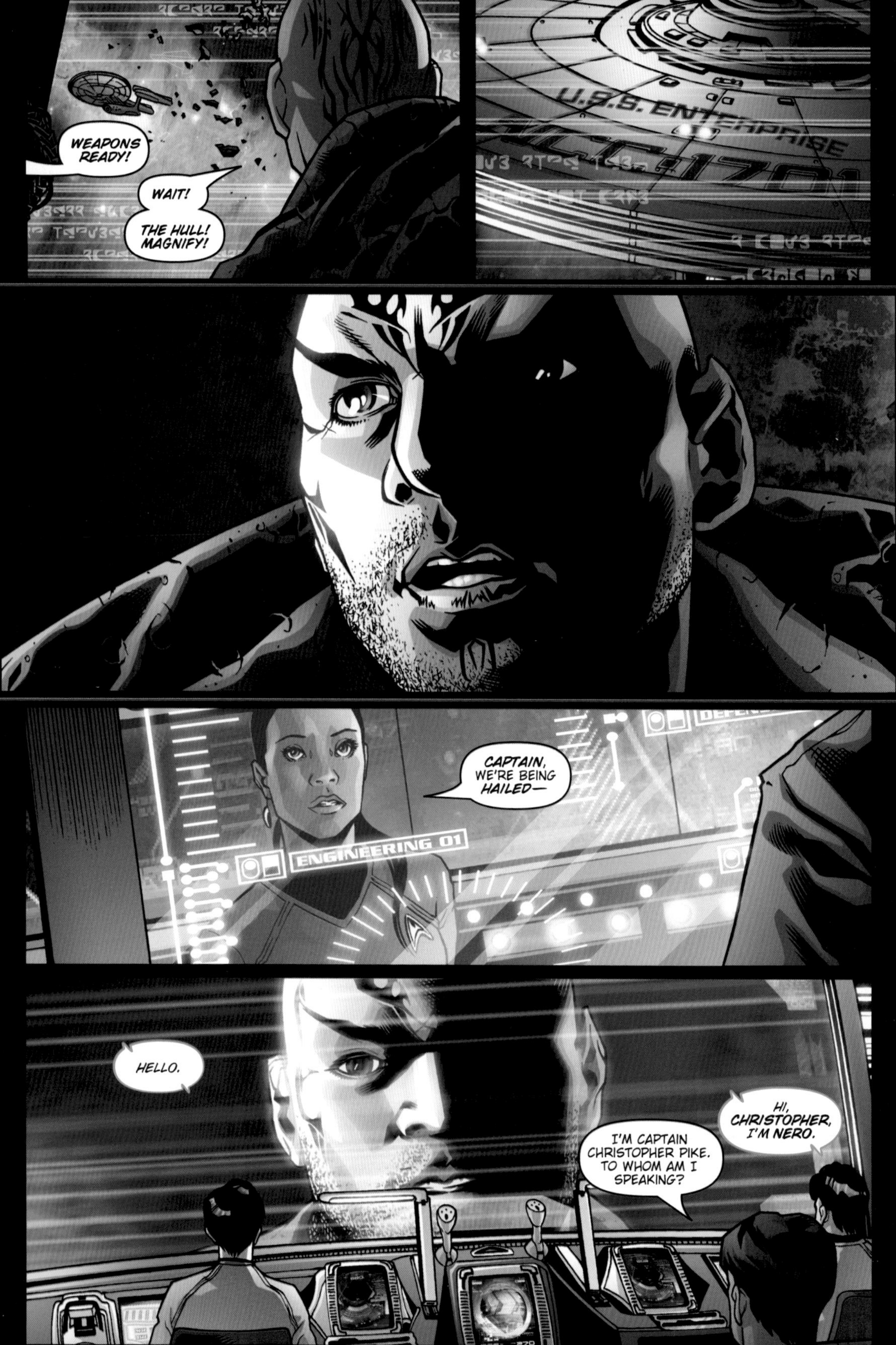
WEAPONS READY!
WAIT!
THE HULL! MAGNIFY!
U.S.S. ENTERPRISE
NCC-1701
CAPTAIN, WE'RE BEING HAILED—
ENGINEERING 01
HELLO.
I'M CAPTAIN CHRISTOPHER PIKE. TO WHOM AM I SPEAKING?
HI, CHRISTOPHER, I'M NERO.

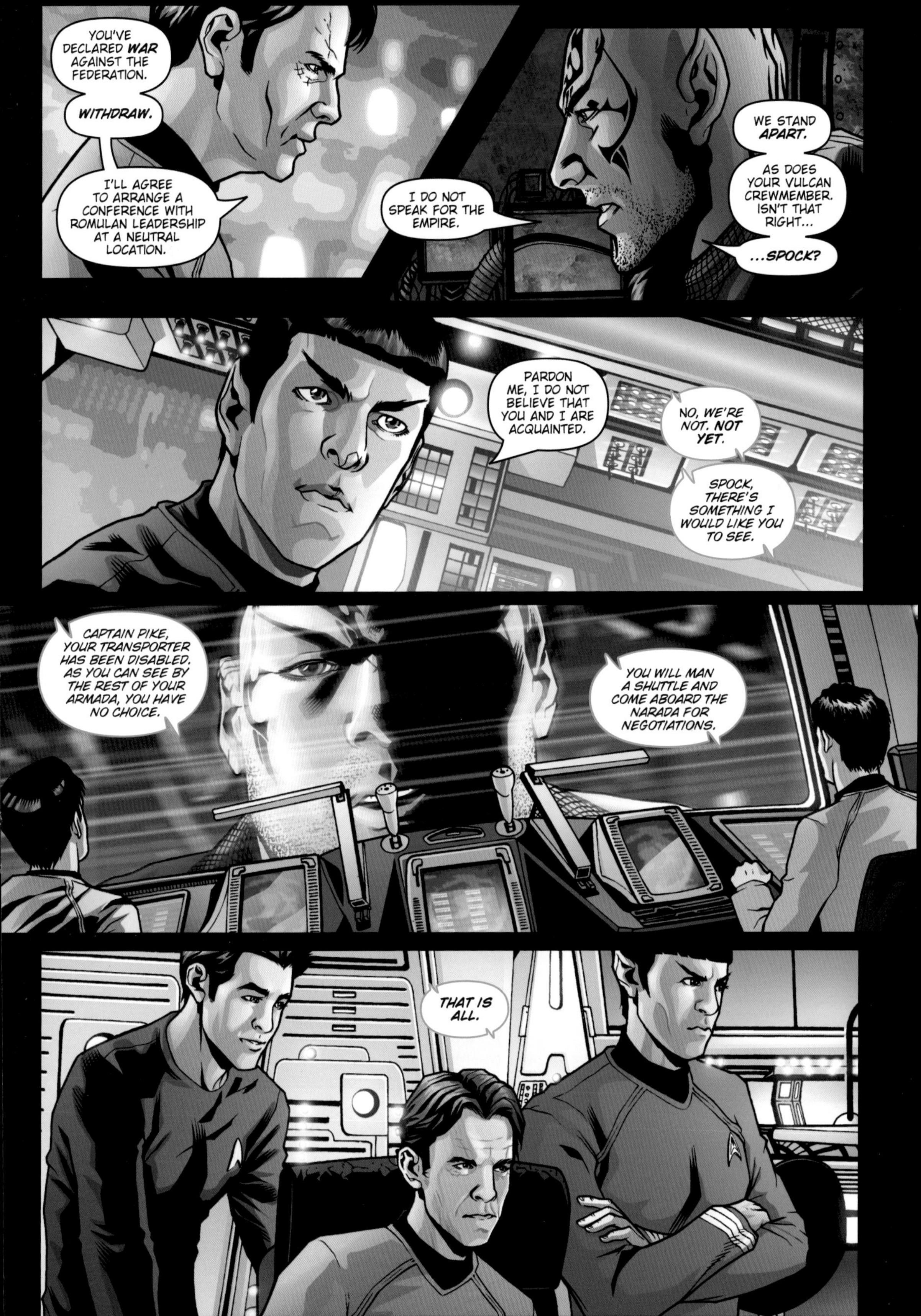
YOU'VE DECLARED **WAR** AGAINST THE FEDERATION.
WITHDRAW.
I'LL AGREE TO ARRANGE A CONFERENCE WITH ROMULAN LEADERSHIP AT A NEUTRAL LOCATION.
I DO NOT SPEAK FOR THE EMPIRE.
WE STAND ***APART.***
AS DOES YOUR VULCAN CREWMEMBER. ISN'T THAT RIGHT...
...SPOCK?
PARDON ME, I DO NOT BELIEVE THAT YOU AND I ARE ACQUAINTED.
NO, WE'RE NOT. ***NOT YET.***
SPOCK, THERE'S SOMETHING I WOULD LIKE YOU TO SEE.
CAPTAIN PIKE, YOUR TRANSPORTER HAS BEEN DISABLED. AS YOU CAN SEE BY THE REST OF YOUR ARMADA, YOU HAVE NO CHOICE.
YOU WILL MAN A SHUTTLE AND COME ABOARD THE NARADA FOR NEGOTIATIONS.
THAT IS ALL.

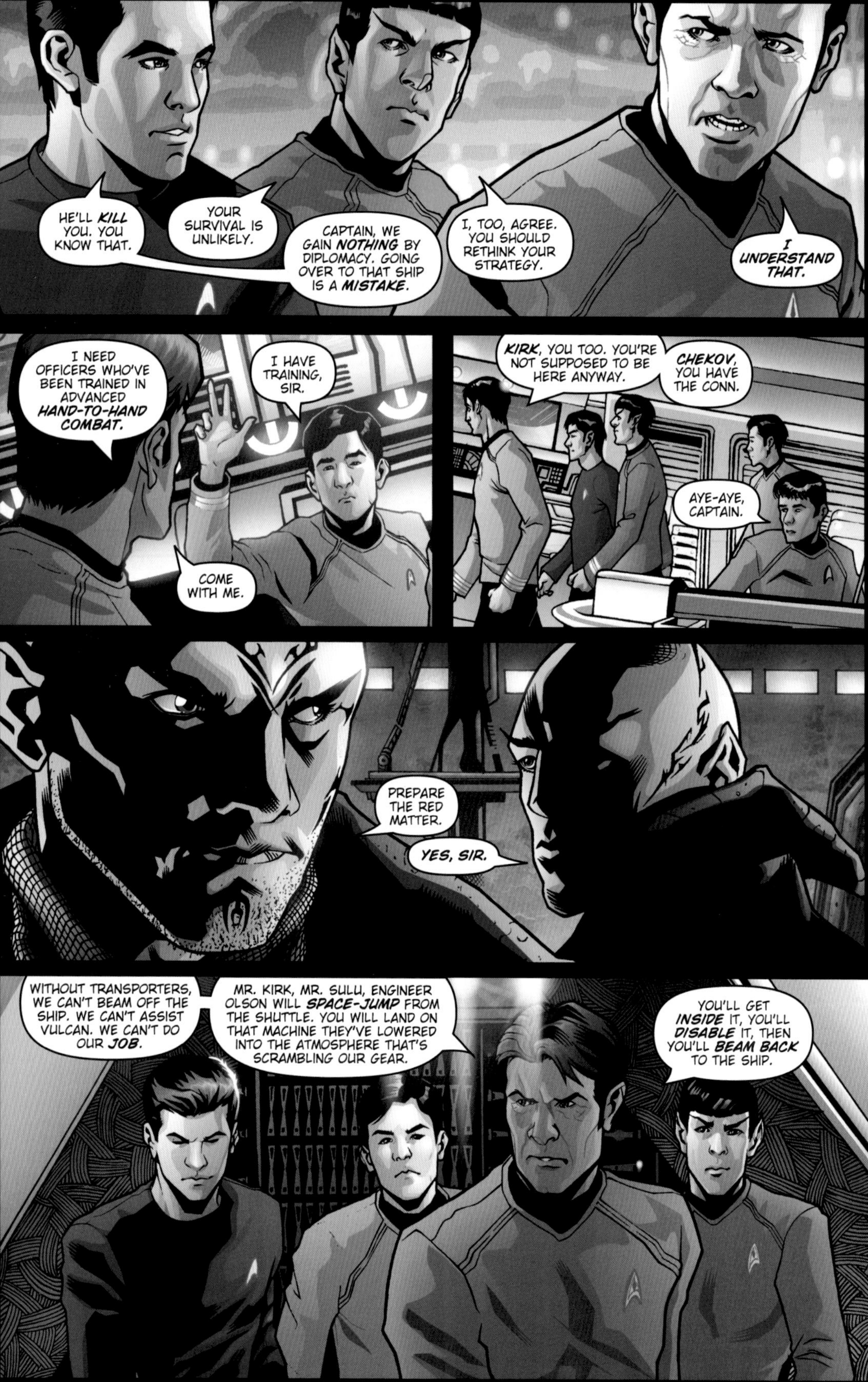
HE'LL KILL YOU. YOU KNOW THAT.
YOUR SURVIVAL IS UNLIKELY.
CAPTAIN, WE GAIN NOTHING BY DIPLOMACY. GOING OVER TO THAT SHIP IS A MISTAKE.
I, TOO, AGREE. YOU SHOULD RETHINK YOUR STRATEGY.
I UNDERSTAND THAT.
I NEED OFFICERS WHO'VE BEEN TRAINED IN ADVANCED HAND-TO-HAND COMBAT.
I HAVE TRAINING, SIR.
COME WITH ME.
KIRK, YOU TOO. YOU'RE NOT SUPPOSED TO BE HERE ANYWAY.
CHEKOV, YOU HAVE THE CONN.
AYE-AYE, CAPTAIN.
PREPARE THE RED MATTER.
YES, SIR.
WITHOUT TRANSPORTERS, WE CAN'T BEAM OFF THE SHIP. WE CAN'T ASSIST VULCAN. WE CAN'T DO OUR JOB.
MR. KIRK, MR. SULU, ENGINEER OLSON WILL SPACE-JUMP FROM THE SHUTTLE. YOU WILL LAND ON THAT MACHINE THEY'VE LOWERED INTO THE ATMOSPHERE THAT'S SCRAMBLING OUR GEAR.
YOU'LL GET INSIDE IT, YOU'LL DISABLE IT, THEN YOU'LL BEAM BACK TO THE SHIP.

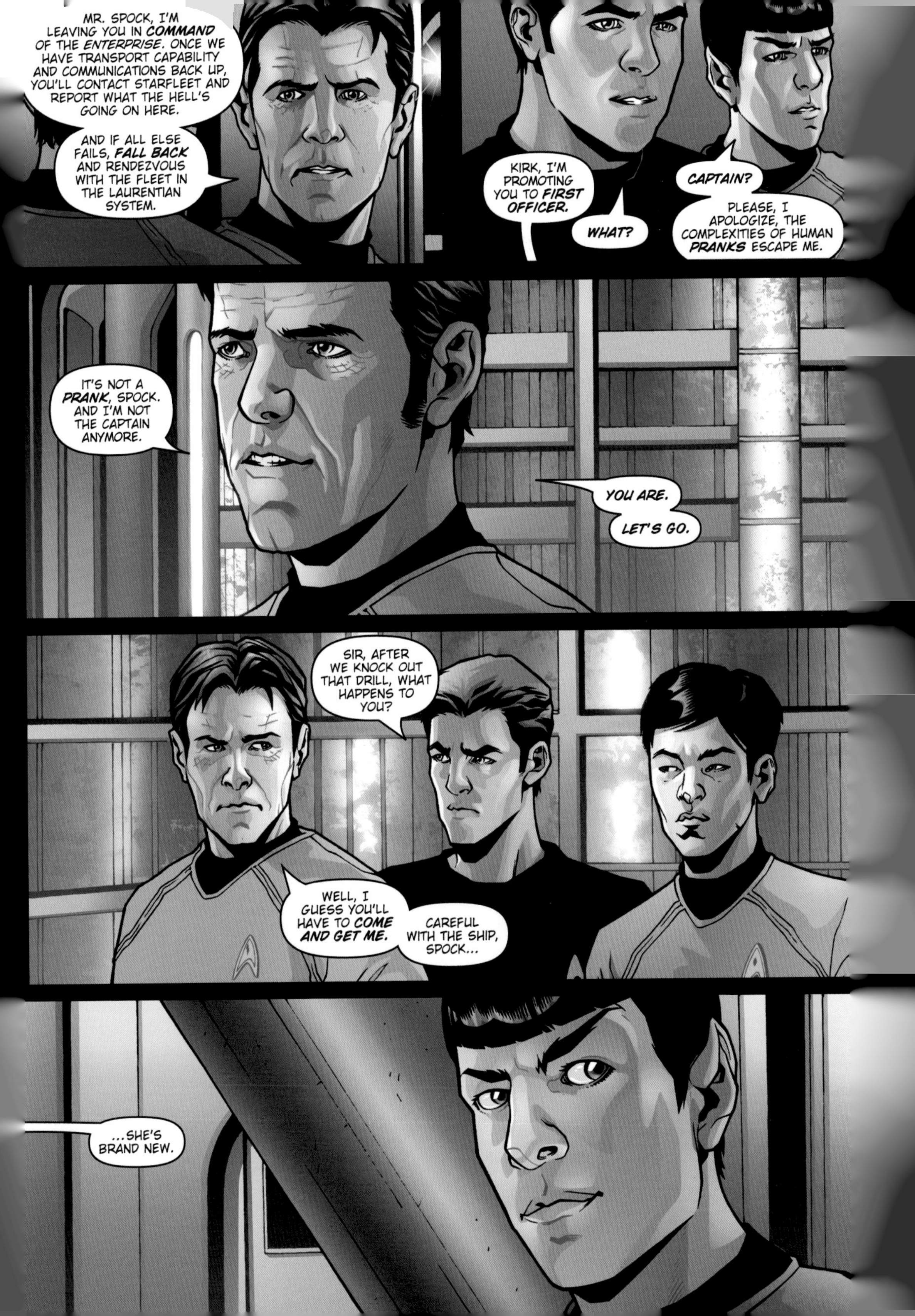
MR. SPOCK, I'M LEAVING YOU IN **COMMAND** OF THE *ENTERPRISE*. ONCE WE HAVE TRANSPORT CAPABILITY AND COMMUNICATIONS BACK UP, YOU'LL CONTACT STARFLEET AND REPORT WHAT THE HELL'S GOING ON HERE.
AND IF ALL ELSE FAILS, **FALL BACK** AND RENDEZVOUS WITH THE FLEET IN THE LAURENTIAN SYSTEM.
KIRK, I'M PROMOTING YOU TO **FIRST OFFICER.**
WHAT?
CAPTAIN?
PLEASE, I APOLOGIZE, THE COMPLEXITIES OF HUMAN **PRANKS** ESCAPE ME.
IT'S NOT A **PRANK,** SPOCK. AND I'M NOT THE CAPTAIN ANYMORE.
YOU ARE.
LET'S GO.
SIR, AFTER WE KNOCK OUT THAT DRILL, WHAT HAPPENS TO YOU?
WELL, I GUESS YOU'LL HAVE TO **COME AND GET ME.**
CAREFUL WITH THE SHIP, SPOCK...
...SHE'S BRAND NEW.

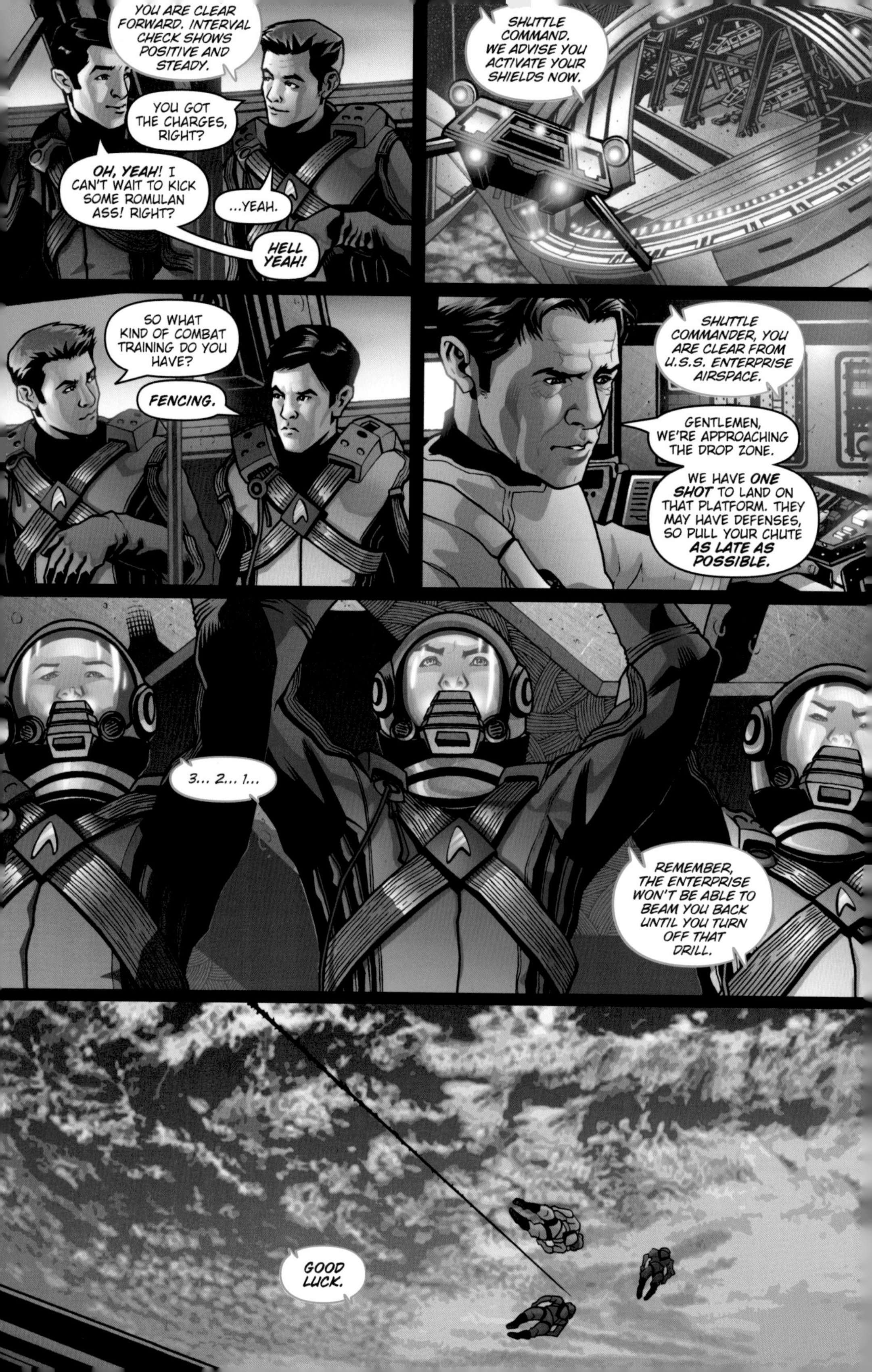
YOU ARE CLEAR FORWARD. INTERVAL CHECK SHOWS POSITIVE AND STEADY.
YOU GOT THE CHARGES, RIGHT?
OH, YEAH! I CAN'T WAIT TO KICK SOME ROMULAN ASS! RIGHT?
...YEAH.
HELL YEAH!
SHUTTLE COMMAND. WE ADVISE YOU ACTIVATE YOUR SHIELDS NOW.
SO WHAT KIND OF COMBAT TRAINING DO YOU HAVE?
FENCING.
SHUTTLE COMMANDER, YOU ARE CLEAR FROM U.S.S. ENTERPRISE AIRSPACE.
GENTLEMEN, WE'RE APPROACHING THE DROP ZONE.
WE HAVE ONE SHOT TO LAND ON THAT PLATFORM. THEY MAY HAVE DEFENSES, SO PULL YOUR CHUTE AS LATE AS POSSIBLE.
3... 2... 1...
REMEMBER, THE ENTERPRISE WON'T BE ABLE TO BEAM YOU BACK UNTIL YOU TURN OFF THAT DRILL.
GOOD LUCK.

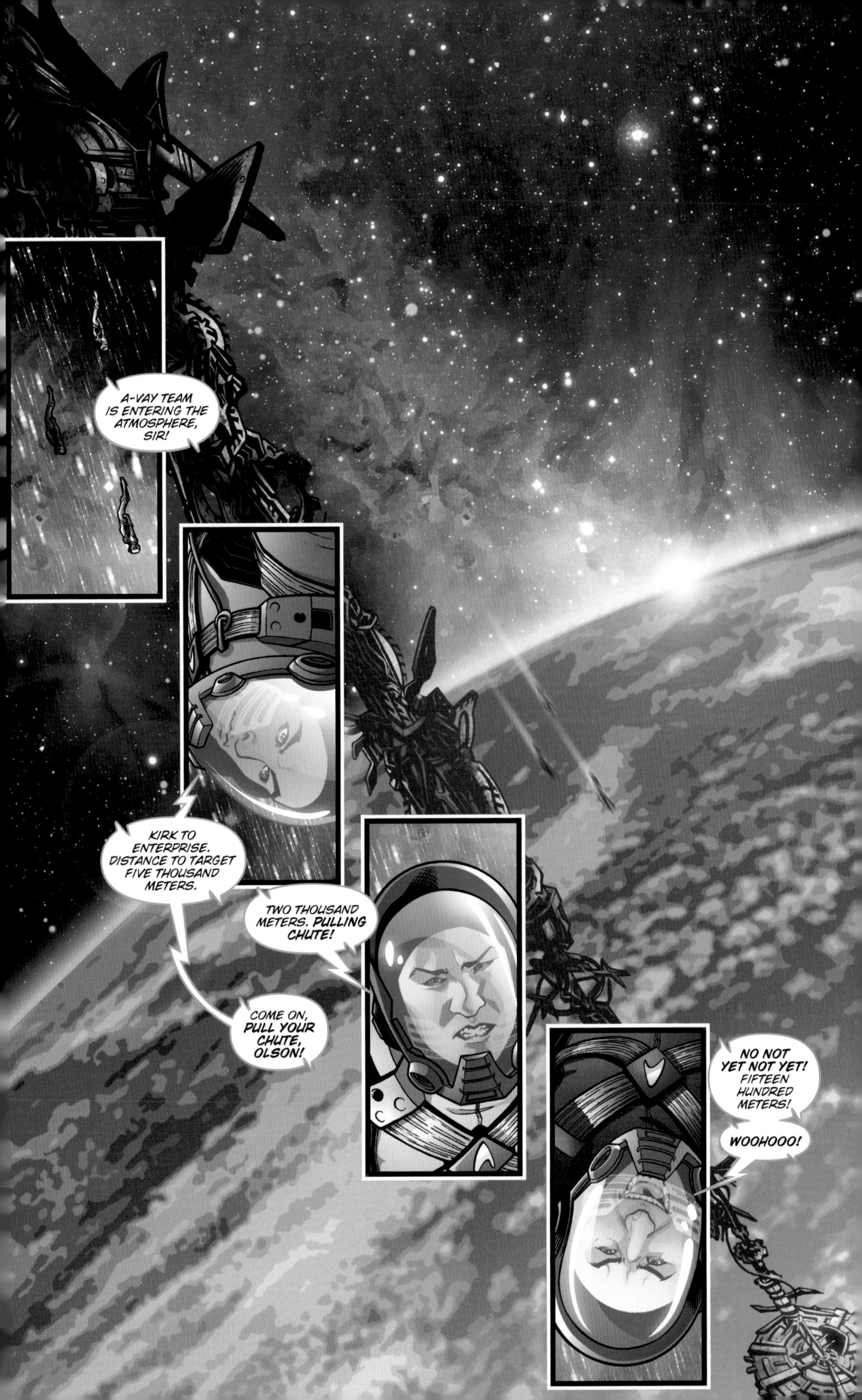
A-VAY TEAM IS ENTERING THE ATMOSPHERE, SIR!
KIRK TO ENTERPRISE. DISTANCE TO TARGET FIVE THOUSAND METERS.
TWO THOUSAND METERS. PULLING CHUTE!
COME ON, PULL YOUR CHUTE, OLSON!
NO NOT YET NOT YET! FIFTEEN HUNDRED METERS!
WOOHOOO!

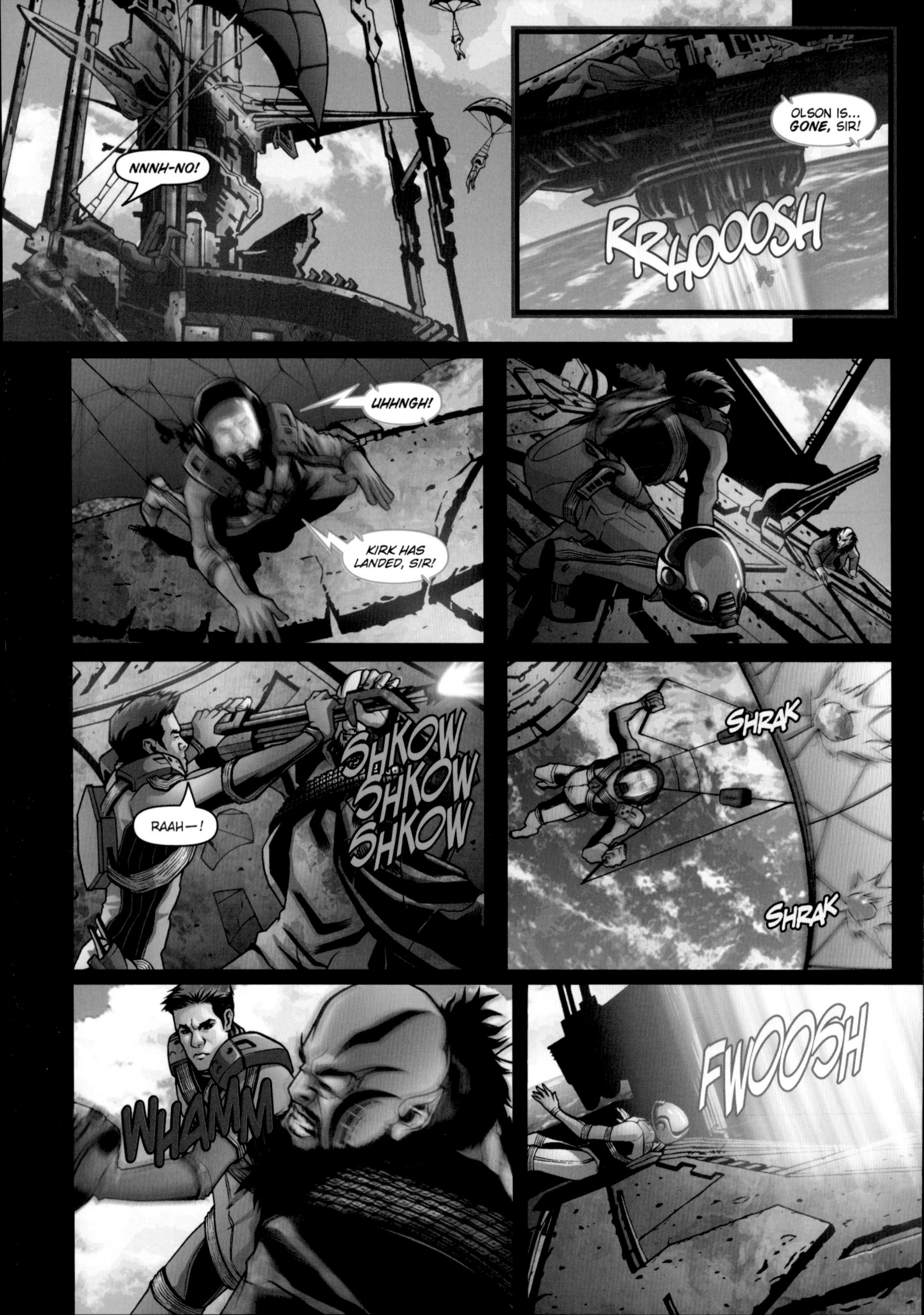
NNNH-NO!
OLSON IS... GONE, SIR!
RRHOOOSH
UHHNGH!
KIRK HAS LANDED, SIR!
RAAH—!
SHKOW SHKOW SHKOW
SHRAK
SHRAK
WHAMM
FWOOSH

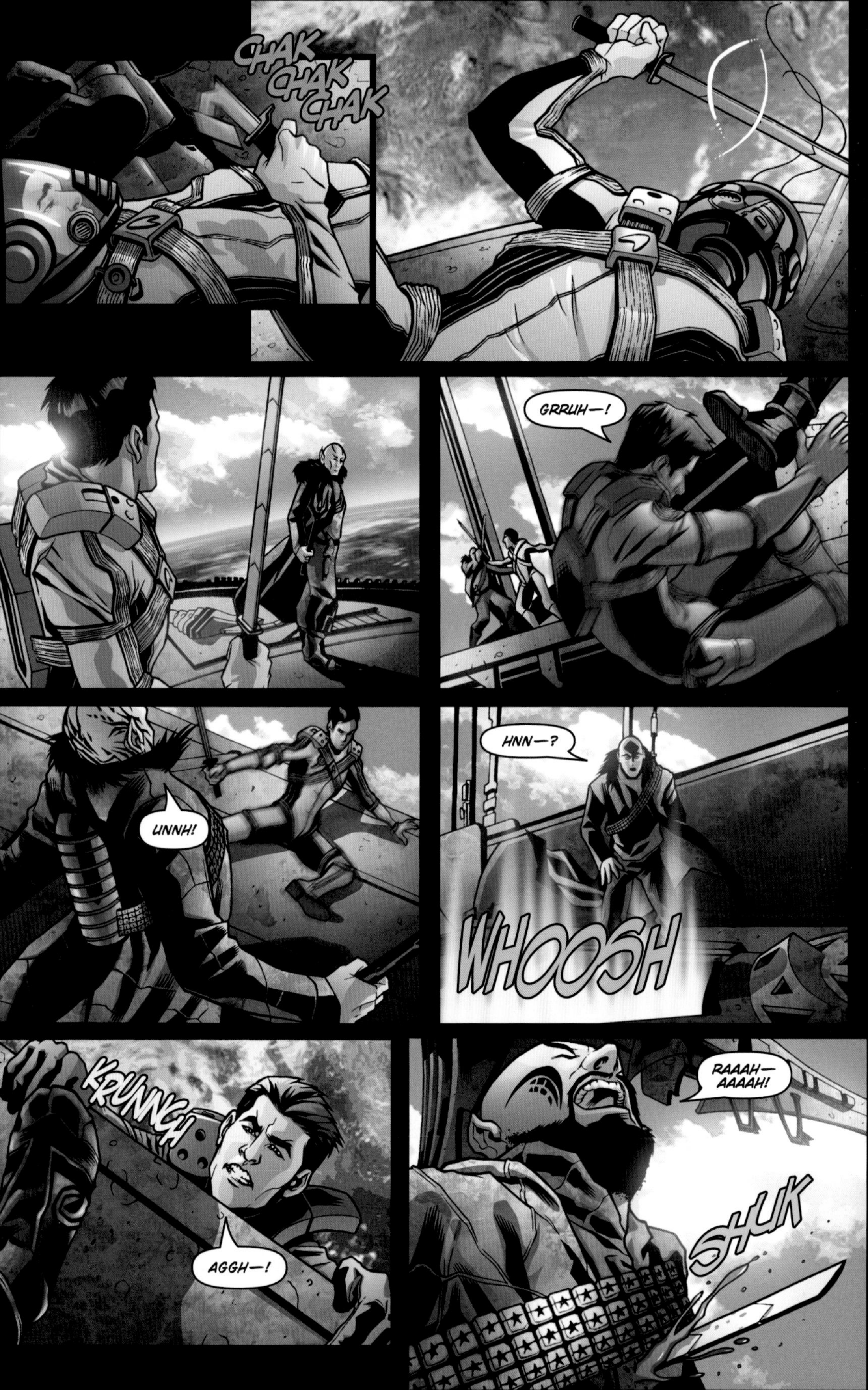
CHAK
CHAK
CHAK
GRRUH—!
UNNH!
HNN—?
WHOOSH
KRUNNCH
AGGH—!
RAAAH—
AAAAH!
SHUK

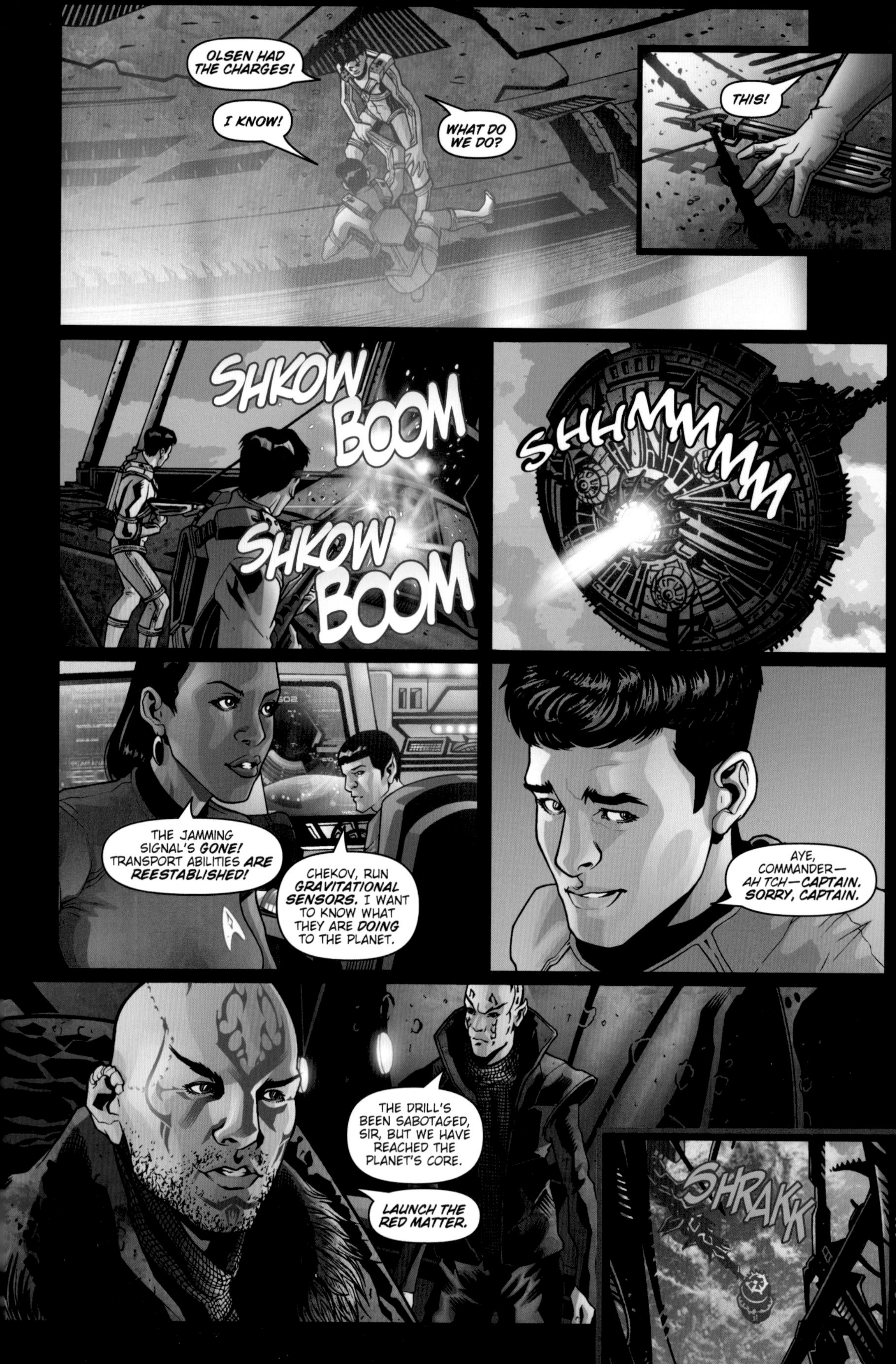

OLSEN HAD THE CHARGES!
I KNOW!
WHAT DO WE DO?
THIS!
SHKOW
BOOM
SHKOW
BOOM
SHHMMMMM
THE JAMMING SIGNAL'S GONE! TRANSPORT ABILITIES ARE REESTABLISHED!
CHEKOV, RUN GRAVITATIONAL SENSORS. I WANT TO KNOW WHAT THEY ARE DOING TO THE PLANET.
AYE, COMMANDER—AH TCH—CAPTAIN. SORRY, CAPTAIN.
THE DRILL'S BEEN SABOTAGED, SIR, BUT WE HAVE REACHED THE PLANET'S CORE.
LAUNCH THE RED MATTER.
SHRAKK

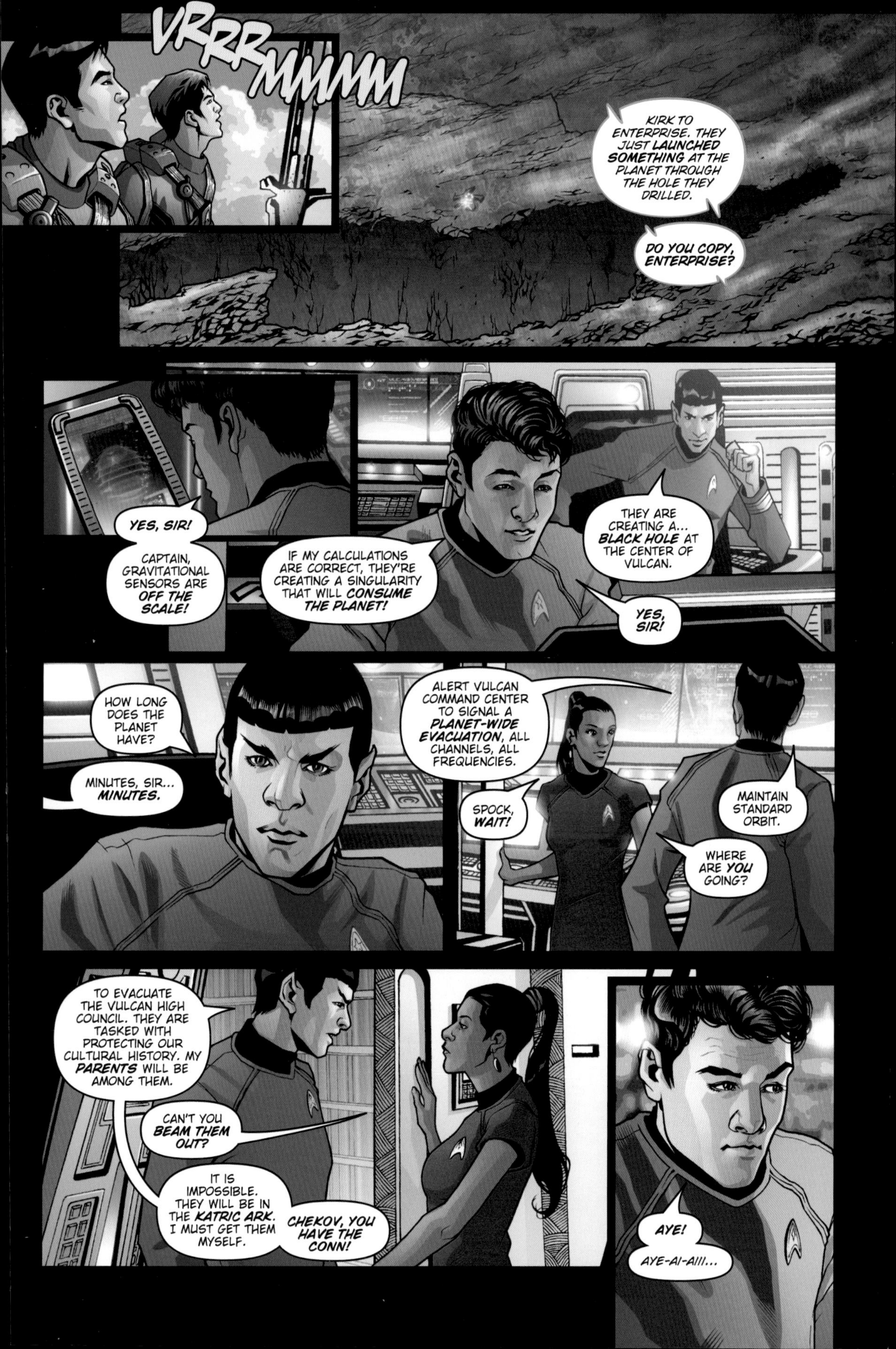
VRRRMMMM
KIRK TO ENTERPRISE. THEY JUST LAUNCHED SOMETHING AT THE PLANET THROUGH THE HOLE THEY DRILLED.
DO YOU COPY, ENTERPRISE?
YES, SIR!
CAPTAIN, GRAVITATIONAL SENSORS ARE OFF THE SCALE!
IF MY CALCULATIONS ARE CORRECT, THEY'RE CREATING A SINGULARITY THAT WILL CONSUME THE PLANET!
THEY ARE CREATING A... BLACK HOLE AT THE CENTER OF VULCAN.
YES, SIR!
HOW LONG DOES THE PLANET HAVE?
MINUTES, SIR... MINUTES.
ALERT VULCAN COMMAND CENTER TO SIGNAL A PLANET-WIDE EVACUATION, ALL CHANNELS, ALL FREQUENCIES.
SPOCK, WAIT!
MAINTAIN STANDARD ORBIT.
WHERE ARE YOU GOING?
TO EVACUATE THE VULCAN HIGH COUNCIL. THEY ARE TASKED WITH PROTECTING OUR CULTURAL HISTORY. MY PARENTS WILL BE AMONG THEM.
CAN'T YOU BEAM THEM OUT?
IT IS IMPOSSIBLE. THEY WILL BE IN THE KATRIC ARK. I MUST GET THEM MYSELF.
CHEKOV, YOU HAVE THE CONN!
AYE!
AYE-AI-AIII...

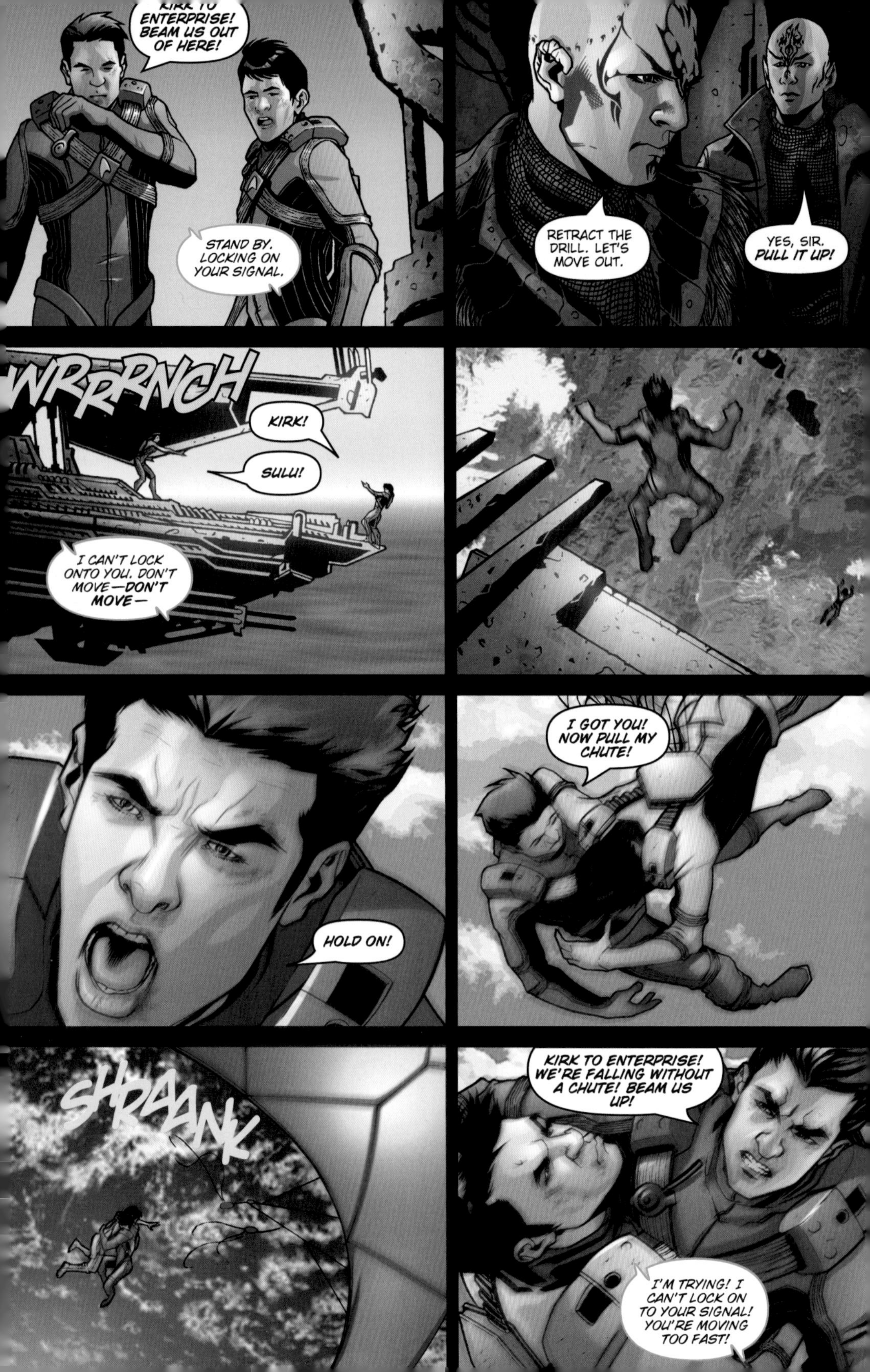

KIRK TO ENTERPRISE! BEAM US OUT OF HERE!
STAND BY. LOCKING ON YOUR SIGNAL.
RETRACT THE DRILL. LET'S MOVE OUT.
YES, SIR. PULL IT UP!
WRRRNCH
KIRK!
SULU!
I CAN'T LOCK ONTO YOU. DON'T MOVE—DON'T MOVE—
HOLD ON!
I GOT YOU! NOW PULL MY CHUTE!
SHRAANK
KIRK TO ENTERPRISE! WE'RE FALLING WITHOUT A CHUTE! BEAM US UP!
I'M TRYING! I CAN'T LOCK ON TO YOUR SIGNAL! YOU'RE MOVING TOO FAST!

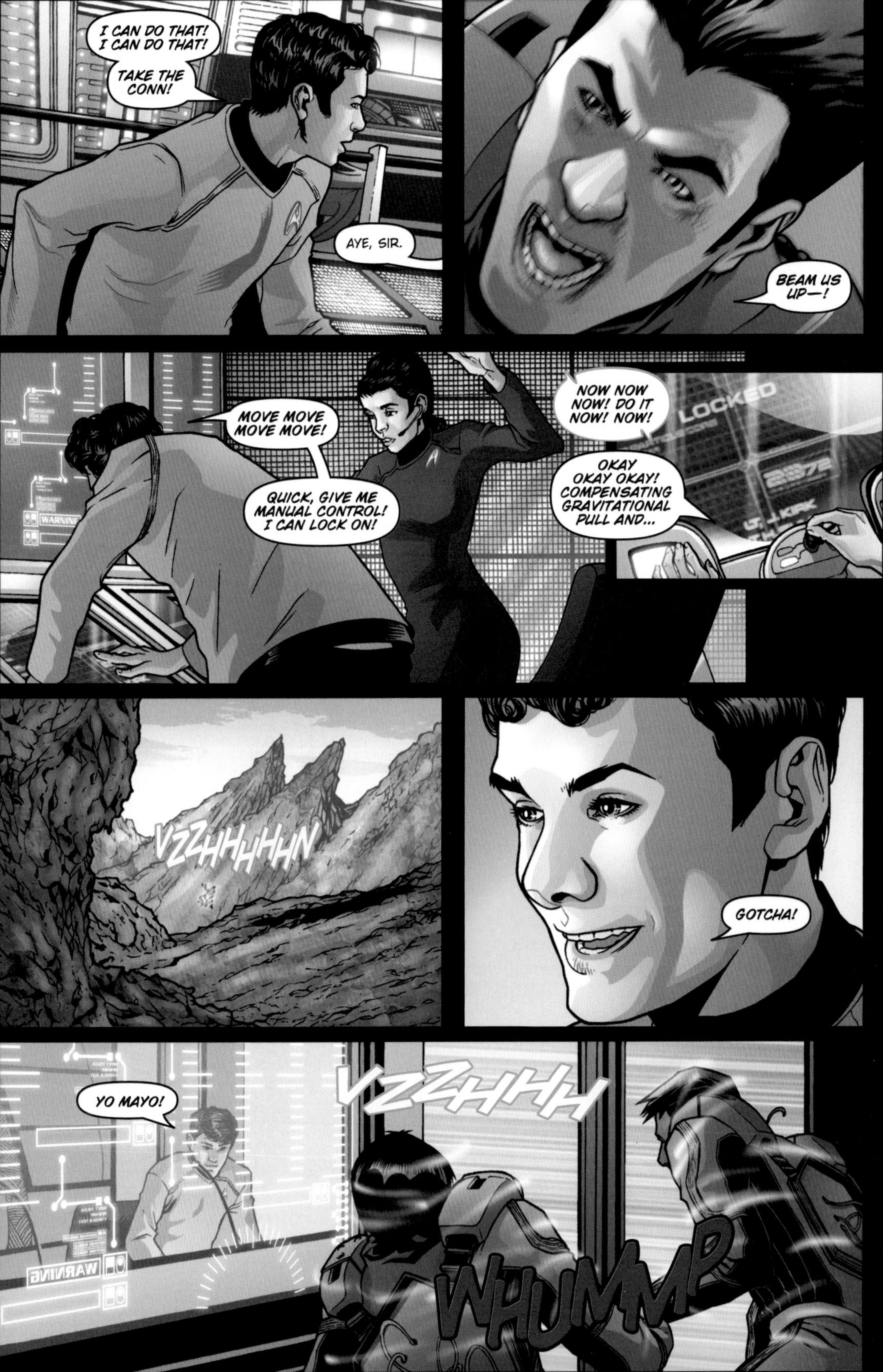
I CAN DO THAT! I CAN DO THAT!
TAKE THE CONN!
AYE, SIR.
BEAM US UP—!
MOVE MOVE MOVE MOVE!
QUICK, GIVE ME MANUAL CONTROL! I CAN LOCK ON!
NOW NOW NOW! DO IT NOW! NOW!
OKAY OKAY OKAY! COMPENSATING GRAVITATIONAL PULL AND...
LOCKED
WARNING
VZZHHHHHN
GOTCHA!
YO MAYO!
VZZHHH
WHUMMP

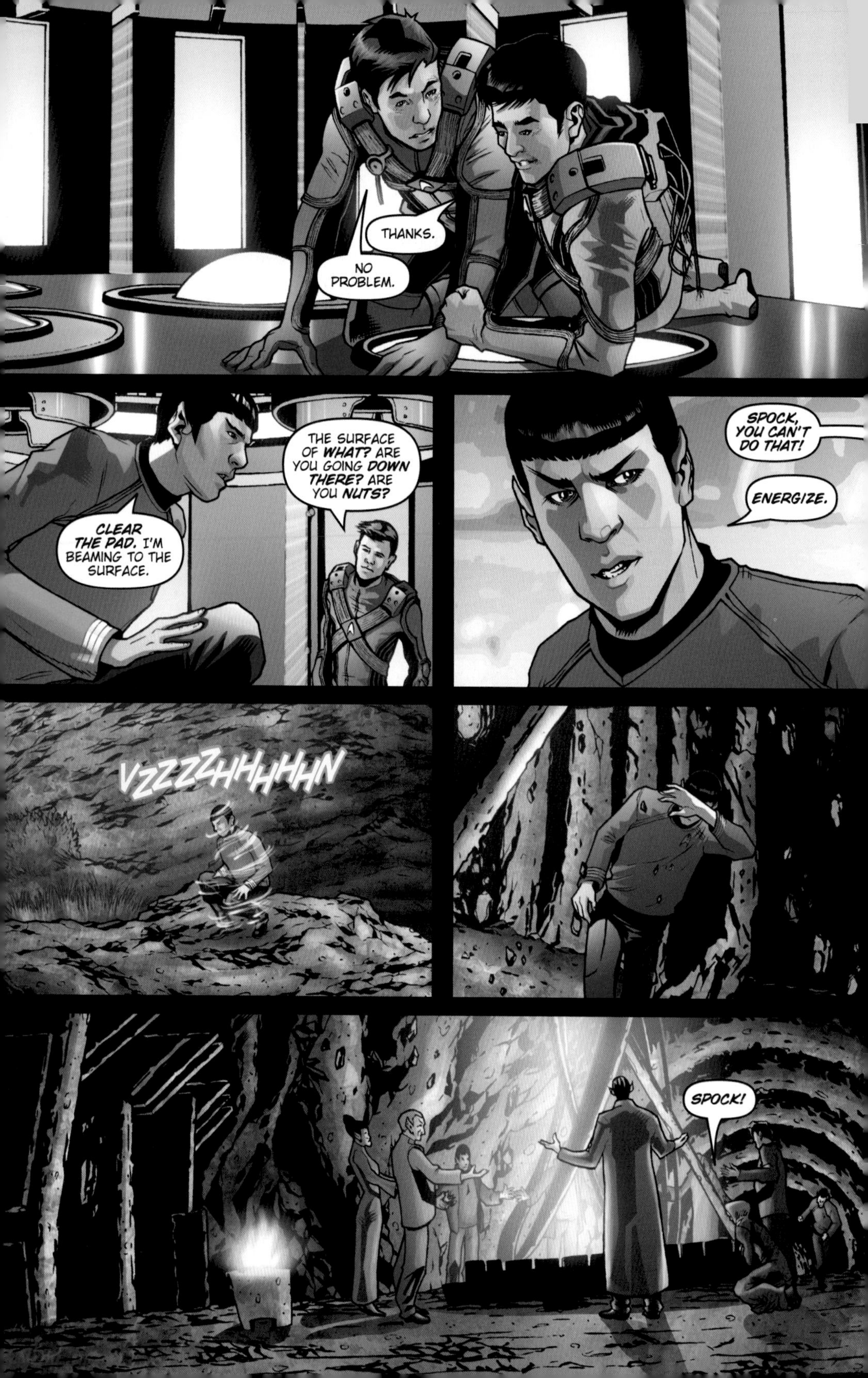
THANKS.
NO PROBLEM.
CLEAR THE PAD. I'M BEAMING TO THE SURFACE.
THE SURFACE OF WHAT? ARE YOU GOING DOWN THERE? ARE YOU NUTS?
SPOCK, YOU CAN'T DO THAT!
ENERGIZE.
VZZZZHHHHHHN
SPOCK!

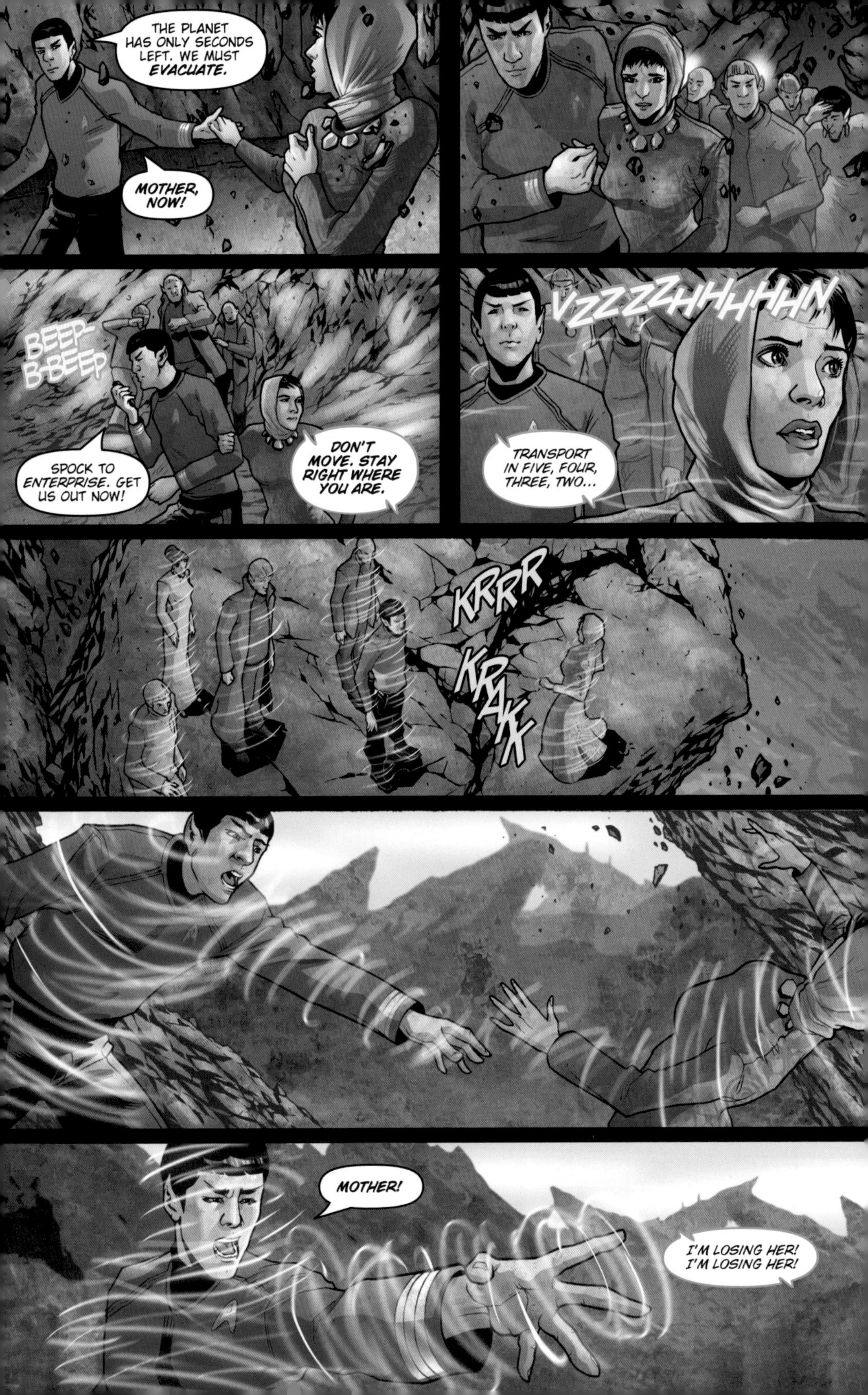
THE PLANET HAS ONLY SECONDS LEFT. WE MUST EVACUATE.
MOTHER, NOW!
BEEP-B-BEEP
SPOCK TO ENTERPRISE. GET US OUT NOW!
DON'T MOVE. STAY RIGHT WHERE YOU ARE.
VZZZZHHHHHN
TRANSPORT IN FIVE, FOUR, THREE, TWO...
KRRR
KRAKK
MOTHER!
I'M LOSING HER! I'M LOSING HER!

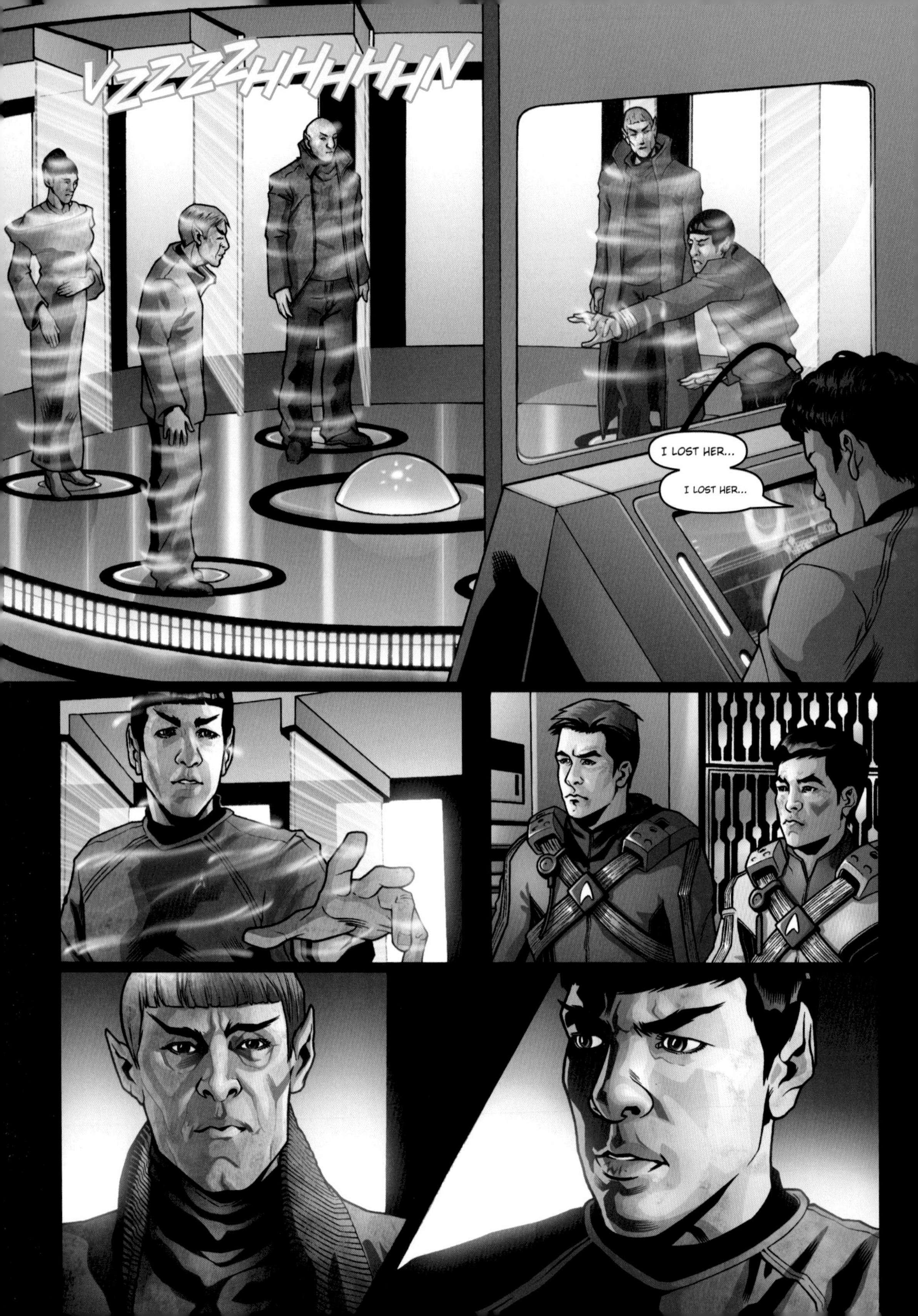
VZZZZHHHHHN
I LOST HER...
I LOST HER...

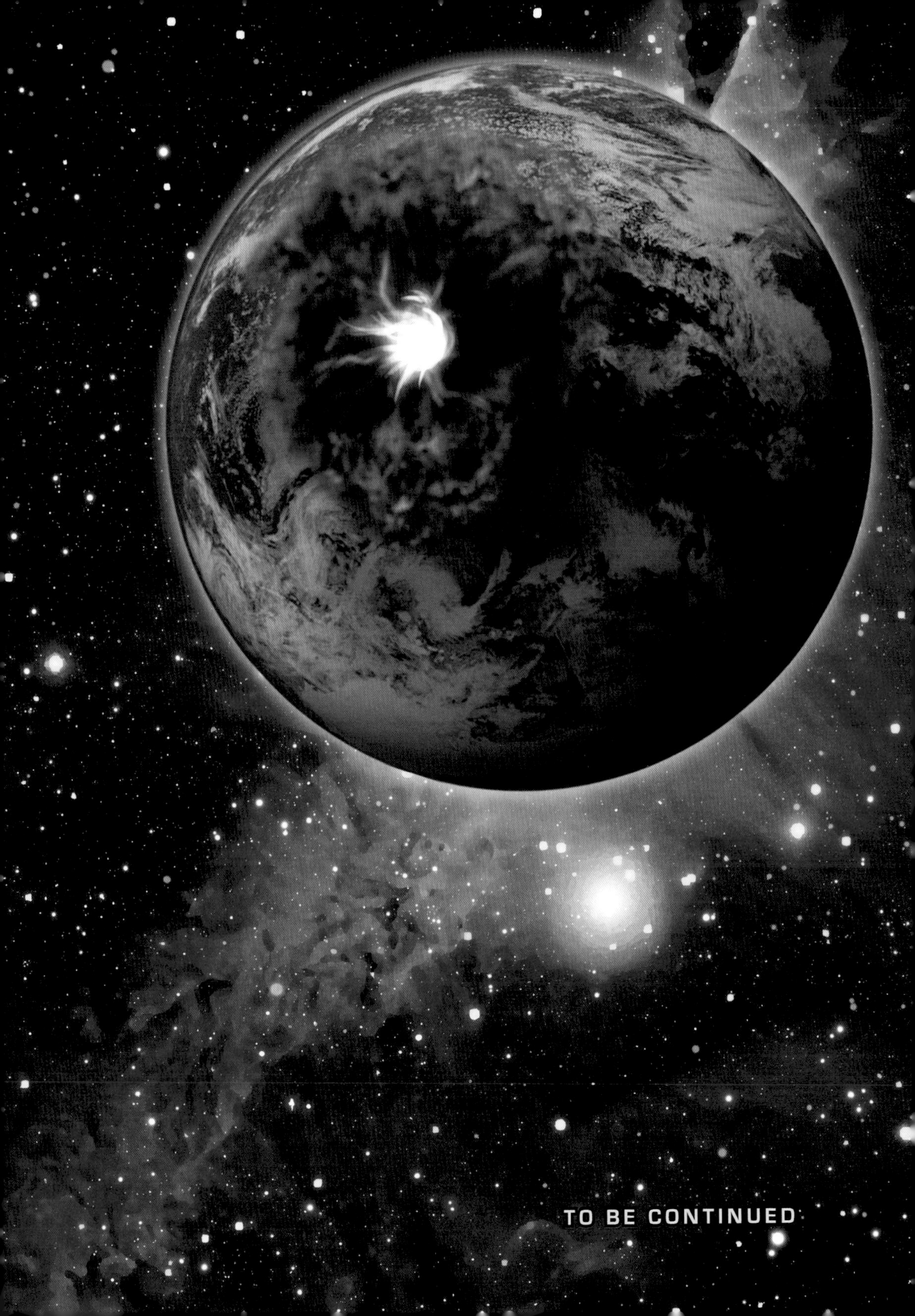
TO BE CONTINUED

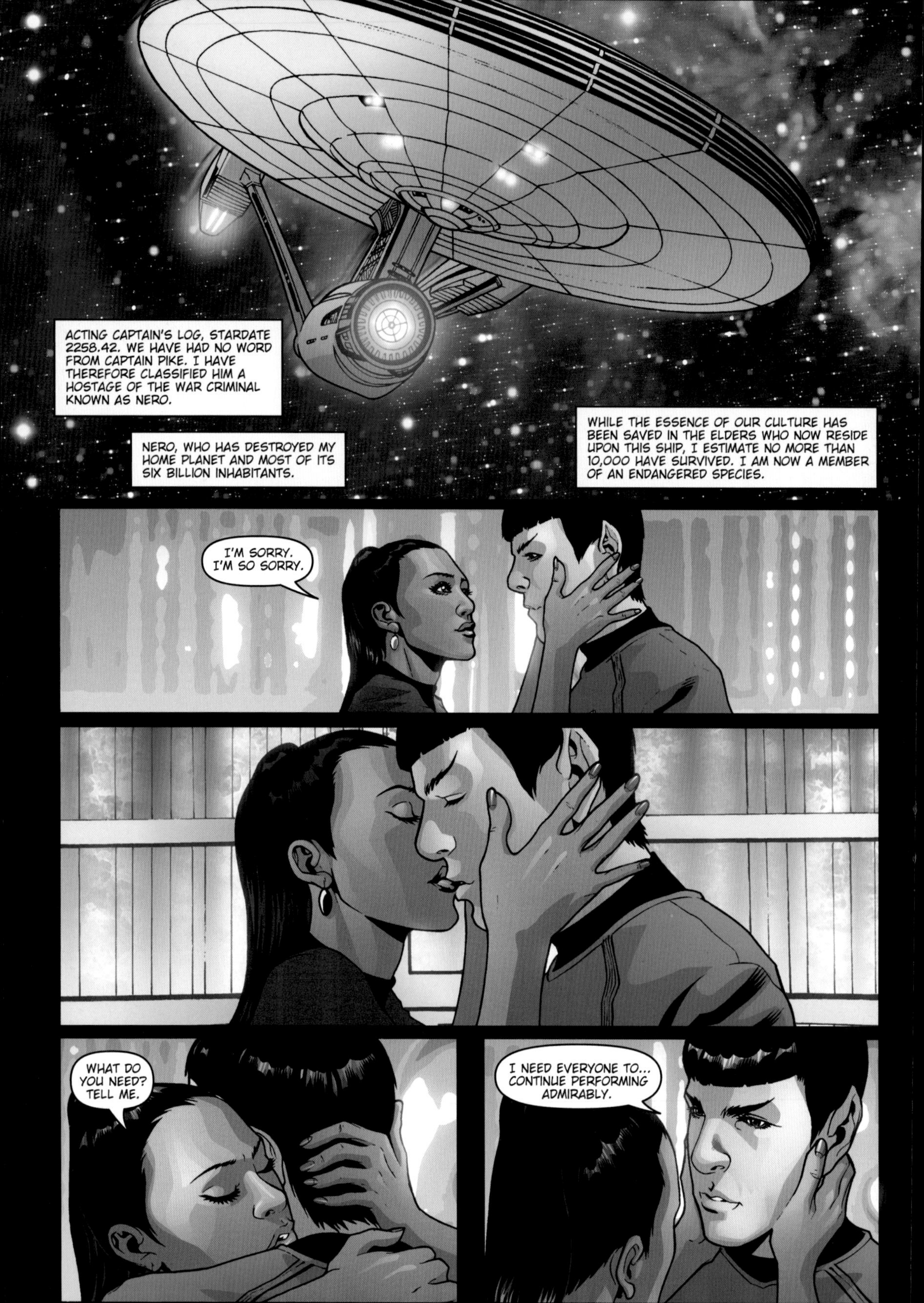
ACTING CAPTAIN'S LOG, STARDATE 2258.42. WE HAVE HAD NO WORD FROM CAPTAIN PIKE. I HAVE THEREFORE CLASSIFIED HIM A HOSTAGE OF THE WAR CRIMINAL KNOWN AS NERO.
NERO, WHO HAS DESTROYED MY HOME PLANET AND MOST OF ITS SIX BILLION INHABITANTS.
WHILE THE ESSENCE OF OUR CULTURE HAS BEEN SAVED IN THE ELDERS WHO NOW RESIDE UPON THIS SHIP, I ESTIMATE NO MORE THAN 10,000 HAVE SURVIVED. I AM NOW A MEMBER OF AN ENDANGERED SPECIES.
I'M SORRY. I'M SO SORRY.
WHAT DO YOU NEED? TELL ME.
I NEED EVERYONE TO... CONTINUE PERFORMING ADMIRABLY.

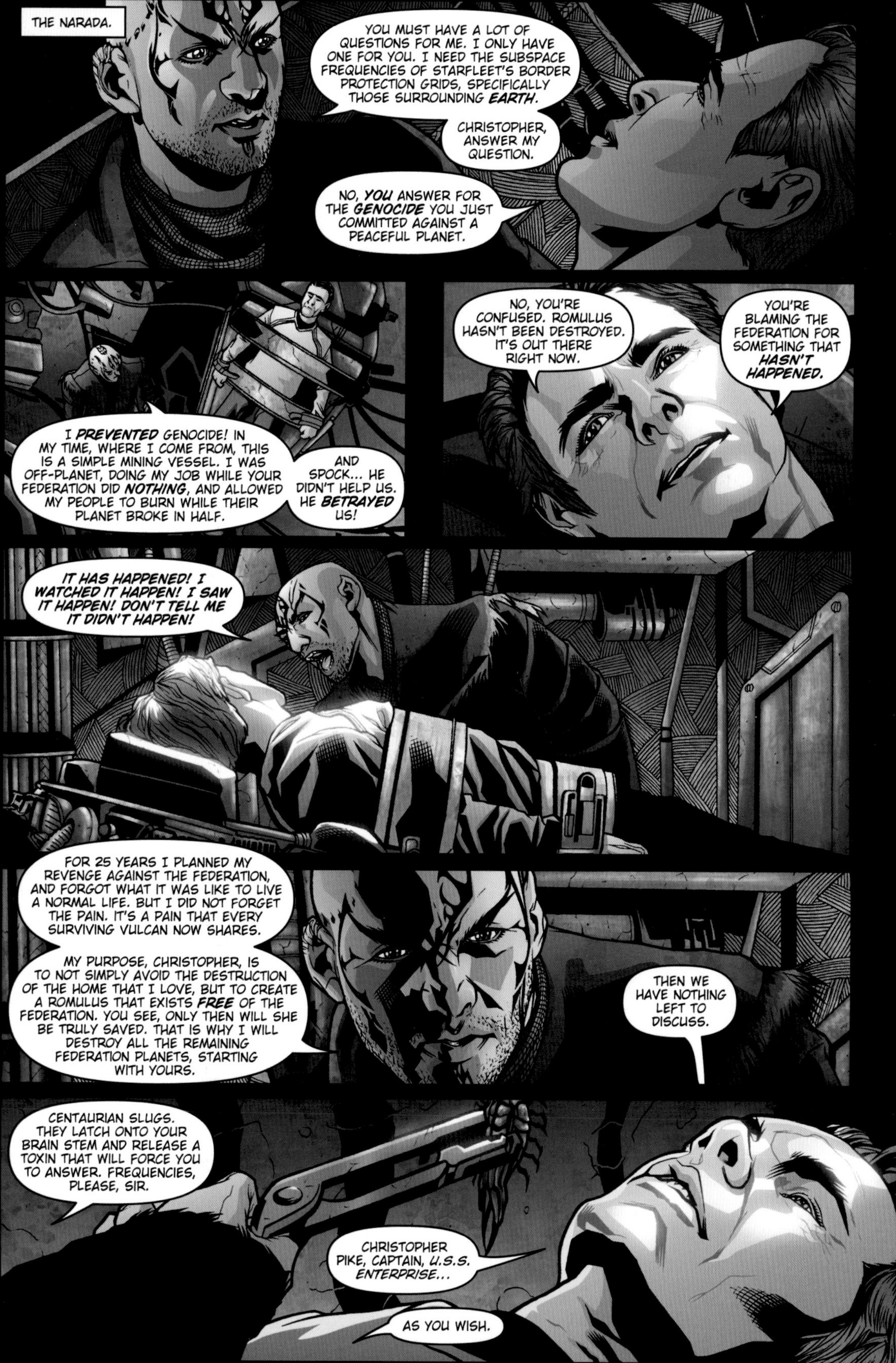
THE NARADA.
YOU MUST HAVE A LOT OF QUESTIONS FOR ME. I ONLY HAVE ONE FOR YOU. I NEED THE SUBSPACE FREQUENCIES OF STARFLEET'S BORDER PROTECTION GRIDS, SPECIFICALLY THOSE SURROUNDING EARTH.
CHRISTOPHER, ANSWER MY QUESTION.
NO, YOU ANSWER FOR THE GENOCIDE YOU JUST COMMITTED AGAINST A PEACEFUL PLANET.
I PREVENTED GENOCIDE! IN MY TIME, WHERE I COME FROM, THIS IS A SIMPLE MINING VESSEL. I WAS OFF-PLANET, DOING MY JOB WHILE YOUR FEDERATION DID NOTHING, AND ALLOWED MY PEOPLE TO BURN WHILE THEIR PLANET BROKE IN HALF.
AND SPOCK... HE DIDN'T HELP US. HE BETRAYED US!
NO, YOU'RE CONFUSED. ROMULUS HASN'T BEEN DESTROYED. IT'S OUT THERE RIGHT NOW.
YOU'RE BLAMING THE FEDERATION FOR SOMETHING THAT HASN'T HAPPENED.
IT HAS HAPPENED! I WATCHED IT HAPPEN! I SAW IT HAPPEN! DON'T TELL ME IT DIDN'T HAPPEN!
FOR 25 YEARS I PLANNED MY REVENGE AGAINST THE FEDERATION, AND FORGOT WHAT IT WAS LIKE TO LIVE A NORMAL LIFE. BUT I DID NOT FORGET THE PAIN. IT'S A PAIN THAT EVERY SURVIVING VULCAN NOW SHARES.
MY PURPOSE, CHRISTOPHER, IS TO NOT SIMPLY AVOID THE DESTRUCTION OF THE HOME THAT I LOVE, BUT TO CREATE A ROMULUS THAT EXISTS FREE OF THE FEDERATION. YOU SEE, ONLY THEN WILL SHE BE TRULY SAVED. THAT IS WHY I WILL DESTROY ALL THE REMAINING FEDERATION PLANETS, STARTING WITH YOURS.
THEN WE HAVE NOTHING LEFT TO DISCUSS.
CENTAURIAN SLUGS. THEY LATCH ONTO YOUR BRAIN STEM AND RELEASE A TOXIN THAT WILL FORCE YOU TO ANSWER. FREQUENCIES, PLEASE, SIR.
CHRISTOPHER PIKE, CAPTAIN, U.S.S. ENTERPRISE...
AS YOU WISH.

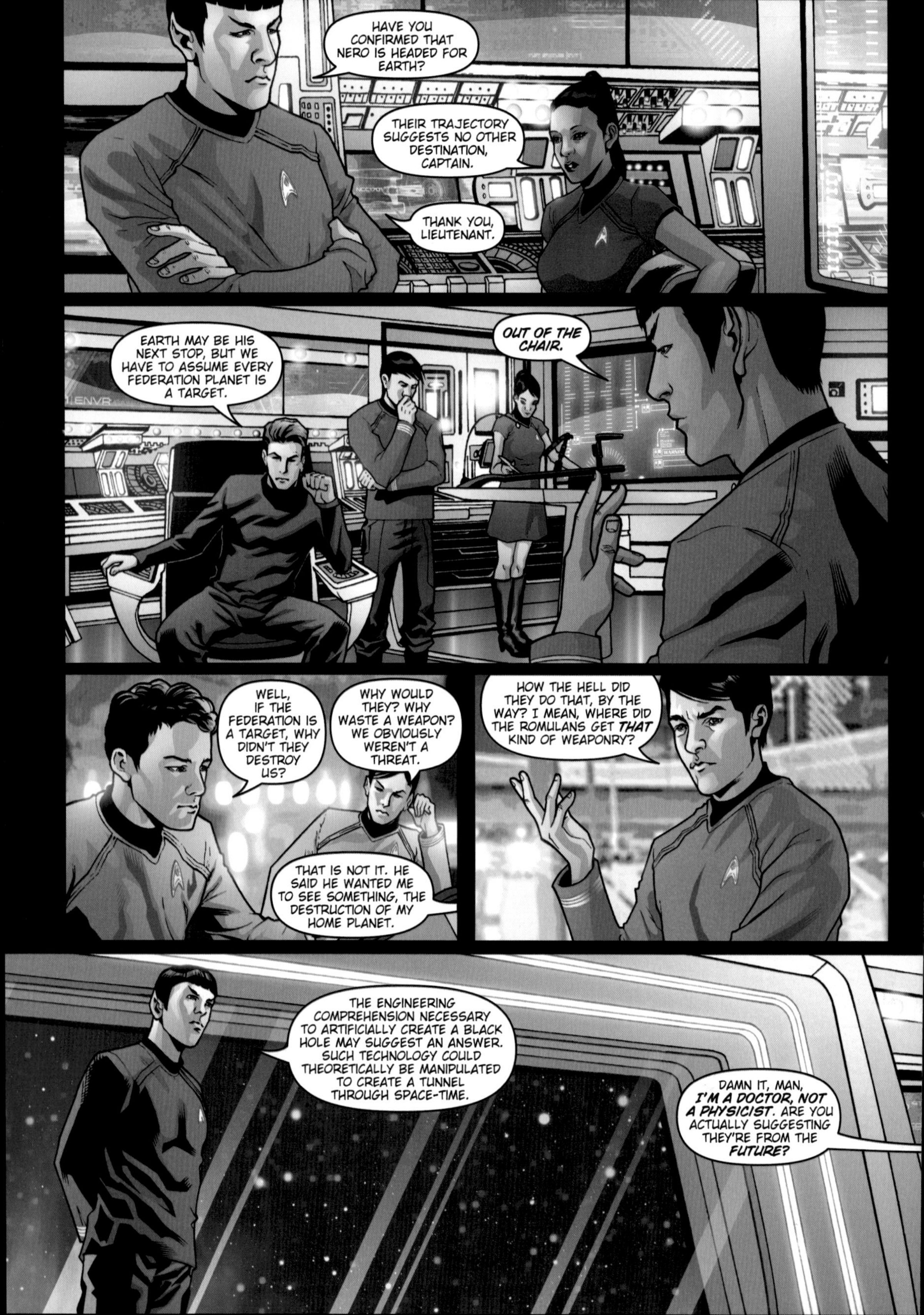
HAVE YOU CONFIRMED THAT NERO IS HEADED FOR EARTH?
THEIR TRAJECTORY SUGGESTS NO OTHER DESTINATION, CAPTAIN.
THANK YOU, LIEUTENANT.
EARTH MAY BE HIS NEXT STOP, BUT WE HAVE TO ASSUME EVERY FEDERATION PLANET IS A TARGET.
OUT OF THE CHAIR.
WELL, IF THE FEDERATION IS A TARGET, WHY DIDN'T THEY DESTROY US?
WHY WOULD THEY? WHY WASTE A WEAPON? WE OBVIOUSLY WEREN'T A THREAT.
THAT IS NOT IT. HE SAID HE WANTED ME TO SEE SOMETHING, THE DESTRUCTION OF MY HOME PLANET.
HOW THE HELL DID THEY DO THAT, BY THE WAY? I MEAN, WHERE DID THE ROMULANS GET *THAT* KIND OF WEAPONRY?
THE ENGINEERING COMPREHENSION NECESSARY TO ARTIFICIALLY CREATE A BLACK HOLE MAY SUGGEST AN ANSWER. SUCH TECHNOLOGY COULD THEORETICALLY BE MANIPULATED TO CREATE A TUNNEL THROUGH SPACE-TIME.
DAMN IT, MAN, ***I'M A DOCTOR, NOT A PHYSICIST***. ARE YOU ACTUALLY SUGGESTING THEY'RE FROM THE ***FUTURE?***

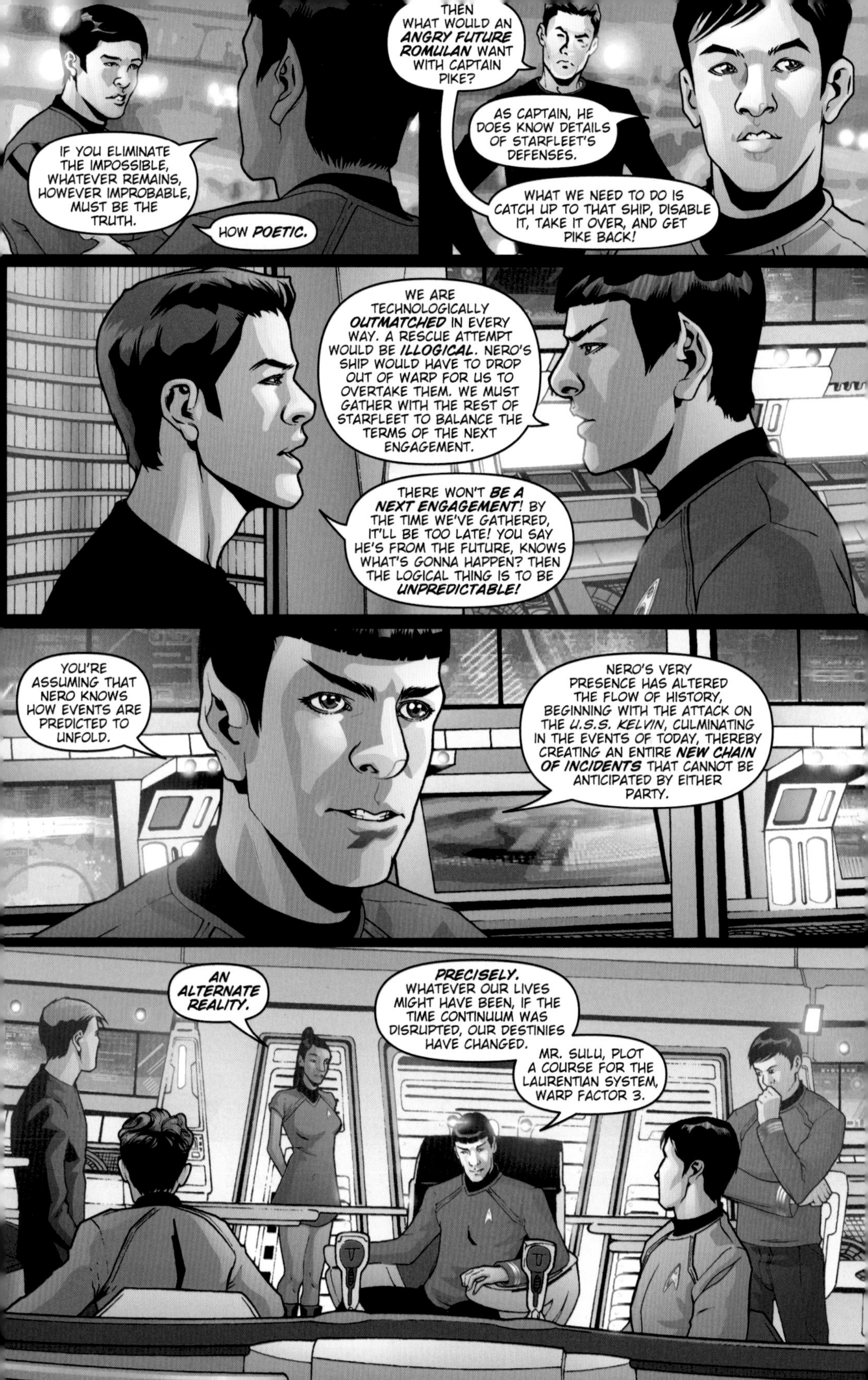
IF YOU ELIMINATE THE IMPOSSIBLE, WHATEVER REMAINS, HOWEVER IMPROBABLE, MUST BE THE TRUTH.
HOW POETIC.
THEN WHAT WOULD AN ANGRY FUTURE ROMULAN WANT WITH CAPTAIN PIKE?
AS CAPTAIN, HE DOES KNOW DETAILS OF STARFLEET'S DEFENSES.
WHAT WE NEED TO DO IS CATCH UP TO THAT SHIP, DISABLE IT, TAKE IT OVER, AND GET PIKE BACK!
WE ARE TECHNOLOGICALLY OUTMATCHED IN EVERY WAY. A RESCUE ATTEMPT WOULD BE ILLOGICAL. NERO'S SHIP WOULD HAVE TO DROP OUT OF WARP FOR US TO OVERTAKE THEM. WE MUST GATHER WITH THE REST OF STARFLEET TO BALANCE THE TERMS OF THE NEXT ENGAGEMENT.
THERE WON'T BE A NEXT ENGAGEMENT! BY THE TIME WE'VE GATHERED, IT'LL BE TOO LATE! YOU SAY HE'S FROM THE FUTURE, KNOWS WHAT'S GONNA HAPPEN? THEN THE LOGICAL THING IS TO BE UNPREDICTABLE!
YOU'RE ASSUMING THAT NERO KNOWS HOW EVENTS ARE PREDICTED TO UNFOLD.
NERO'S VERY PRESENCE HAS ALTERED THE FLOW OF HISTORY, BEGINNING WITH THE ATTACK ON THE U.S.S. KELVIN, CULMINATING IN THE EVENTS OF TODAY, THEREBY CREATING AN ENTIRE NEW CHAIN OF INCIDENTS THAT CANNOT BE ANTICIPATED BY EITHER PARTY.
AN ALTERNATE REALITY.
PRECISELY. WHATEVER OUR LIVES MIGHT HAVE BEEN, IF THE TIME CONTINUUM WAS DISRUPTED, OUR DESTINIES HAVE CHANGED.
MR. SULU, PLOT A COURSE FOR THE LAURENTIAN SYSTEM, WARP FACTOR 3.

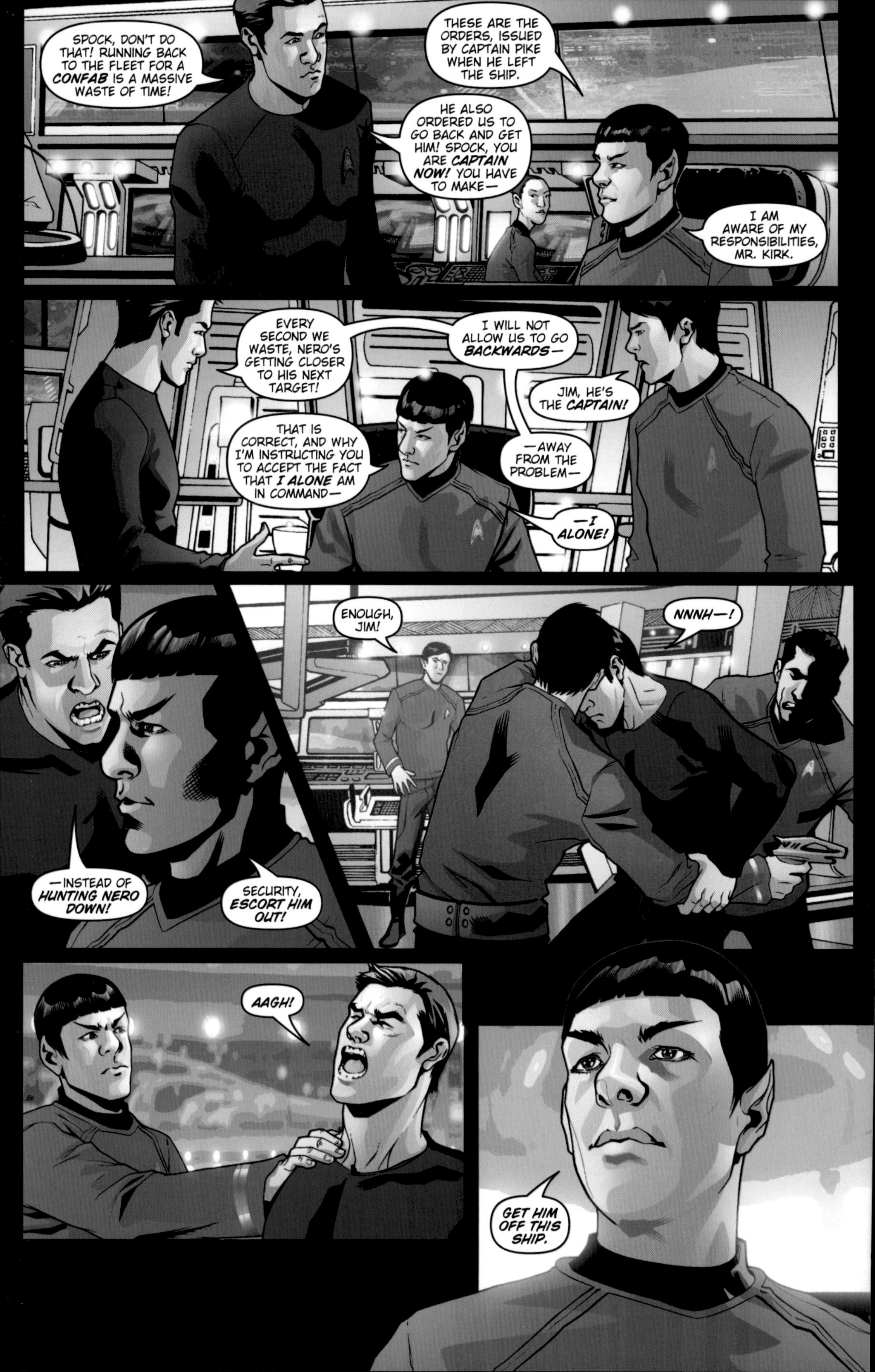
SPOCK, DON'T DO THAT! RUNNING BACK TO THE FLEET FOR A CONFAB IS A MASSIVE WASTE OF TIME!
THESE ARE THE ORDERS, ISSUED BY CAPTAIN PIKE WHEN HE LEFT THE SHIP.
HE ALSO ORDERED US TO GO BACK AND GET HIM! SPOCK, YOU ARE CAPTAIN NOW! YOU HAVE TO MAKE—
I AM AWARE OF MY RESPONSIBILITIES, MR. KIRK.
EVERY SECOND WE WASTE, NERO'S GETTING CLOSER TO HIS NEXT TARGET!
I WILL NOT ALLOW US TO GO BACKWARDS—
—AWAY FROM THE PROBLEM—
JIM, HE'S THE CAPTAIN!
THAT IS CORRECT, AND WHY I'M INSTRUCTING YOU TO ACCEPT THE FACT THAT I ALONE AM IN COMMAND—
—I ALONE!
—INSTEAD OF HUNTING NERO DOWN!
SECURITY, ESCORT HIM OUT!
ENOUGH, JIM!
NNNH—!
AAGH!
GET HIM OFF THIS SHIP.

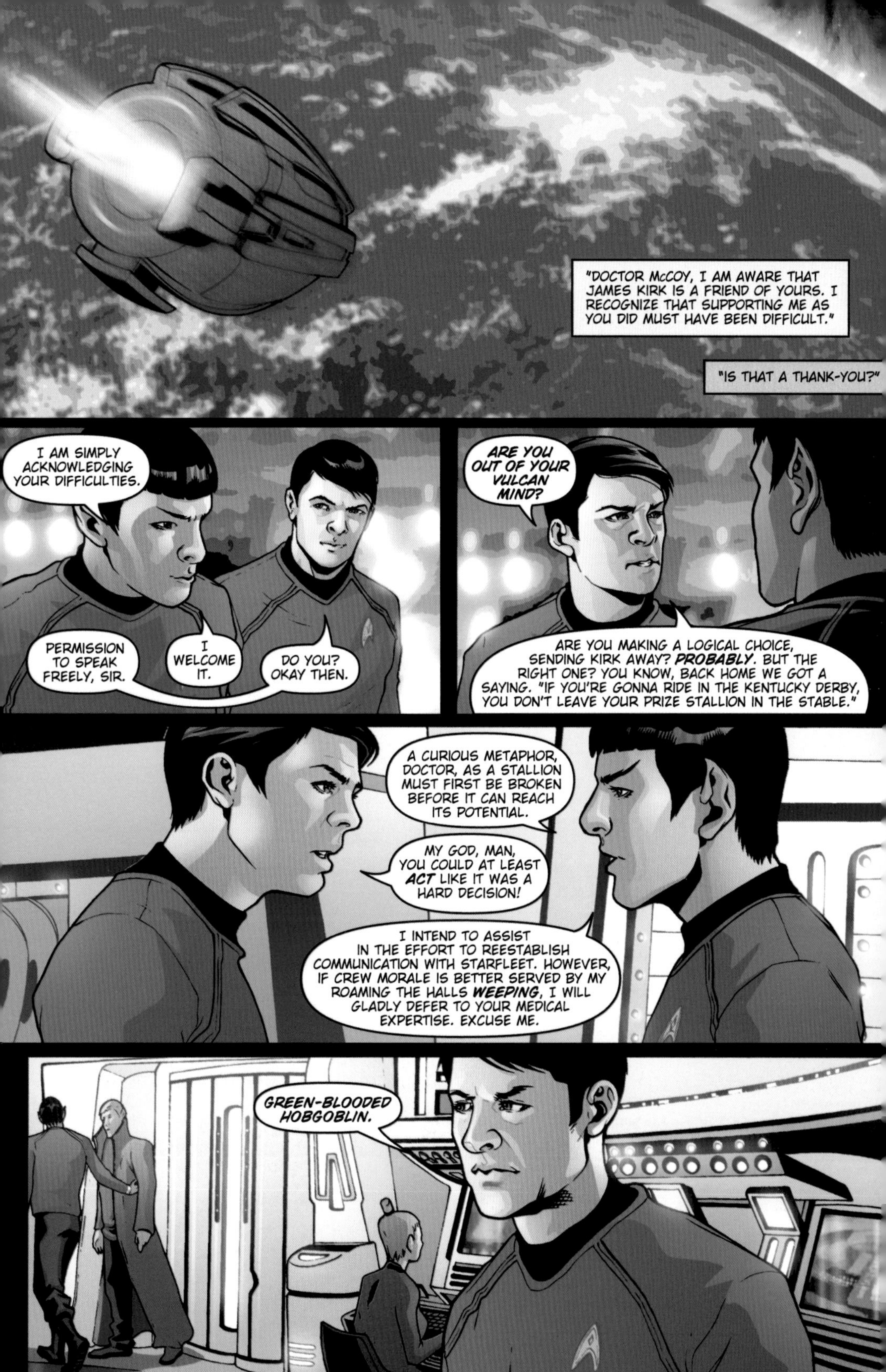

"DOCTOR McCOY, I AM AWARE THAT JAMES KIRK IS A FRIEND OF YOURS. I RECOGNIZE THAT SUPPORTING ME AS YOU DID MUST HAVE BEEN DIFFICULT."
"IS THAT A THANK-YOU?"
I AM SIMPLY ACKNOWLEDGING YOUR DIFFICULTIES.
PERMISSION TO SPEAK FREELY, SIR.
I WELCOME IT.
DO YOU? OKAY THEN.
ARE YOU OUT OF YOUR VULCAN MIND?
ARE YOU MAKING A LOGICAL CHOICE, SENDING KIRK AWAY? PROBABLY. BUT THE RIGHT ONE? YOU KNOW, BACK HOME WE GOT A SAYING. "IF YOU'RE GONNA RIDE IN THE KENTUCKY DERBY, YOU DON'T LEAVE YOUR PRIZE STALLION IN THE STABLE."
A CURIOUS METAPHOR, DOCTOR, AS A STALLION MUST FIRST BE BROKEN BEFORE IT CAN REACH ITS POTENTIAL.
MY GOD, MAN, YOU COULD AT LEAST ACT LIKE IT WAS A HARD DECISION!
I INTEND TO ASSIST IN THE EFFORT TO REESTABLISH COMMUNICATION WITH STARFLEET. HOWEVER, IF CREW MORALE IS BETTER SERVED BY MY ROAMING THE HALLS WEEPING, I WILL GLADLY DEFER TO YOUR MEDICAL EXPERTISE. EXCUSE ME.
GREEN-BLOODED HOBGOBLIN.

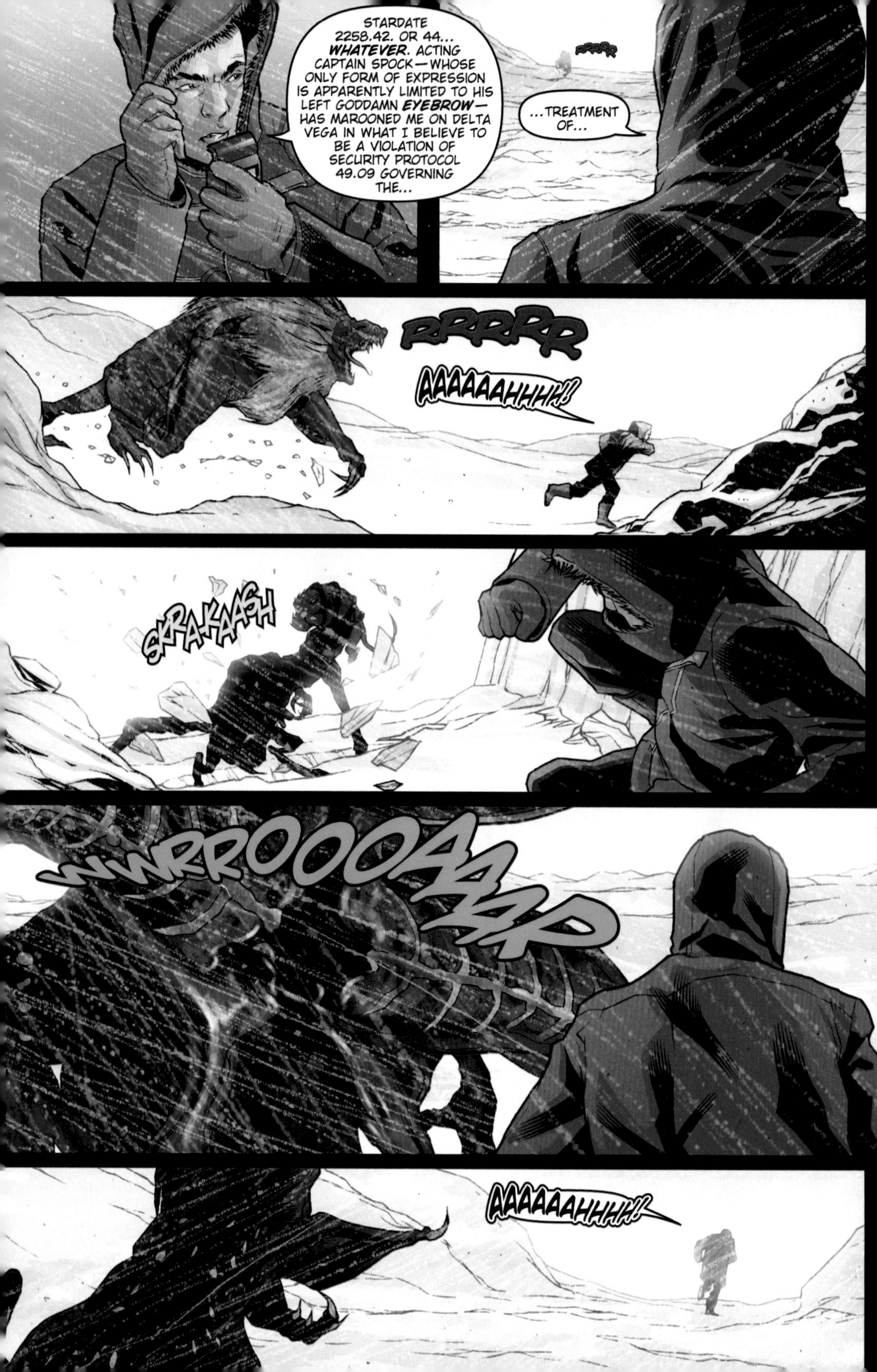
STARDATE 2258.42. OR 44... WHATEVER. ACTING CAPTAIN SPOCK—WHOSE ONLY FORM OF EXPRESSION IS APPARENTLY LIMITED TO HIS LEFT GODDAMN EYEBROW—HAS MAROONED ME ON DELTA VEGA IN WHAT I BELIEVE TO BE A VIOLATION OF SECURITY PROTOCOL 49.09 GOVERNING THE...
RRRR
...TREATMENT OF...
RRRRR
AAAAAAHHHH!
SKRAKAASH
WWRROOOAAAAR
AAAAAAHHHH!

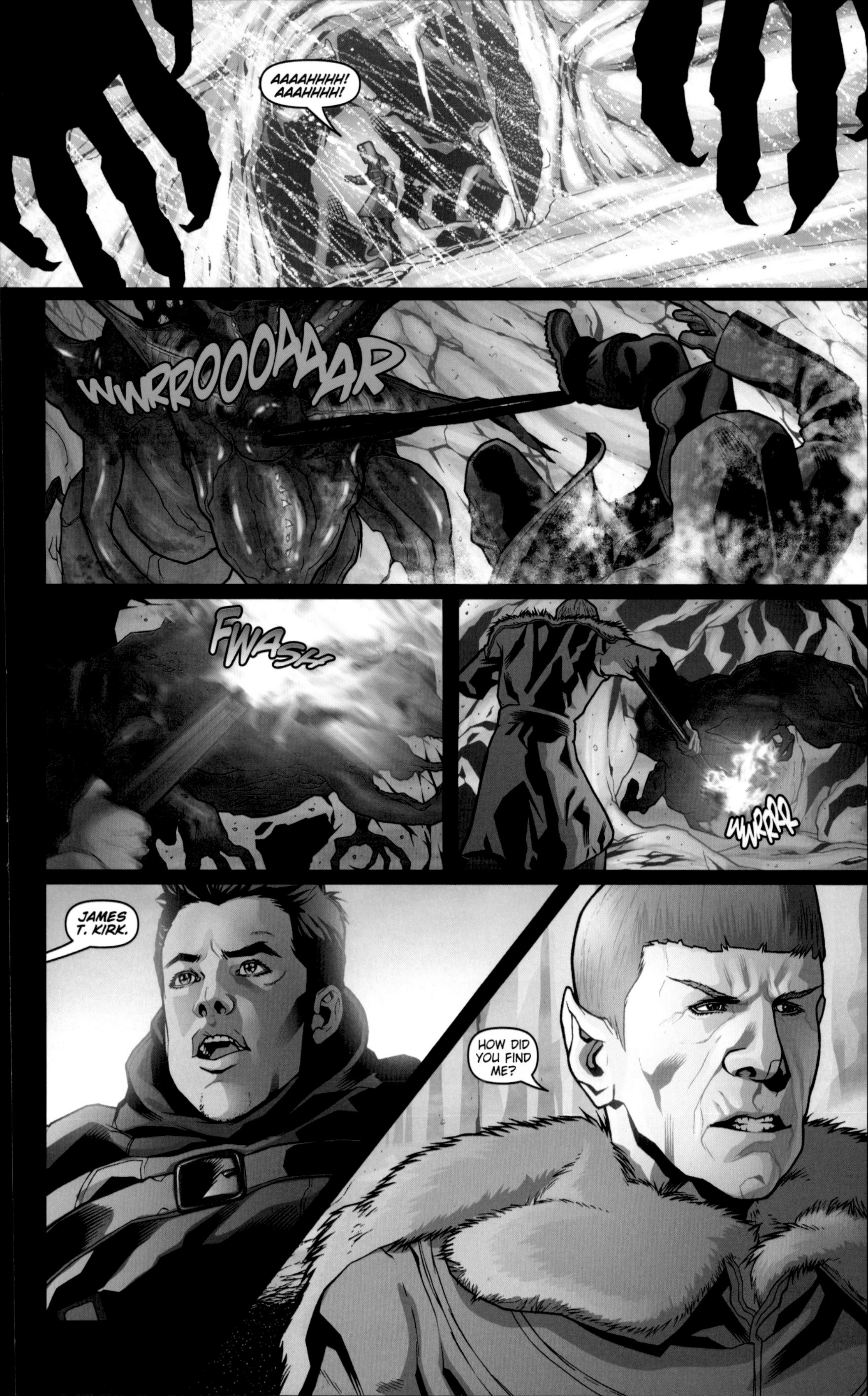
AAAAHHHH!
AAAHHHH!
WWRROOOAAAAR
FWASH
WWRRRR
JAMES T. KIRK.
HOW DID YOU FIND ME?

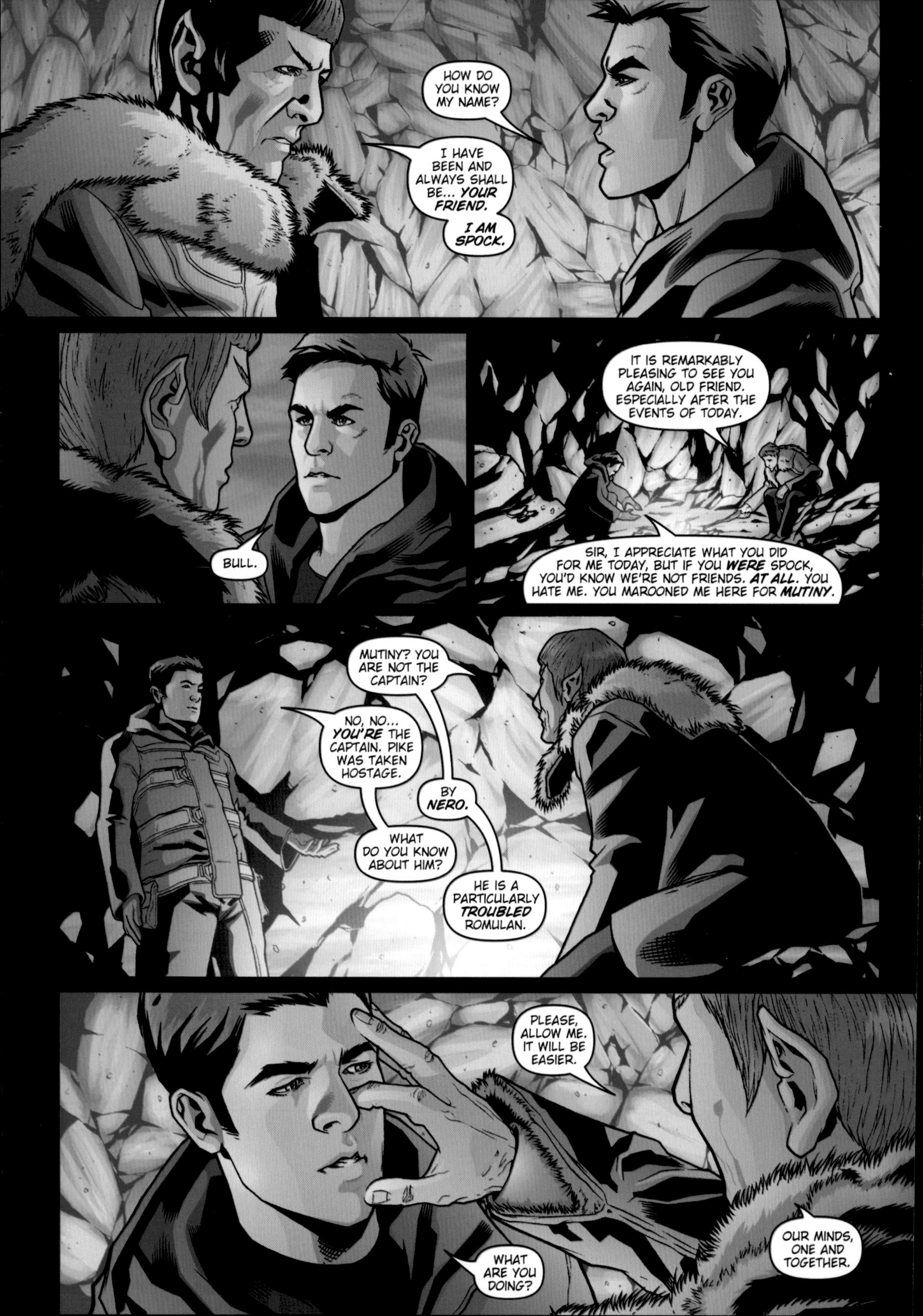
HOW DO YOU KNOW MY NAME?
I HAVE BEEN AND ALWAYS SHALL BE... **YOUR FRIEND.**
I AM SPOCK.
BULL.
IT IS REMARKABLY PLEASING TO SEE YOU AGAIN, OLD FRIEND. ESPECIALLY AFTER THE EVENTS OF TODAY.
SIR, I APPRECIATE WHAT YOU DID FOR ME TODAY, BUT IF YOU **WERE** SPOCK, YOU'D KNOW WE'RE NOT FRIENDS. **AT ALL.** YOU HATE ME. YOU MAROONED ME HERE FOR **MUTINY**.
MUTINY? YOU ARE NOT THE CAPTAIN?
NO, NO... **YOU'RE** THE CAPTAIN. PIKE WAS TAKEN HOSTAGE.
BY **NERO.**
WHAT DO YOU KNOW ABOUT HIM?
HE IS A PARTICULARLY **TROUBLED** ROMULAN.
PLEASE, ALLOW ME. IT WILL BE EASIER.
WHAT ARE YOU DOING?
OUR MINDS, ONE AND TOGETHER.

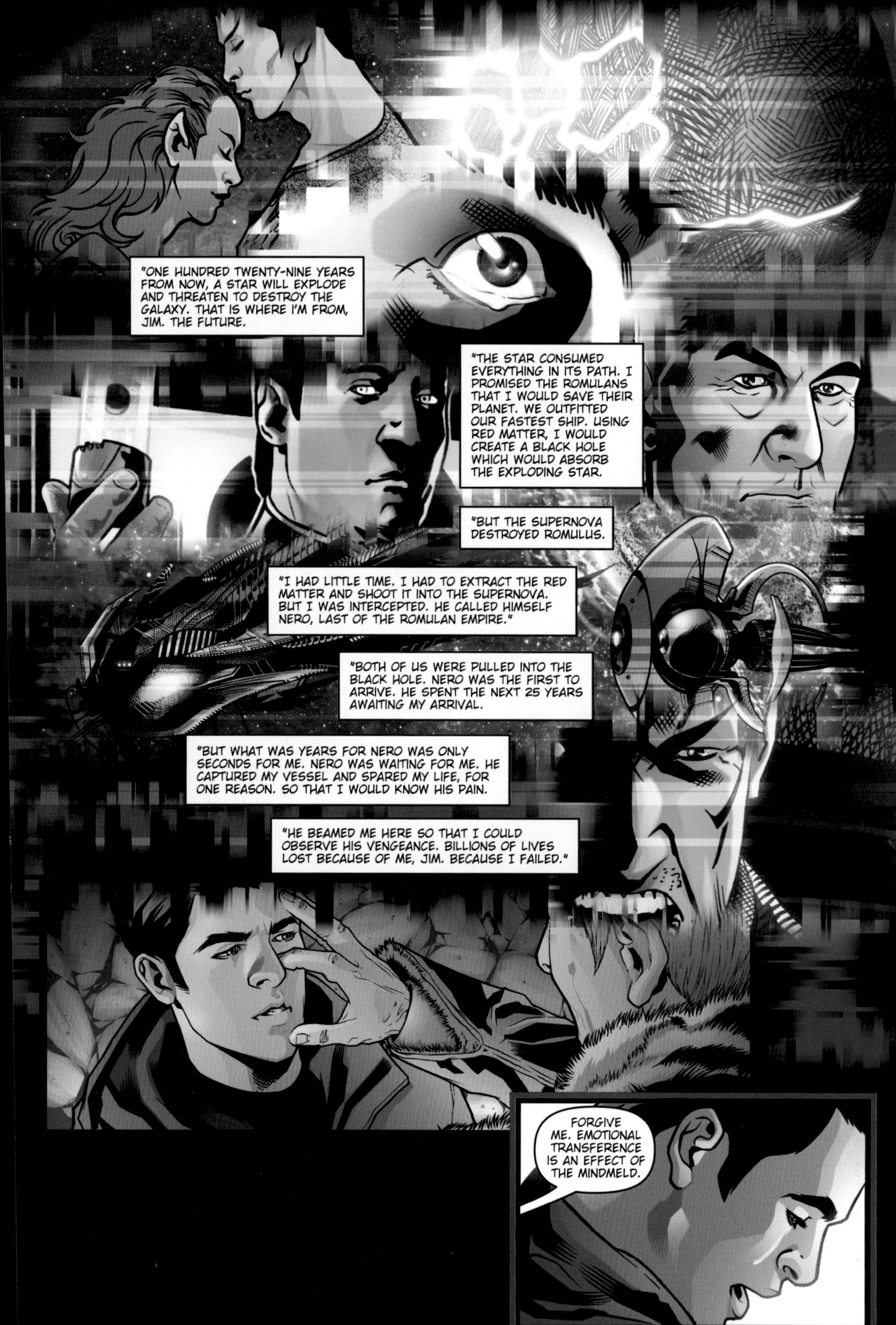
"ONE HUNDRED TWENTY-NINE YEARS FROM NOW, A STAR WILL EXPLODE AND THREATEN TO DESTROY THE GALAXY. THAT IS WHERE I'M FROM, JIM. THE FUTURE.
"THE STAR CONSUMED EVERYTHING IN ITS PATH. I PROMISED THE ROMULANS THAT I WOULD SAVE THEIR PLANET. WE OUTFITTED OUR FASTEST SHIP. USING RED MATTER, I WOULD CREATE A BLACK HOLE WHICH WOULD ABSORB THE EXPLODING STAR.
"BUT THE SUPERNOVA DESTROYED ROMULUS.
"I HAD LITTLE TIME. I HAD TO EXTRACT THE RED MATTER AND SHOOT IT INTO THE SUPERNOVA. BUT I WAS INTERCEPTED. HE CALLED HIMSELF NERO, LAST OF THE ROMULAN EMPIRE."
"BOTH OF US WERE PULLED INTO THE BLACK HOLE. NERO WAS THE FIRST TO ARRIVE. HE SPENT THE NEXT 25 YEARS AWAITING MY ARRIVAL.
"BUT WHAT WAS YEARS FOR NERO WAS ONLY SECONDS FOR ME. NERO WAS WAITING FOR ME. HE CAPTURED MY VESSEL AND SPARED MY LIFE, FOR ONE REASON. SO THAT I WOULD KNOW HIS PAIN.
"HE BEAMED ME HERE SO THAT I COULD OBSERVE HIS VENGEANCE. BILLIONS OF LIVES LOST BECAUSE OF ME, JIM. BECAUSE I FAILED."
FORGIVE ME. EMOTIONAL TRANSFERENCE IS AN EFFECT OF THE MINDMELD.

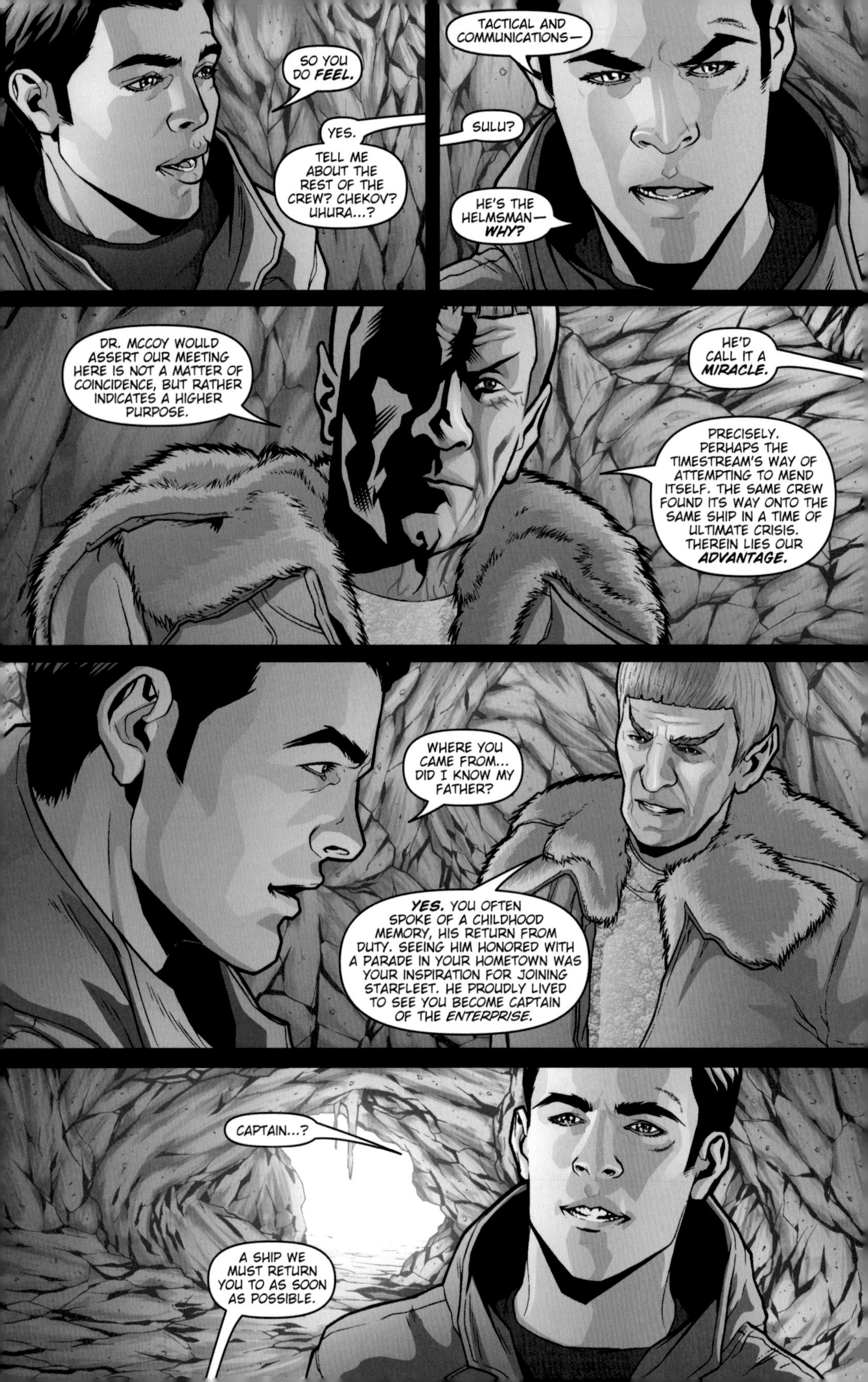
SO YOU DO FEEL.
YES.
TELL ME ABOUT THE REST OF THE CREW? CHEKOV? UHURA...?
TACTICAL AND COMMUNICATIONS—
SULU?
HE'S THE HELMSMAN— WHY?
DR. MCCOY WOULD ASSERT OUR MEETING HERE IS NOT A MATTER OF COINCIDENCE, BUT RATHER INDICATES A HIGHER PURPOSE.
HE'D CALL IT A MIRACLE.
PRECISELY. PERHAPS THE TIMESTREAM'S WAY OF ATTEMPTING TO MEND ITSELF. THE SAME CREW FOUND ITS WAY ONTO THE SAME SHIP IN A TIME OF ULTIMATE CRISIS. THEREIN LIES OUR ADVANTAGE.
WHERE YOU CAME FROM... DID I KNOW MY FATHER?
YES. YOU OFTEN SPOKE OF A CHILDHOOD MEMORY, HIS RETURN FROM DUTY. SEEING HIM HONORED WITH A PARADE IN YOUR HOMETOWN WAS YOUR INSPIRATION FOR JOINING STARFLEET. HE PROUDLY LIVED TO SEE YOU BECOME CAPTAIN OF THE ENTERPRISE.
CAPTAIN...?
A SHIP WE MUST RETURN YOU TO AS SOON AS POSSIBLE.

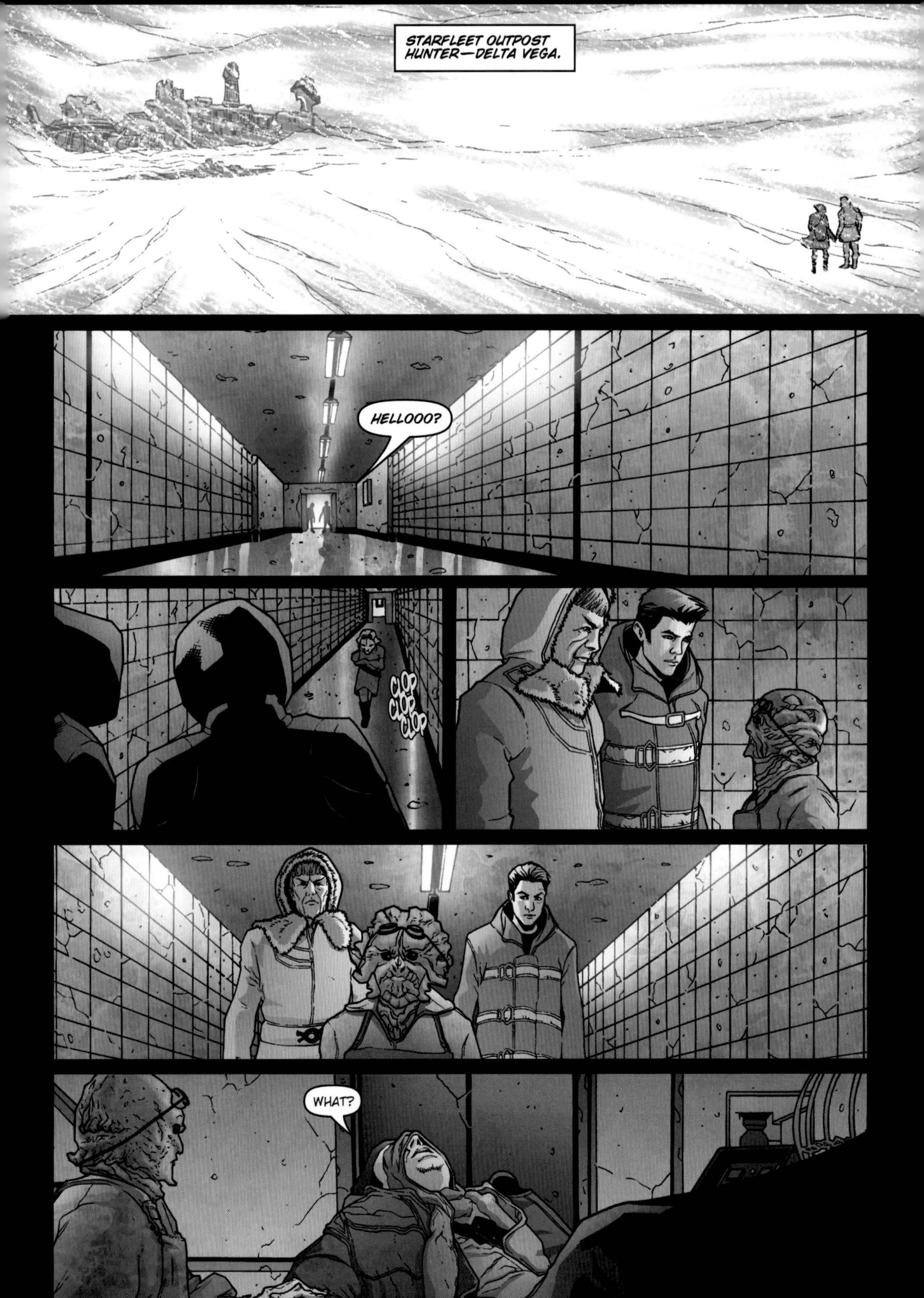
STARFLEET OUTPOST HUNTER—DELTA VEGA.
HELLOOO?
CLOP CLOP CLOP
WHAT?

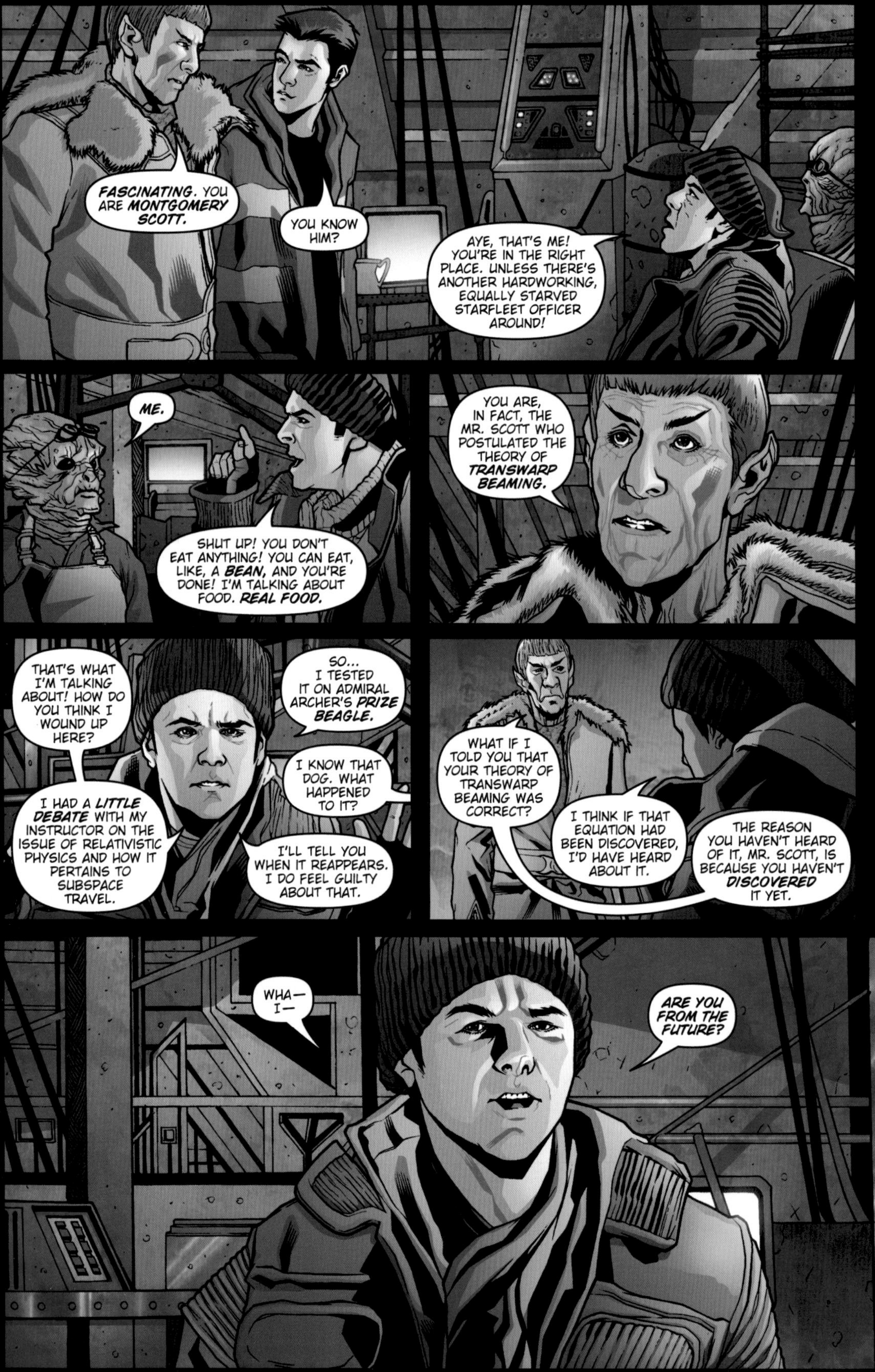
FASCINATING. YOU ARE MONTGOMERY SCOTT.
YOU KNOW HIM?
AYE, THAT'S ME! YOU'RE IN THE RIGHT PLACE. UNLESS THERE'S ANOTHER HARDWORKING, EQUALLY STARVED STARFLEET OFFICER AROUND!
ME.
SHUT UP! YOU DON'T EAT ANYTHING! YOU CAN EAT, LIKE, A BEAN, AND YOU'RE DONE! I'M TALKING ABOUT FOOD. REAL FOOD.
YOU ARE, IN FACT, THE MR. SCOTT WHO POSTULATED THE THEORY OF TRANSWARP BEAMING.
THAT'S WHAT I'M TALKING ABOUT! HOW DO YOU THINK I WOUND UP HERE?
I HAD A LITTLE DEBATE WITH MY INSTRUCTOR ON THE ISSUE OF RELATIVISTIC PHYSICS AND HOW IT PERTAINS TO SUBSPACE TRAVEL.
SO... I TESTED IT ON ADMIRAL ARCHER'S PRIZE BEAGLE.
I KNOW THAT DOG. WHAT HAPPENED TO IT?
I'LL TELL YOU WHEN IT REAPPEARS. I DO FEEL GUILTY ABOUT THAT.
WHAT IF I TOLD YOU THAT YOUR THEORY OF TRANSWARP BEAMING WAS CORRECT?
I THINK IF THAT EQUATION HAD BEEN DISCOVERED, I'D HAVE HEARD ABOUT IT.
THE REASON YOU HAVEN'T HEARD OF IT, MR. SCOTT, IS BECAUSE YOU HAVEN'T DISCOVERED IT YET.
WHA— I—
ARE YOU FROM THE FUTURE?

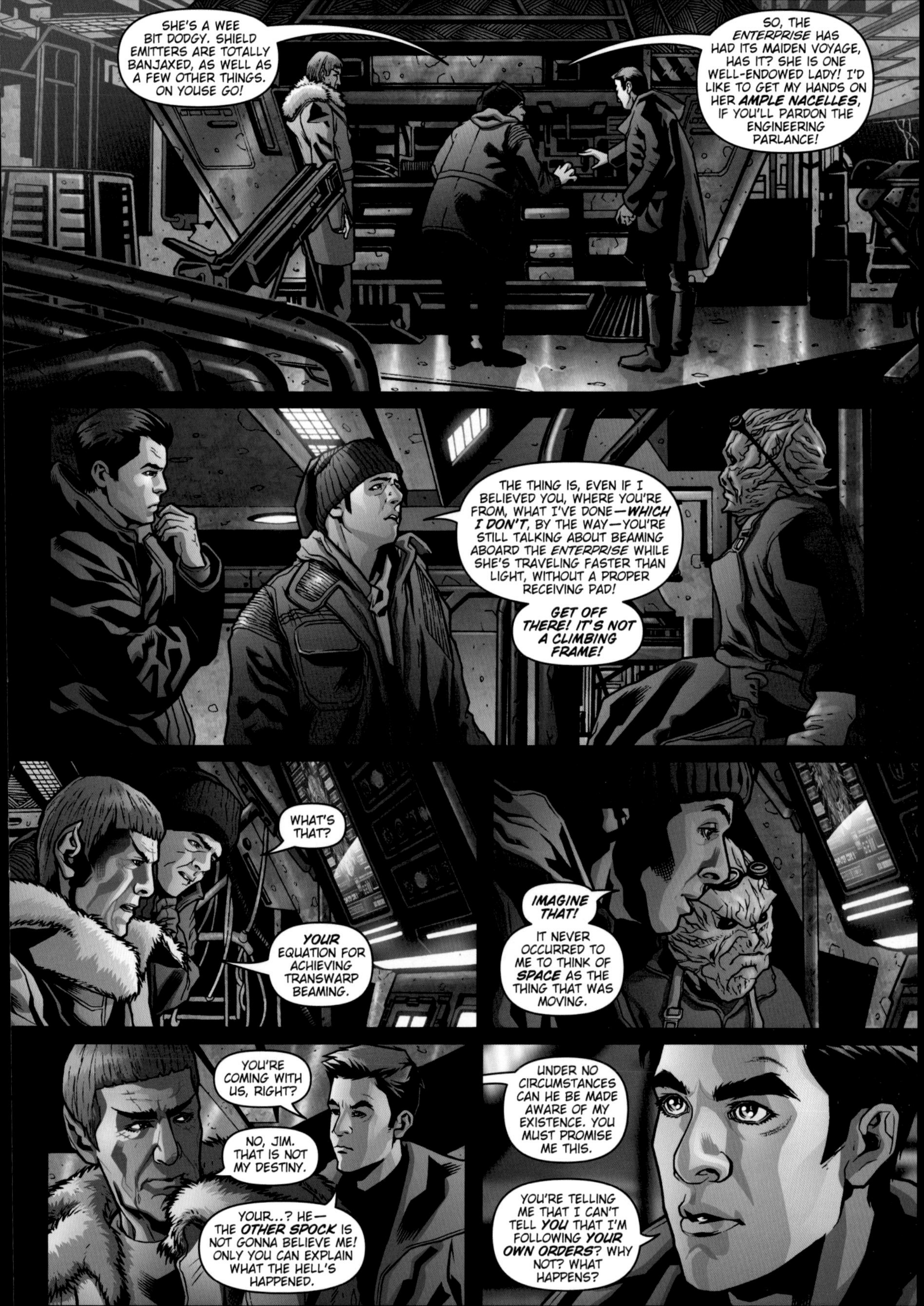
SHE'S A WEE BIT DODGY. SHIELD EMITTERS ARE TOTALLY BANJAXED, AS WELL AS A FEW OTHER THINGS. ON YOUSE GO!
SO, THE ENTERPRISE HAS HAD ITS MAIDEN VOYAGE, HAS IT? SHE IS ONE WELL-ENDOWED LADY! I'D LIKE TO GET MY HANDS ON HER AMPLE NACELLES, IF YOU'LL PARDON THE ENGINEERING PARLANCE!
THE THING IS, EVEN IF I BELIEVED YOU, WHERE YOU'RE FROM, WHAT I'VE DONE—WHICH I DON'T, BY THE WAY—YOU'RE STILL TALKING ABOUT BEAMING ABOARD THE ENTERPRISE WHILE SHE'S TRAVELING FASTER THAN LIGHT, WITHOUT A PROPER RECEIVING PAD!
GET OFF THERE! IT'S NOT A CLIMBING FRAME!
WHAT'S THAT?
YOUR EQUATION FOR ACHIEVING TRANSWARP BEAMING.
IMAGINE THAT!
IT NEVER OCCURRED TO ME TO THINK OF SPACE AS THE THING THAT WAS MOVING.
YOU'RE COMING WITH US, RIGHT?
NO, JIM. THAT IS NOT MY DESTINY.
YOUR...? HE— THE OTHER SPOCK IS NOT GONNA BELIEVE ME! ONLY YOU CAN EXPLAIN WHAT THE HELL'S HAPPENED.
UNDER NO CIRCUMSTANCES CAN HE BE MADE AWARE OF MY EXISTENCE. YOU MUST PROMISE ME THIS.
YOU'RE TELLING ME THAT I CAN'T TELL YOU THAT I'M FOLLOWING YOUR OWN ORDERS? WHY NOT? WHAT HAPPENS?

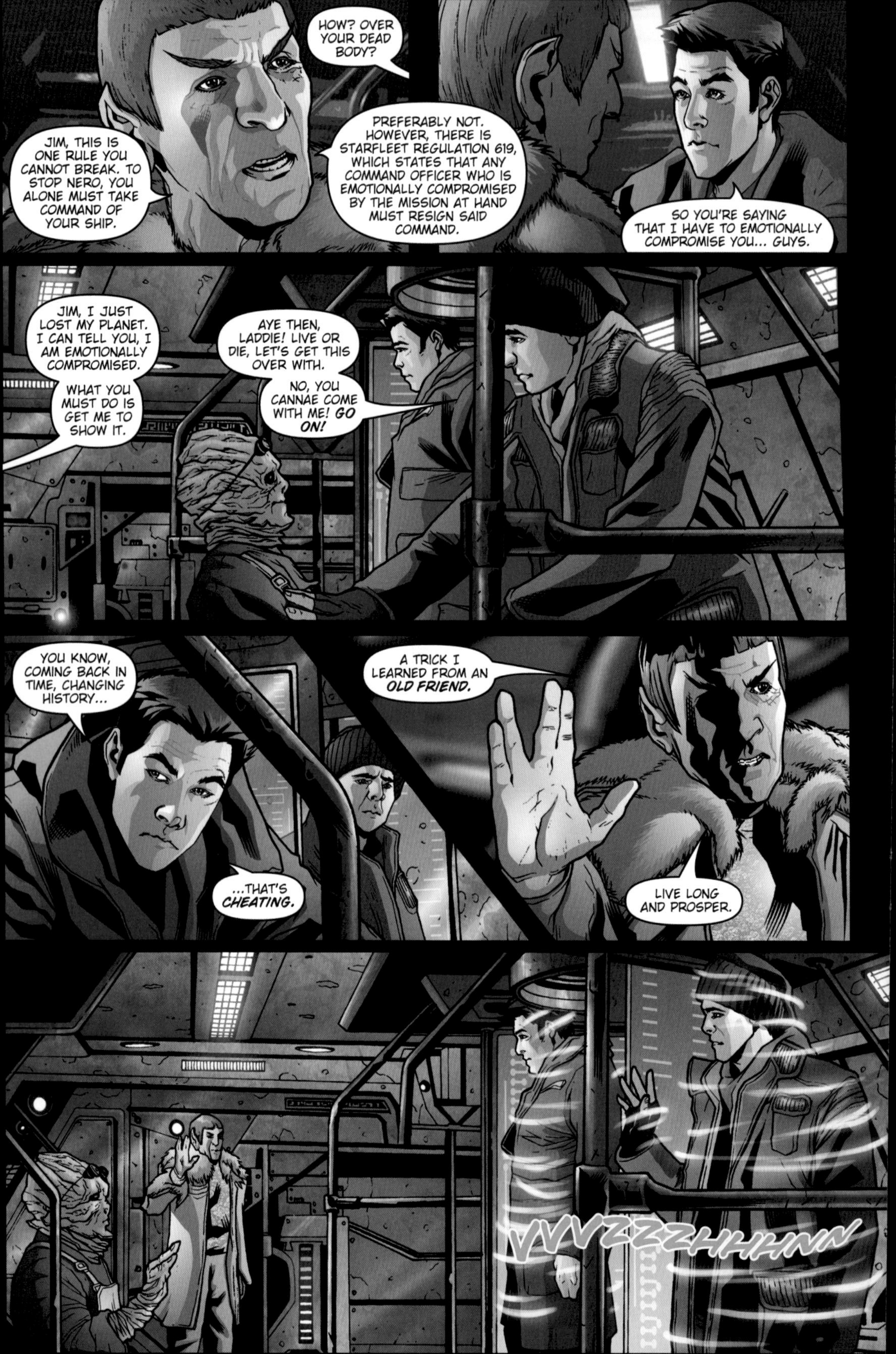
JIM, THIS IS ONE RULE YOU CANNOT BREAK. TO STOP NERO, YOU ALONE MUST TAKE COMMAND OF YOUR SHIP.
HOW? OVER YOUR DEAD BODY?
PREFERABLY NOT. HOWEVER, THERE IS STARFLEET REGULATION 619, WHICH STATES THAT ANY COMMAND OFFICER WHO IS EMOTIONALLY COMPROMISED BY THE MISSION AT HAND MUST RESIGN SAID COMMAND.
SO YOU'RE SAYING THAT I HAVE TO EMOTIONALLY COMPROMISE YOU... GUYS.
JIM, I JUST LOST MY PLANET. I CAN TELL YOU, I AM EMOTIONALLY COMPROMISED.
WHAT YOU MUST DO IS GET ME TO SHOW IT.
AYE THEN, LADDIE! LIVE OR DIE, LET'S GET THIS OVER WITH.
NO, YOU CANNAE COME WITH ME! GO ON!
YOU KNOW, COMING BACK IN TIME, CHANGING HISTORY...
...THAT'S CHEATING.
A TRICK I LEARNED FROM AN OLD FRIEND.
LIVE LONG AND PROSPER.
VVVZZZHHHNN

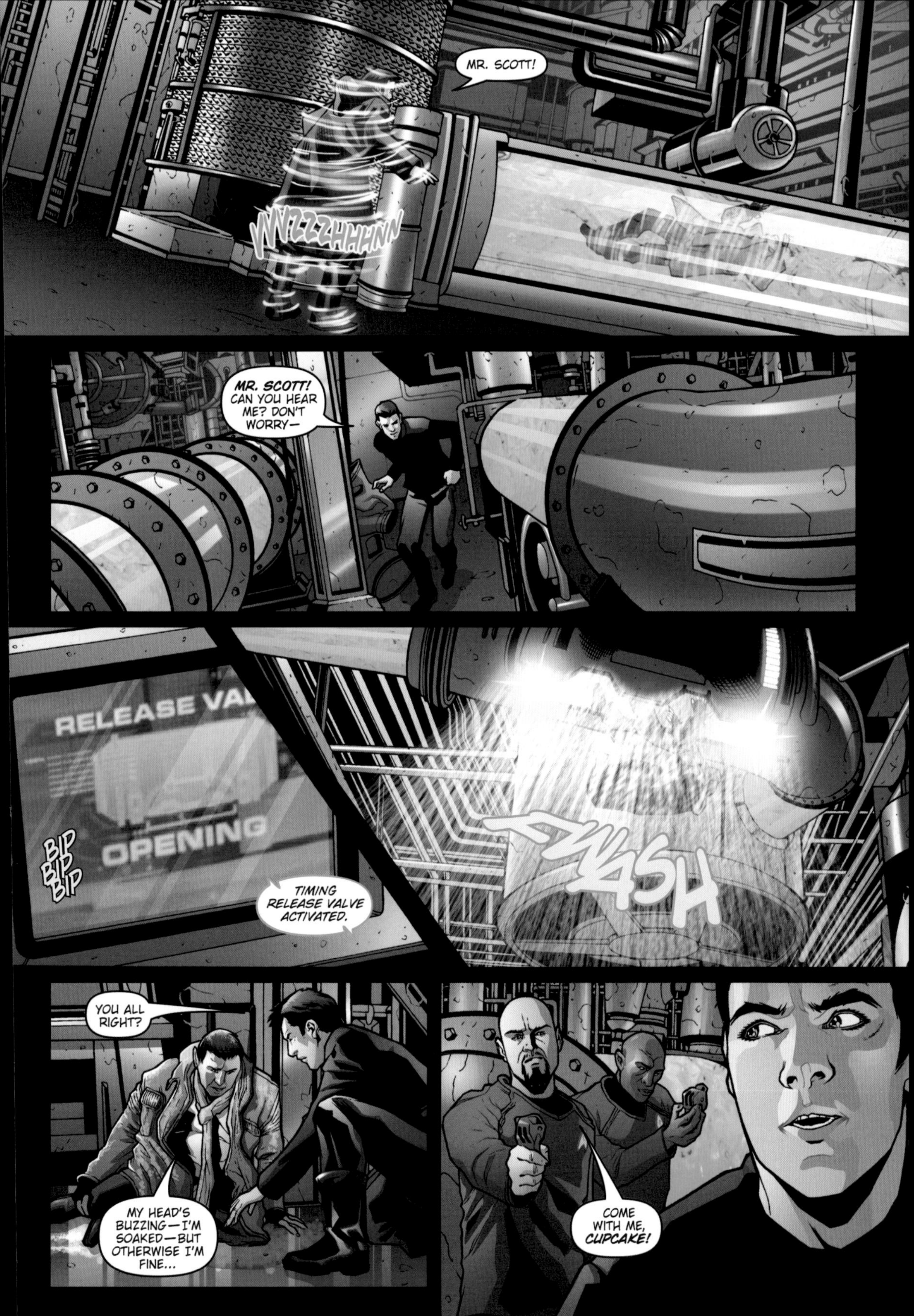
MR. SCOTT!
VVVZZZZHHHNN
MR. SCOTT! CAN YOU HEAR ME? DON'T WORRY—
RELEASE VA
OPENING
BIP BIP BIP
TIMING RELEASE VALVE ACTIVATED.
FWASH
YOU ALL RIGHT?
MY HEAD'S BUZZING—I'M SOAKED—BUT OTHERWISE I'M FINE...
COME WITH ME, CUPCAKE!

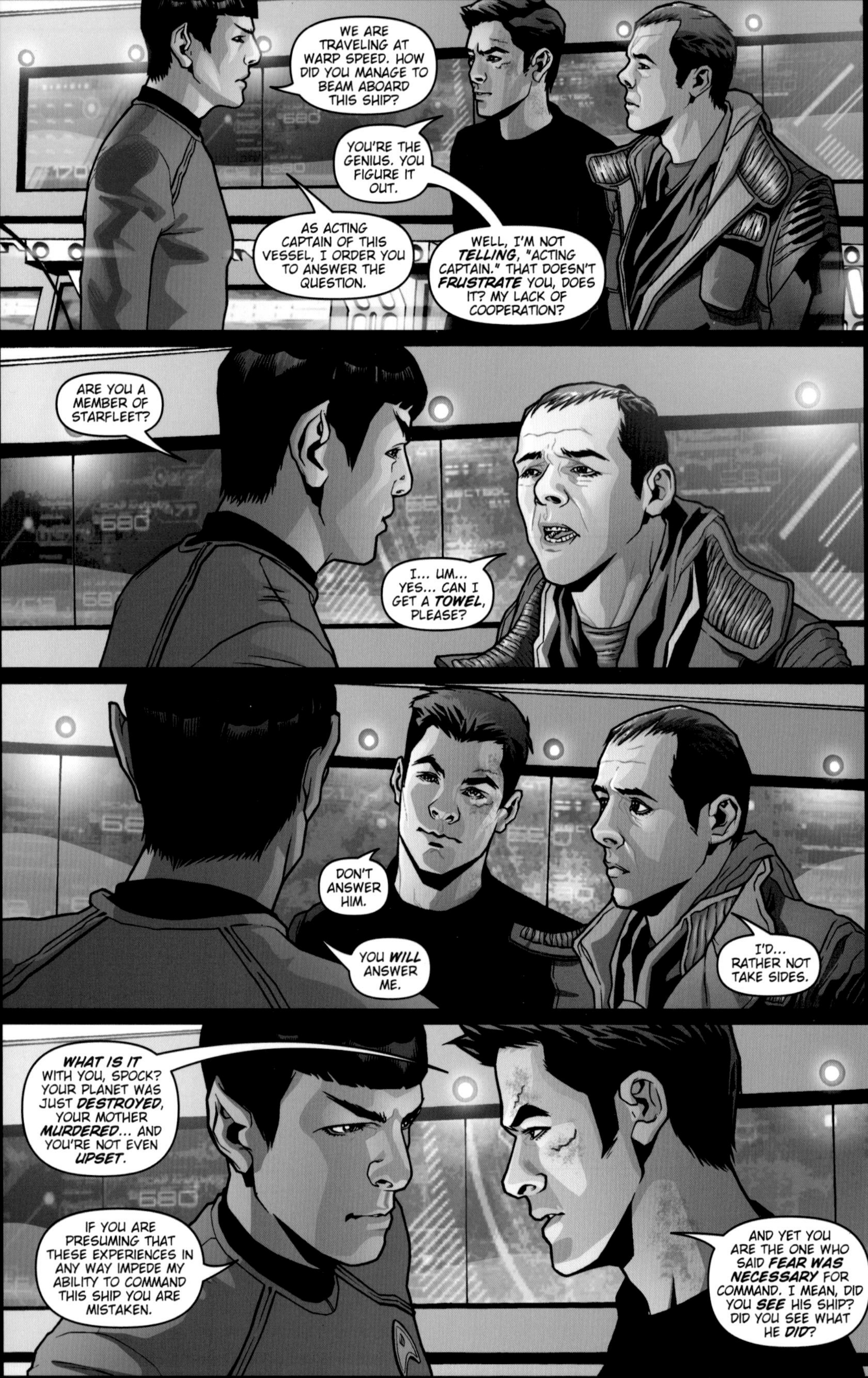
WE ARE TRAVELING AT WARP SPEED. HOW DID YOU MANAGE TO BEAM ABOARD THIS SHIP?
YOU'RE THE GENIUS. YOU FIGURE IT OUT.
AS ACTING CAPTAIN OF THIS VESSEL, I ORDER YOU TO ANSWER THE QUESTION.
WELL, I'M NOT TELLING, "ACTING CAPTAIN." THAT DOESN'T FRUSTRATE YOU, DOES IT? MY LACK OF COOPERATION?
ARE YOU A MEMBER OF STARFLEET?
I... UM... YES... CAN I GET A TOWEL, PLEASE?
DON'T ANSWER HIM.
YOU WILL ANSWER ME.
I'D... RATHER NOT TAKE SIDES.
WHAT IS IT WITH YOU, SPOCK? YOUR PLANET WAS JUST DESTROYED, YOUR MOTHER MURDERED... AND YOU'RE NOT EVEN UPSET.
IF YOU ARE PRESUMING THAT THESE EXPERIENCES IN ANY WAY IMPEDE MY ABILITY TO COMMAND THIS SHIP YOU ARE MISTAKEN.
AND YET YOU ARE THE ONE WHO SAID FEAR WAS NECESSARY FOR COMMAND. I MEAN, DID YOU SEE HIS SHIP? DID YOU SEE WHAT HE DID?

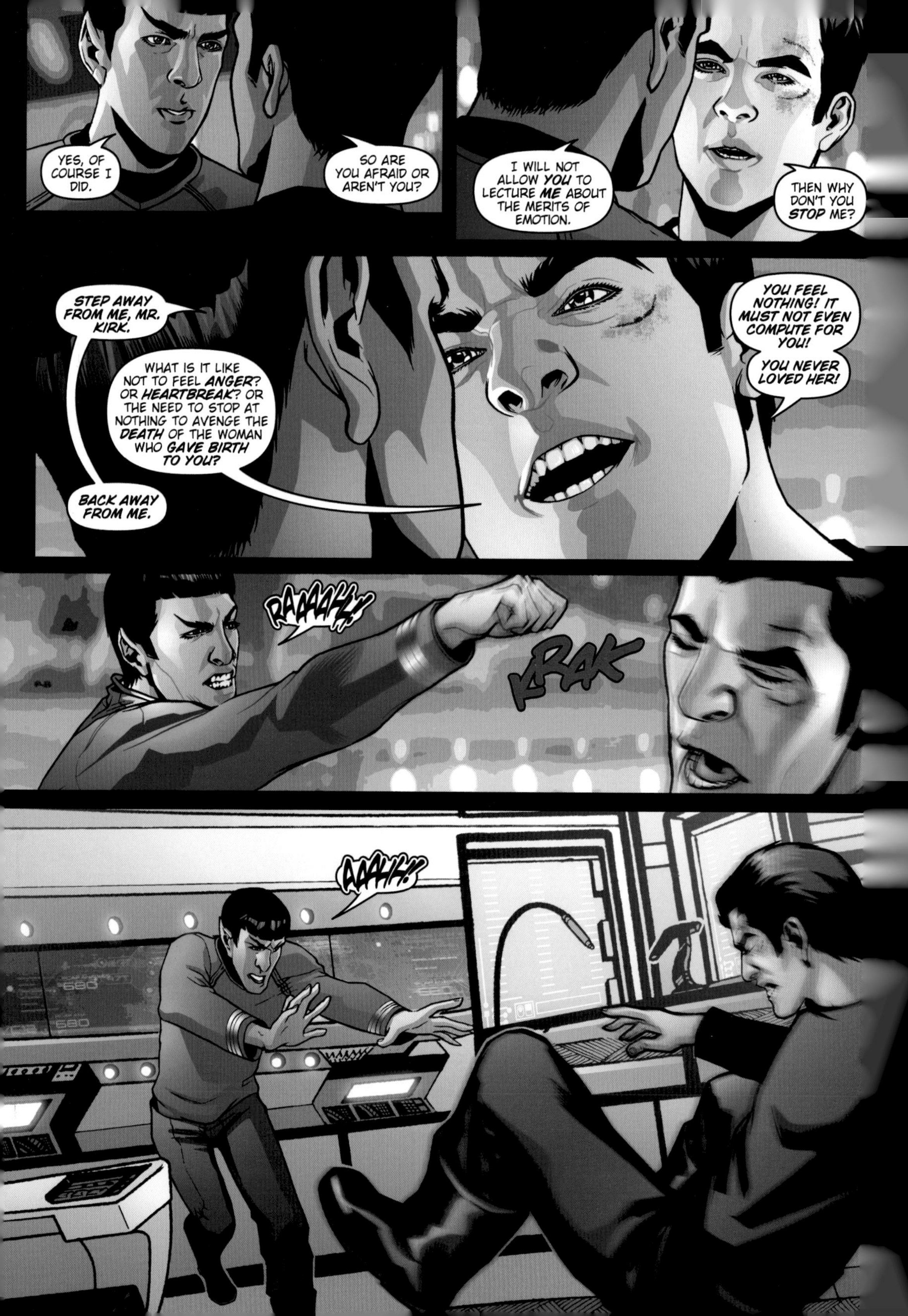

YES, OF COURSE I DID.
SO ARE YOU AFRAID OR AREN'T YOU?
I WILL NOT ALLOW YOU TO LECTURE ME ABOUT THE MERITS OF EMOTION.
THEN WHY DON'T YOU STOP ME?
STEP AWAY FROM ME, MR. KIRK.
WHAT IS IT LIKE NOT TO FEEL ANGER? OR HEARTBREAK? OR THE NEED TO STOP AT NOTHING TO AVENGE THE DEATH OF THE WOMAN WHO GAVE BIRTH TO YOU?
BACK AWAY FROM ME.
YOU FEEL NOTHING! IT MUST NOT EVEN COMPUTE FOR YOU!
YOU NEVER LOVED HER!
RAAAAH!!
KRAK
AAAHH!!

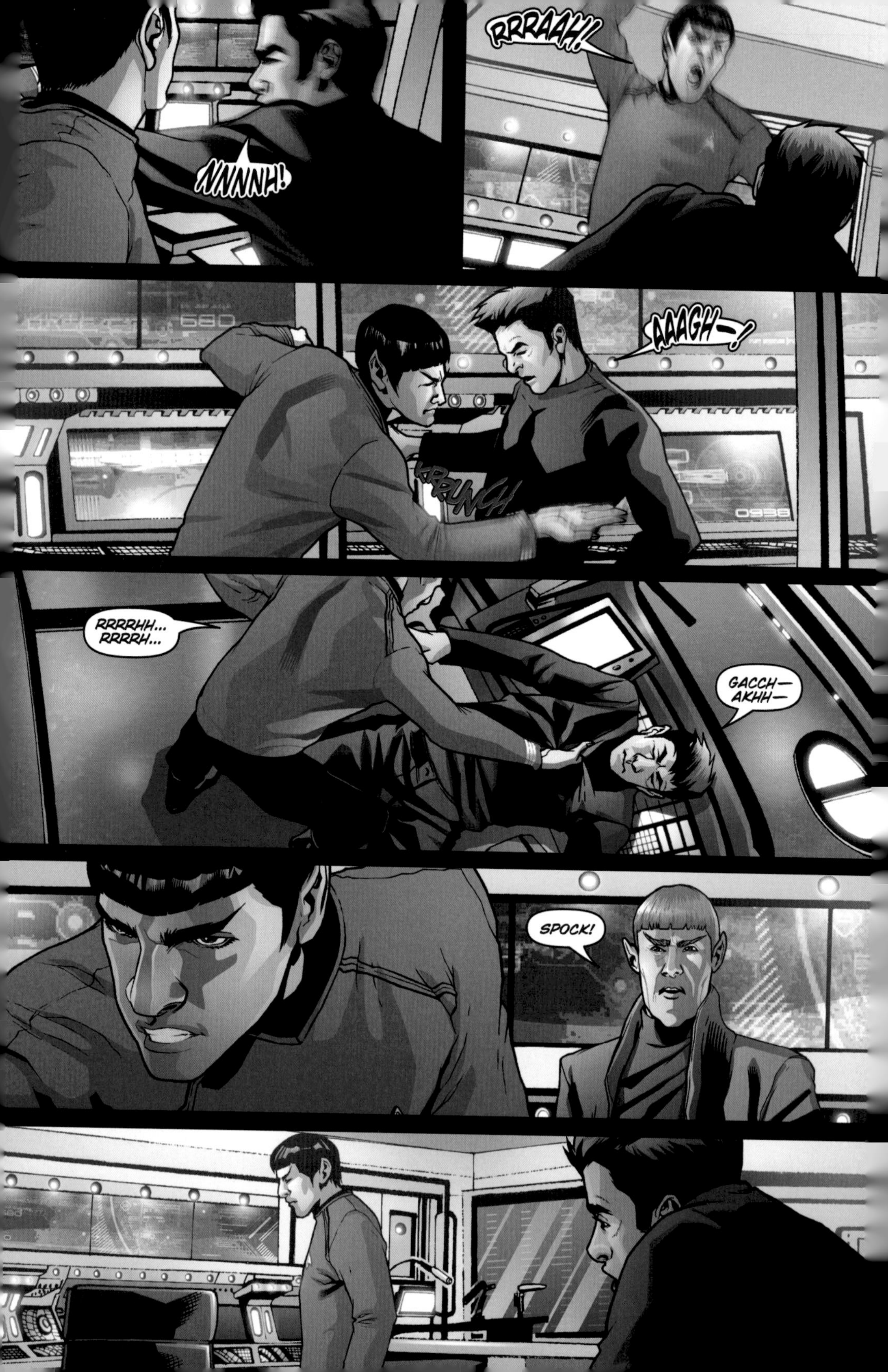
NNNNH!
RRRAAH!
AAAGH—!
KRRUNCH
RRRRHH... RRRRH...
GACCH— AKHH—
SPOCK!

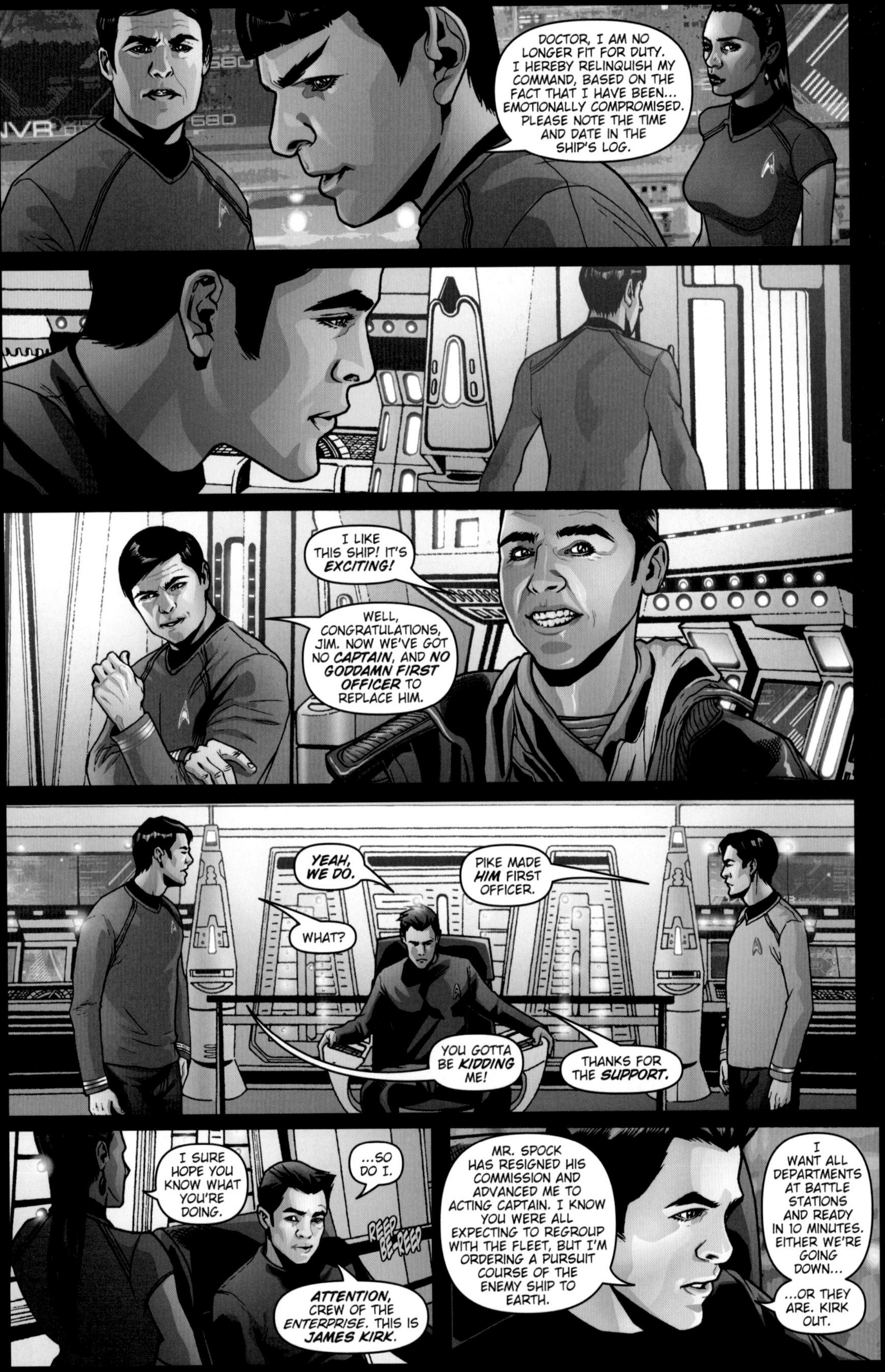
DOCTOR, I AM NO LONGER FIT FOR DUTY. I HEREBY RELINQUISH MY COMMAND, BASED ON THE FACT THAT I HAVE BEEN... EMOTIONALLY COMPROMISED. PLEASE NOTE THE TIME AND DATE IN THE SHIP'S LOG.
I LIKE THIS SHIP! IT'S EXCITING!
WELL, CONGRATULATIONS, JIM. NOW WE'VE GOT NO CAPTAIN, AND NO GODDAMN FIRST OFFICER TO REPLACE HIM.
YEAH, WE DO.
PIKE MADE HIM FIRST OFFICER.
WHAT?
YOU GOTTA BE KIDDING ME!
THANKS FOR THE SUPPORT.
I SURE HOPE YOU KNOW WHAT YOU'RE DOING.
...SO DO I.
REEP BE-REEP
ATTENTION, CREW OF THE ENTERPRISE. THIS IS JAMES KIRK.
MR. SPOCK HAS RESIGNED HIS COMMISSION AND ADVANCED ME TO ACTING CAPTAIN. I KNOW YOU WERE ALL EXPECTING TO REGROUP WITH THE FLEET, BUT I'M ORDERING A PURSUIT COURSE OF THE ENEMY SHIP TO EARTH.
I WANT ALL DEPARTMENTS AT BATTLE STATIONS AND READY IN 10 MINUTES. EITHER WE'RE GOING DOWN...
...OR THEY ARE. KIRK OUT.

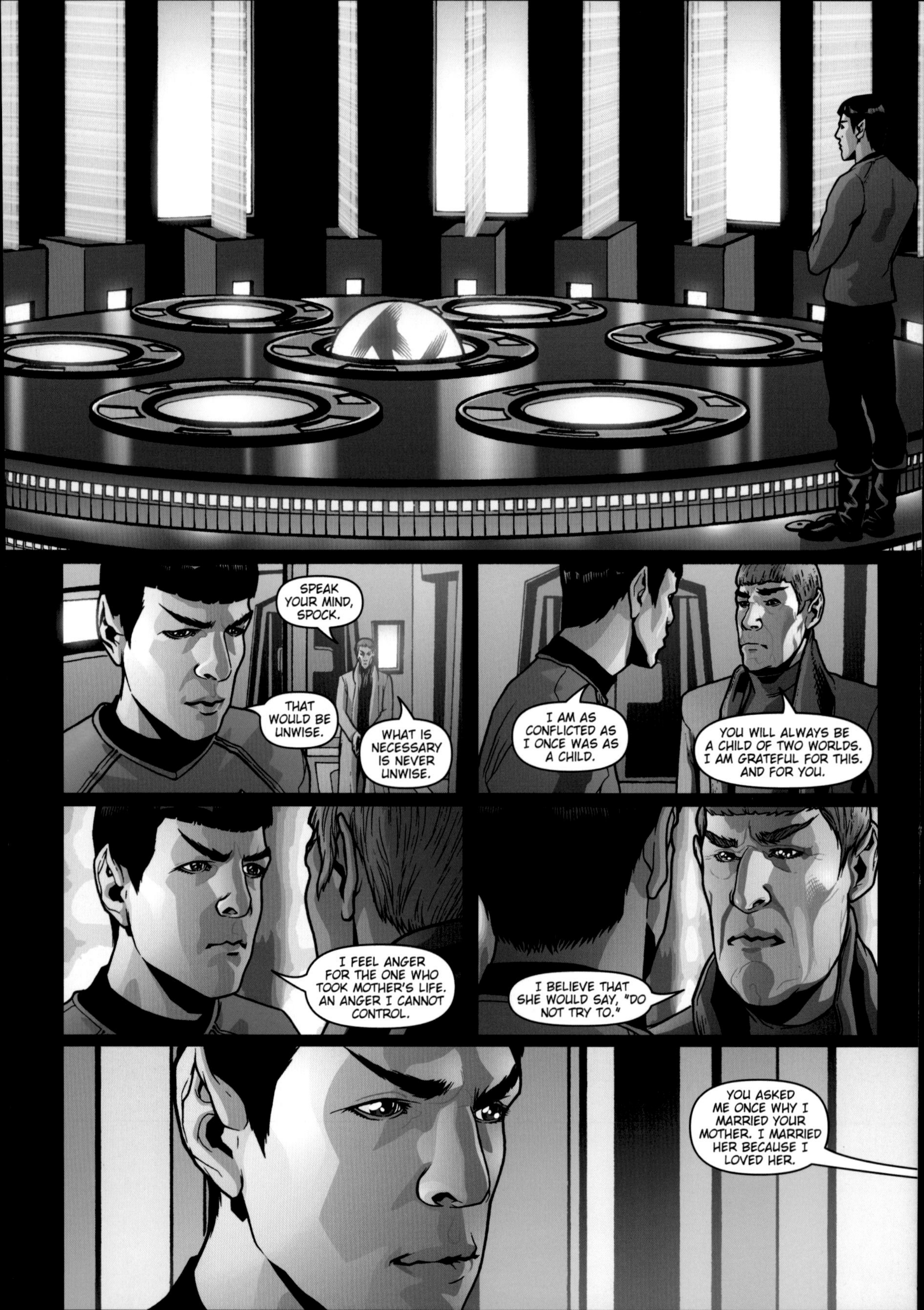
SPEAK YOUR MIND, SPOCK.
THAT WOULD BE UNWISE.
WHAT IS NECESSARY IS NEVER UNWISE.
I AM AS CONFLICTED AS I ONCE WAS AS A CHILD.
YOU WILL ALWAYS BE A CHILD OF TWO WORLDS. I AM GRATEFUL FOR THIS. AND FOR YOU.
I FEEL ANGER FOR THE ONE WHO TOOK MOTHER'S LIFE. AN ANGER I CANNOT CONTROL.
I BELIEVE THAT SHE WOULD SAY, "DO NOT TRY TO."
YOU ASKED ME ONCE WHY I MARRIED YOUR MOTHER. I MARRIED HER BECAUSE I LOVED HER.

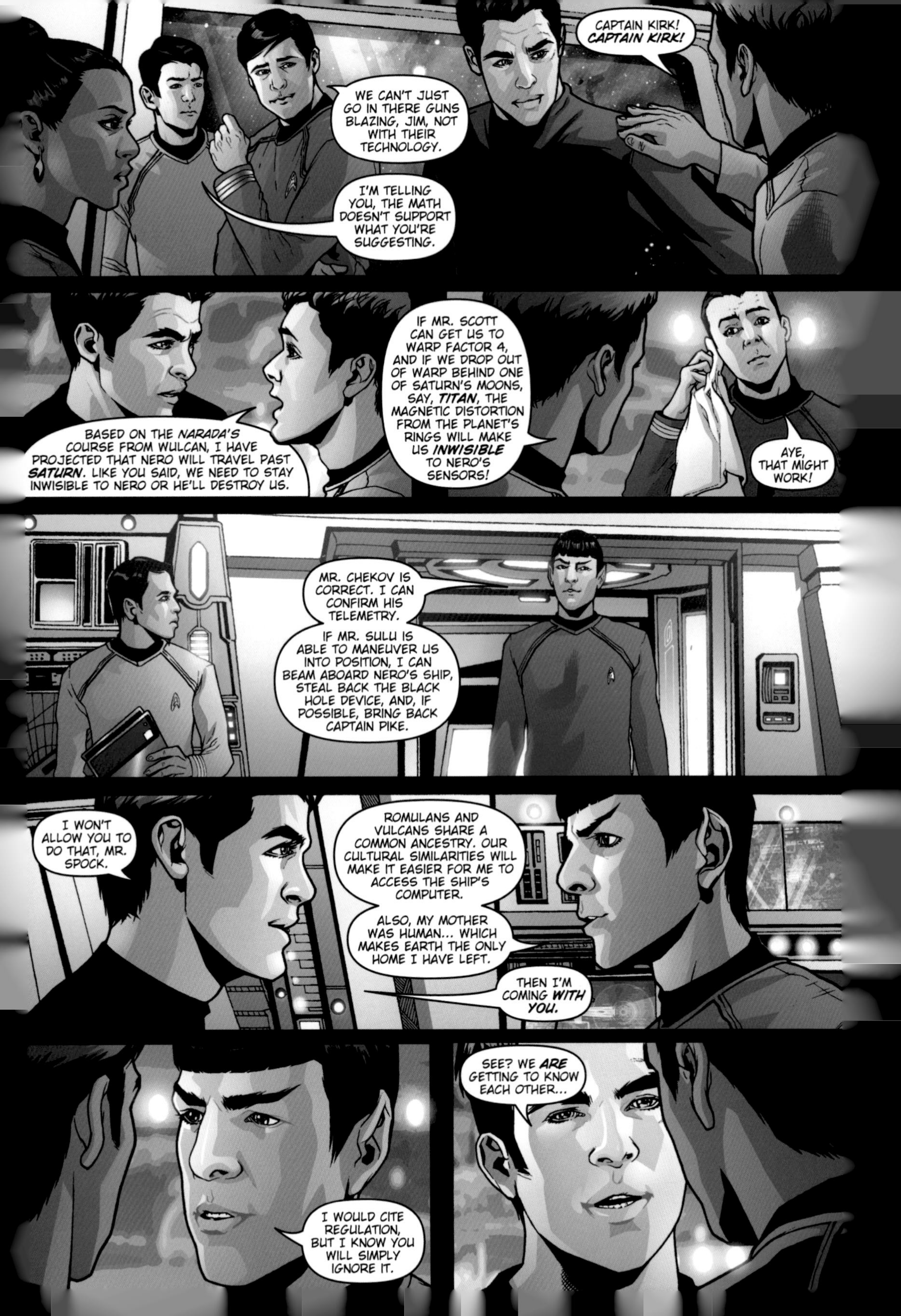
CAPTAIN KIRK! CAPTAIN KIRK!
WE CAN'T JUST GO IN THERE GUNS BLAZING, JIM, NOT WITH THEIR TECHNOLOGY.
I'M TELLING YOU, THE MATH DOESN'T SUPPORT WHAT YOU'RE SUGGESTING.
BASED ON THE NARADA'S COURSE FROM WULCAN, I HAVE PROJECTED THAT NERO WILL TRAVEL PAST SATURN. LIKE YOU SAID, WE NEED TO STAY INWISIBLE TO NERO OR HE'LL DESTROY US.
IF MR. SCOTT CAN GET US TO WARP FACTOR 4, AND IF WE DROP OUT OF WARP BEHIND ONE OF SATURN'S MOONS, SAY, TITAN, THE MAGNETIC DISTORTION FROM THE PLANET'S RINGS WILL MAKE US INWISIBLE TO NERO'S SENSORS!
AYE, THAT MIGHT WORK!
MR. CHEKOV IS CORRECT. I CAN CONFIRM HIS TELEMETRY.
IF MR. SULU IS ABLE TO MANEUVER US INTO POSITION, I CAN BEAM ABOARD NERO'S SHIP, STEAL BACK THE BLACK HOLE DEVICE, AND, IF POSSIBLE, BRING BACK CAPTAIN PIKE.
I WON'T ALLOW YOU TO DO THAT, MR. SPOCK.
ROMULANS AND VULCANS SHARE A COMMON ANCESTRY. OUR CULTURAL SIMILARITIES WILL MAKE IT EASIER FOR ME TO ACCESS THE SHIP'S COMPUTER.
ALSO, MY MOTHER WAS HUMAN... WHICH MAKES EARTH THE ONLY HOME I HAVE LEFT.
THEN I'M COMING WITH YOU.
I WOULD CITE REGULATION, BUT I KNOW YOU WILL SIMPLY IGNORE IT.
SEE? WE ARE GETTING TO KNOW EACH OTHER...

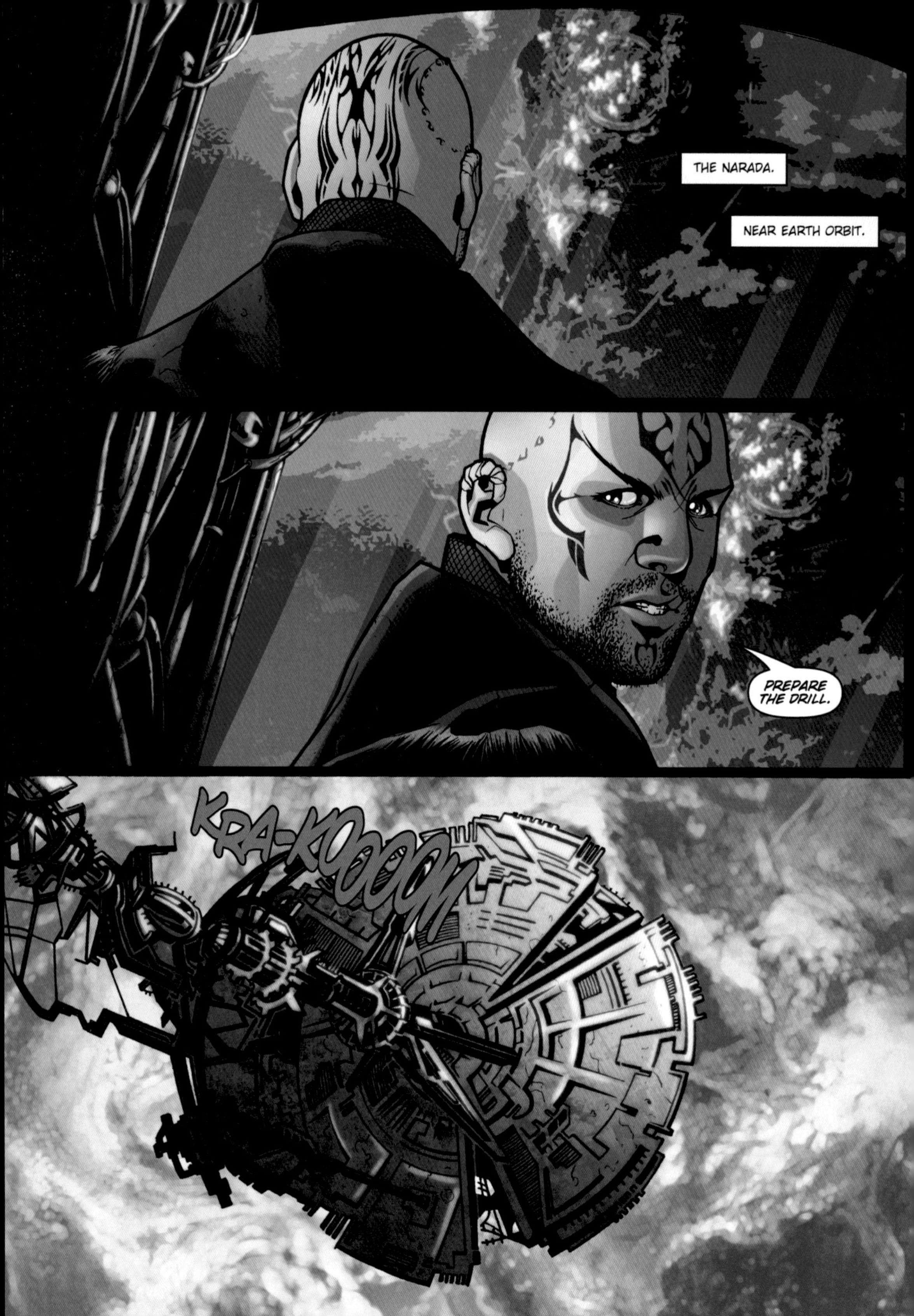
THE NARADA.
NEAR EARTH ORBIT.
PREPARE THE DRILL.
KRA-KOOOOM

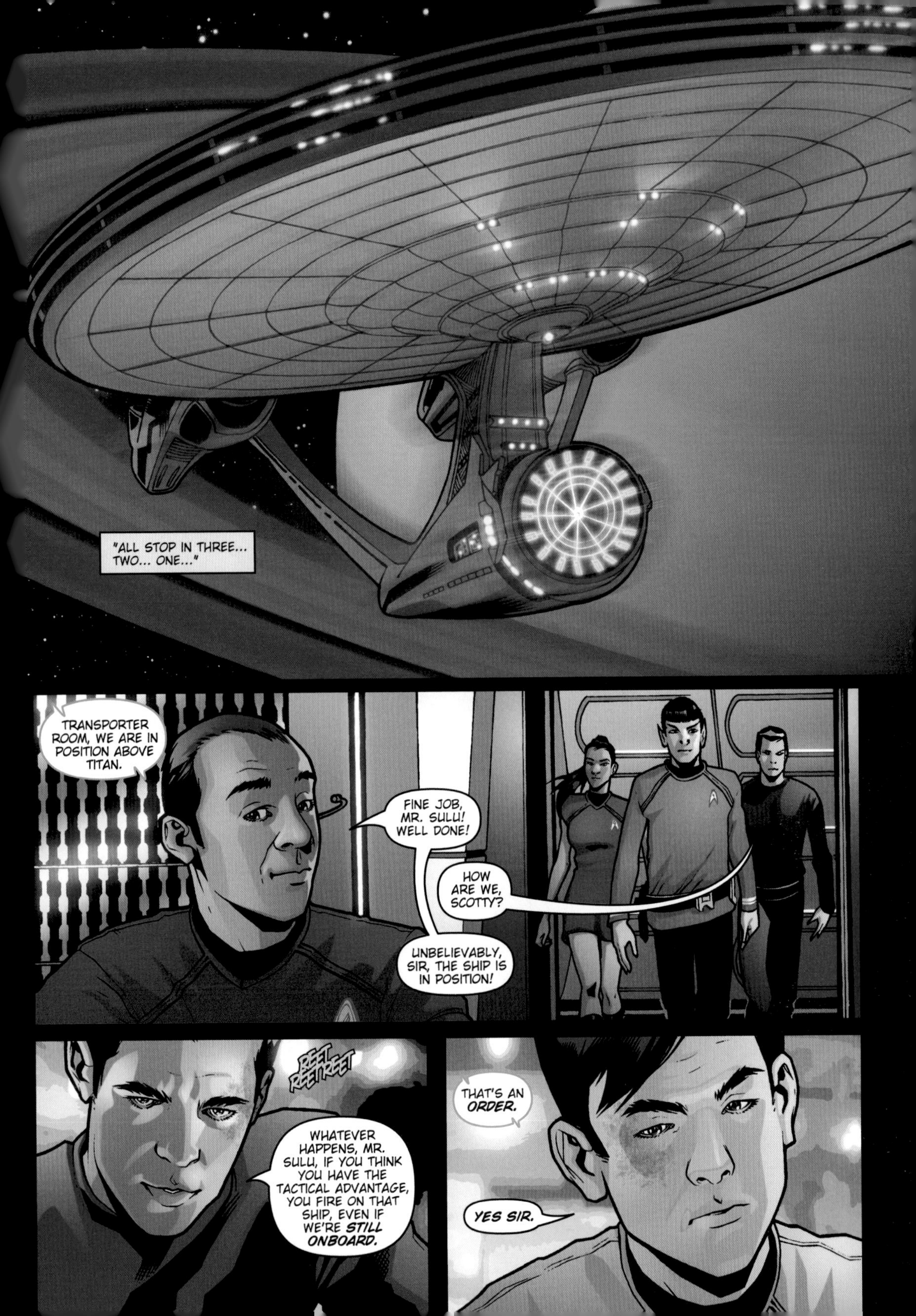
"ALL STOP IN THREE... TWO... ONE..."
TRANSPORTER ROOM, WE ARE IN POSITION ABOVE TITAN.
FINE JOB, MR. SULU! WELL DONE!
HOW ARE WE, SCOTTY?
UNBELIEVABLY, SIR, THE SHIP IS IN POSITION!
REET REETREET
WHATEVER HAPPENS, MR. SULU, IF YOU THINK YOU HAVE THE TACTICAL ADVANTAGE, YOU FIRE ON THAT SHIP, EVEN IF WE'RE ***STILL ONBOARD.***
THAT'S AN ***ORDER.***
YES SIR.

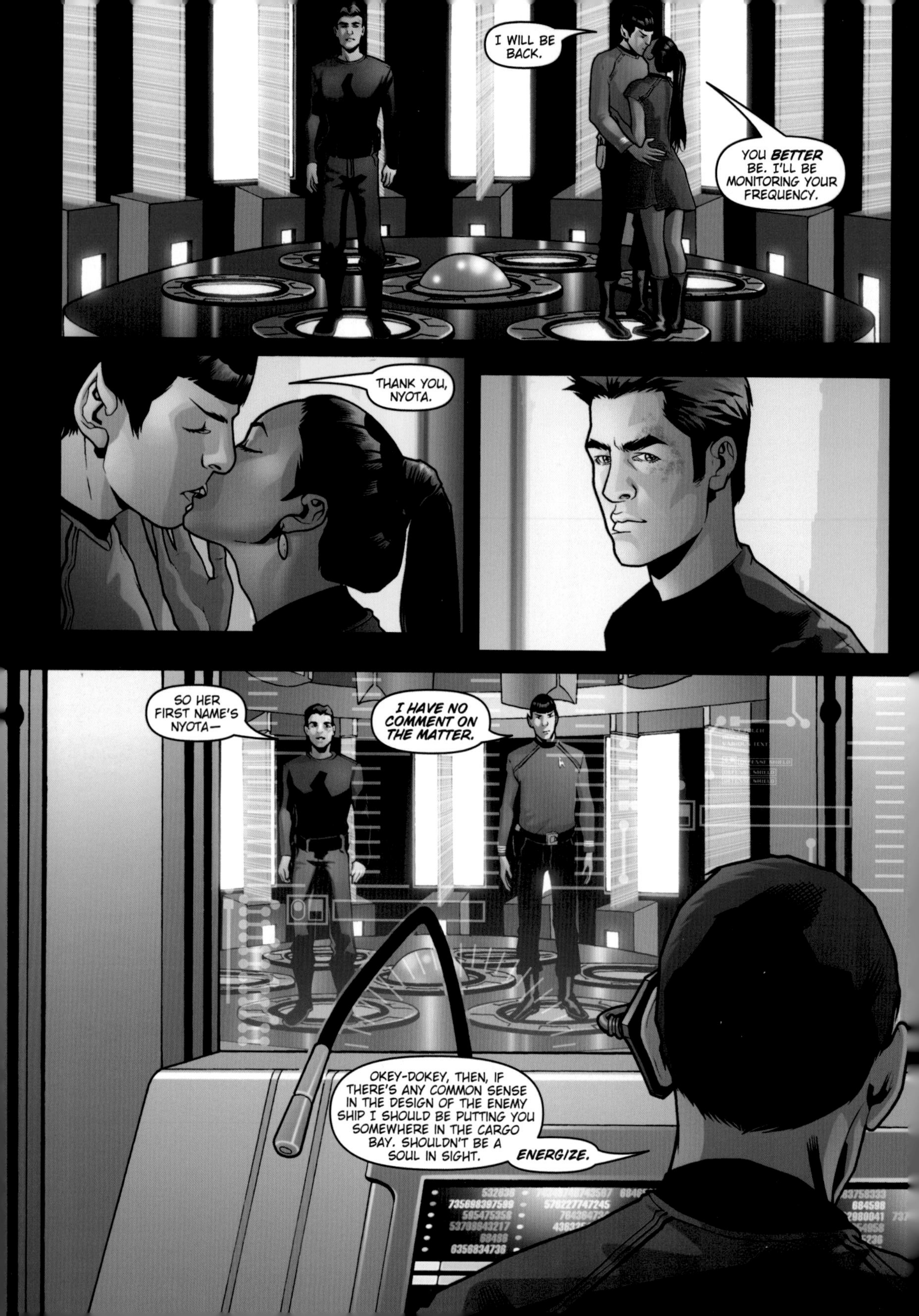
I WILL BE BACK.
YOU *BETTER* BE. I'LL BE MONITORING YOUR FREQUENCY.
THANK YOU, NYOTA.
SO HER FIRST NAME'S NYOTA—
I HAVE NO COMMENT ON THE MATTER.
OKEY-DOKEY, THEN, IF THERE'S ANY COMMON SENSE IN THE DESIGN OF THE ENEMY SHIP I SHOULD BE PUTTING YOU SOMEWHERE IN THE CARGO BAY. SHOULDN'T BE A SOUL IN SIGHT.
ENERGIZE.

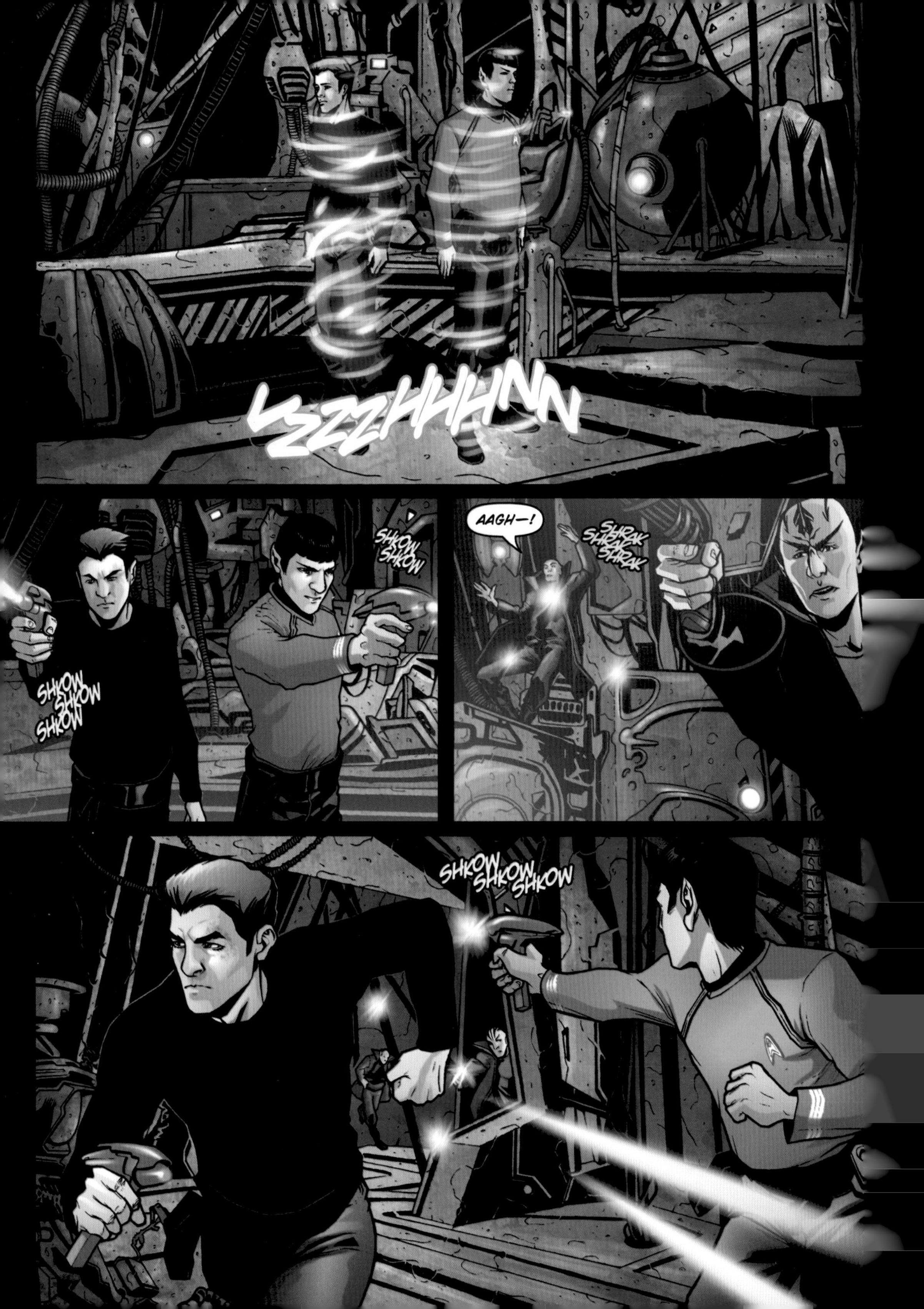
SZZZHHHNN
SHKOW SHKOW
SHKOW SHKOW SHKOW
AAGH—!
SHRAK SHRAK SHRAK
SHKOW SHKOW SHKOW

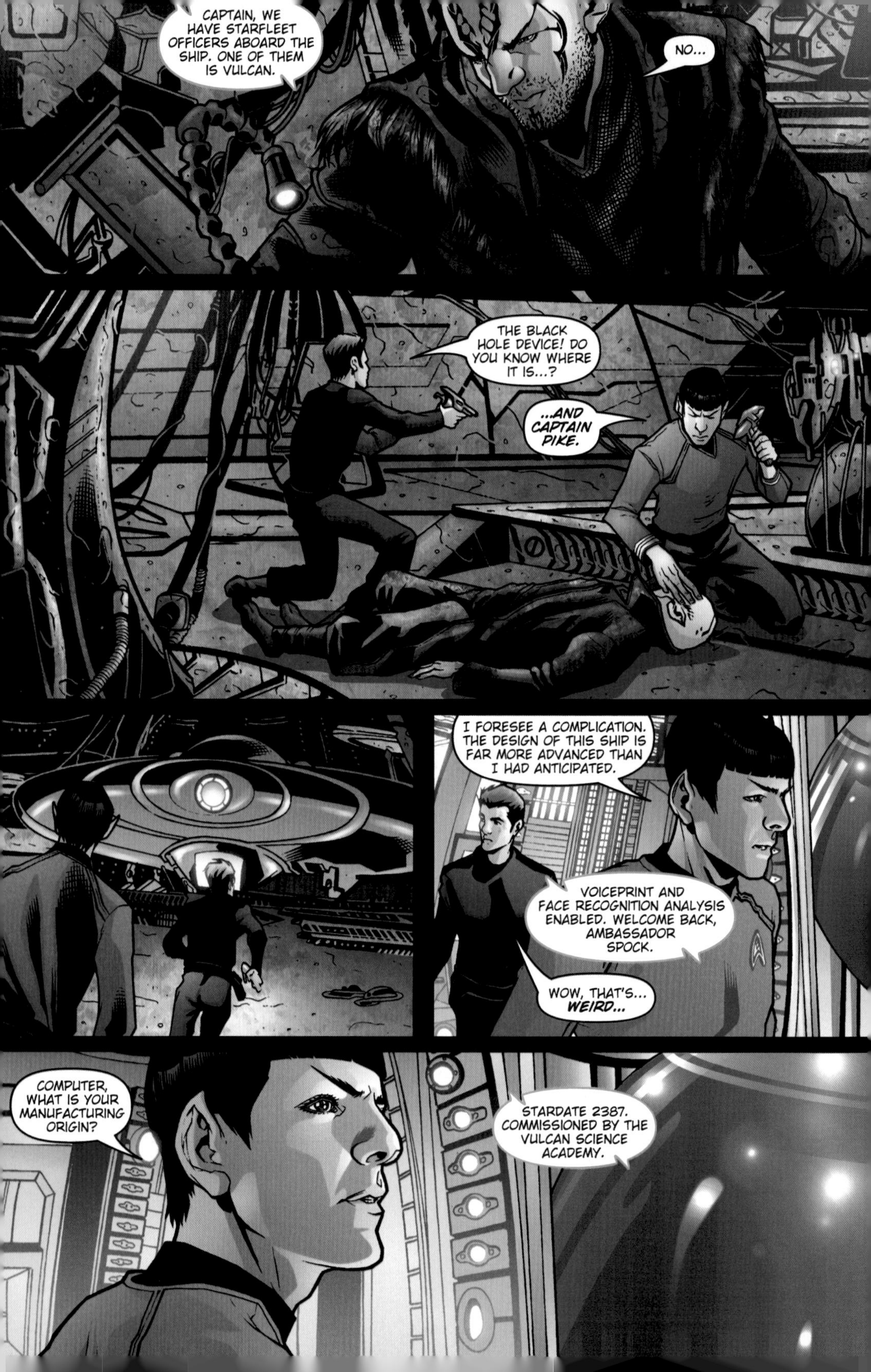
CAPTAIN, WE HAVE STARFLEET OFFICERS ABOARD THE SHIP. ONE OF THEM IS VULCAN.
NO...
THE BLACK HOLE DEVICE! DO YOU KNOW WHERE IT IS...?
...AND CAPTAIN PIKE.
I FORESEE A COMPLICATION. THE DESIGN OF THIS SHIP IS FAR MORE ADVANCED THAN I HAD ANTICIPATED.
VOICEPRINT AND FACE RECOGNITION ANALYSIS ENABLED. WELCOME BACK, AMBASSADOR SPOCK.
WOW, THAT'S... WEIRD...
COMPUTER, WHAT IS YOUR MANUFACTURING ORIGIN?
STARDATE 2387. COMMISSIONED BY THE VULCAN SCIENCE ACADEMY.

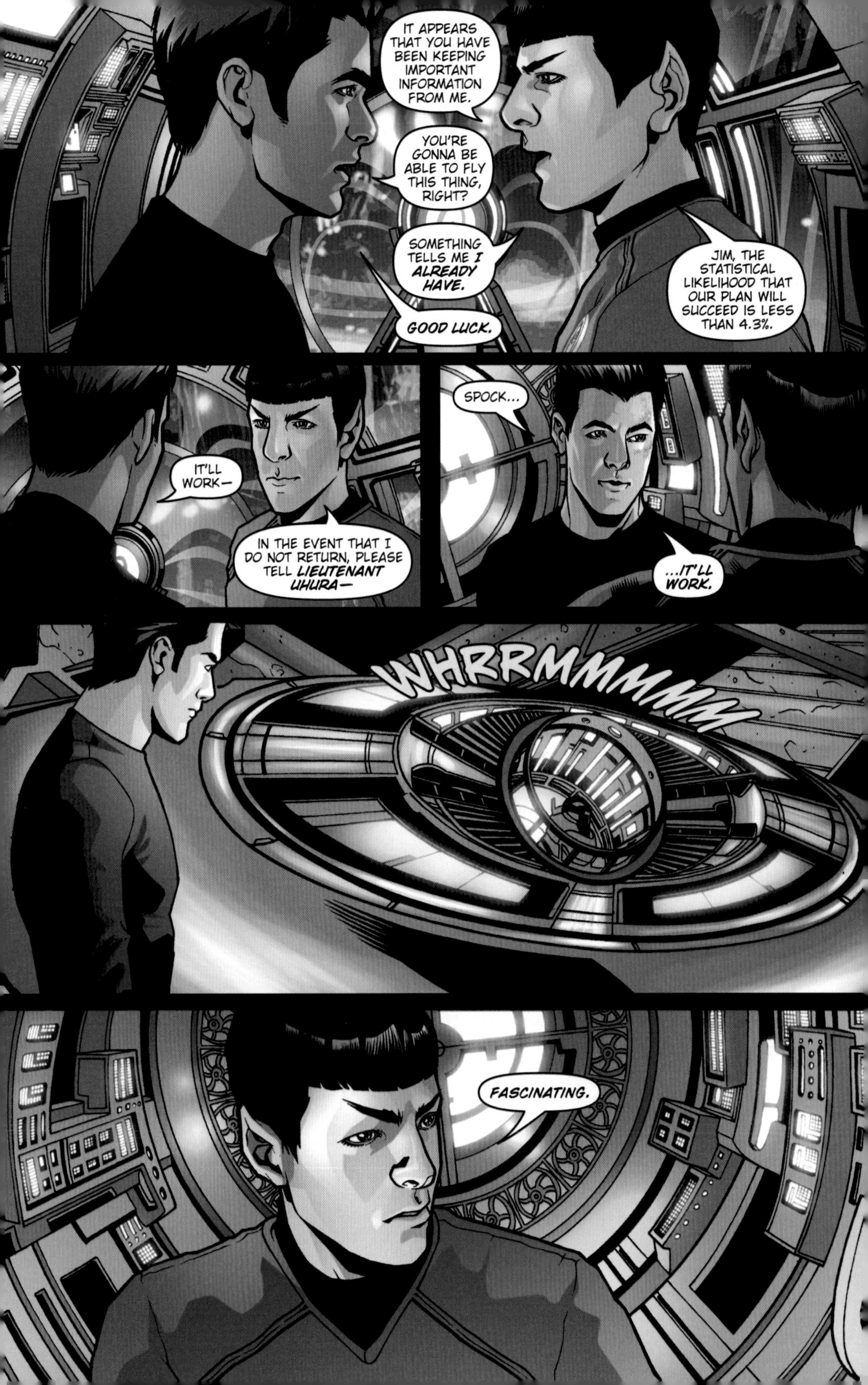
IT APPEARS THAT YOU HAVE BEEN KEEPING IMPORTANT INFORMATION FROM ME.
YOU'RE GONNA BE ABLE TO FLY THIS THING, RIGHT?
SOMETHING TELLS ME *I ALREADY HAVE.*
JIM, THE STATISTICAL LIKELIHOOD THAT OUR PLAN WILL SUCCEED IS LESS THAN 4.3%.
GOOD LUCK.
IT'LL WORK—
IN THE EVENT THAT I DO NOT RETURN, PLEASE TELL *LIEUTENANT UHURA*—
SPOCK...
...IT'LL WORK.
WHRRMMMMMM
FASCINATING.

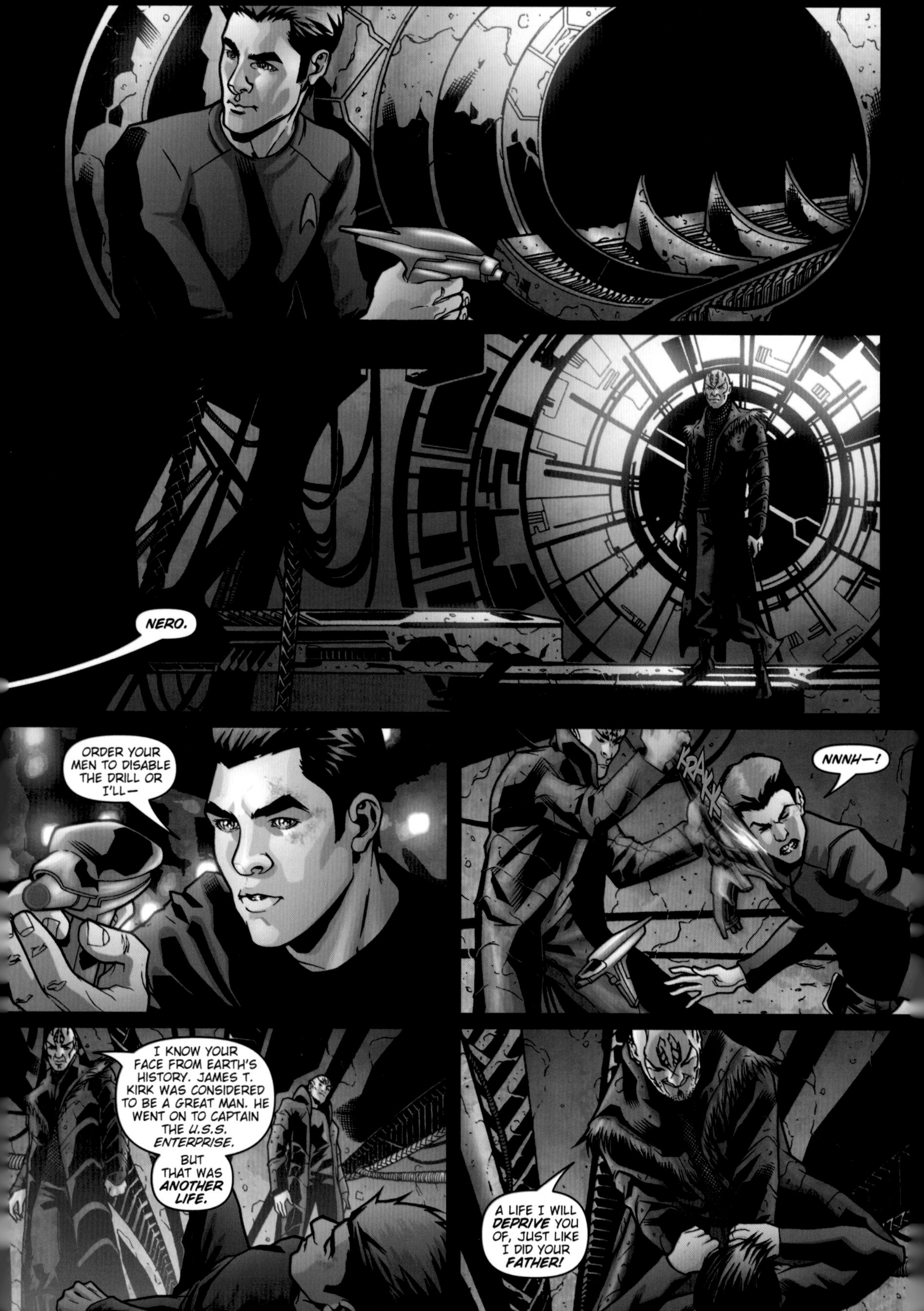
NERO.
ORDER YOUR MEN TO DISABLE THE DRILL OR I'LL—
KRAKK
NNNH—!
I KNOW YOUR FACE FROM EARTH'S HISTORY. JAMES T. KIRK WAS CONSIDERED TO BE A GREAT MAN. HE WENT ON TO CAPTAIN THE U.S.S. ENTERPRISE.
BUT THAT WAS ANOTHER LIFE.
A LIFE I WILL DEPRIVE YOU OF, JUST LIKE I DID YOUR FATHER!

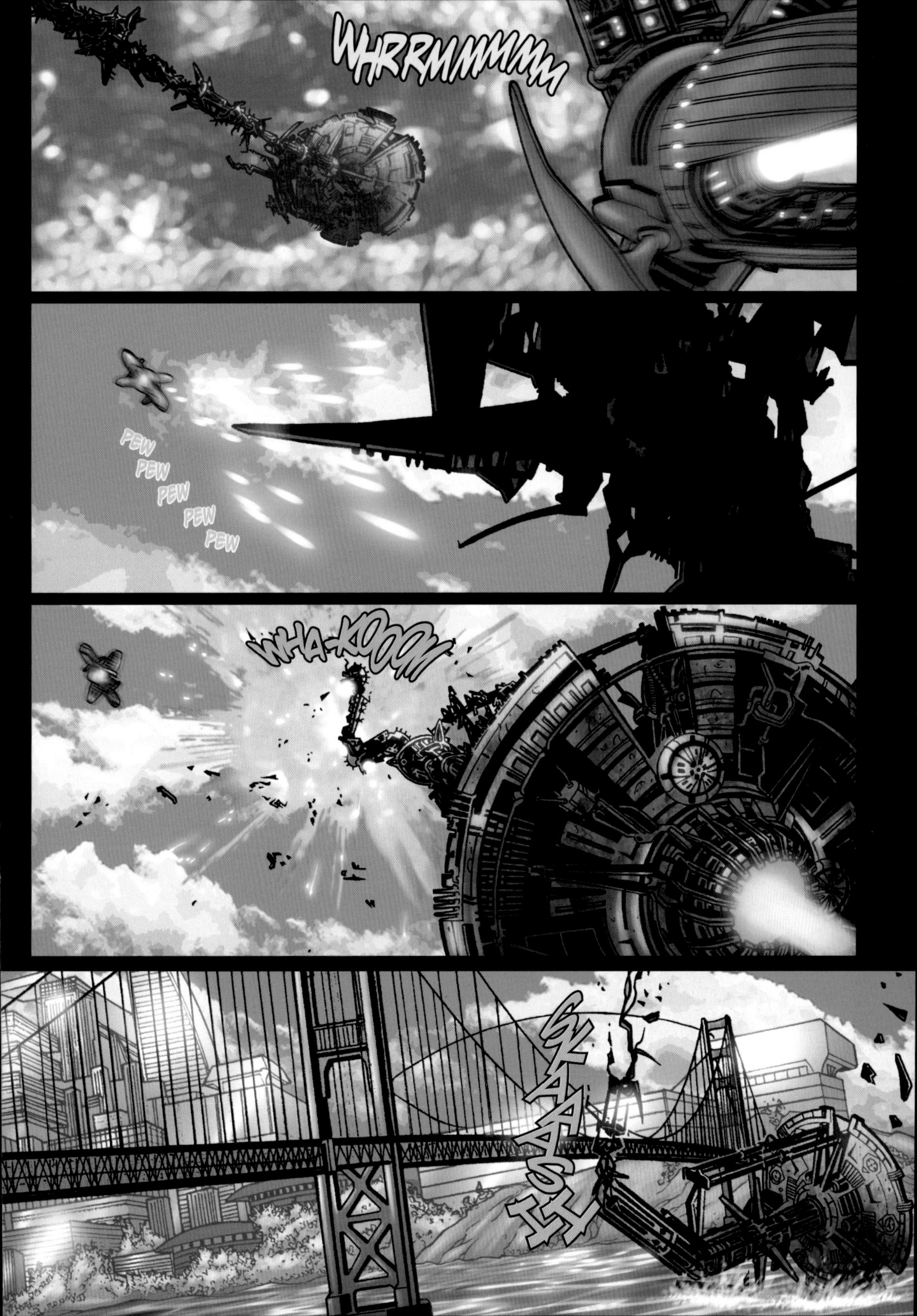
WHRRMMMMMM
PEW
PEW
PEW
PEW
PEW
WHA-KOOOM
SKAAASHH

CAPTAIN NERO, THE VULCAN SHIP HAS BEEN TAKEN! *THE DRILL HAS BEEN DESTROYED!*

SPOCK!

SPOCK!

OPEN A CHANNEL!

YESSIR!

SPOCK! I KNEW I SHOULD HAVE KILLED YOU WHEN I HAD THE CHANCE!

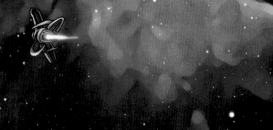

HE WENT TO WARP, SIR!

GO AFTER HIM!

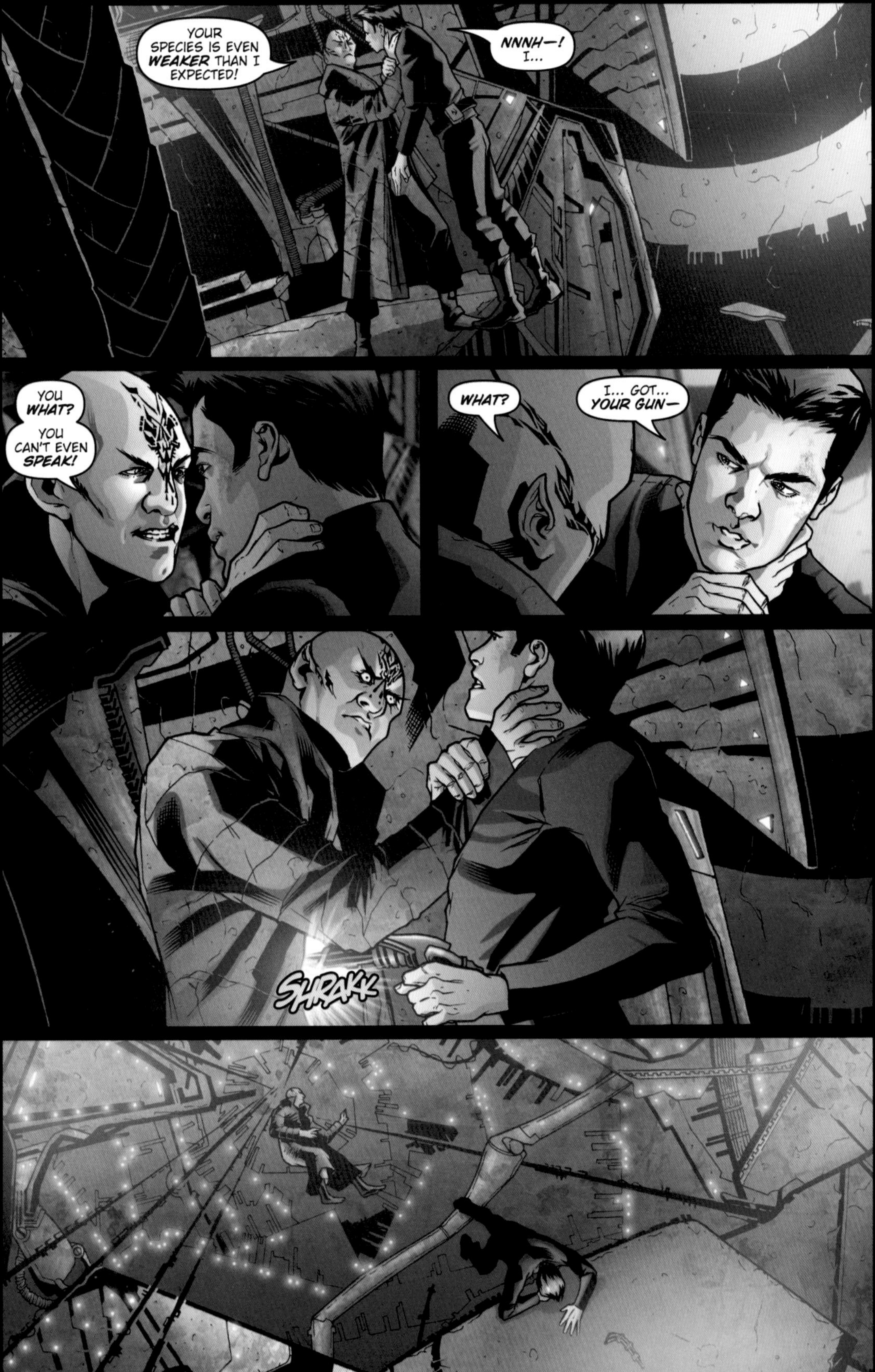
YOUR SPECIES IS EVEN WEAKER THAN I EXPECTED!
NNNH—! I...
YOU WHAT? YOU CAN'T EVEN SPEAK!
WHAT?
I... GOT... YOUR GUN—
SHRAKK

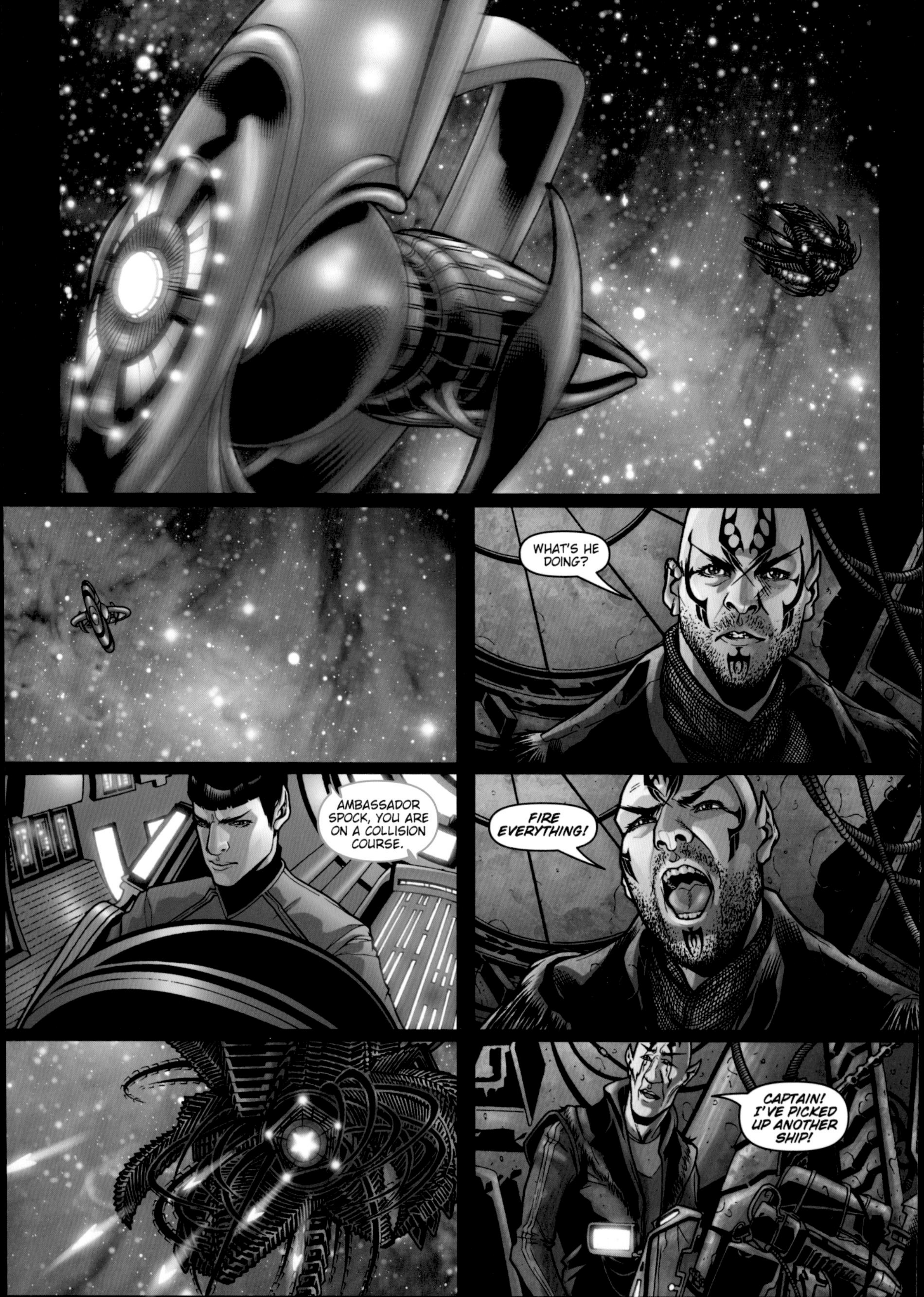
WHAT'S HE DOING?
AMBASSADOR SPOCK, YOU ARE ON A COLLISION COURSE.
FIRE EVERYTHING!
CAPTAIN! I'VE PICKED UP ANOTHER SHIP!

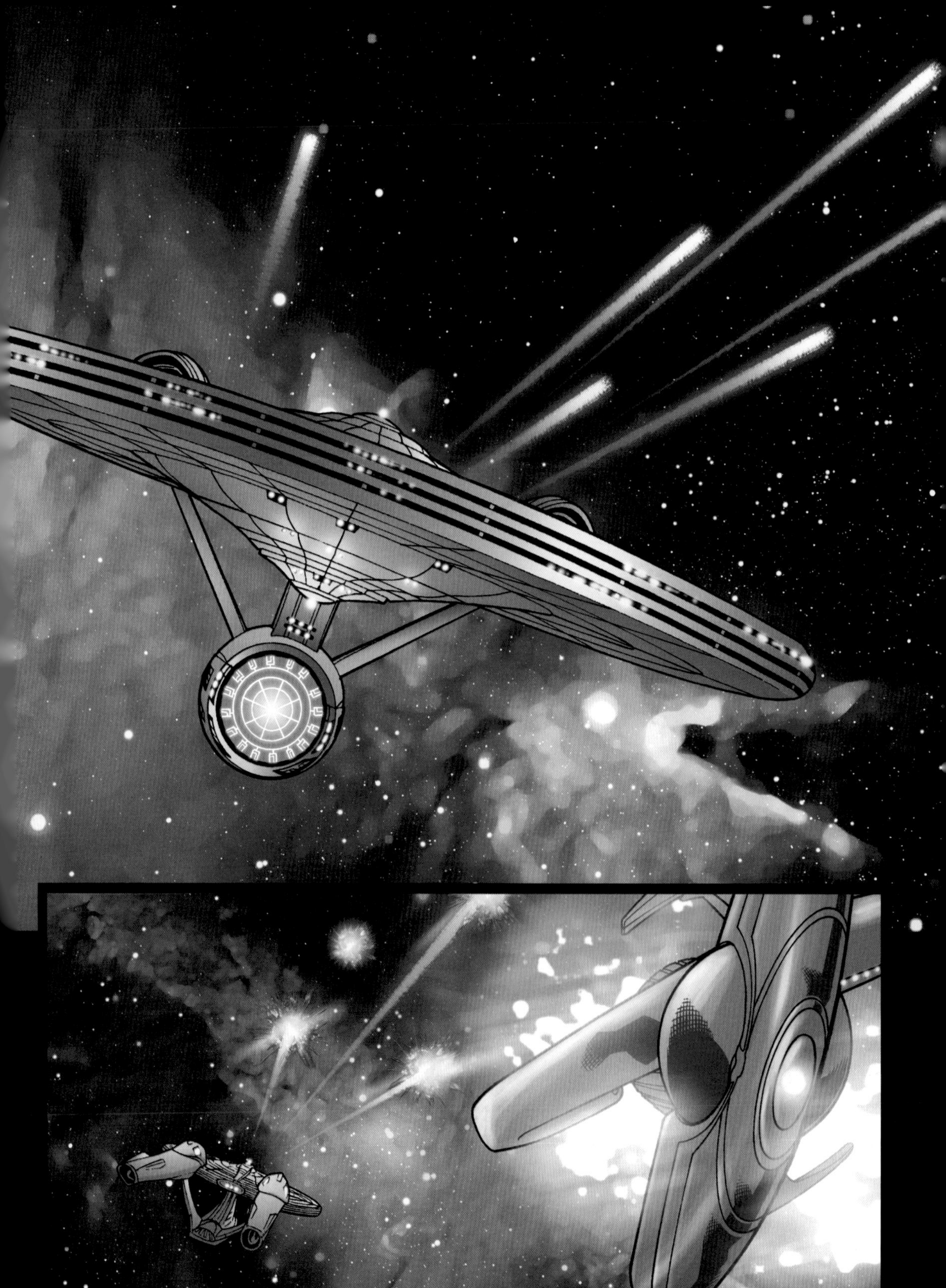

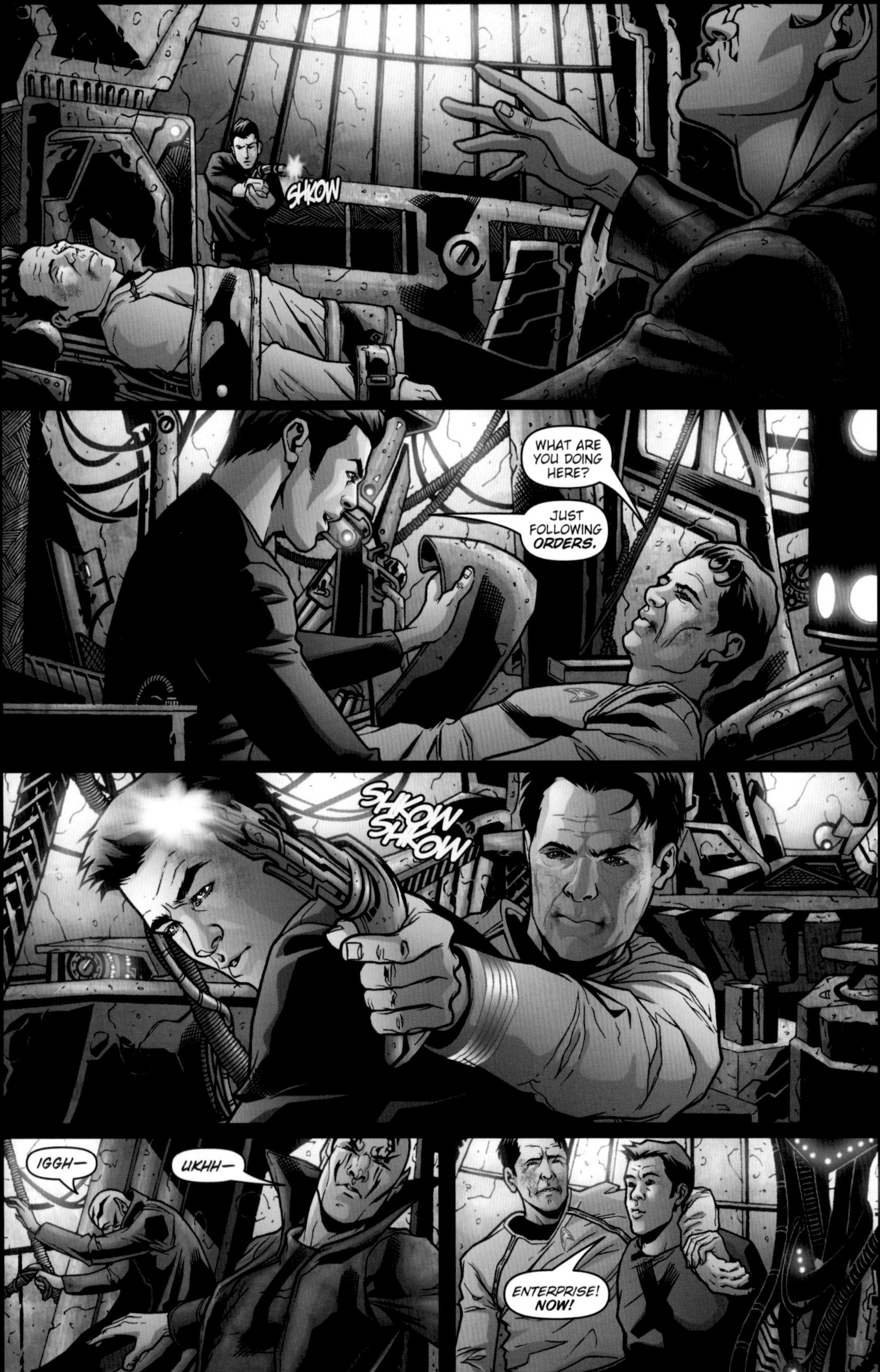
SHKOW
WHAT ARE YOU DOING HERE?
JUST FOLLOWING **ORDERS.**
SHKOW SHKOW
IGGH—
UKHH—
ENTERPRISE! NOW!

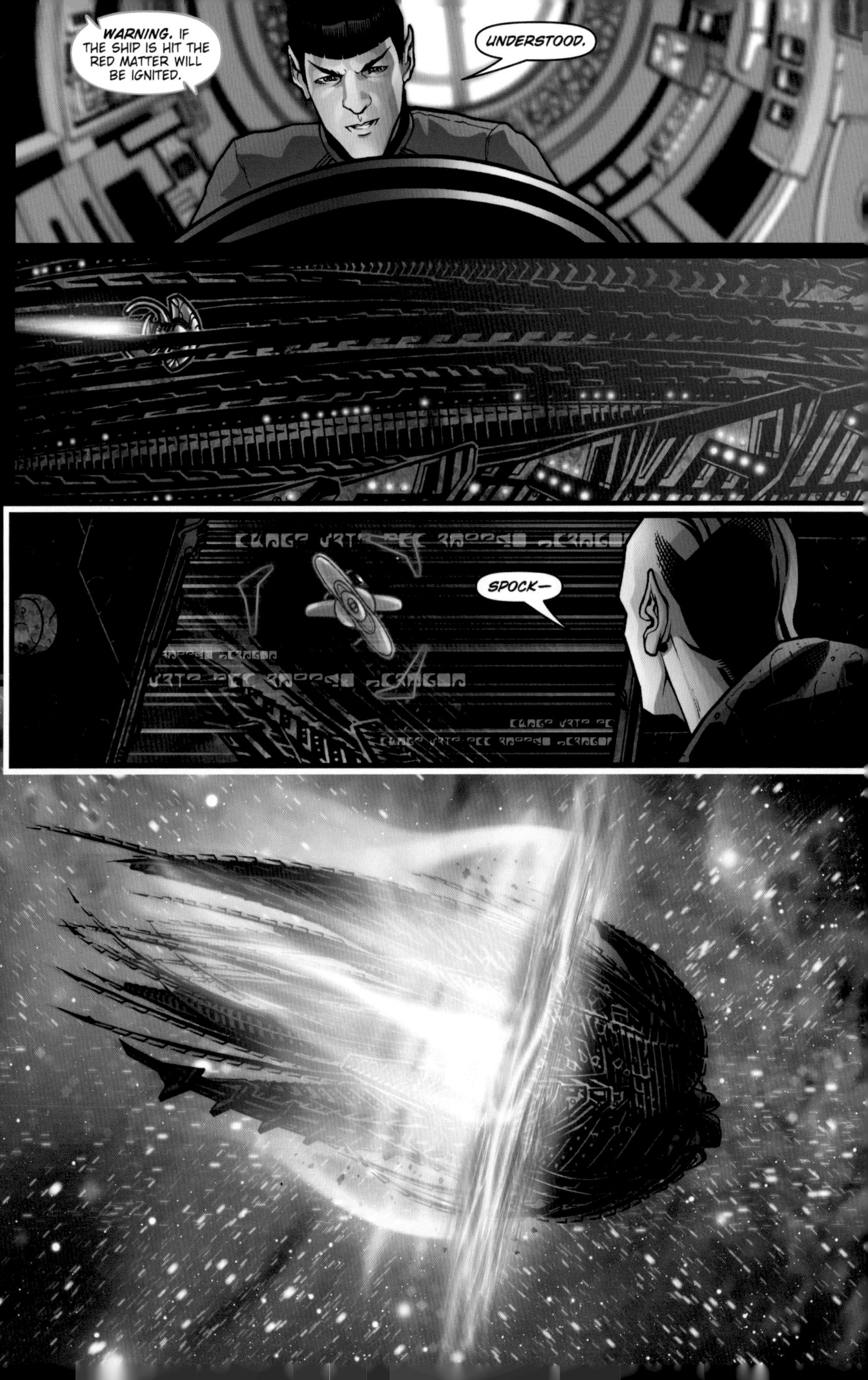
WARNING. IF THE SHIP IS HIT THE RED MATTER WILL BE IGNITED.
UNDERSTOOD.
SPOCK—

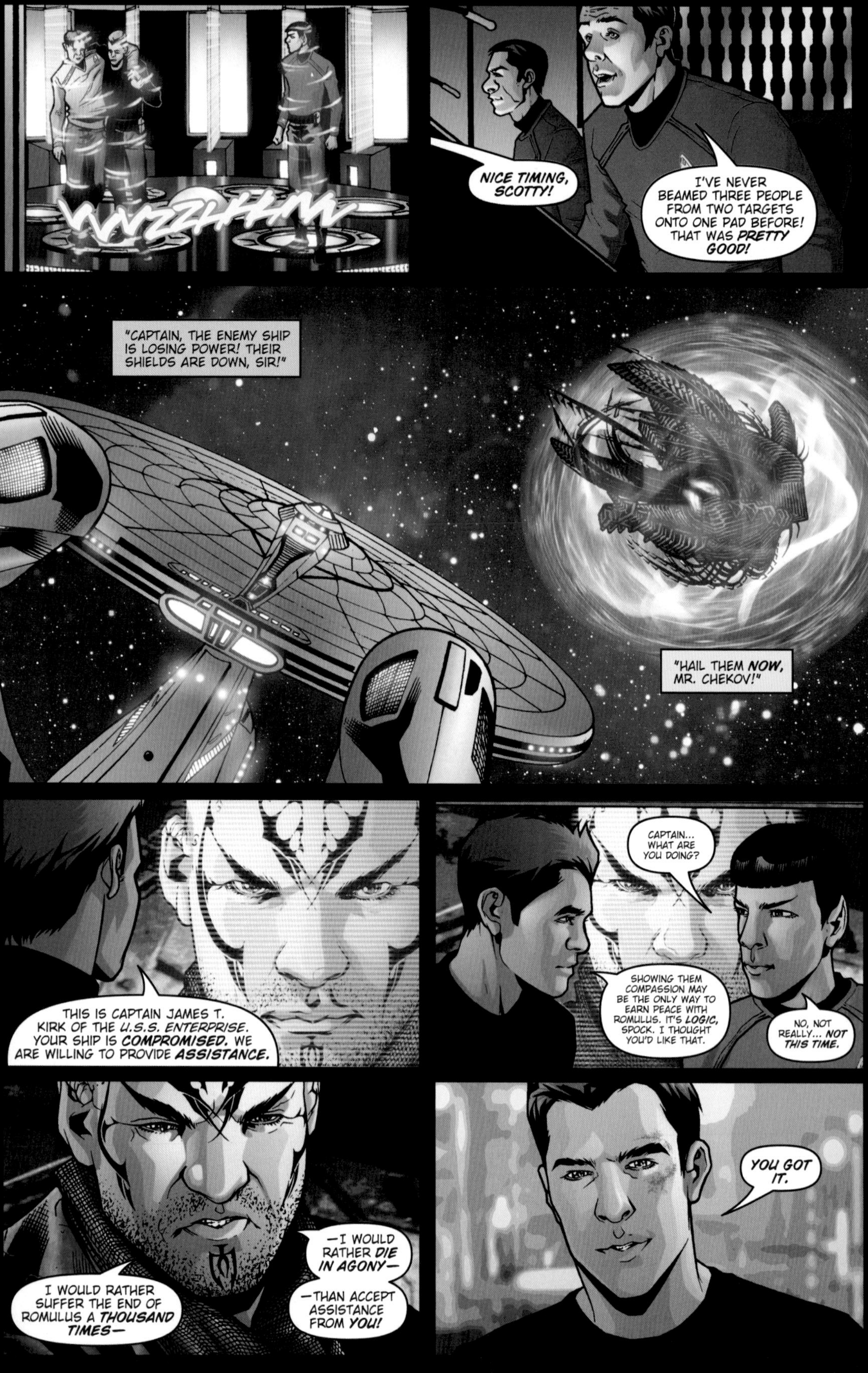
VVVZZHHHMM
NICE TIMING, SCOTTY!
I'VE NEVER BEAMED THREE PEOPLE FROM TWO TARGETS ONTO ONE PAD BEFORE! THAT WAS PRETTY GOOD!
"CAPTAIN, THE ENEMY SHIP IS LOSING POWER! THEIR SHIELDS ARE DOWN, SIR!"
"HAIL THEM NOW, MR. CHEKOV!"
THIS IS CAPTAIN JAMES T. KIRK OF THE U.S.S. ENTERPRISE. YOUR SHIP IS COMPROMISED. WE ARE WILLING TO PROVIDE ASSISTANCE.
CAPTAIN... WHAT ARE YOU DOING?
SHOWING THEM COMPASSION MAY BE THE ONLY WAY TO EARN PEACE WITH ROMULUS. IT'S LOGIC, SPOCK. I THOUGHT YOU'D LIKE THAT.
NO, NOT REALLY... NOT THIS TIME.
I WOULD RATHER SUFFER THE END OF ROMULUS A THOUSAND TIMES—
—I WOULD RATHER DIE IN AGONY—
—THAN ACCEPT ASSISTANCE FROM YOU!
YOU GOT IT.

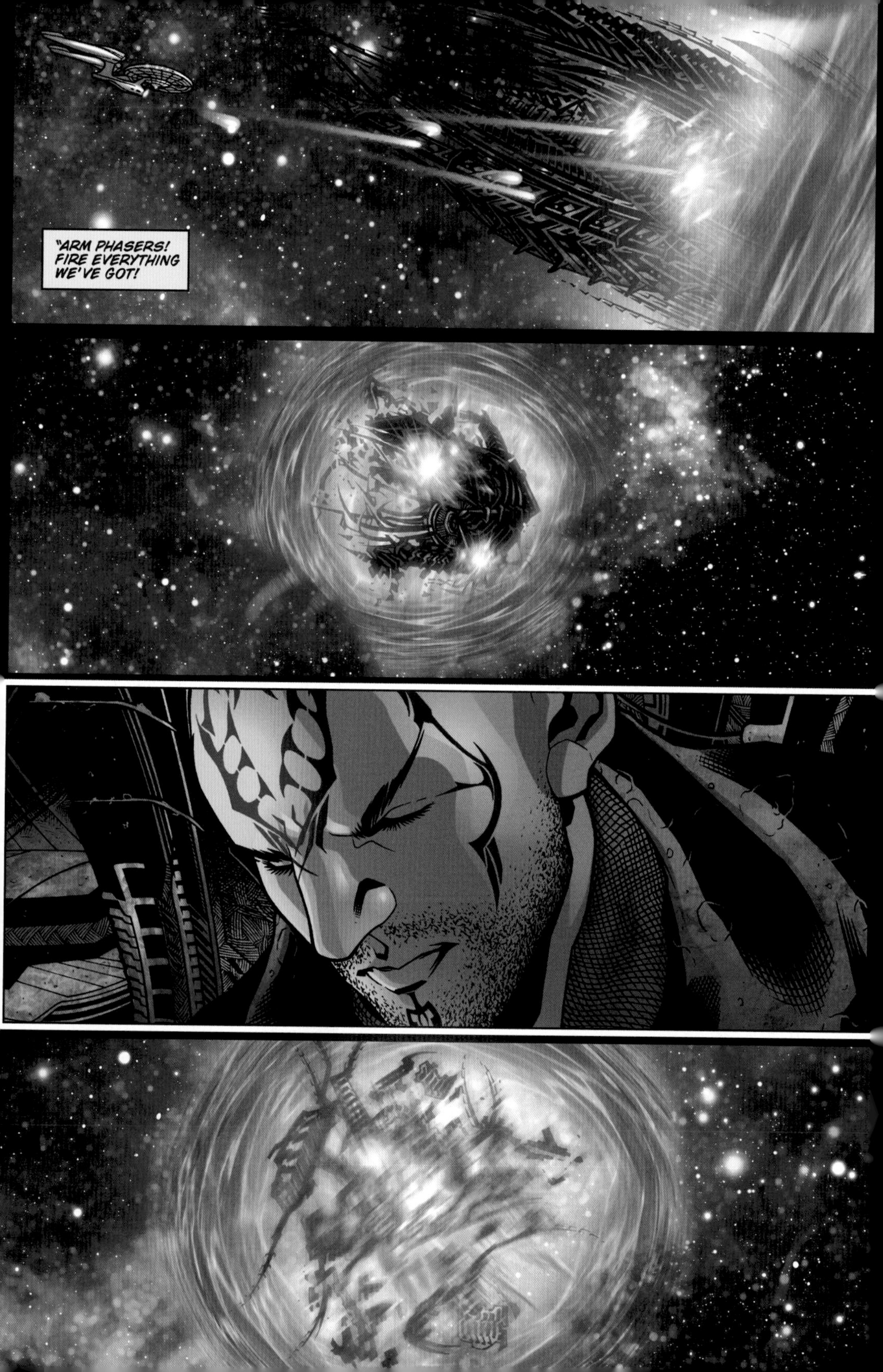
"ARM PHASERS! FIRE EVERYTHING WE'VE GOT!

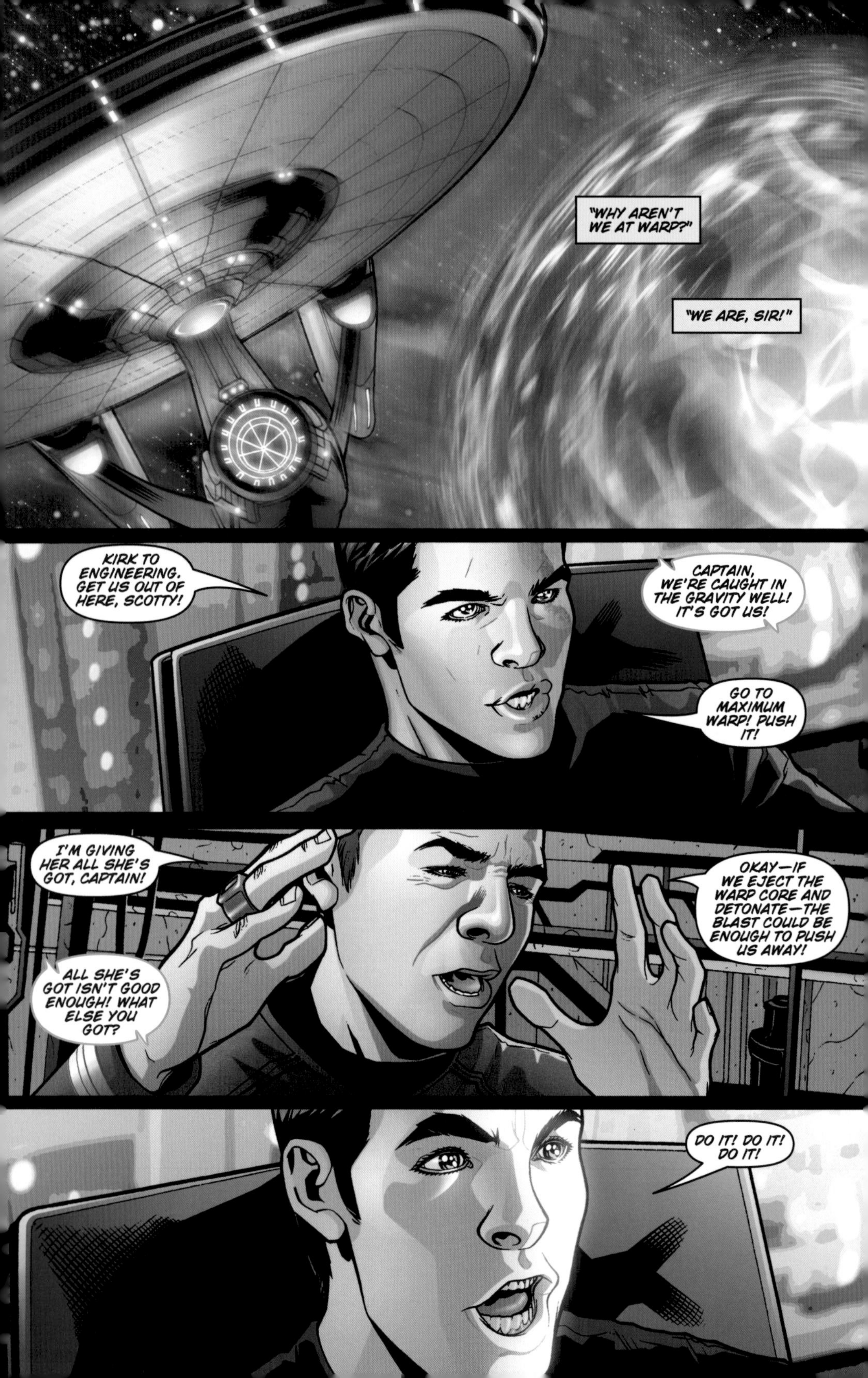
"WHY AREN'T WE AT WARP?"
"WE ARE, SIR!"
KIRK TO ENGINEERING. GET US OUT OF HERE, SCOTTY!
CAPTAIN, WE'RE CAUGHT IN THE GRAVITY WELL! IT'S GOT US!
GO TO MAXIMUM WARP! PUSH IT!
I'M GIVING HER ALL SHE'S GOT, CAPTAIN!
ALL SHE'S GOT ISN'T GOOD ENOUGH! WHAT ELSE YOU GOT?
OKAY—IF WE EJECT THE WARP CORE AND DETONATE—THE BLAST COULD BE ENOUGH TO PUSH US AWAY!
DO IT! DO IT! DO IT!

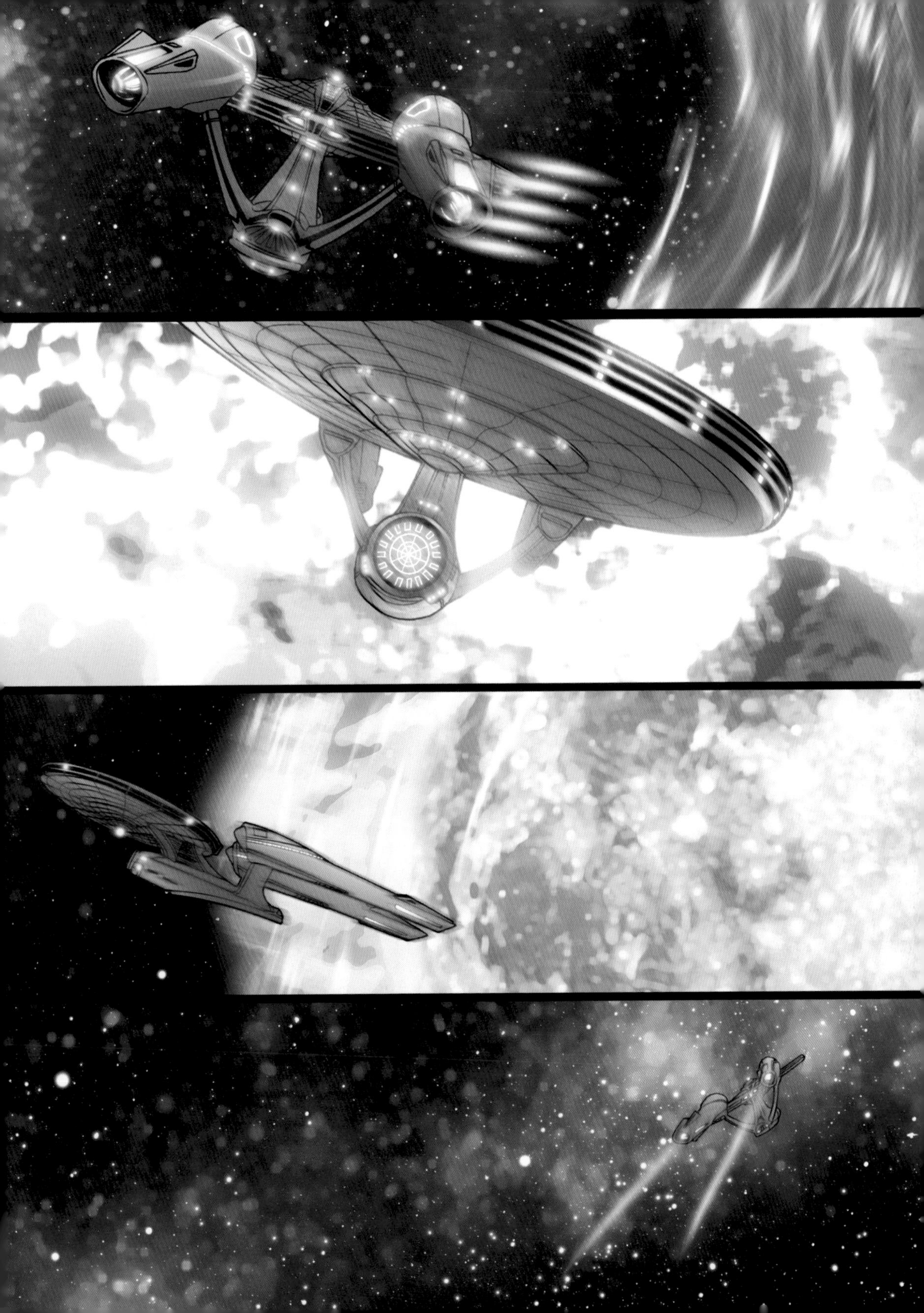

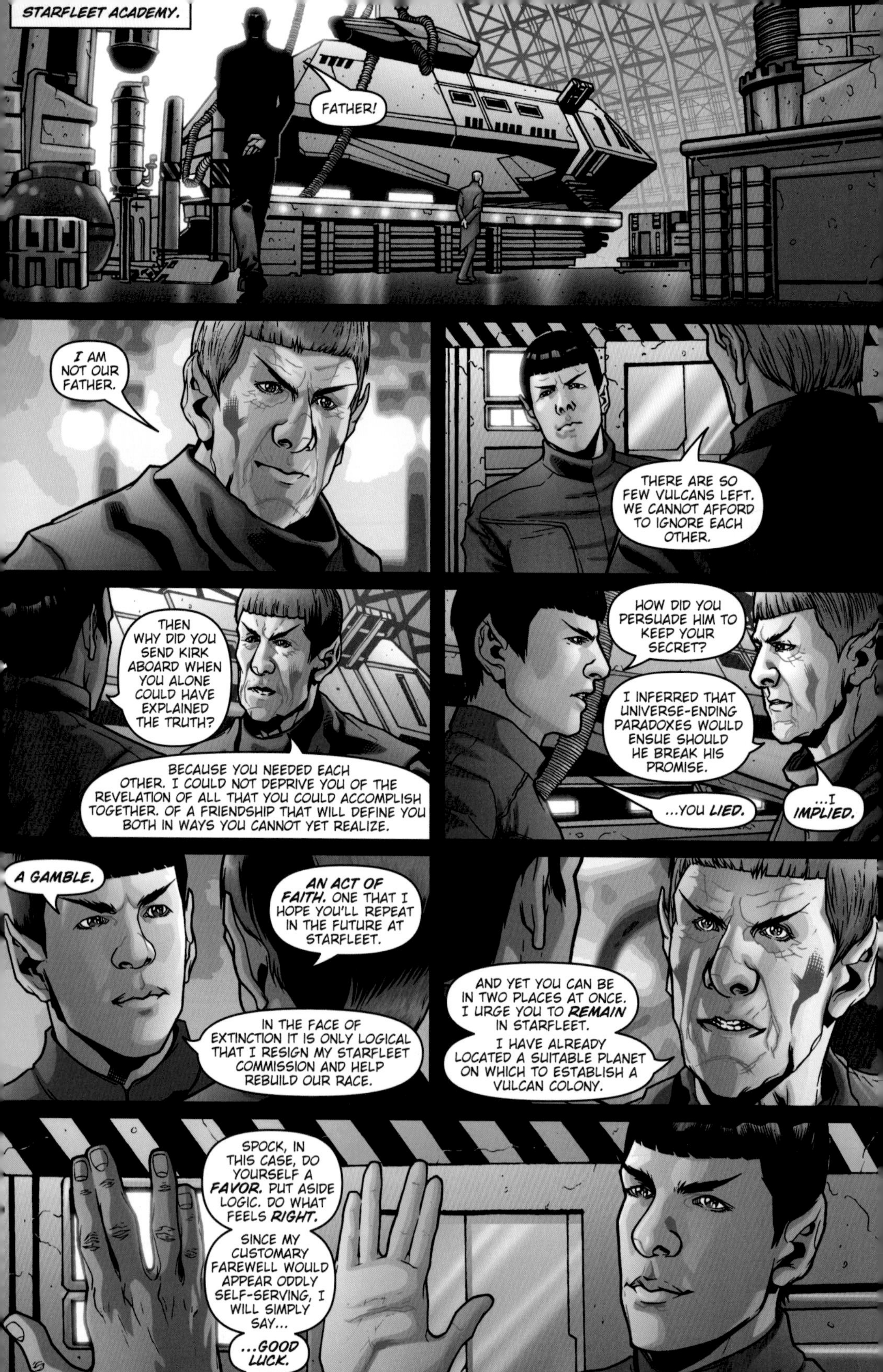
STARFLEET ACADEMY.
FATHER!
I AM NOT OUR FATHER.
THERE ARE SO FEW VULCANS LEFT. WE CANNOT AFFORD TO IGNORE EACH OTHER.
THEN WHY DID YOU SEND KIRK ABOARD WHEN YOU ALONE COULD HAVE EXPLAINED THE TRUTH?
BECAUSE YOU NEEDED EACH OTHER. I COULD NOT DEPRIVE YOU OF THE REVELATION OF ALL THAT YOU COULD ACCOMPLISH TOGETHER. OF A FRIENDSHIP THAT WILL DEFINE YOU BOTH IN WAYS YOU CANNOT YET REALIZE.
HOW DID YOU PERSUADE HIM TO KEEP YOUR SECRET?
I INFERRED THAT UNIVERSE-ENDING PARADOXES WOULD ENSUE SHOULD HE BREAK HIS PROMISE.
...YOU **LIED.**
...I **IMPLIED.**
A GAMBLE.
AN ACT OF FAITH. ONE THAT I HOPE YOU'LL REPEAT IN THE FUTURE AT STARFLEET.
IN THE FACE OF EXTINCTION IT IS ONLY LOGICAL THAT I RESIGN MY STARFLEET COMMISSION AND HELP REBUILD OUR RACE.
AND YET YOU CAN BE IN TWO PLACES AT ONCE. I URGE YOU TO ***REMAIN*** IN STARFLEET.
I HAVE ALREADY LOCATED A SUITABLE PLANET ON WHICH TO ESTABLISH A VULCAN COLONY.
SPOCK, IN THIS CASE, DO YOURSELF A ***FAVOR.*** PUT ASIDE LOGIC. DO WHAT FEELS ***RIGHT.***
SINCE MY CUSTOMARY FAREWELL WOULD APPEAR ODDLY SELF-SERVING, I WILL SIMPLY SAY...
...GOOD LUCK.

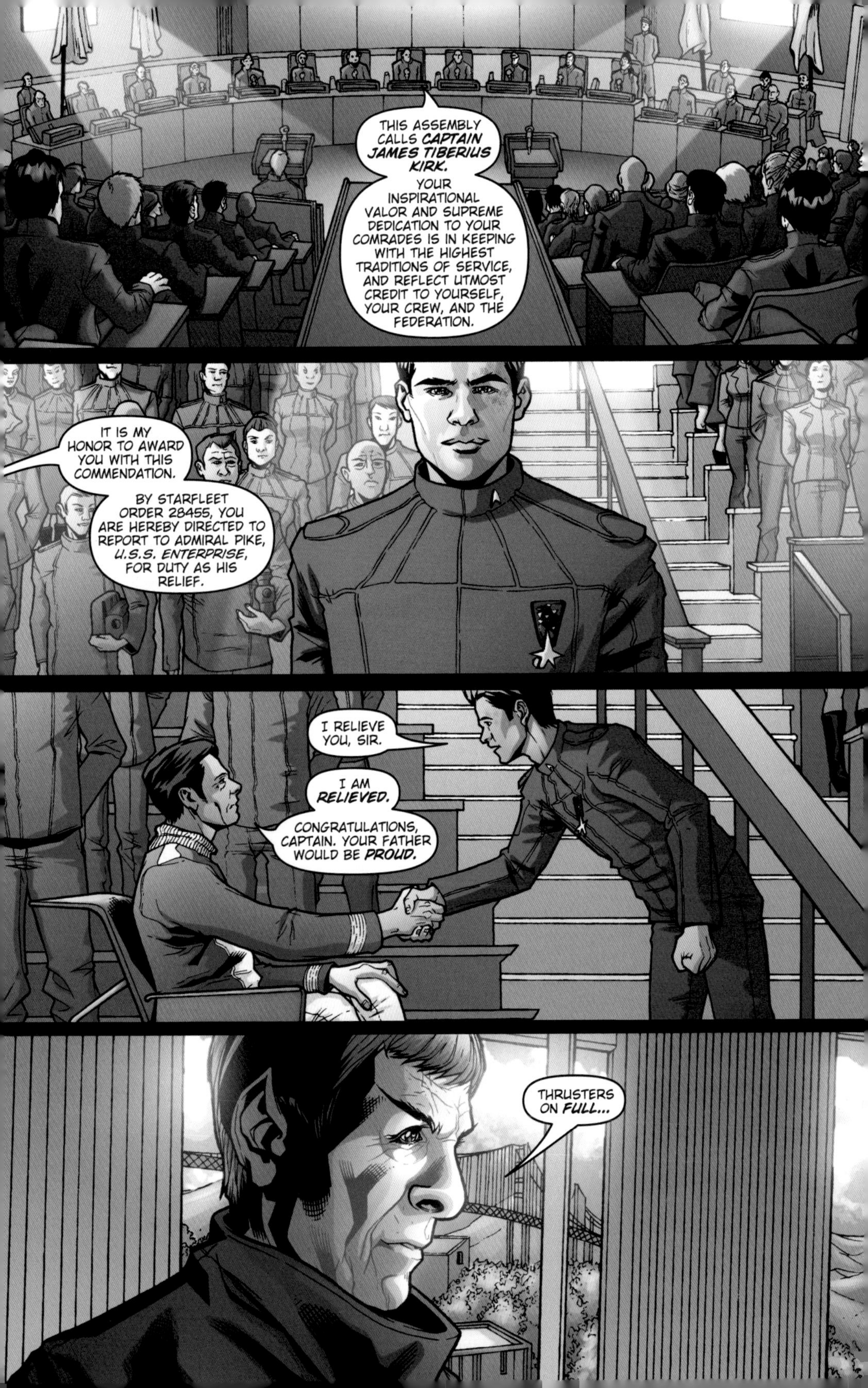
THIS ASSEMBLY CALLS CAPTAIN JAMES TIBERIUS KIRK.
YOUR INSPIRATIONAL VALOR AND SUPREME DEDICATION TO YOUR COMRADES IS IN KEEPING WITH THE HIGHEST TRADITIONS OF SERVICE, AND REFLECT UTMOST CREDIT TO YOURSELF, YOUR CREW, AND THE FEDERATION.
IT IS MY HONOR TO AWARD YOU WITH THIS COMMENDATION.
BY STARFLEET ORDER 28455, YOU ARE HEREBY DIRECTED TO REPORT TO ADMIRAL PIKE, U.S.S. ENTERPRISE, FOR DUTY AS HIS RELIEF.
I RELIEVE YOU, SIR.
I AM RELIEVED.
CONGRATULATIONS, CAPTAIN. YOUR FATHER WOULD BE PROUD.
THRUSTERS ON FULL...

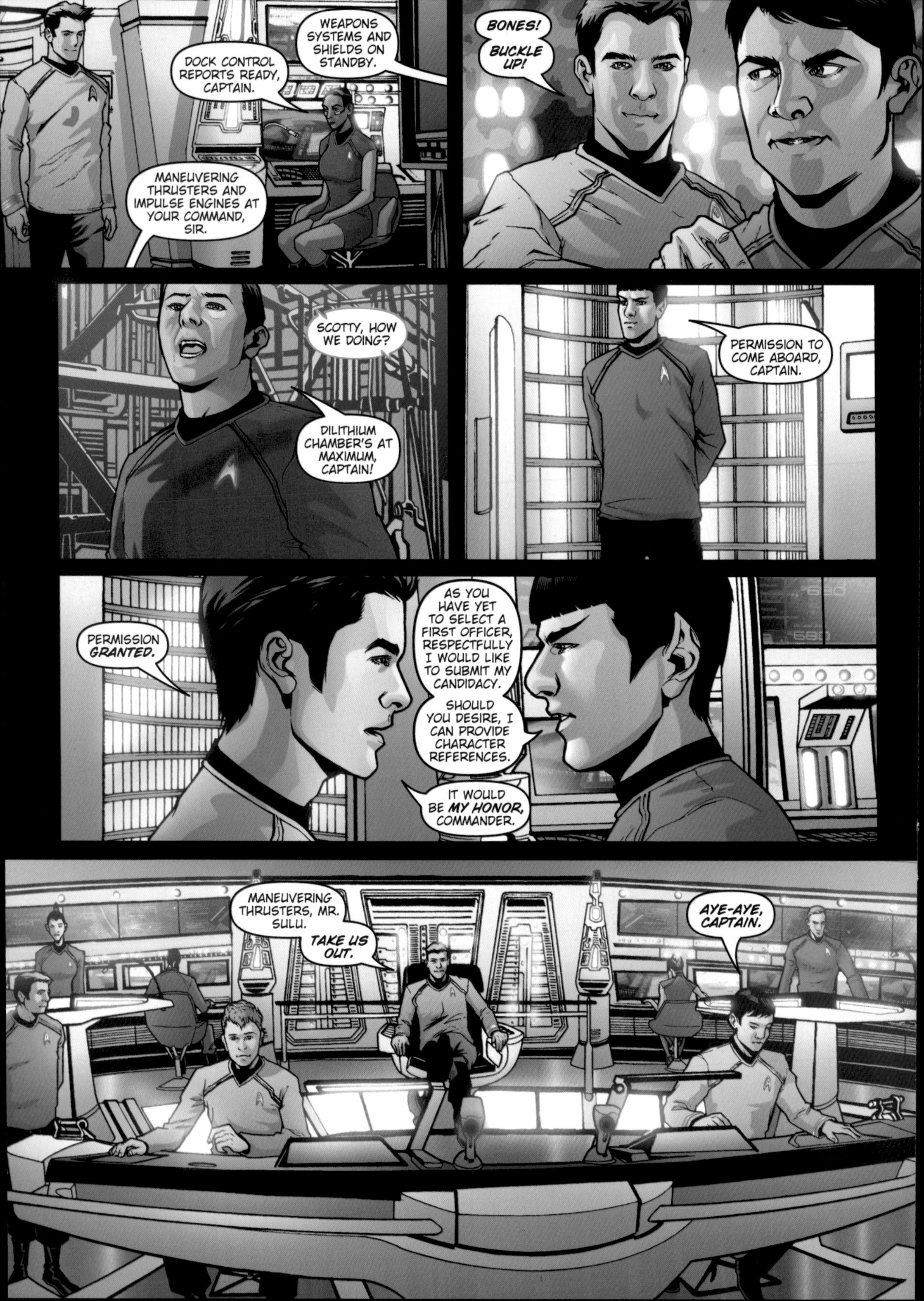
DOCK CONTROL REPORTS READY, CAPTAIN.
WEAPONS SYSTEMS AND SHIELDS ON STANDBY.
MANEUVERING THRUSTERS AND IMPULSE ENGINES AT YOUR COMMAND, SIR.
BONES! BUCKLE UP!
SCOTTY, HOW WE DOING?
DILITHIUM CHAMBER'S AT MAXIMUM, CAPTAIN!
PERMISSION TO COME ABOARD, CAPTAIN.
PERMISSION GRANTED.
AS YOU HAVE YET TO SELECT A FIRST OFFICER, RESPECTFULLY I WOULD LIKE TO SUBMIT MY CANDIDACY.
SHOULD YOU DESIRE, I CAN PROVIDE CHARACTER REFERENCES.
IT WOULD BE MY HONOR, COMMANDER.
MANEUVERING THRUSTERS, MR. SULU.
TAKE US OUT.
AYE-AYE, CAPTAIN.

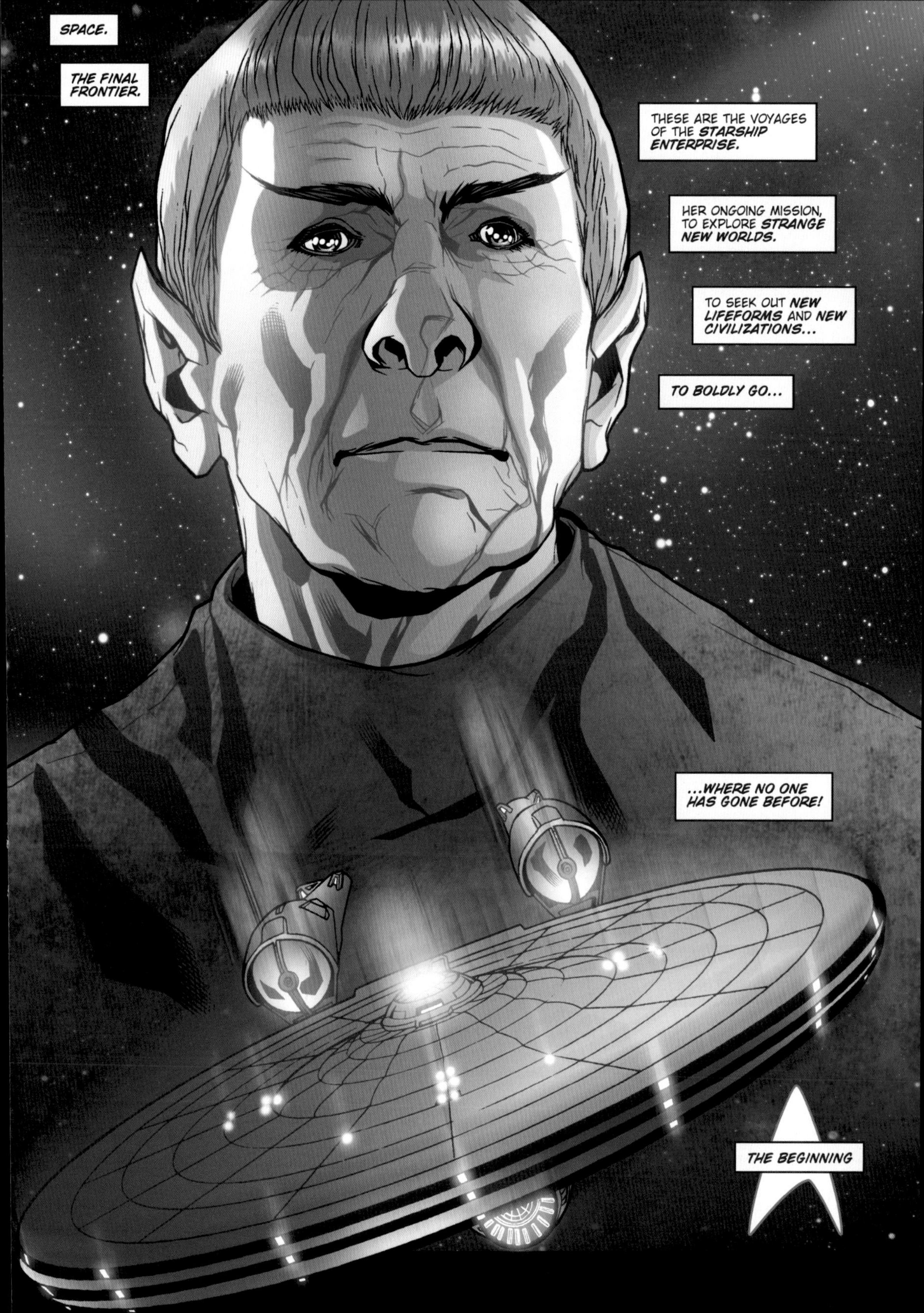
SPACE.
THE FINAL FRONTIER.
THESE ARE THE VOYAGES OF THE STARSHIP ENTERPRISE.
HER ONGOING MISSION, TO EXPLORE STRANGE NEW WORLDS.
TO SEEK OUT NEW LIFEFORMS AND NEW CIVILIZATIONS...
TO BOLDLY GO...
...WHERE NO ONE HAS GONE BEFORE!
THE BEGINNING

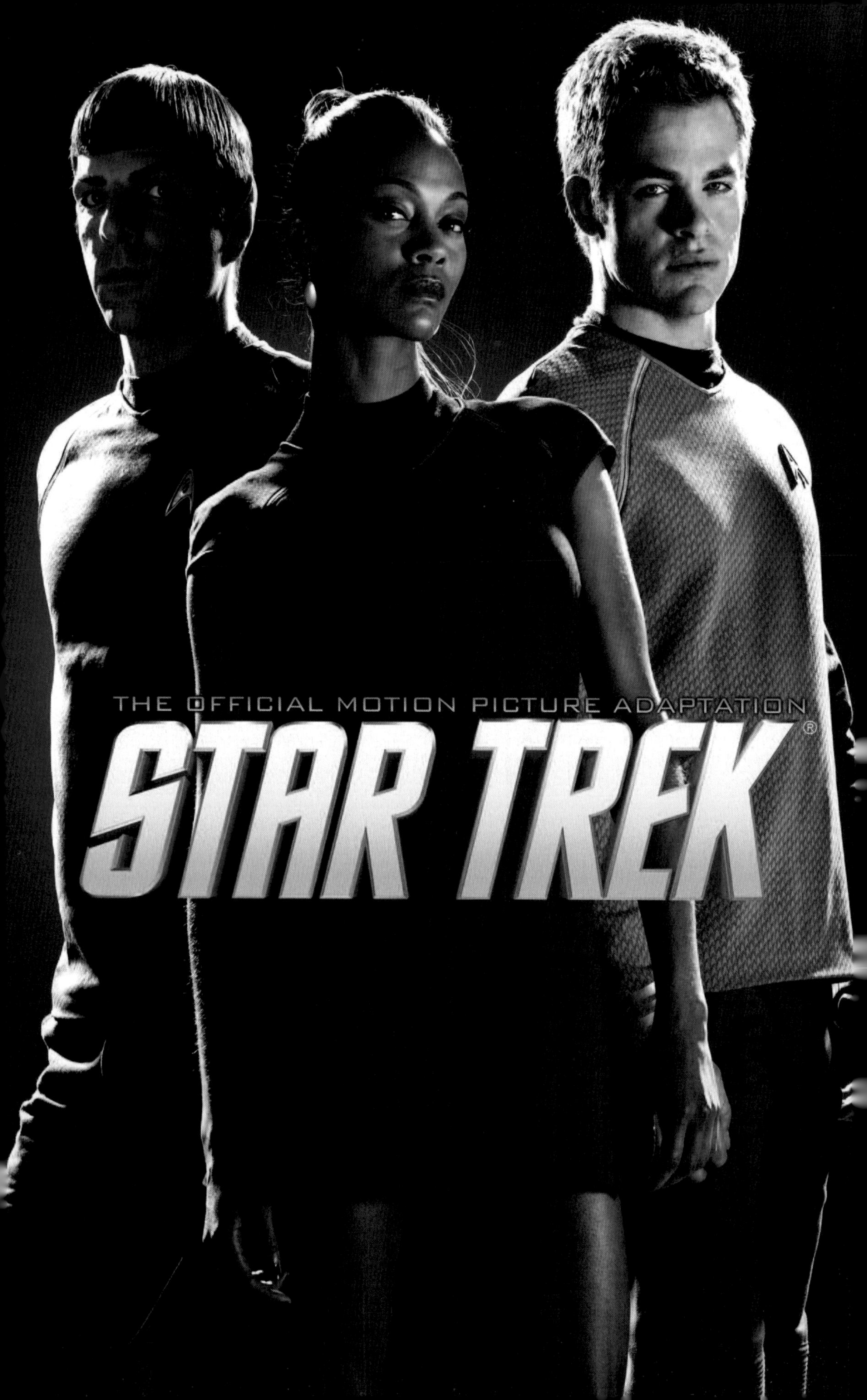
THE OFFICIAL MOTION PICTURE ADAPTATION
STAR TREK®

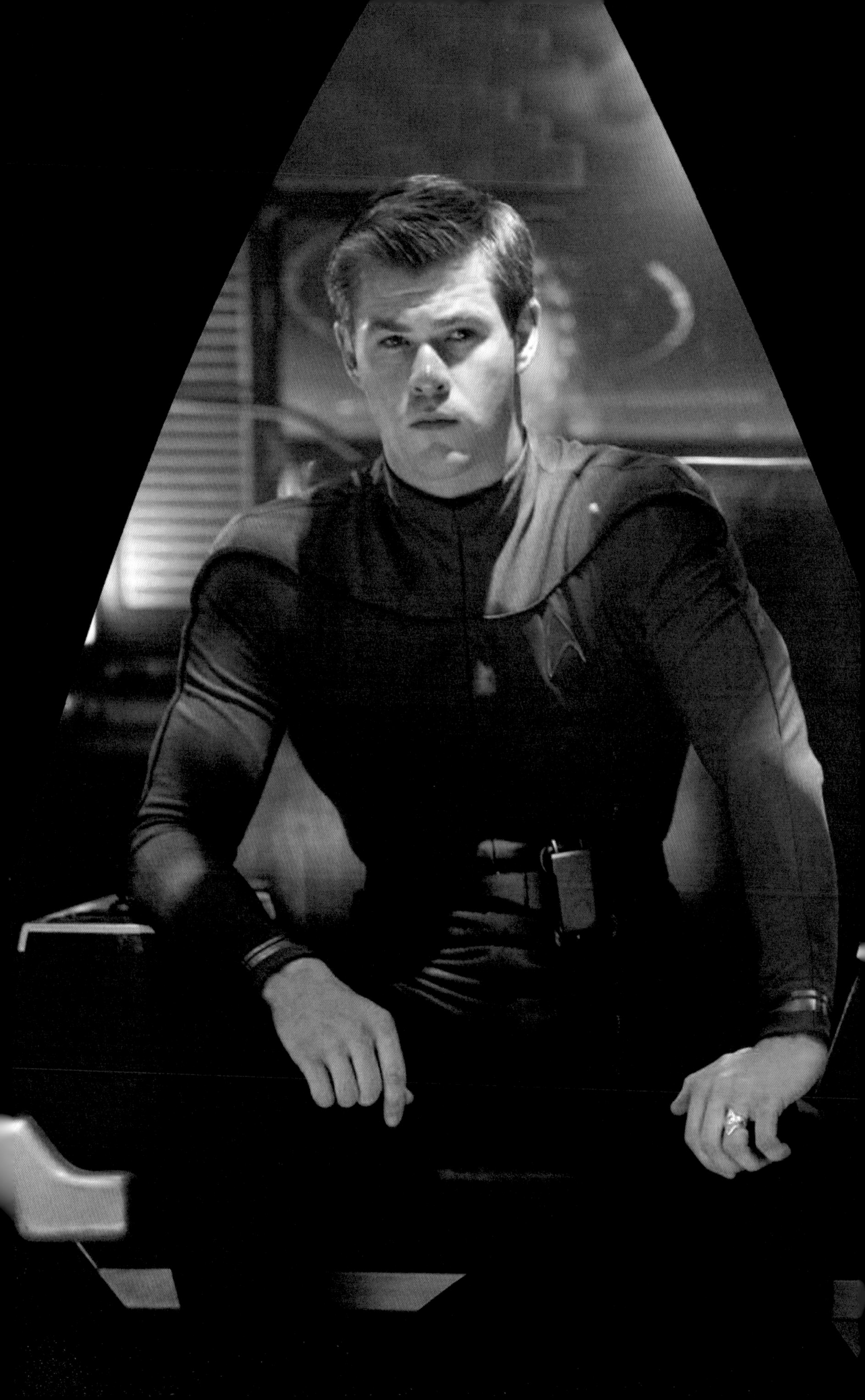

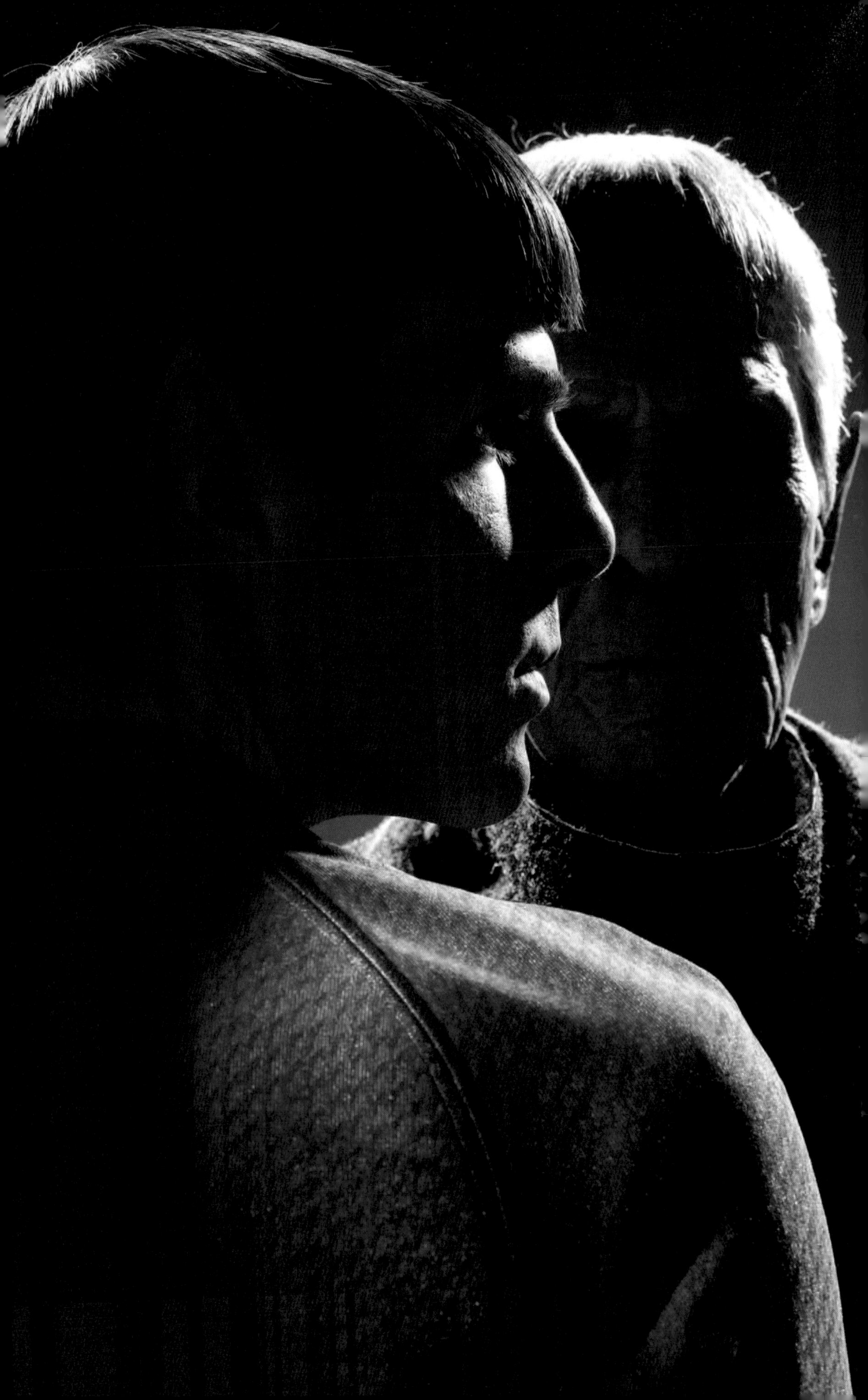

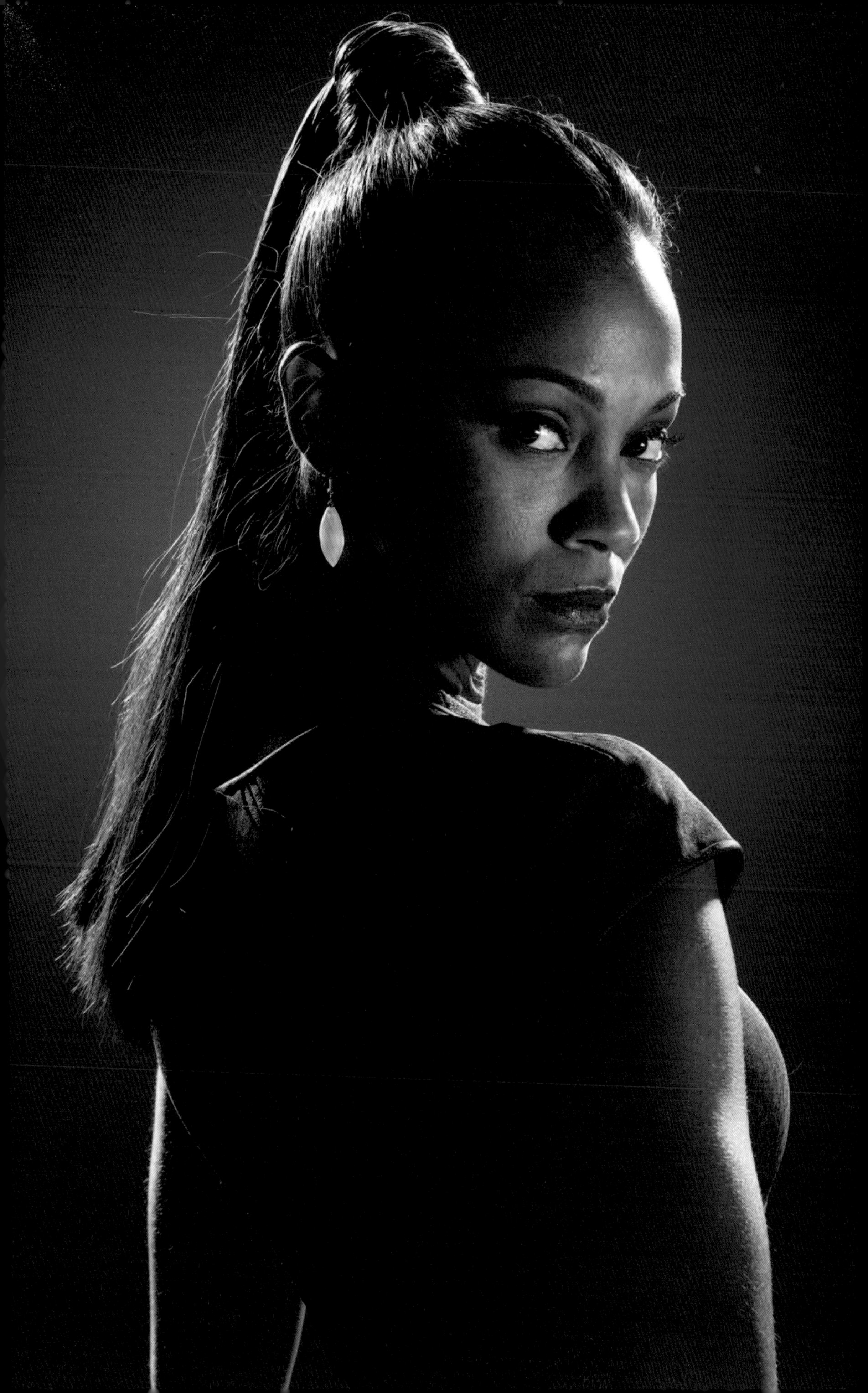

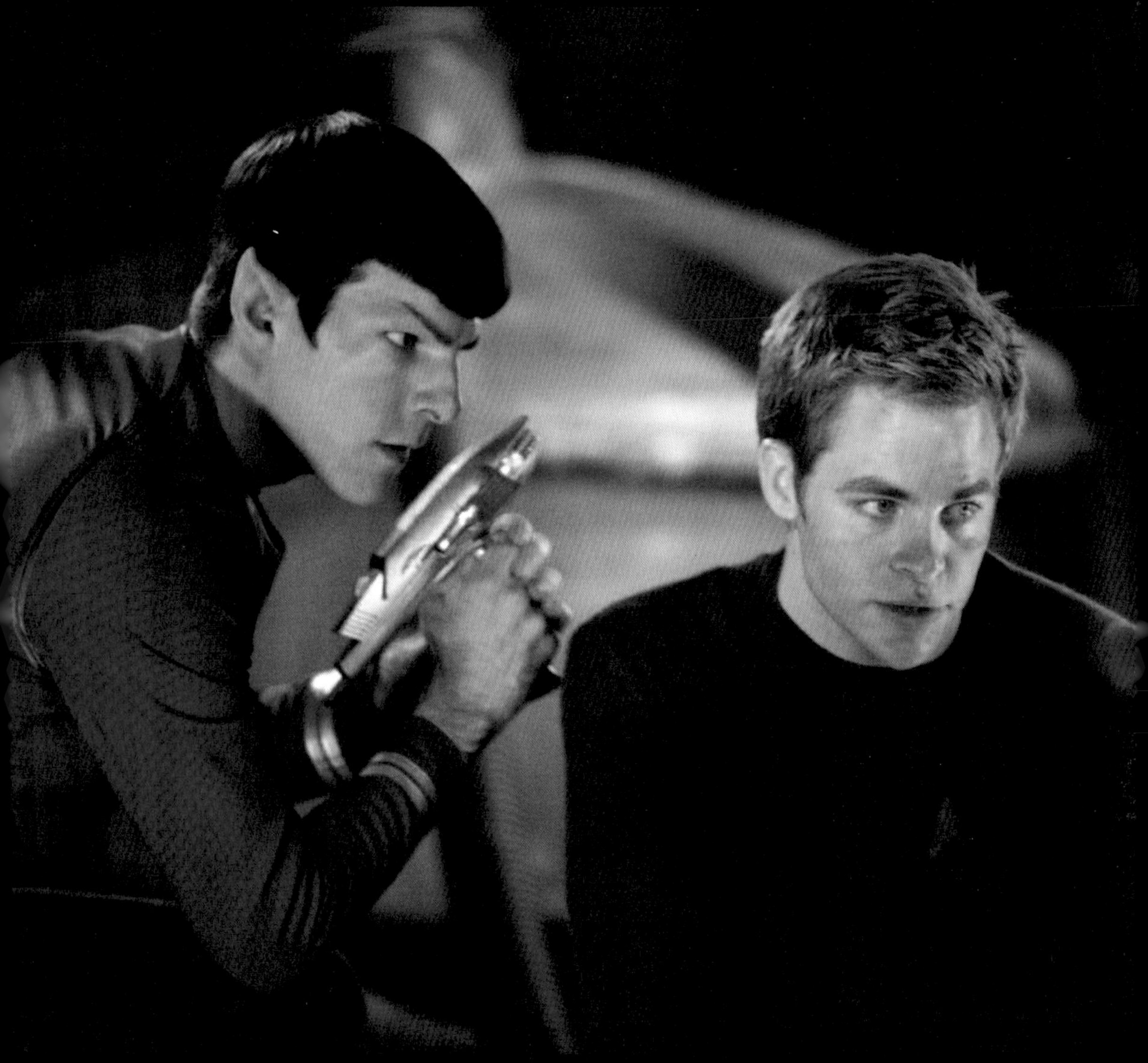

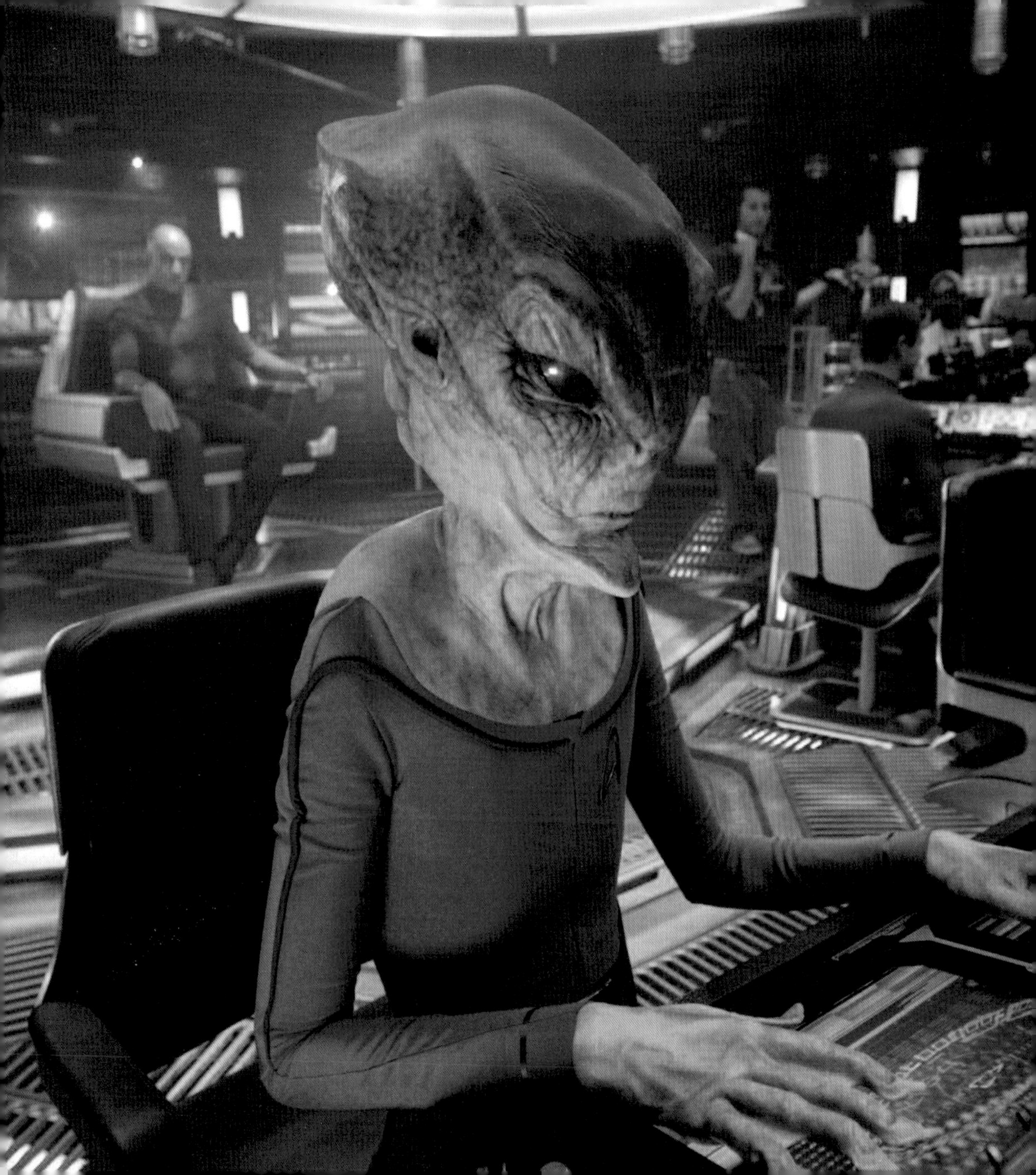

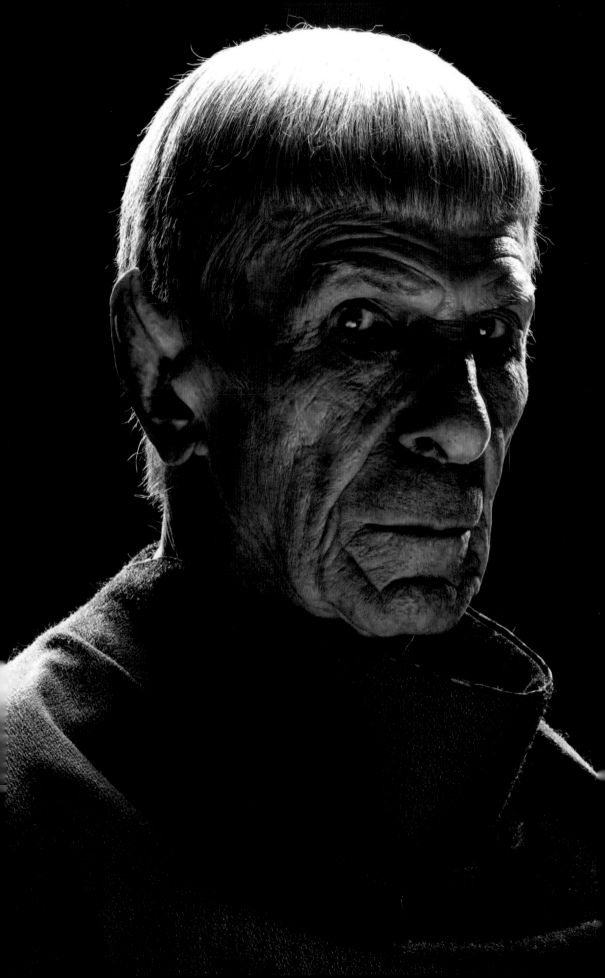

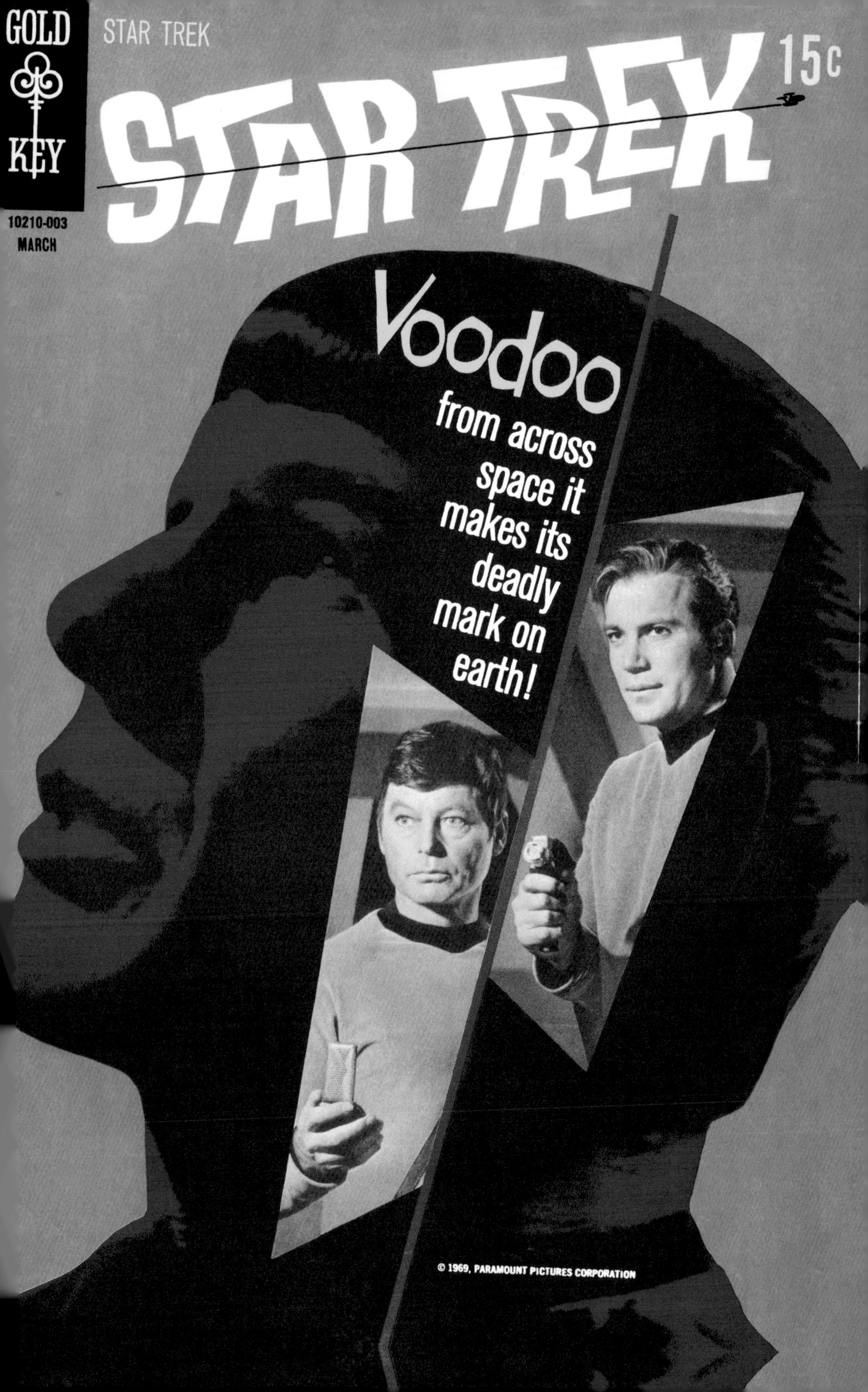
GOLD KEY
STAR TREK
15c
STAR TREK
10210-003
MARCH
Voodoo
from across space it makes its deadly mark on earth!
© 1969, PARAMOUNT PICTURES CORPORATION

STAR TREK #7 (Gold Key)

THE VOODOO PLANET

The *Enterprise* crew encountered individuals with incredible powers of the mind and apparent supernatural abilities on more than one occasion during the TV series (in episodes such as *Catspaw* and *Plato's Stepchildren*), but in issue #7 of the Gold Key comic from March 1970, they faced what might be one of their most 'way-out' adventures on an entire planet dedicated to sympathetic 'voodoo' magic!

Writer Dick Wood plays fast and loose with the tropes of *STAR TREK* once more and here Kirk and Spock find themselves up against a monocle-wearing dictator who fled Earth (shades of Khan Noonien Singh) to craft another world into an exact duplicate, complete with fake cities and landmarks made from...papier maché! Using occult secrets learned from the natives, he strikes at Earth's major cities and uses voodoo dolls of Kirk and Spock to take them prisoner. Rescued by Doctor McCoy, they return to the *Enterprise,* where Spock reveals that not only did the ancient Vulcans practise their own form of voodoo, but that he also has a library of occult books from which to duplicate their spells and potions. Fighting fire with fire, the *Enterprise* crew are victorious... even if their solution strains the credibility of even the most generous reader!

Wood's story is worth the ride, however, if only for the crazy, hokey twists of it – and while artist Alberto Giolitti wasn't always accurate with his depiction of the interiors of the *U.S.S. Enterprise* or Starfleet's technology, he was known for his scrupulous attention to detail with reference models and photographs – which can clearly be seen in *The Voodoo Planet* with its representations of Earth locations such as Paris's Eiffel Tower, the Sphinx of Egypt, or the Colosseum of Rome and the Leaning Tower of Pisa from Giolitti's native Italy.

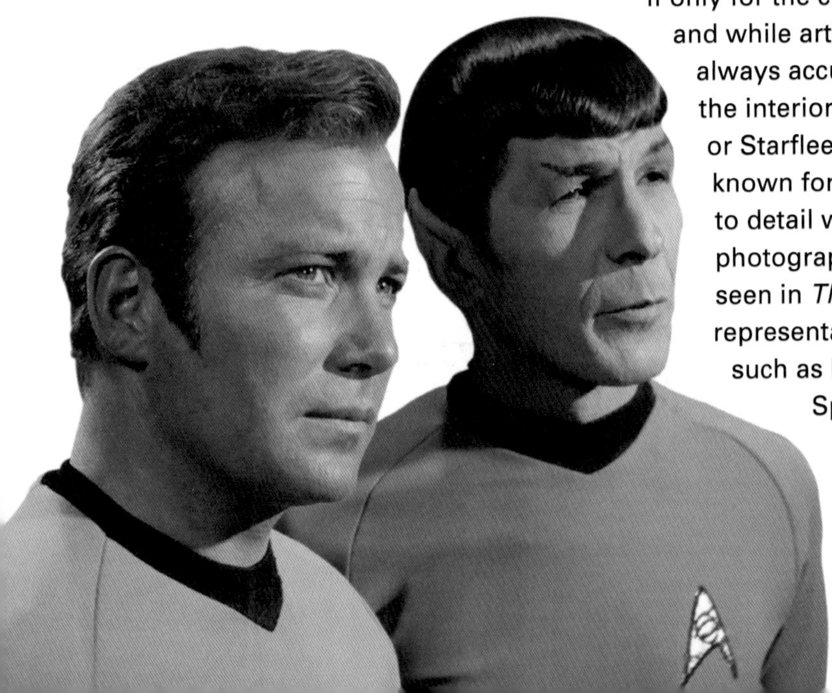

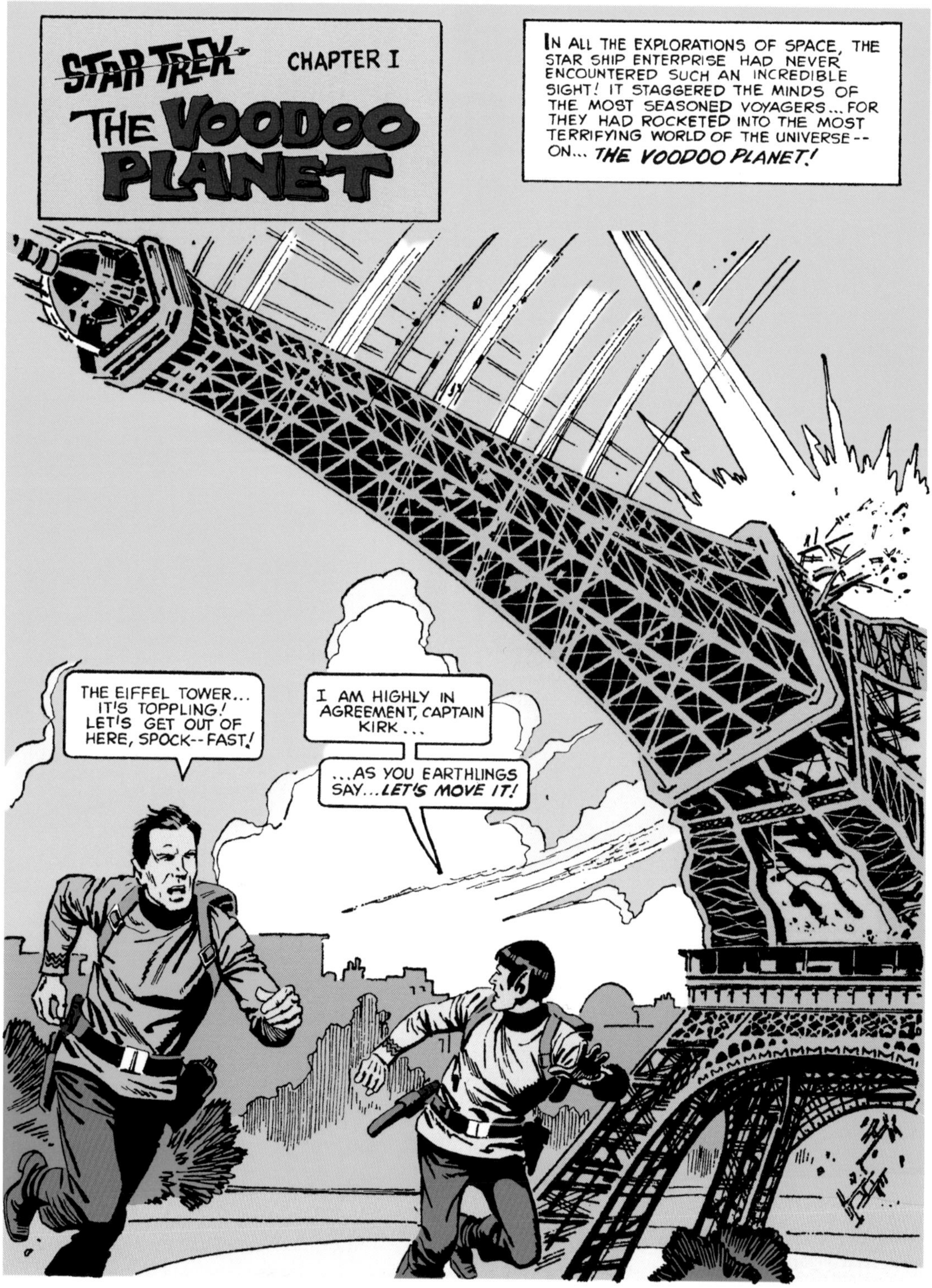
STAR TREK CHAPTER I
THE VOODOO PLANET
IN ALL THE EXPLORATIONS OF SPACE, THE STAR SHIP ENTERPRISE HAD NEVER ENCOUNTERED SUCH AN INCREDIBLE SIGHT! IT STAGGERED THE MINDS OF THE MOST SEASONED VOYAGERS... FOR THEY HAD ROCKETED INTO THE MOST TERRIFYING WORLD OF THE UNIVERSE-- ON... THE VOODOO PLANET!
THE EIFFEL TOWER... IT'S TOPPLING! LET'S GET OUT OF HERE, SPOCK--FAST!
I AM HIGHLY IN AGREEMENT, CAPTAIN KIRK...
...AS YOU EARTHLINGS SAY... LET'S MOVE IT!

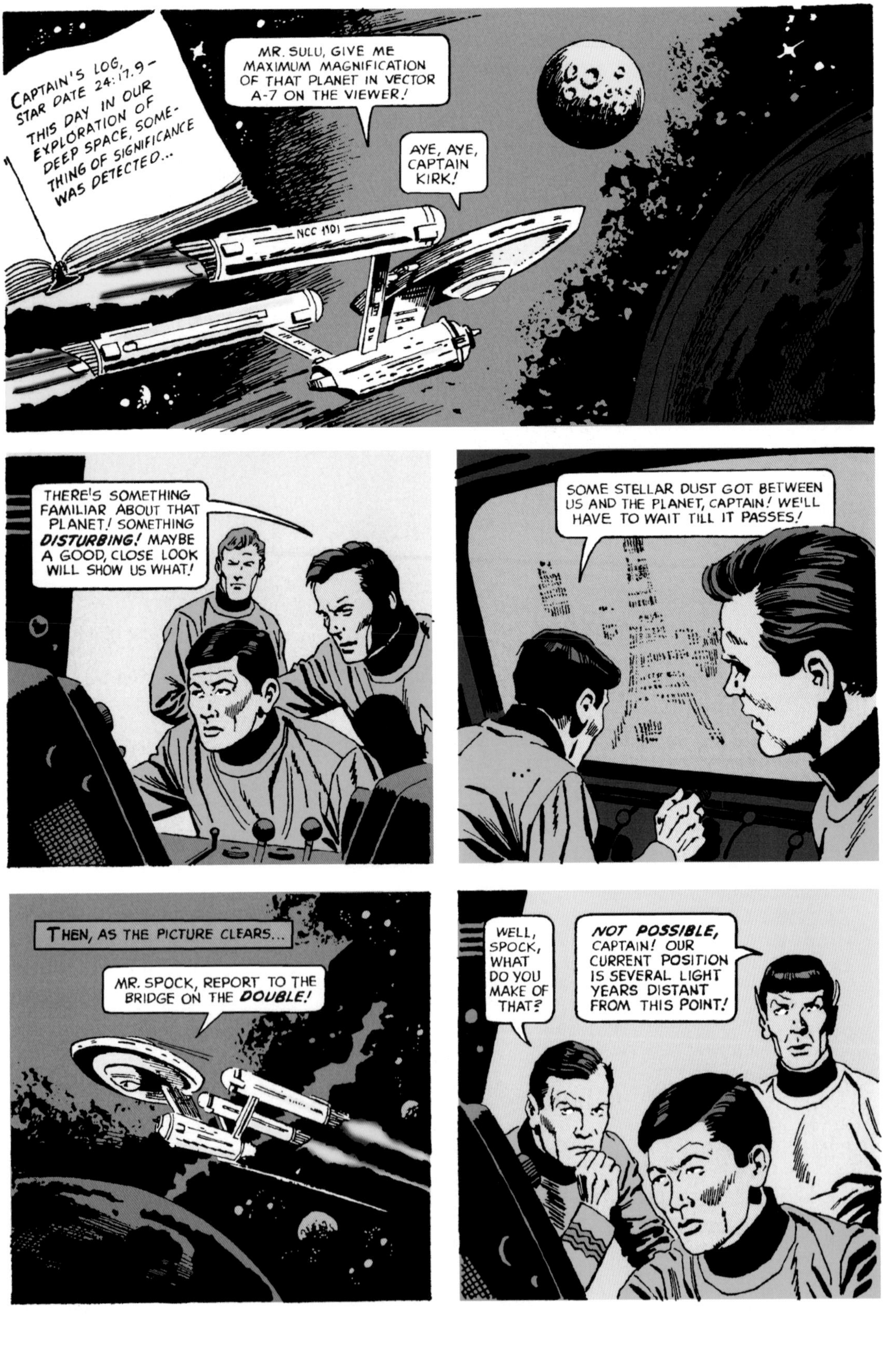
CAPTAIN'S LOG, STAR DATE 24:17.9 - THIS DAY IN OUR EXPLORATION OF DEEP SPACE, SOMETHING OF SIGNIFICANCE WAS DETECTED...
MR. SULU, GIVE ME MAXIMUM MAGNIFICATION OF THAT PLANET IN VECTOR A-7 ON THE VIEWER!
AYE, AYE, CAPTAIN KIRK!
NCC 1701
THERE'S SOMETHING FAMILIAR ABOUT THAT PLANET! SOMETHING DISTURBING! MAYBE A GOOD, CLOSE LOOK WILL SHOW US WHAT!
SOME STELLAR DUST GOT BETWEEN US AND THE PLANET, CAPTAIN! WE'LL HAVE TO WAIT TILL IT PASSES!
THEN, AS THE PICTURE CLEARS...
MR. SPOCK, REPORT TO THE BRIDGE ON THE DOUBLE!
WELL, SPOCK, WHAT DO YOU MAKE OF THAT?
NOT POSSIBLE, CAPTAIN! OUR CURRENT POSITION IS SEVERAL LIGHT YEARS DISTANT FROM THIS POINT!

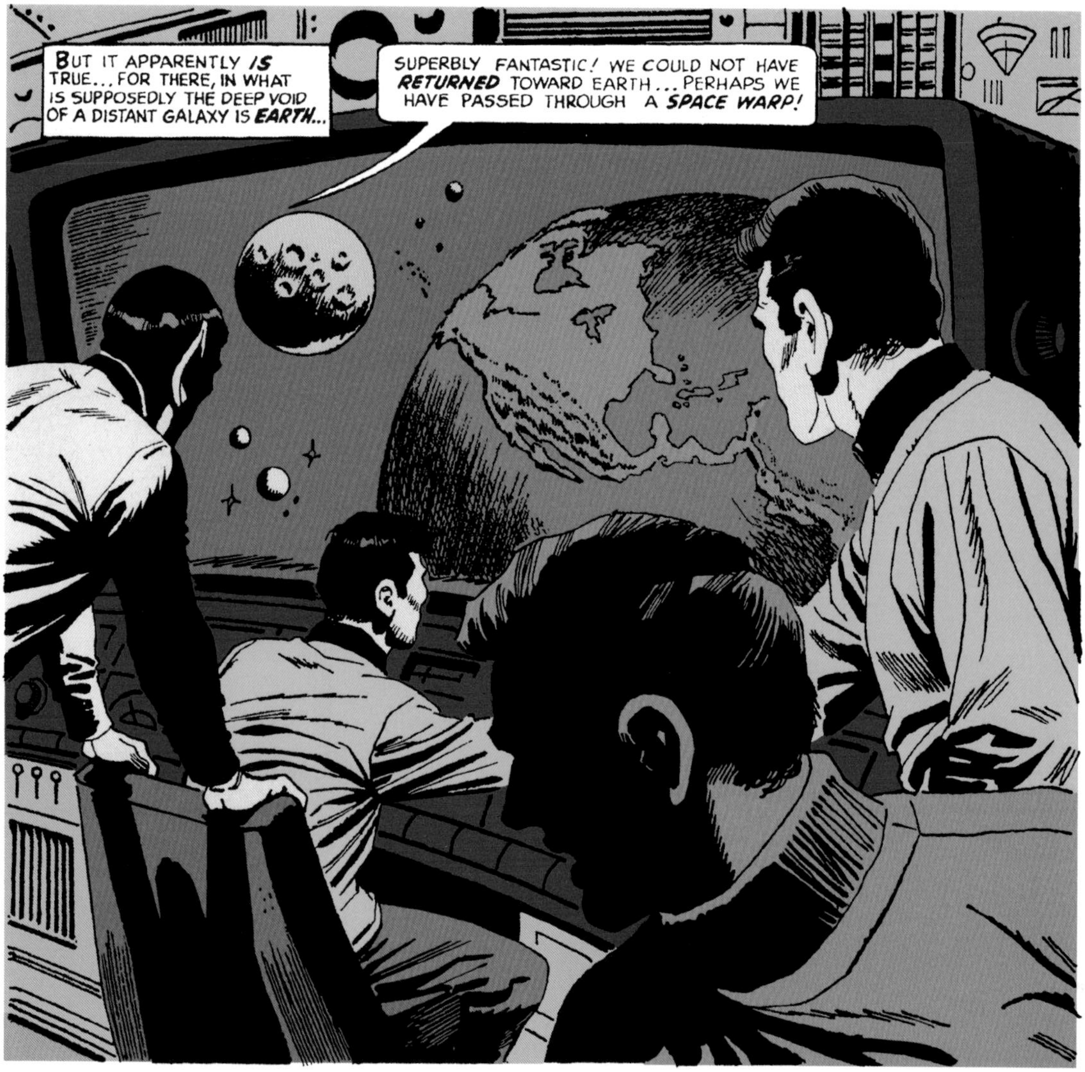
BUT IT APPARENTLY IS TRUE... FOR THERE, IN WHAT IS SUPPOSEDLY THE DEEP VOID OF A DISTANT GALAXY IS EARTH...
SUPERBLY FANTASTIC! WE COULD NOT HAVE RETURNED TOWARD EARTH... PERHAPS WE HAVE PASSED THROUGH A SPACE WARP!

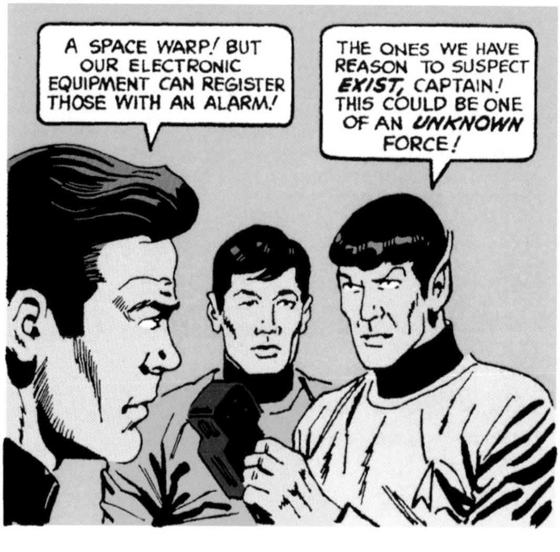
A SPACE WARP! BUT OUR ELECTRONIC EQUIPMENT CAN REGISTER THOSE WITH AN ALARM!
THE ONES WE HAVE REASON TO SUSPECT EXIST, CAPTAIN! THIS COULD BE ONE OF AN UNKNOWN FORCE!

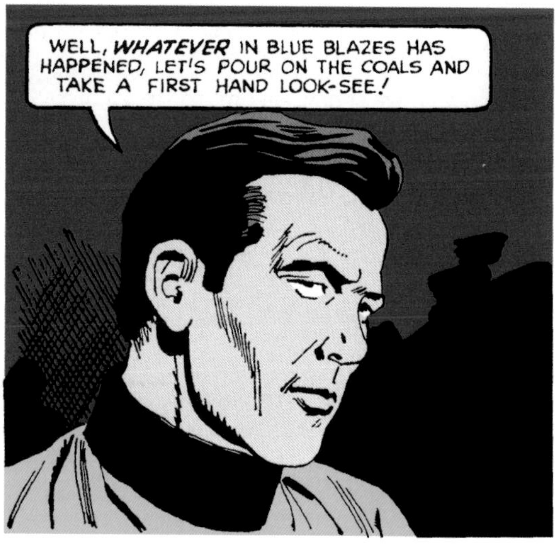
WELL, WHATEVER IN BLUE BLAZES HAS HAPPENED, LET'S POUR ON THE COALS AND TAKE A FIRST HAND LOOK-SEE!

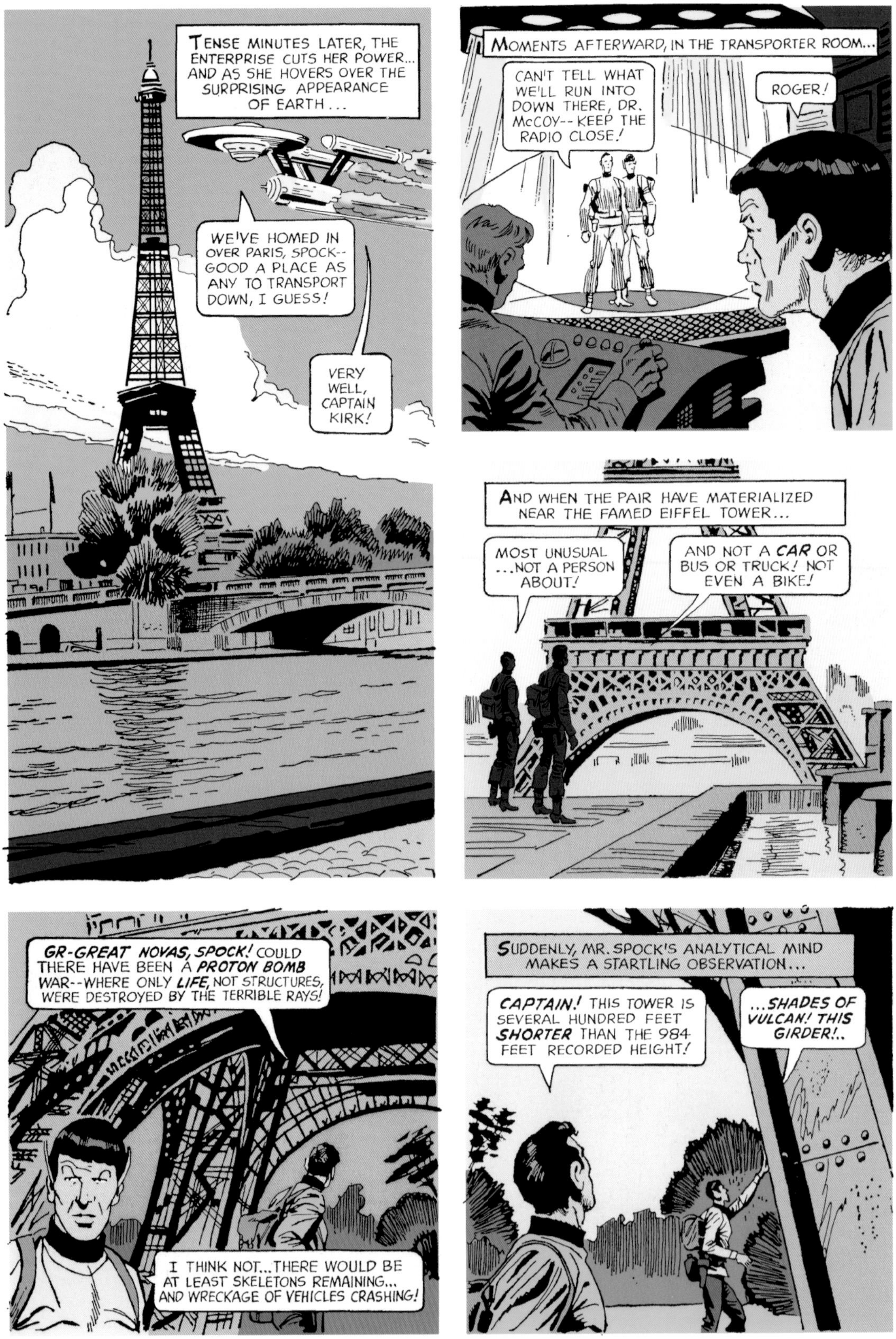
TENSE MINUTES LATER, THE ENTERPRISE CUTS HER POWER... AND AS SHE HOVERS OVER THE SURPRISING APPEARANCE OF EARTH...
WE'VE HOMED IN OVER PARIS, SPOCK-- GOOD A PLACE AS ANY TO TRANSPORT DOWN, I GUESS!
VERY WELL, CAPTAIN KIRK!
MOMENTS AFTERWARD, IN THE TRANSPORTER ROOM...
CAN'T TELL WHAT WE'LL RUN INTO DOWN THERE, DR. McCOY-- KEEP THE RADIO CLOSE!
ROGER!
AND WHEN THE PAIR HAVE MATERIALIZED NEAR THE FAMED EIFFEL TOWER...
MOST UNUSUAL ...NOT A PERSON ABOUT!
AND NOT A CAR OR BUS OR TRUCK! NOT EVEN A BIKE!
GR-GREAT NOVAS, SPOCK! COULD THERE HAVE BEEN A PROTON BOMB WAR--WHERE ONLY LIFE, NOT STRUCTURES, WERE DESTROYED BY THE TERRIBLE RAYS!
I THINK NOT...THERE WOULD BE AT LEAST SKELETONS REMAINING... AND WRECKAGE OF VEHICLES CRASHING!
SUDDENLY, MR. SPOCK'S ANALYTICAL MIND MAKES A STARTLING OBSERVATION...
CAPTAIN! THIS TOWER IS SEVERAL HUNDRED FEET SHORTER THAN THE 984 FEET RECORDED HEIGHT!
...SHADES OF VULCAN! THIS GIRDER!..

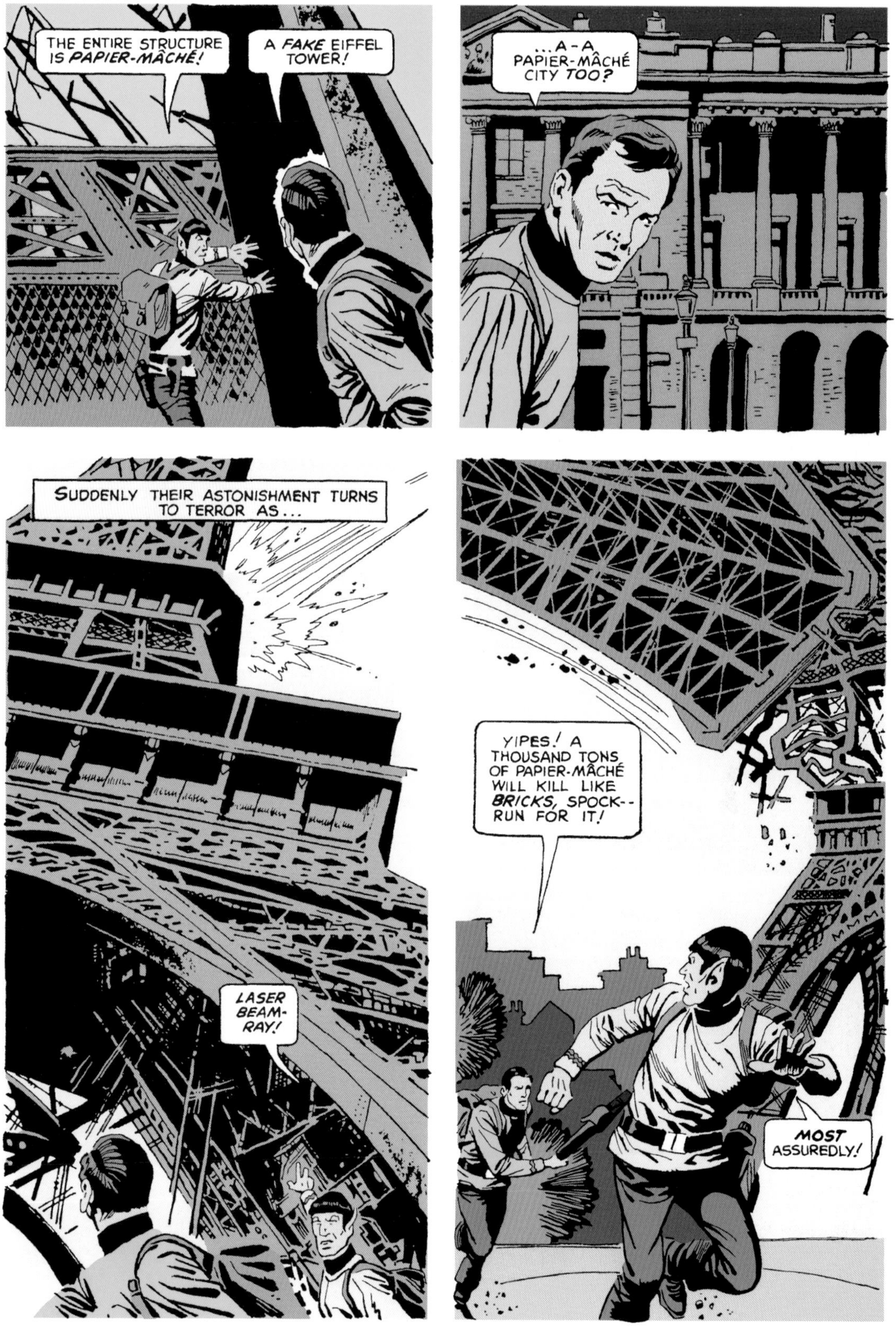
THE ENTIRE STRUCTURE IS PAPIER-MÂCHÉ!
A FAKE EIFFEL TOWER!
...A-A PAPIER-MÂCHÉ CITY TOO?
SUDDENLY THEIR ASTONISHMENT TURNS TO TERROR AS...
LASER BEAM-RAY!
YIPES! A THOUSAND TONS OF PAPIER-MÂCHÉ WILL KILL LIKE BRICKS, SPOCK--RUN FOR IT!
MOST ASSUREDLY!

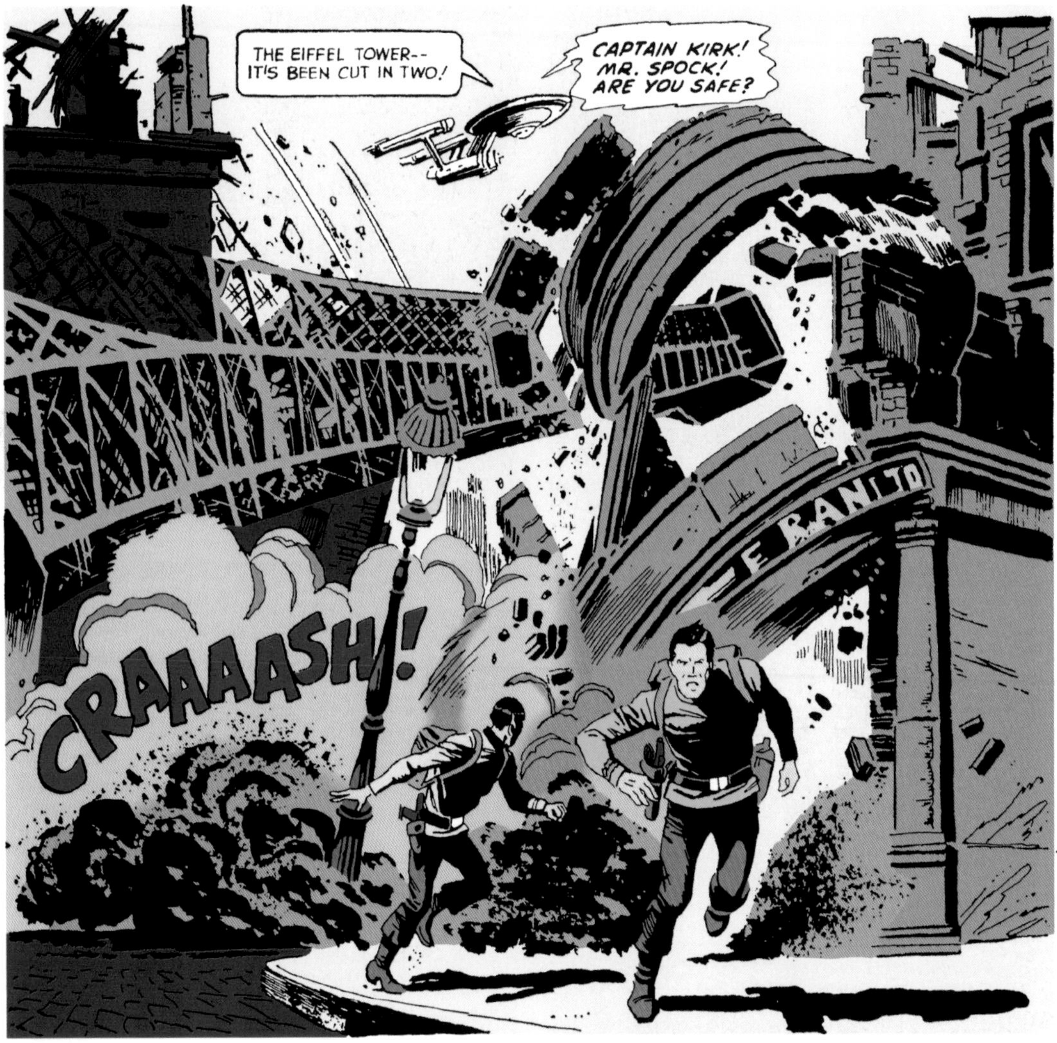
THE EIFFEL TOWER-- IT'S BEEN CUT IN TWO!
CAPTAIN KIRK! MR. SPOCK! ARE YOU SAFE?
CRAAAASH!

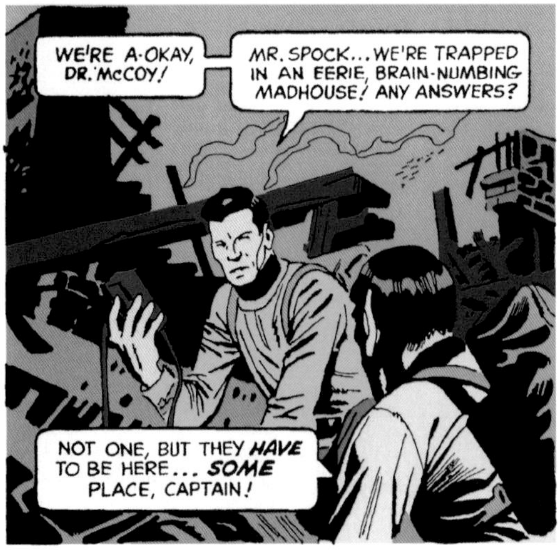
WE'RE A-OKAY, DR. McCOY!
MR. SPOCK... WE'RE TRAPPED IN AN EERIE, BRAIN-NUMBING MADHOUSE! ANY ANSWERS?
NOT ONE, BUT THEY HAVE TO BE HERE... SOME PLACE, CAPTAIN!

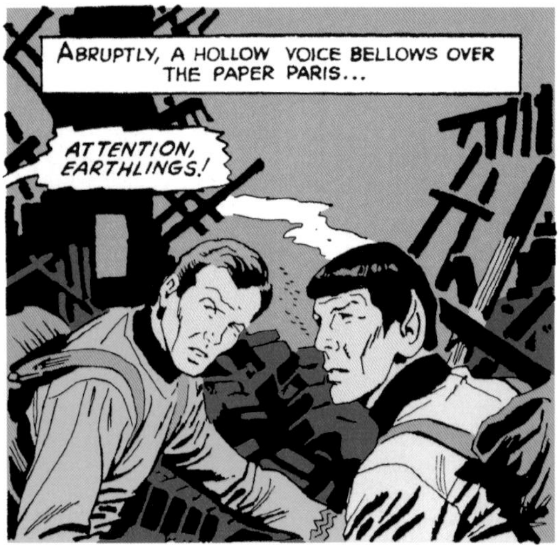
ABRUPTLY, A HOLLOW VOICE BELLOWS OVER THE PAPER PARIS...
ATTENTION, EARTHLINGS!

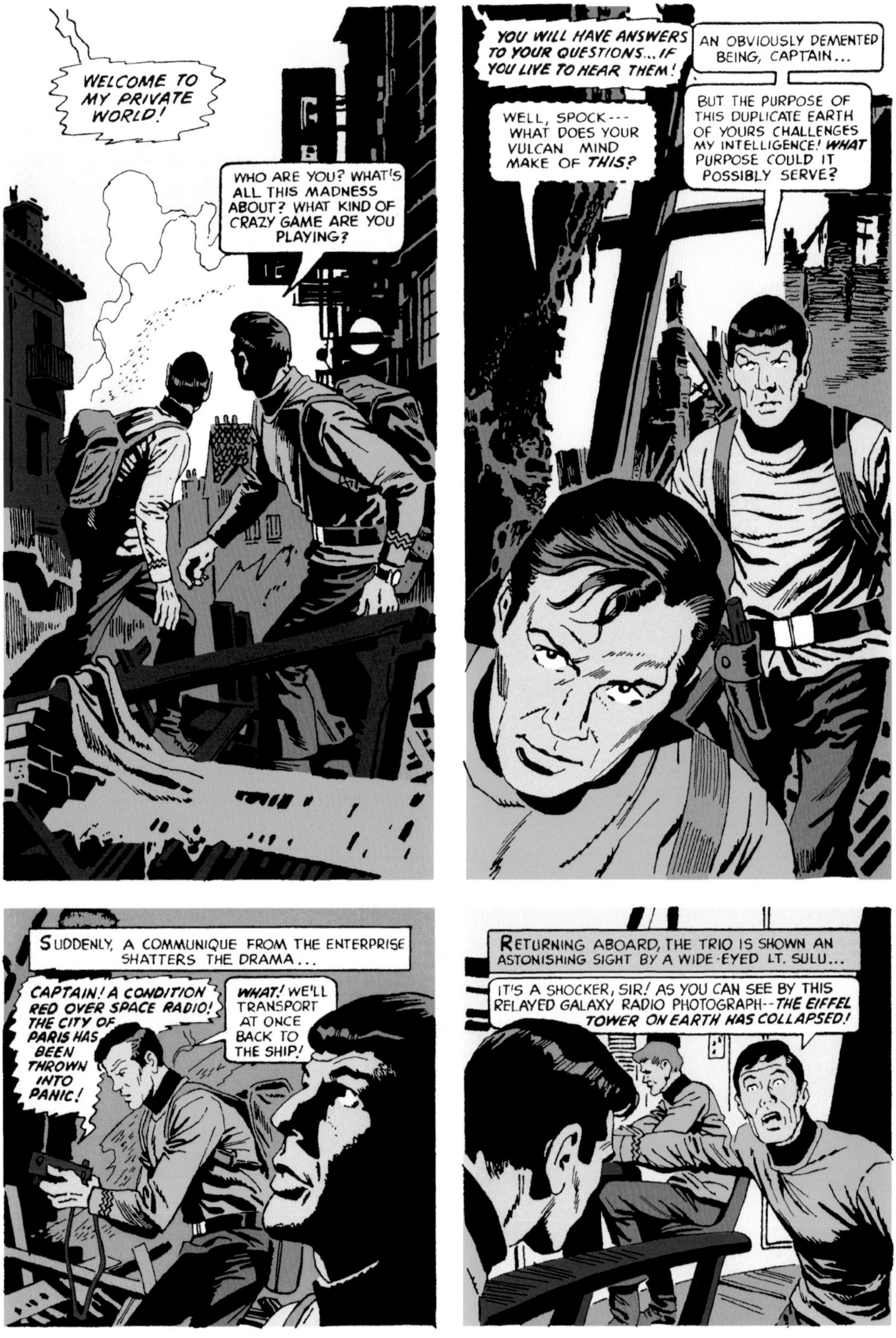
WELCOME TO MY PRIVATE WORLD!
WHO ARE YOU? WHAT'S ALL THIS MADNESS ABOUT? WHAT KIND OF CRAZY GAME ARE YOU PLAYING?
YOU WILL HAVE ANSWERS TO YOUR QUESTIONS... IF YOU LIVE TO HEAR THEM!
WELL, SPOCK--- WHAT DOES YOUR VULCAN MIND MAKE OF THIS?
AN OBVIOUSLY DEMENTED BEING, CAPTAIN...
BUT THE PURPOSE OF THIS DUPLICATE EARTH OF YOURS CHALLENGES MY INTELLIGENCE! WHAT PURPOSE COULD IT POSSIBLY SERVE?
SUDDENLY, A COMMUNIQUE FROM THE ENTERPRISE SHATTERS THE DRAMA...
CAPTAIN! A CONDITION RED OVER SPACE RADIO! THE CITY OF PARIS HAS BEEN THROWN INTO PANIC!
WHAT! WE'LL TRANSPORT AT ONCE BACK TO THE SHIP!
RETURNING ABOARD, THE TRIO IS SHOWN AN ASTONISHING SIGHT BY A WIDE-EYED LT. SULU...
IT'S A SHOCKER, SIR! AS YOU CAN SEE BY THIS RELAYED GALAXY RADIO PHOTOGRAPH--THE EIFFEL TOWER ON EARTH HAS COLLAPSED!

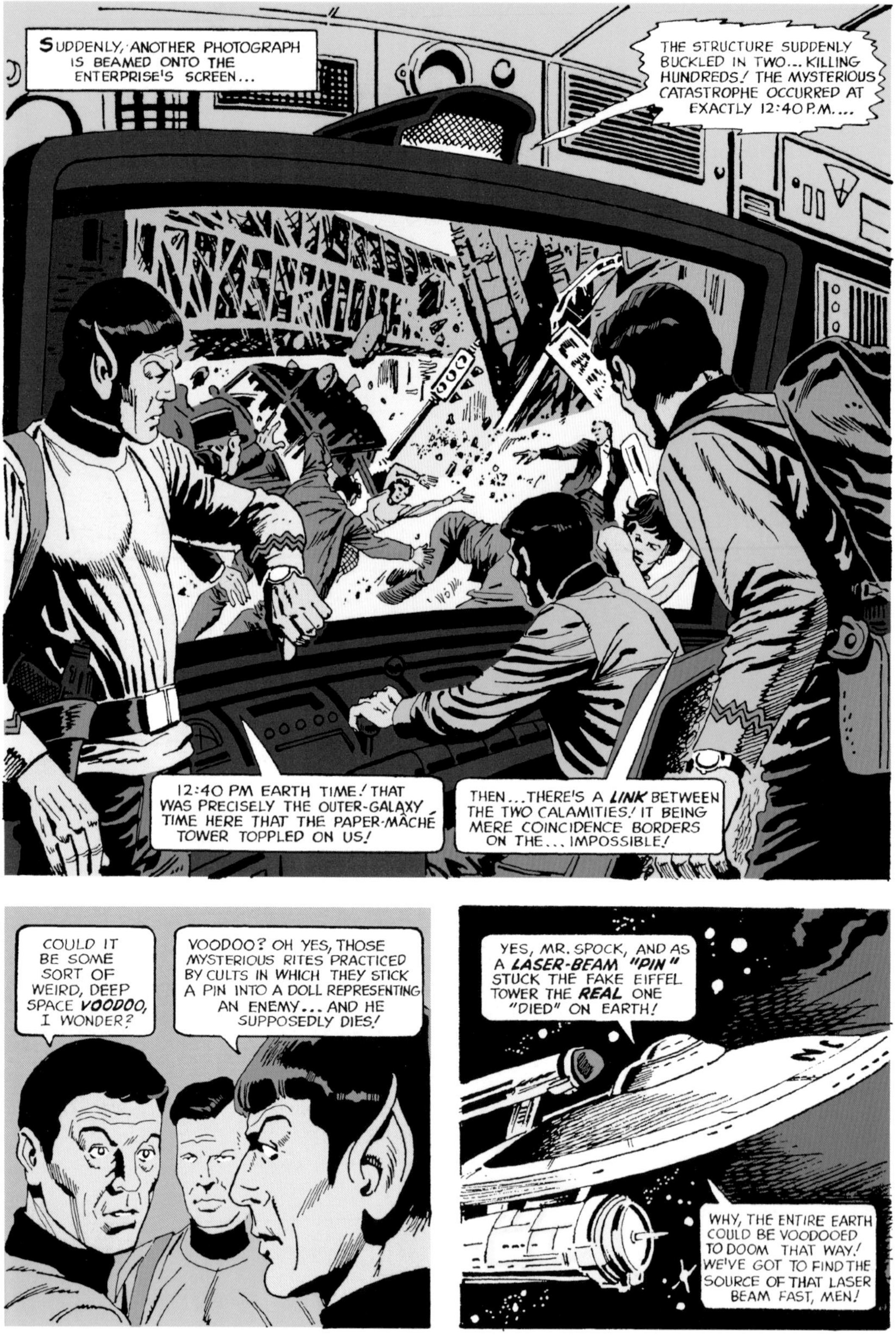
SUDDENLY, ANOTHER PHOTOGRAPH IS BEAMED ONTO THE ENTERPRISE'S SCREEN...
THE STRUCTURE SUDDENLY BUCKLED IN TWO... KILLING HUNDREDS! THE MYSTERIOUS CATASTROPHE OCCURRED AT EXACTLY 12:40 P.M....
12:40 PM EARTH TIME! THAT WAS PRECISELY THE OUTER-GALAXY TIME HERE THAT THE PAPER-MÂCHÉ TOWER TOPPLED ON US!
THEN... THERE'S A **LINK** BETWEEN THE TWO CALAMITIES! IT BEING MERE COINCIDENCE BORDERS ON THE... IMPOSSIBLE!
COULD IT BE SOME SORT OF WEIRD, DEEP SPACE **VOODOO**, I WONDER?
VOODOO? OH YES, THOSE MYSTERIOUS RITES PRACTICED BY CULTS IN WHICH THEY STICK A PIN INTO A DOLL REPRESENTING AN ENEMY... AND HE SUPPOSEDLY DIES!
YES, MR. SPOCK, AND AS A **LASER-BEAM "PIN"** STUCK THE FAKE EIFFEL TOWER THE **REAL** ONE "DIED" ON EARTH!
WHY, THE ENTIRE EARTH COULD BE VOODOOED TO DOOM THAT WAY! WE'VE GOT TO FIND THE SOURCE OF THAT LASER BEAM FAST, MEN!

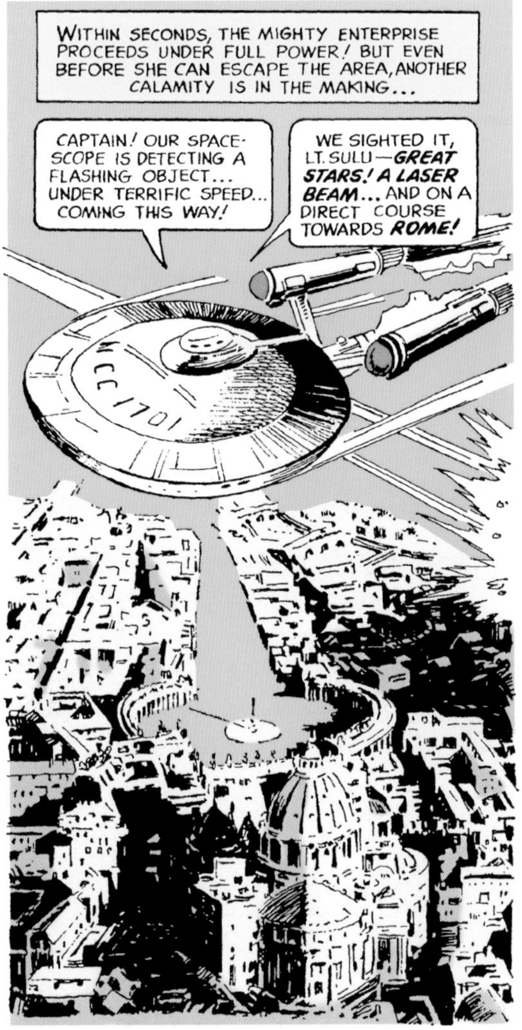
WITHIN SECONDS, THE MIGHTY ENTERPRISE PROCEEDS UNDER FULL POWER! BUT EVEN BEFORE SHE CAN ESCAPE THE AREA, ANOTHER CALAMITY IS IN THE MAKING...
CAPTAIN! OUR SPACE-SCOPE IS DETECTING A FLASHING OBJECT... UNDER TERRIFIC SPEED... COMING THIS WAY!
WE SIGHTED IT, LT. SULU—GREAT STARS! A LASER BEAM... AND ON A DIRECT COURSE TOWARDS ROME!
NCC 1701

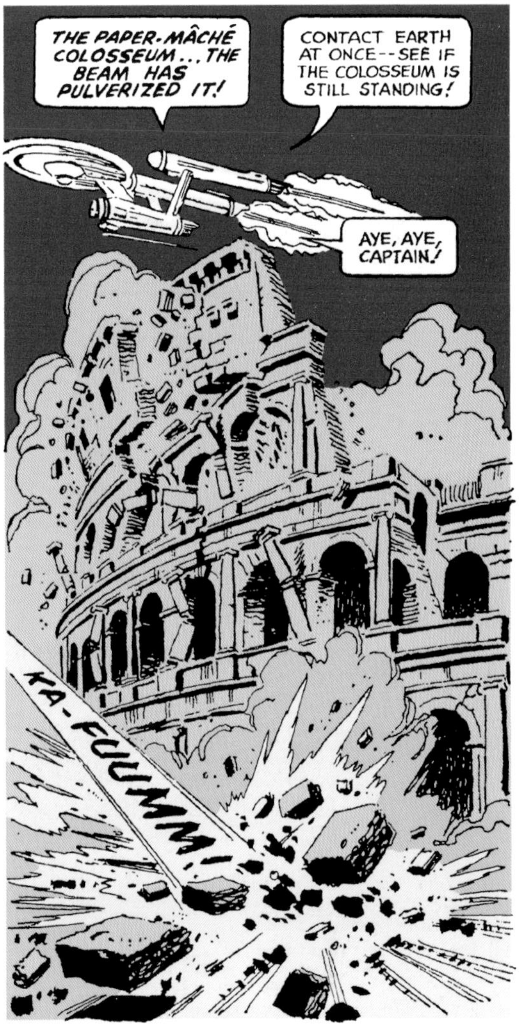
THE PAPER-MÂCHÉ COLOSSEUM... THE BEAM HAS PULVERIZED IT!
CONTACT EARTH AT ONCE--SEE IF THE COLOSSEUM IS STILL STANDING!
AYE, AYE, CAPTAIN!
KA-FUUMM!

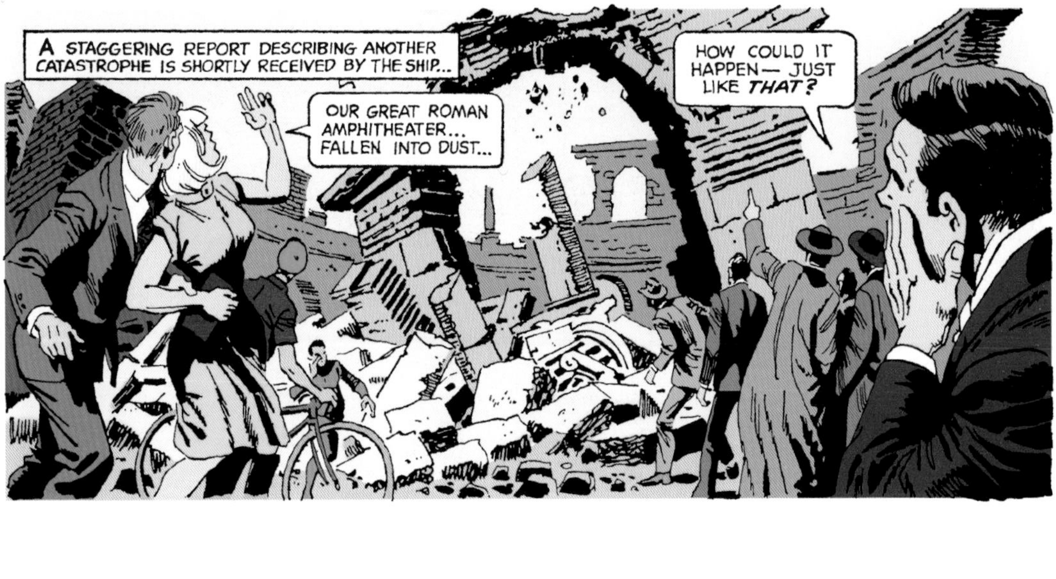
A STAGGERING REPORT DESCRIBING ANOTHER CATASTROPHE IS SHORTLY RECEIVED BY THE SHIP...
OUR GREAT ROMAN AMPHITHEATER... FALLEN INTO DUST...
HOW COULD IT HAPPEN— JUST LIKE THAT?

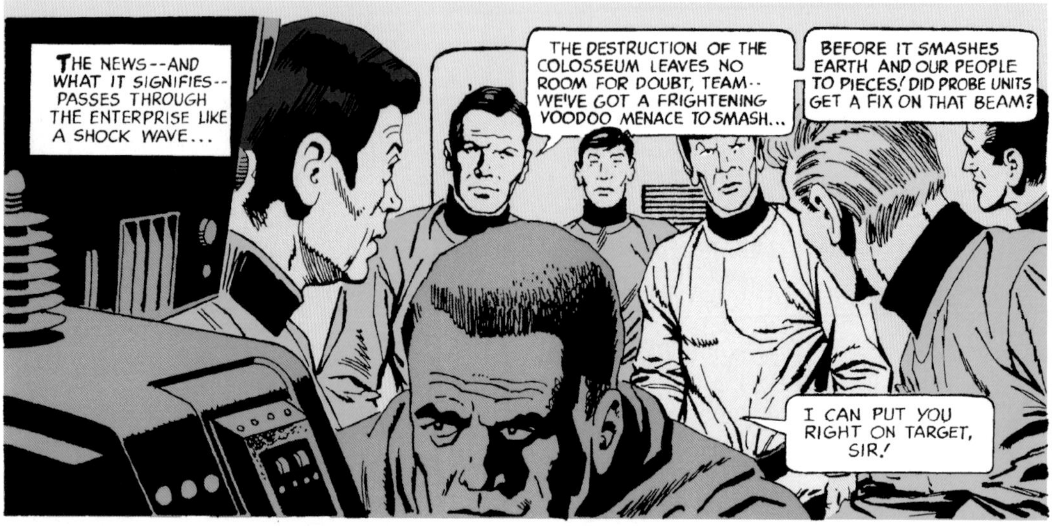
THE NEWS--AND WHAT IT SIGNIFIES--PASSES THROUGH THE ENTERPRISE LIKE A SHOCK WAVE...
THE DESTRUCTION OF THE COLOSSEUM LEAVES NO ROOM FOR DOUBT, TEAM--WE'VE GOT A FRIGHTENING VOODOO MENACE TO SMASH...
BEFORE IT SMASHES EARTH AND OUR PEOPLE TO PIECES! DID PROBE UNITS GET A FIX ON THAT BEAM?
I CAN PUT YOU RIGHT ON TARGET, SIR!

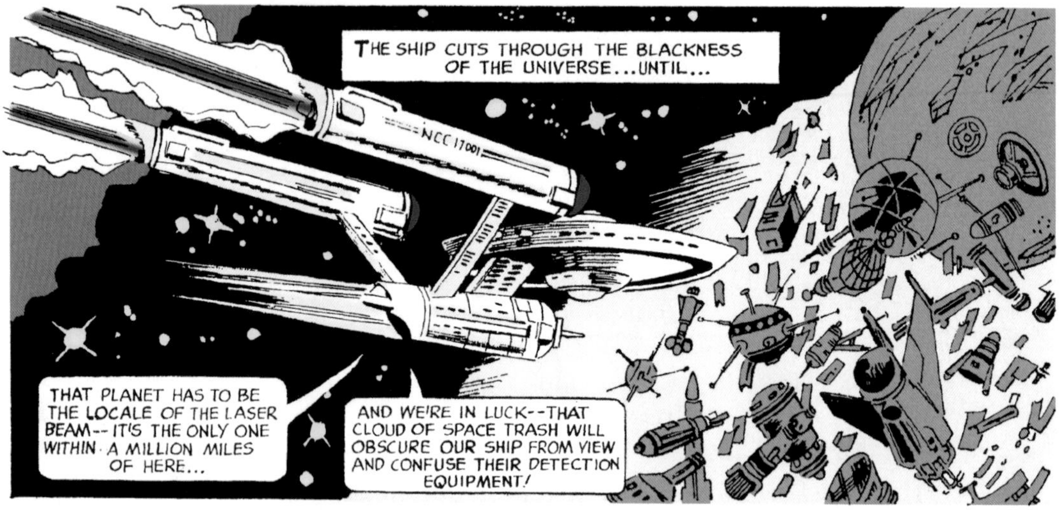
THE SHIP CUTS THROUGH THE BLACKNESS OF THE UNIVERSE...UNTIL...
NCC 1700
THAT PLANET HAS TO BE THE LOCALE OF THE LASER BEAM--IT'S THE ONLY ONE WITHIN A MILLION MILES OF HERE...
AND WE'RE IN LUCK--THAT CLOUD OF SPACE TRASH WILL OBSCURE OUR SHIP FROM VIEW AND CONFUSE THEIR DETECTION EQUIPMENT!

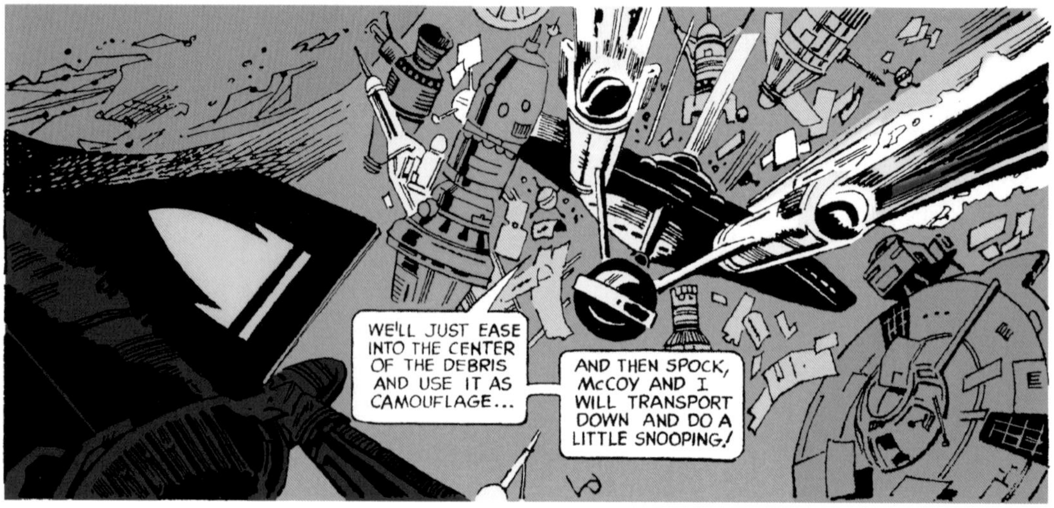
WE'LL JUST EASE INTO THE CENTER OF THE DEBRIS AND USE IT AS CAMOUFLAGE...
AND THEN SPOCK, McCOY AND I WILL TRANSPORT DOWN AND DO A LITTLE SNOOPING!

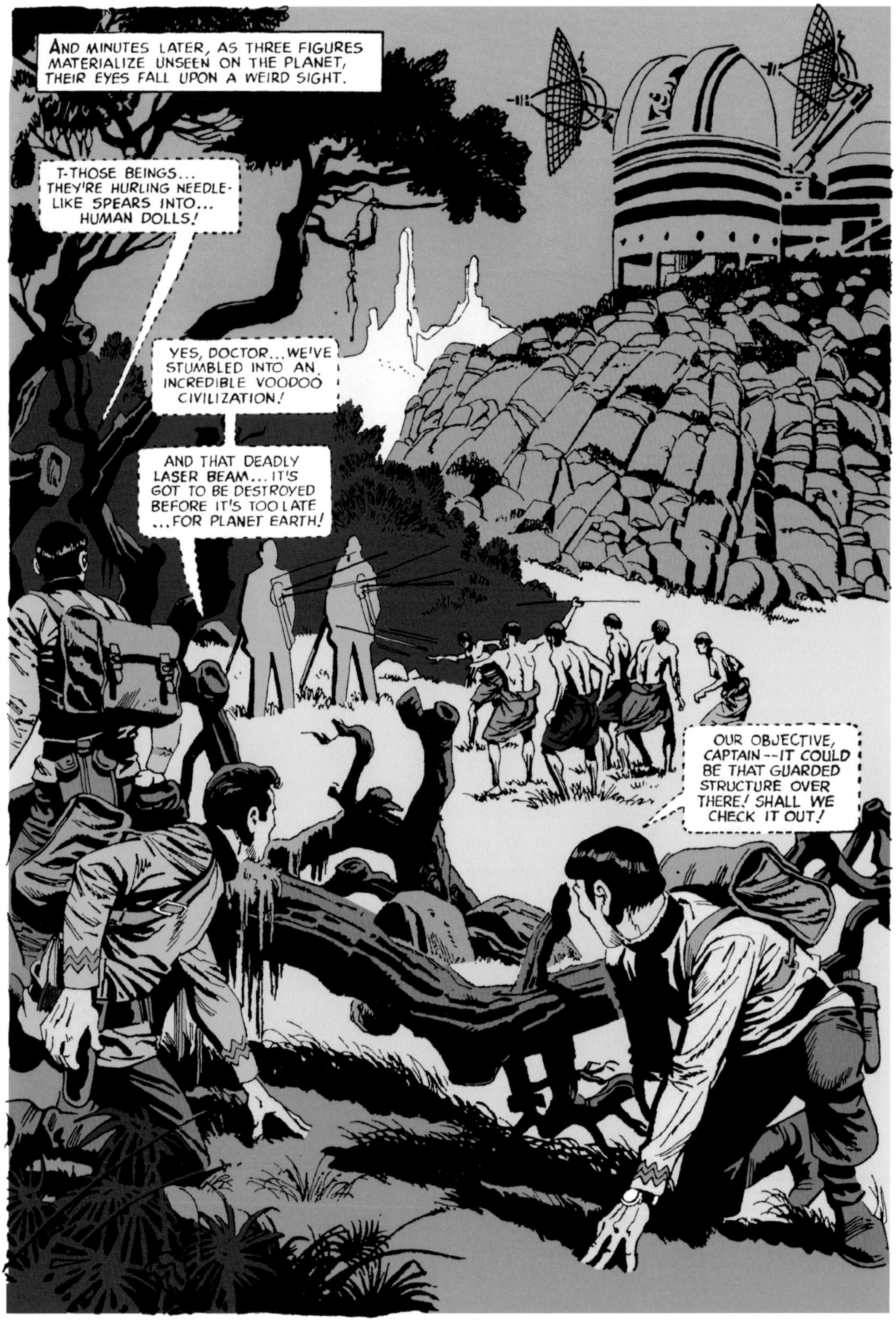
AND MINUTES LATER, AS THREE FIGURES MATERIALIZE UNSEEN ON THE PLANET, THEIR EYES FALL UPON A WEIRD SIGHT.
T-THOSE BEINGS... THEY'RE HURLING NEEDLE-LIKE SPEARS INTO... HUMAN DOLLS!
YES, DOCTOR... WE'VE STUMBLED INTO AN INCREDIBLE VOODOO CIVILIZATION!
AND THAT DEADLY LASER BEAM... IT'S GOT TO BE DESTROYED BEFORE IT'S TOO LATE ...FOR PLANET EARTH!
OUR OBJECTIVE, CAPTAIN--IT COULD BE THAT GUARDED STRUCTURE OVER THERE! SHALL WE CHECK IT OUT!

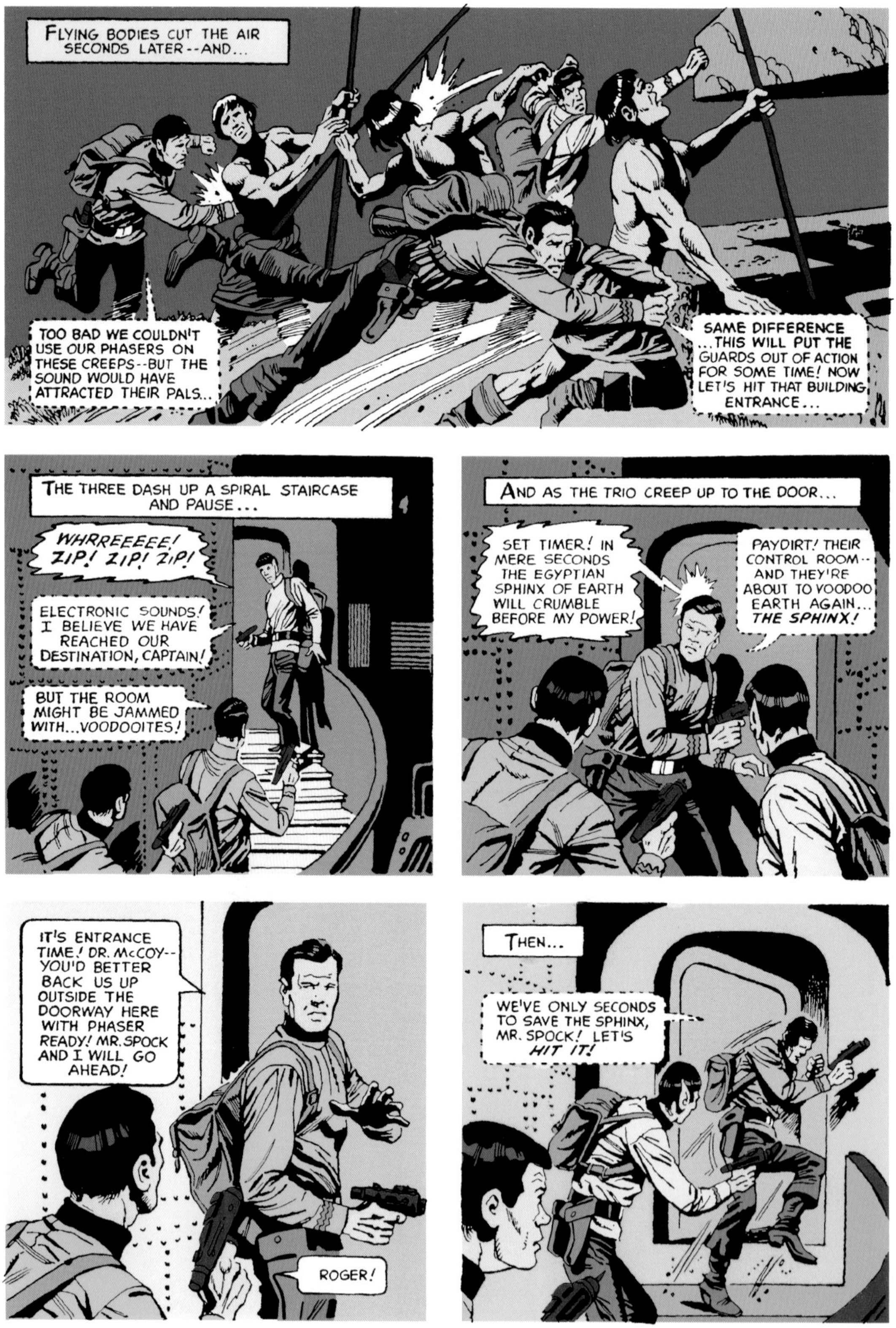
FLYING BODIES CUT THE AIR SECONDS LATER--AND...
TOO BAD WE COULDN'T USE OUR PHASERS ON THESE CREEPS--BUT THE SOUND WOULD HAVE ATTRACTED THEIR PALS...
SAME DIFFERENCE ...THIS WILL PUT THE GUARDS OUT OF ACTION FOR SOME TIME! NOW LET'S HIT THAT BUILDING ENTRANCE...
THE THREE DASH UP A SPIRAL STAIRCASE AND PAUSE...
WHRREEEEEE! ZIP! ZIP! ZIP!
ELECTRONIC SOUNDS! I BELIEVE WE HAVE REACHED OUR DESTINATION, CAPTAIN!
BUT THE ROOM MIGHT BE JAMMED WITH...VOODOOITES!
AND AS THE TRIO CREEP UP TO THE DOOR...
SET TIMER! IN MERE SECONDS THE EGYPTIAN SPHINX OF EARTH WILL CRUMBLE BEFORE MY POWER!
PAYDIRT! THEIR CONTROL ROOM--AND THEY'RE ABOUT TO VOODOO EARTH AGAIN... THE SPHINX!
IT'S ENTRANCE TIME! DR. McCOY--YOU'D BETTER BACK US UP OUTSIDE THE DOORWAY HERE WITH PHASER READY! MR. SPOCK AND I WILL GO AHEAD!
ROGER!
THEN...
WE'VE ONLY SECONDS TO SAVE THE SPHINX, MR. SPOCK! LET'S HIT IT!

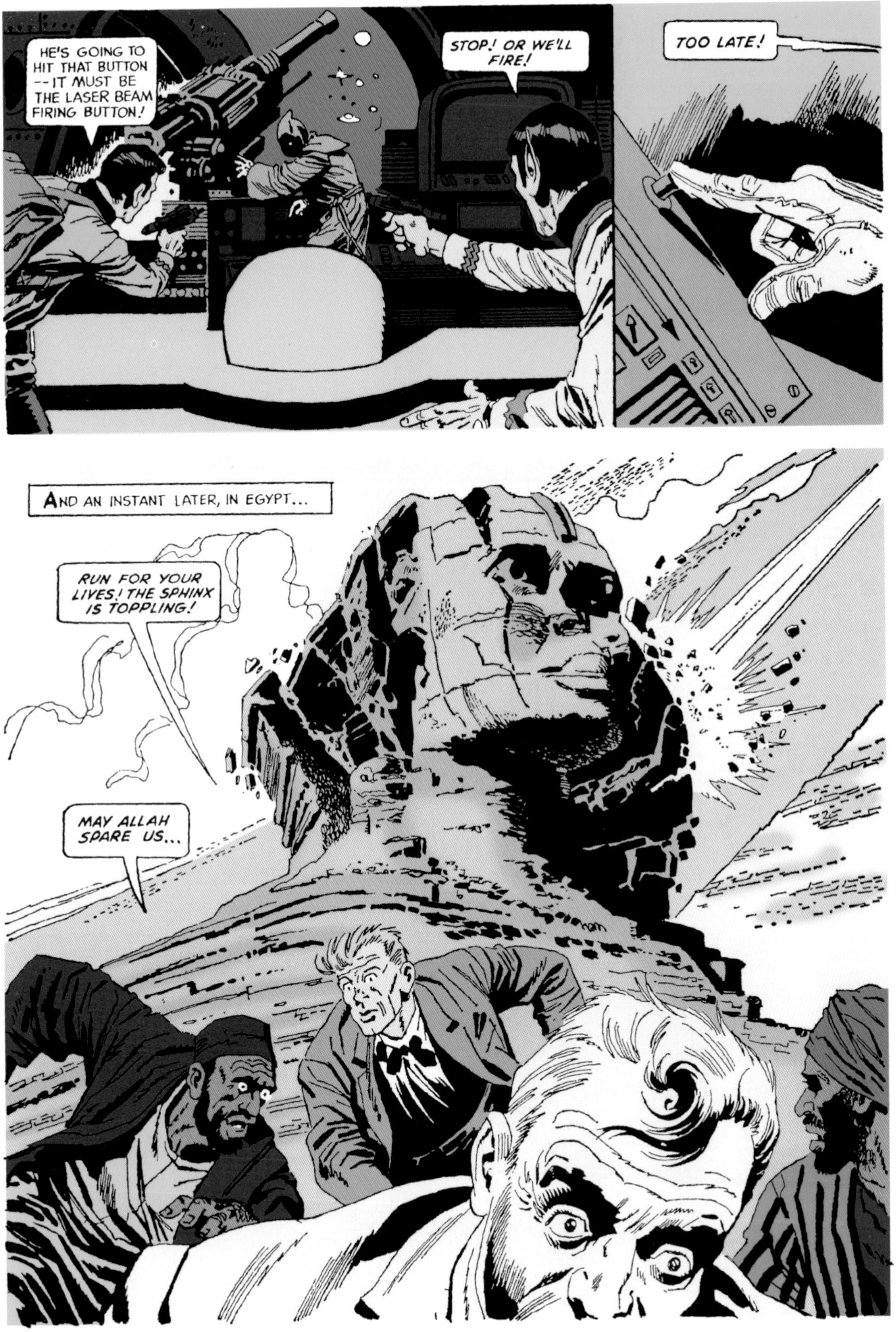
HE'S GOING TO HIT THAT BUTTON --IT MUST BE THE LASER BEAM FIRING BUTTON!
STOP! OR WE'LL FIRE!
TOO LATE!
AND AN INSTANT LATER, IN EGYPT...
RUN FOR YOUR LIVES! THE SPHINX IS TOPPLING!
MAY ALLAH SPARE US...

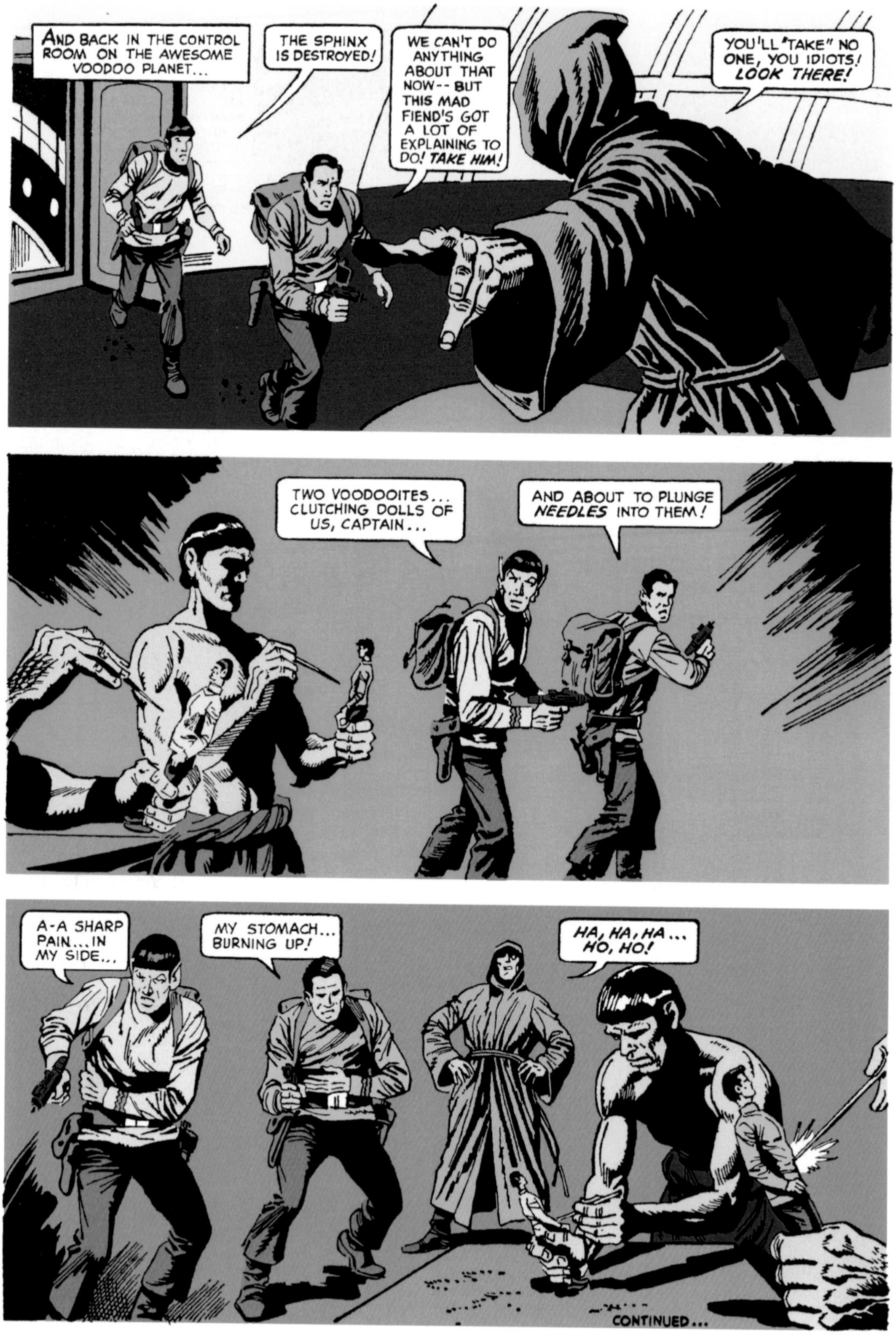
AND BACK IN THE CONTROL ROOM ON THE AWESOME VOODOO PLANET...
THE SPHINX IS DESTROYED!
WE CAN'T DO ANYTHING ABOUT THAT NOW-- BUT THIS MAD FIEND'S GOT A LOT OF EXPLAINING TO DO! TAKE HIM!
YOU'LL "TAKE" NO ONE, YOU IDIOTS! LOOK THERE!
TWO VOODOOITES... CLUTCHING DOLLS OF US, CAPTAIN...
AND ABOUT TO PLUNGE NEEDLES INTO THEM!
A-A SHARP PAIN... IN MY SIDE...
MY STOMACH... BURNING UP!
HA, HA, HA... HO, HO!
CONTINUED...

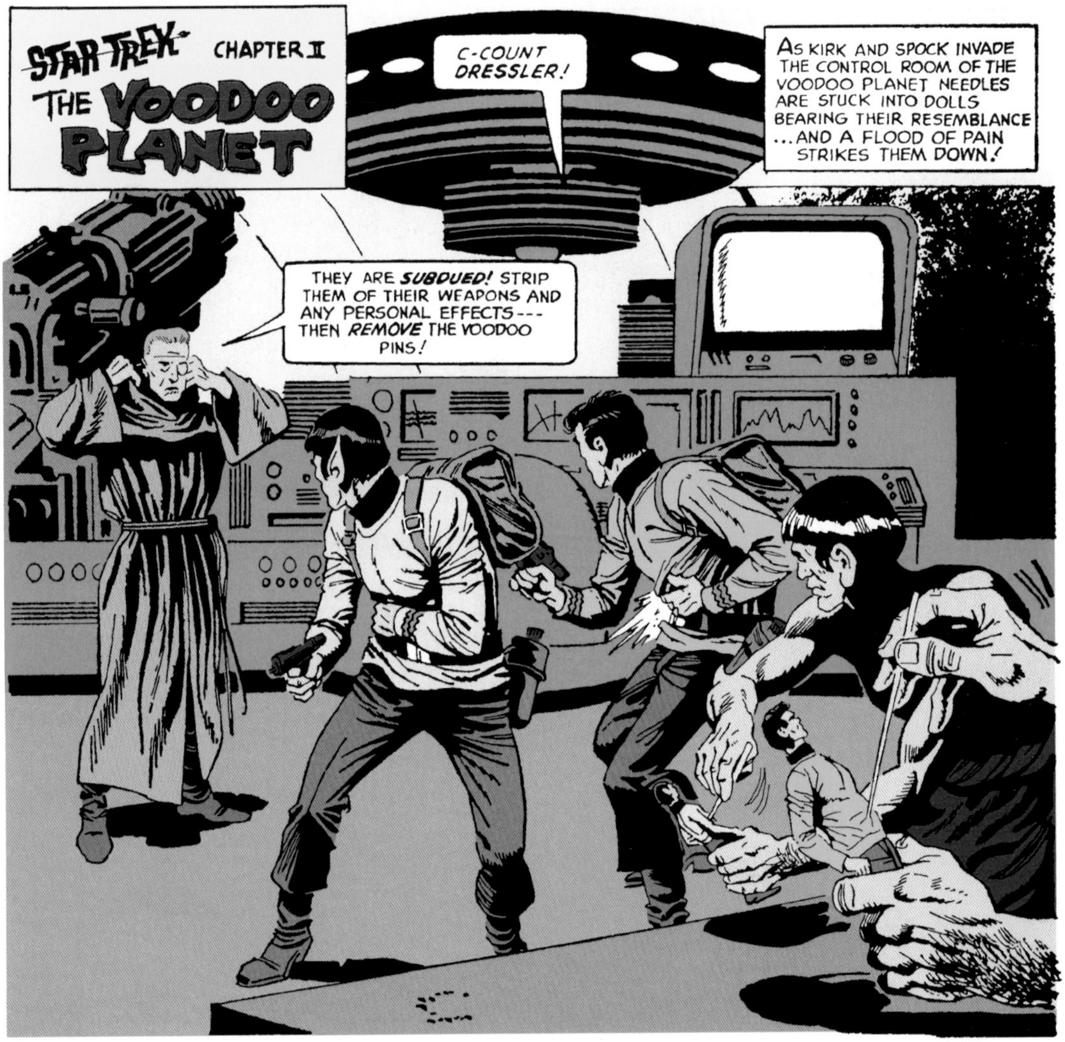
STAR TREK CHAPTER II
THE VOODOO PLANET
C-COUNT DRESSLER!
AS KIRK AND SPOCK INVADE THE CONTROL ROOM OF THE VOODOO PLANET NEEDLES ARE STUCK INTO DOLLS BEARING THEIR RESEMBLANCE ...AND A FLOOD OF PAIN STRIKES THEM DOWN!
THEY ARE SUBDUED! STRIP THEM OF THEIR WEAPONS AND ANY PERSONAL EFFECTS--- THEN REMOVE THE VOODOO PINS!

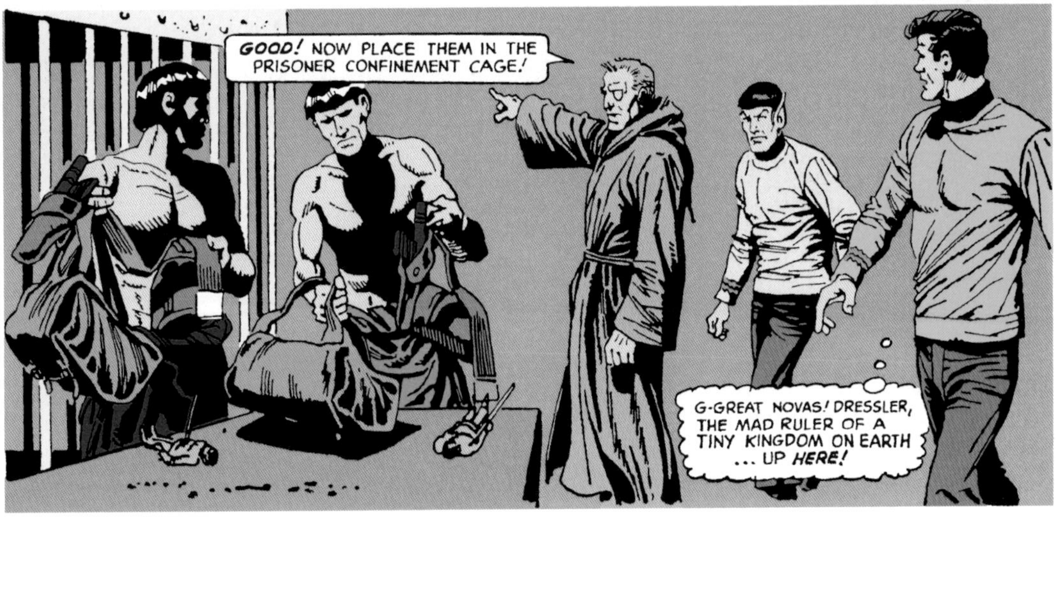
GOOD! NOW PLACE THEM IN THE PRISONER CONFINEMENT CAGE!
G-GREAT NOVAS! DRESSLER, THE MAD RULER OF A TINY KINGDOM ON EARTH ... UP HERE!

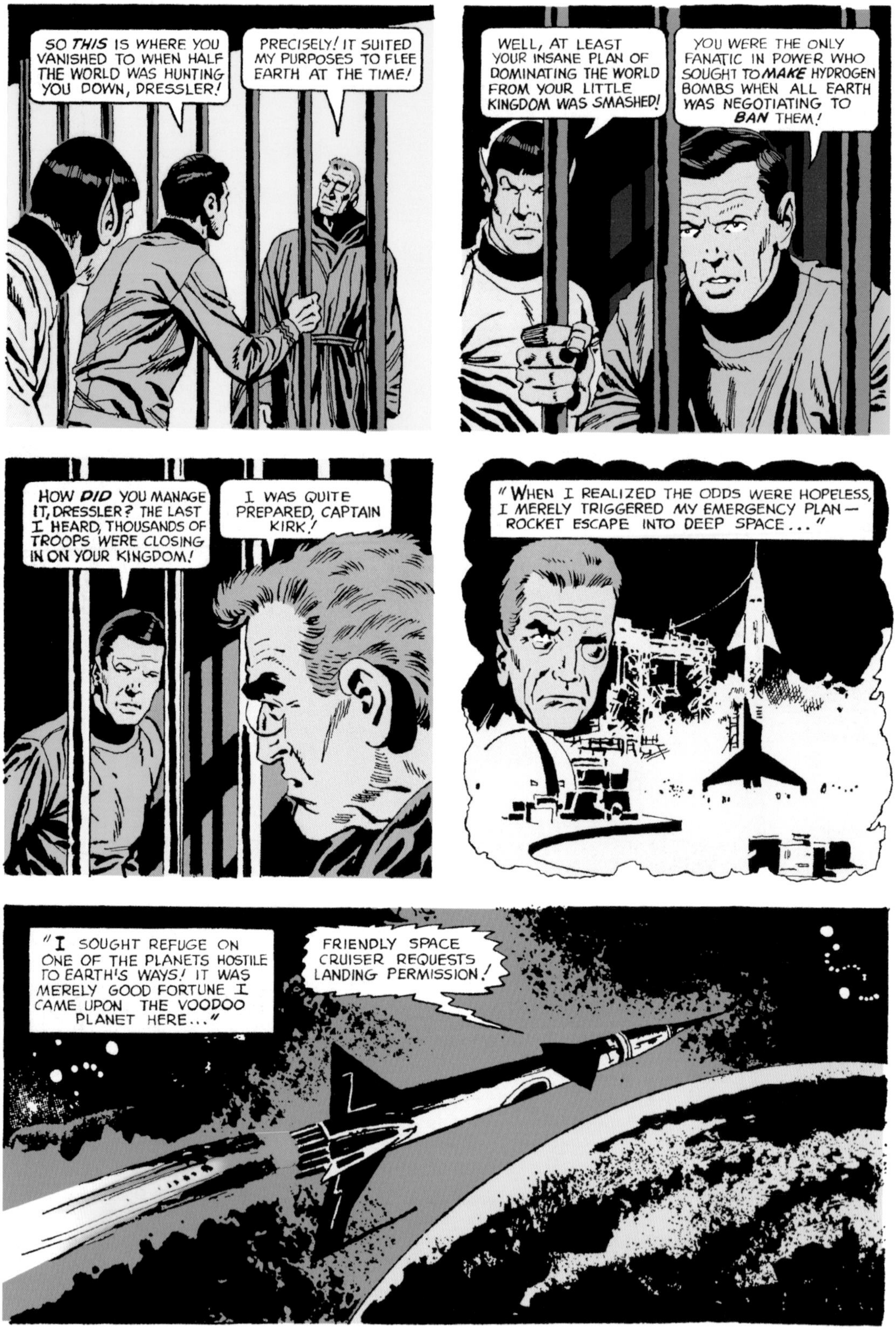

SO THIS IS WHERE YOU VANISHED TO WHEN HALF THE WORLD WAS HUNTING YOU DOWN, DRESSLER!
PRECISELY! IT SUITED MY PURPOSES TO FLEE EARTH AT THE TIME!
WELL, AT LEAST YOUR INSANE PLAN OF DOMINATING THE WORLD FROM YOUR LITTLE KINGDOM WAS SMASHED!
YOU WERE THE ONLY FANATIC IN POWER WHO SOUGHT TO MAKE HYDROGEN BOMBS WHEN ALL EARTH WAS NEGOTIATING TO BAN THEM!
HOW DID YOU MANAGE IT, DRESSLER? THE LAST I HEARD, THOUSANDS OF TROOPS WERE CLOSING IN ON YOUR KINGDOM!
I WAS QUITE PREPARED, CAPTAIN KIRK!
"WHEN I REALIZED THE ODDS WERE HOPELESS, I MERELY TRIGGERED MY EMERGENCY PLAN— ROCKET ESCAPE INTO DEEP SPACE..."
"I SOUGHT REFUGE ON ONE OF THE PLANETS HOSTILE TO EARTH'S WAYS! IT WAS MERELY GOOD FORTUNE I CAME UPON THE VOODOO PLANET HERE..."
FRIENDLY SPACE CRUISER REQUESTS LANDING PERMISSION!

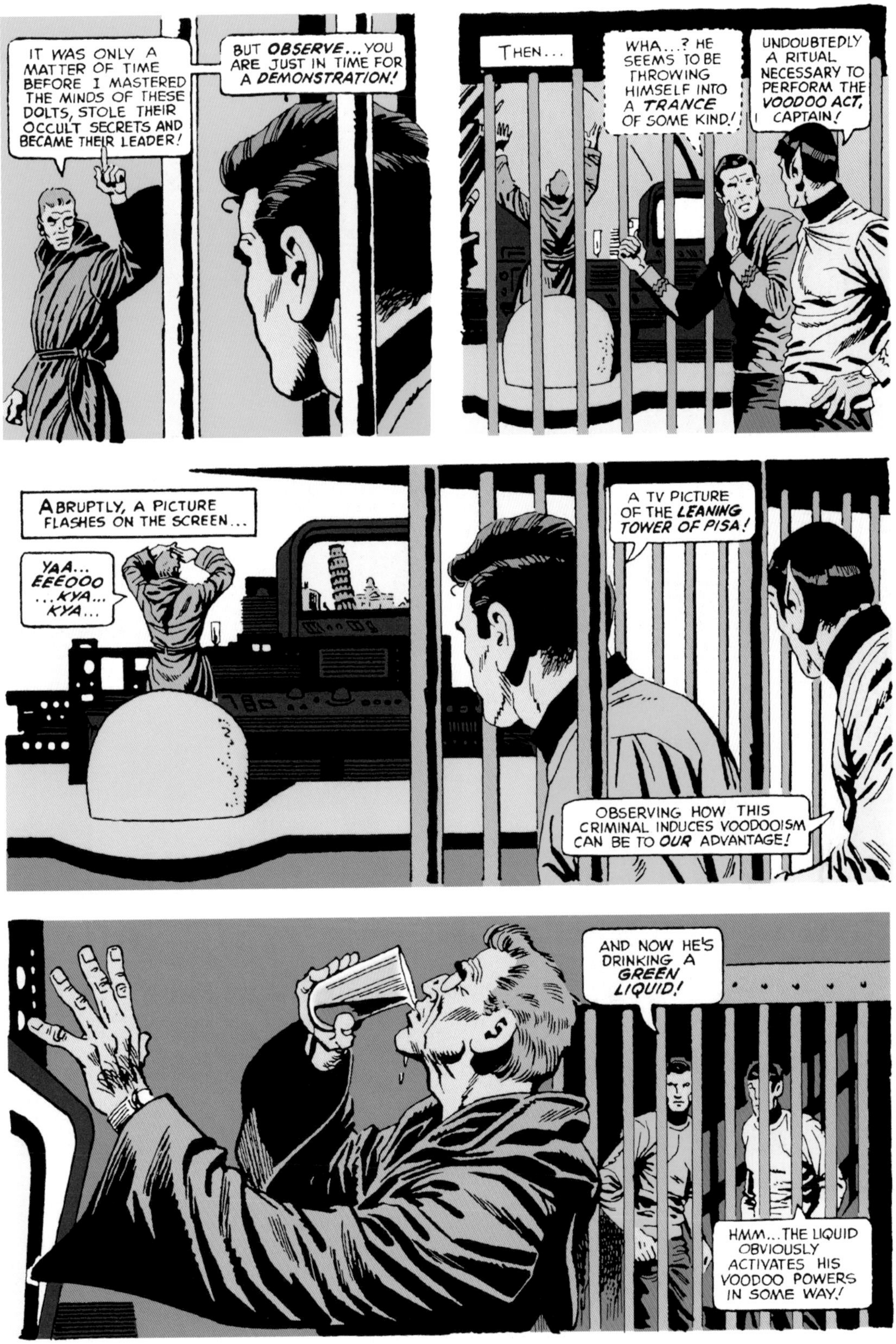
IT WAS ONLY A MATTER OF TIME BEFORE I MASTERED THE MINDS OF THESE DOLTS, STOLE THEIR OCCULT SECRETS AND BECAME THEIR LEADER!
BUT OBSERVE... YOU ARE JUST IN TIME FOR A DEMONSTRATION!
THEN...
WHA...? HE SEEMS TO BE THROWING HIMSELF INTO A TRANCE OF SOME KIND!
UNDOUBTEDLY A RITUAL NECESSARY TO PERFORM THE VOODOO ACT, CAPTAIN!
ABRUPTLY, A PICTURE FLASHES ON THE SCREEN...
YAA... EEEOOO ...KYA... KYA...
A TV PICTURE OF THE LEANING TOWER OF PISA!
OBSERVING HOW THIS CRIMINAL INDUCES VOODOOISM CAN BE TO OUR ADVANTAGE!
AND NOW HE'S DRINKING A GREEN LIQUID!
HMM... THE LIQUID OBVIOUSLY ACTIVATES HIS VOODOO POWERS IN SOME WAY!

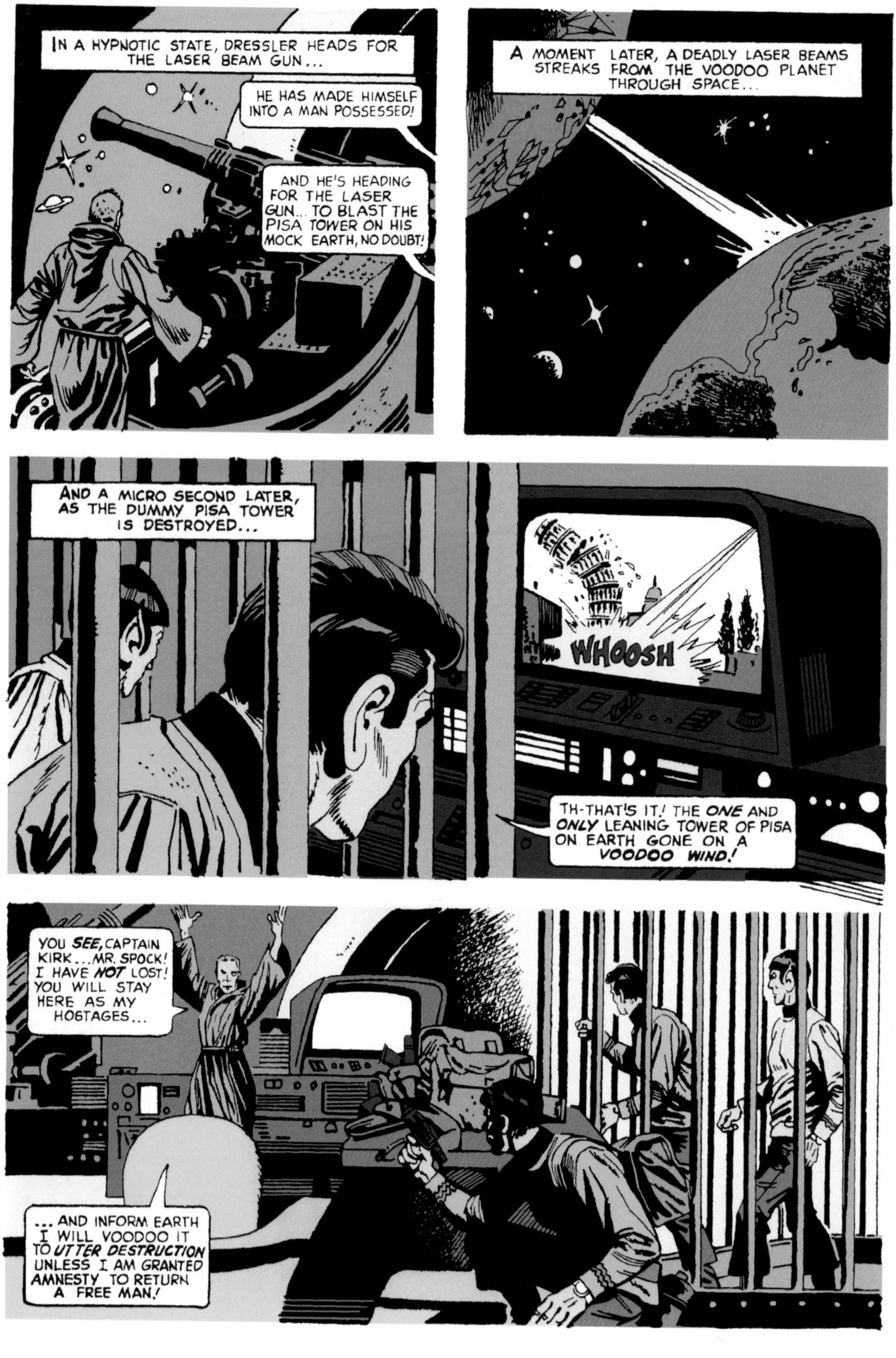
IN A HYPNOTIC STATE, DRESSLER HEADS FOR THE LASER BEAM GUN...
HE HAS MADE HIMSELF INTO A MAN POSSESSED!
AND HE'S HEADING FOR THE LASER GUN... TO BLAST THE PISA TOWER ON HIS MOCK EARTH, NO DOUBT!
A MOMENT LATER, A DEADLY LASER BEAMS STREAKS FROM THE VOODOO PLANET THROUGH SPACE...
AND A MICRO SECOND LATER, AS THE DUMMY PISA TOWER IS DESTROYED...
WHOOSH
TH-THAT'S IT! THE ONE AND ONLY LEANING TOWER OF PISA ON EARTH GONE ON A VOODOO WIND!
YOU SEE, CAPTAIN KIRK... MR. SPOCK! I HAVE NOT LOST! YOU WILL STAY HERE AS MY HOSTAGES...
... AND INFORM EARTH I WILL VOODOO IT TO UTTER DESTRUCTION UNLESS I AM GRANTED AMNESTY TO RETURN A FREE MAN!

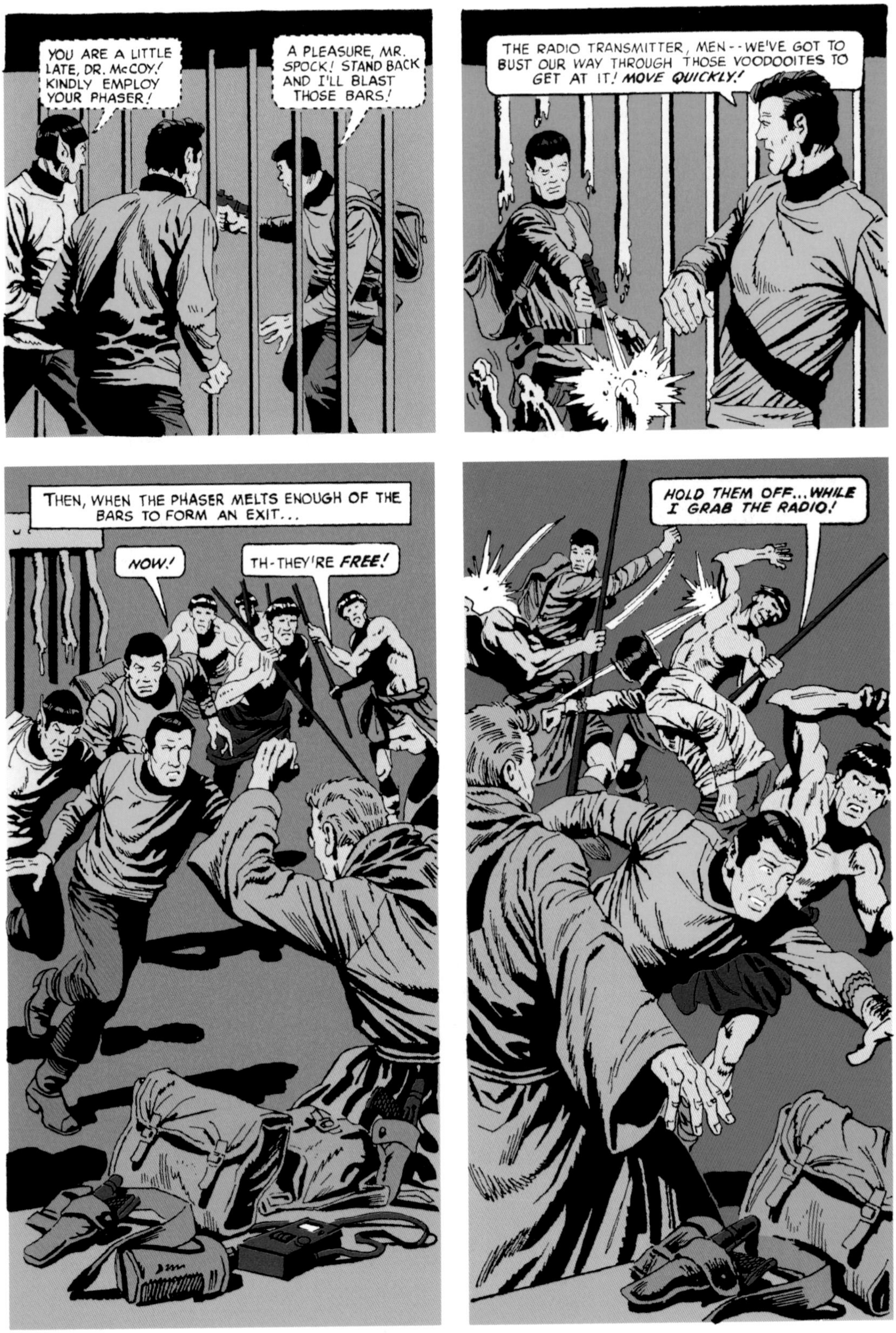
YOU ARE A LITTLE LATE, DR. McCOY! KINDLY EMPLOY YOUR PHASER!
A PLEASURE, MR. SPOCK! STAND BACK AND I'LL BLAST THOSE BARS!
THE RADIO TRANSMITTER, MEN--WE'VE GOT TO BUST OUR WAY THROUGH THOSE VOODOOITES TO GET AT IT! MOVE QUICKLY!
THEN, WHEN THE PHASER MELTS ENOUGH OF THE BARS TO FORM AN EXIT...
NOW!
TH-THEY'RE FREE!
HOLD THEM OFF...WHILE I GRAB THE RADIO!

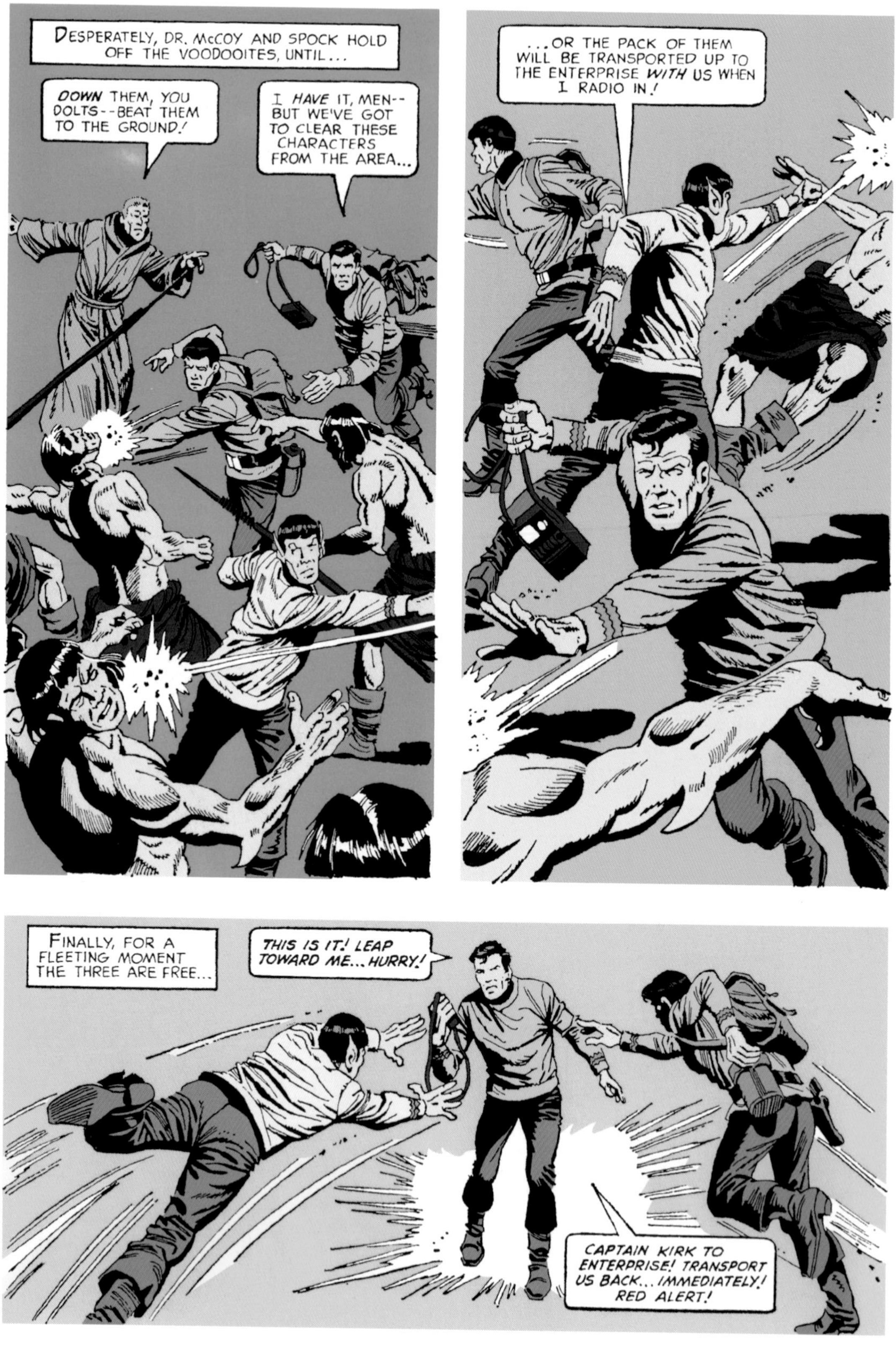
DESPERATELY, DR. McCOY AND SPOCK HOLD OFF THE VOODOOITES, UNTIL...
DOWN THEM, YOU DOLTS--BEAT THEM TO THE GROUND!
I HAVE IT, MEN--BUT WE'VE GOT TO CLEAR THESE CHARACTERS FROM THE AREA...
...OR THE PACK OF THEM WILL BE TRANSPORTED UP TO THE ENTERPRISE WITH US WHEN I RADIO IN!
FINALLY, FOR A FLEETING MOMENT THE THREE ARE FREE...
THIS IS IT! LEAP TOWARD ME... HURRY!
CAPTAIN KIRK TO ENTERPRISE! TRANSPORT US BACK... IMMEDIATELY! RED ALERT!

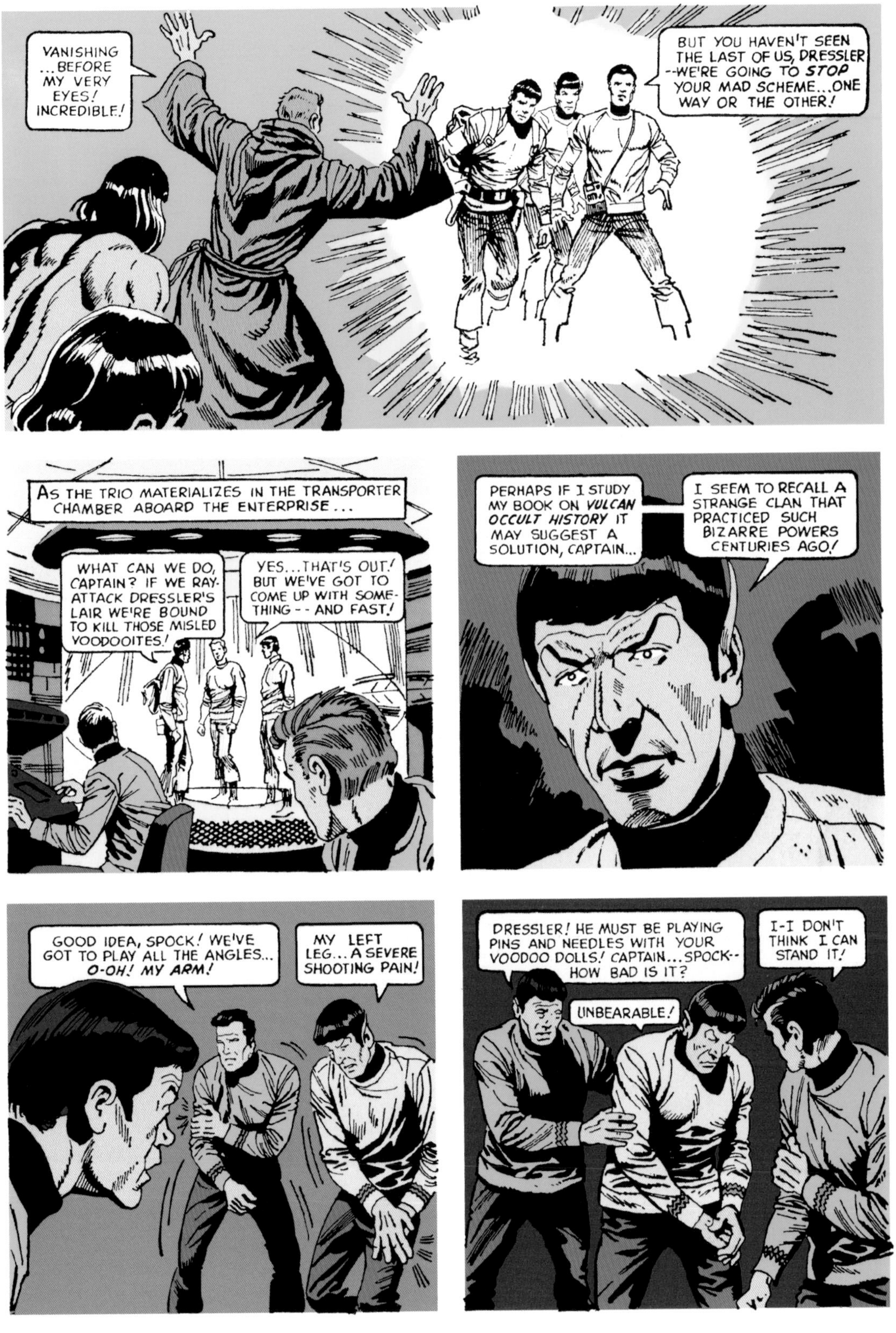
VANISHING ...BEFORE MY VERY EYES! INCREDIBLE!
BUT YOU HAVEN'T SEEN THE LAST OF US, DRESSLER --WE'RE GOING TO STOP YOUR MAD SCHEME...ONE WAY OR THE OTHER!
AS THE TRIO MATERIALIZES IN THE TRANSPORTER CHAMBER ABOARD THE ENTERPRISE...
WHAT CAN WE DO, CAPTAIN? IF WE RAY-ATTACK DRESSLER'S LAIR WE'RE BOUND TO KILL THOSE MISLED VOODOOITES!
YES...THAT'S OUT! BUT WE'VE GOT TO COME UP WITH SOMETHING -- AND FAST!
PERHAPS IF I STUDY MY BOOK ON VULCAN OCCULT HISTORY IT MAY SUGGEST A SOLUTION, CAPTAIN...
I SEEM TO RECALL A STRANGE CLAN THAT PRACTICED SUCH BIZARRE POWERS CENTURIES AGO!
GOOD IDEA, SPOCK! WE'VE GOT TO PLAY ALL THE ANGLES... O-OH! MY ARM!
MY LEFT LEG...A SEVERE SHOOTING PAIN!
DRESSLER! HE MUST BE PLAYING PINS AND NEEDLES WITH YOUR VOODOO DOLLS! CAPTAIN...SPOCK-- HOW BAD IS IT?
I-I DON'T THINK I CAN STAND IT!
UNBEARABLE!

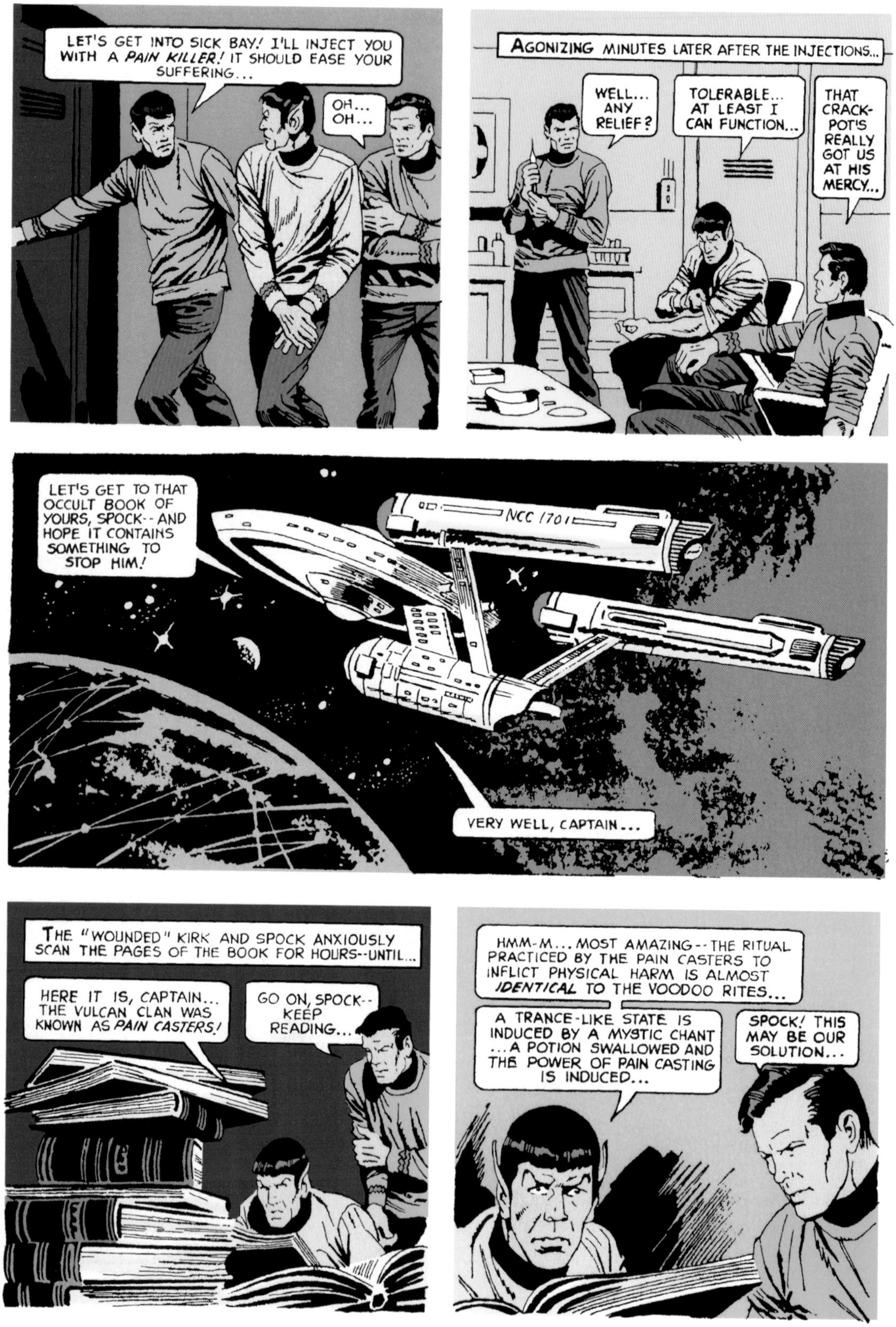

LET'S GET INTO SICK BAY! I'LL INJECT YOU WITH A PAIN KILLER! IT SHOULD EASE YOUR SUFFERING...
OH... OH...
AGONIZING MINUTES LATER AFTER THE INJECTIONS...
WELL... ANY RELIEF?
TOLERABLE... AT LEAST I CAN FUNCTION...
THAT CRACK-POT'S REALLY GOT US AT HIS MERCY...
LET'S GET TO THAT OCCULT BOOK OF YOURS, SPOCK-- AND HOPE IT CONTAINS SOMETHING TO STOP HIM!
NCC 1701
VERY WELL, CAPTAIN...
THE "WOUNDED" KIRK AND SPOCK ANXIOUSLY SCAN THE PAGES OF THE BOOK FOR HOURS--UNTIL...
HERE IT IS, CAPTAIN... THE VULCAN CLAN WAS KNOWN AS PAIN CASTERS!
GO ON, SPOCK-- KEEP READING...
HMM-M... MOST AMAZING-- THE RITUAL PRACTICED BY THE PAIN CASTERS TO INFLICT PHYSICAL HARM IS ALMOST IDENTICAL TO THE VOODOO RITES...
A TRANCE-LIKE STATE IS INDUCED BY A MYSTIC CHANT ...A POTION SWALLOWED AND THE POWER OF PAIN CASTING IS INDUCED...
SPOCK! THIS MAY BE OUR SOLUTION...

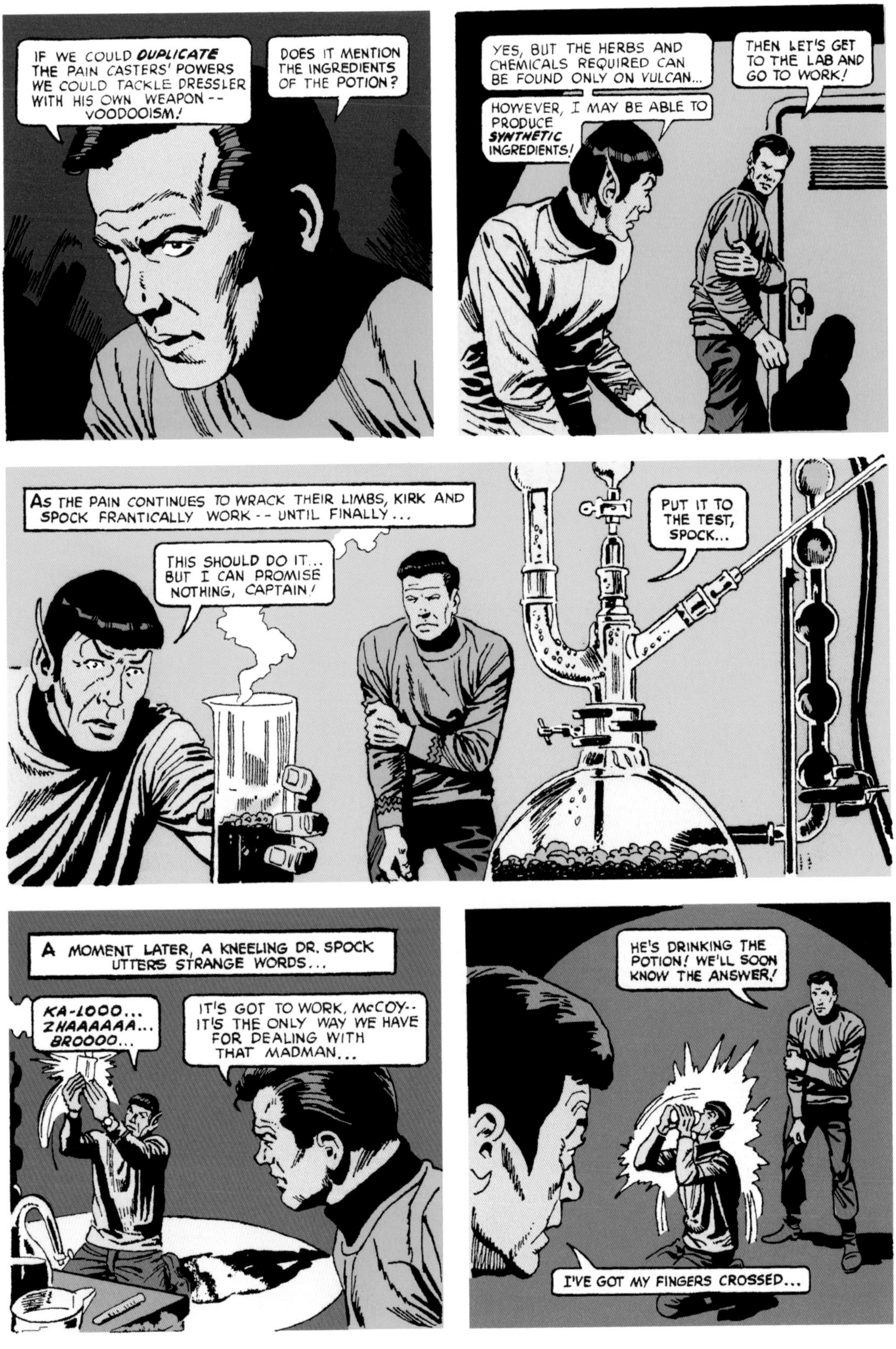
IF WE COULD DUPLICATE THE PAIN CASTERS' POWERS WE COULD TACKLE DRESSLER WITH HIS OWN WEAPON -- VOODOOISM!
DOES IT MENTION THE INGREDIENTS OF THE POTION?
YES, BUT THE HERBS AND CHEMICALS REQUIRED CAN BE FOUND ONLY ON VULCAN...
HOWEVER, I MAY BE ABLE TO PRODUCE SYNTHETIC INGREDIENTS!
THEN LET'S GET TO THE LAB AND GO TO WORK!
AS THE PAIN CONTINUES TO WRACK THEIR LIMBS, KIRK AND SPOCK FRANTICALLY WORK -- UNTIL FINALLY...
THIS SHOULD DO IT... BUT I CAN PROMISE NOTHING, CAPTAIN!
PUT IT TO THE TEST, SPOCK...
A MOMENT LATER, A KNEELING DR. SPOCK UTTERS STRANGE WORDS...
KA-LOOO... ZHAAAAAA... BROOOO...
IT'S GOT TO WORK, McCOY-- IT'S THE ONLY WAY WE HAVE FOR DEALING WITH THAT MADMAN...
HE'S DRINKING THE POTION! WE'LL SOON KNOW THE ANSWER!
I'VE GOT MY FINGERS CROSSED...

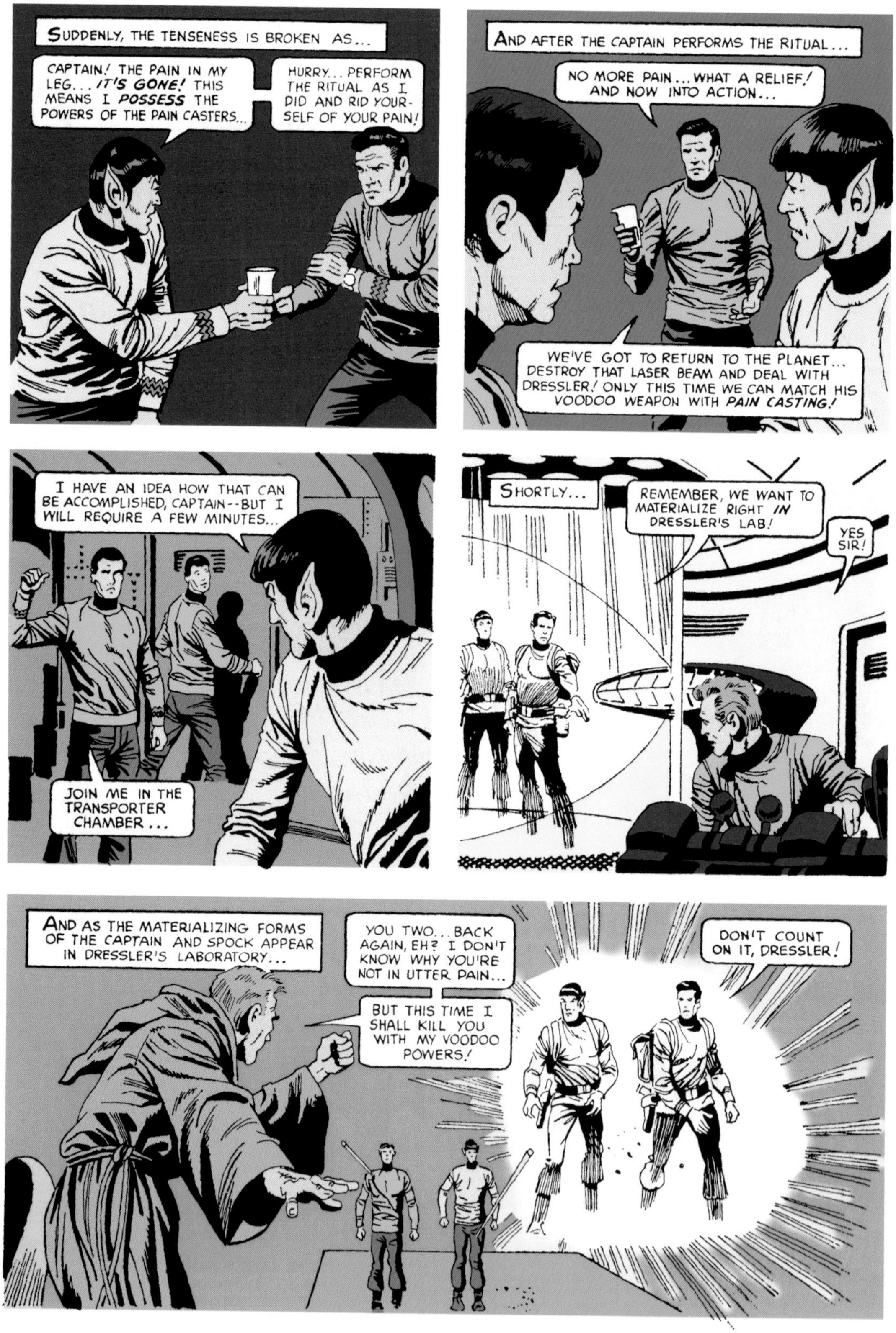
SUDDENLY, THE TENSENESS IS BROKEN AS...
CAPTAIN! THE PAIN IN MY LEG... IT'S GONE! THIS MEANS I POSSESS THE POWERS OF THE PAIN CASTERS...
HURRY... PERFORM THE RITUAL AS I DID AND RID YOURSELF OF YOUR PAIN!
AND AFTER THE CAPTAIN PERFORMS THE RITUAL...
NO MORE PAIN... WHAT A RELIEF! AND NOW INTO ACTION...
WE'VE GOT TO RETURN TO THE PLANET... DESTROY THAT LASER BEAM AND DEAL WITH DRESSLER! ONLY THIS TIME WE CAN MATCH HIS VOODOO WEAPON WITH PAIN CASTING!
I HAVE AN IDEA HOW THAT CAN BE ACCOMPLISHED, CAPTAIN--BUT I WILL REQUIRE A FEW MINUTES...
JOIN ME IN THE TRANSPORTER CHAMBER...
SHORTLY...
REMEMBER, WE WANT TO MATERIALIZE RIGHT IN DRESSLER'S LAB!
YES SIR!
AND AS THE MATERIALIZING FORMS OF THE CAPTAIN AND SPOCK APPEAR IN DRESSLER'S LABORATORY...
YOU TWO... BACK AGAIN, EH? I DON'T KNOW WHY YOU'RE NOT IN UTTER PAIN...
BUT THIS TIME I SHALL KILL YOU WITH MY VOODOO POWERS!
DON'T COUNT ON IT, DRESSLER!

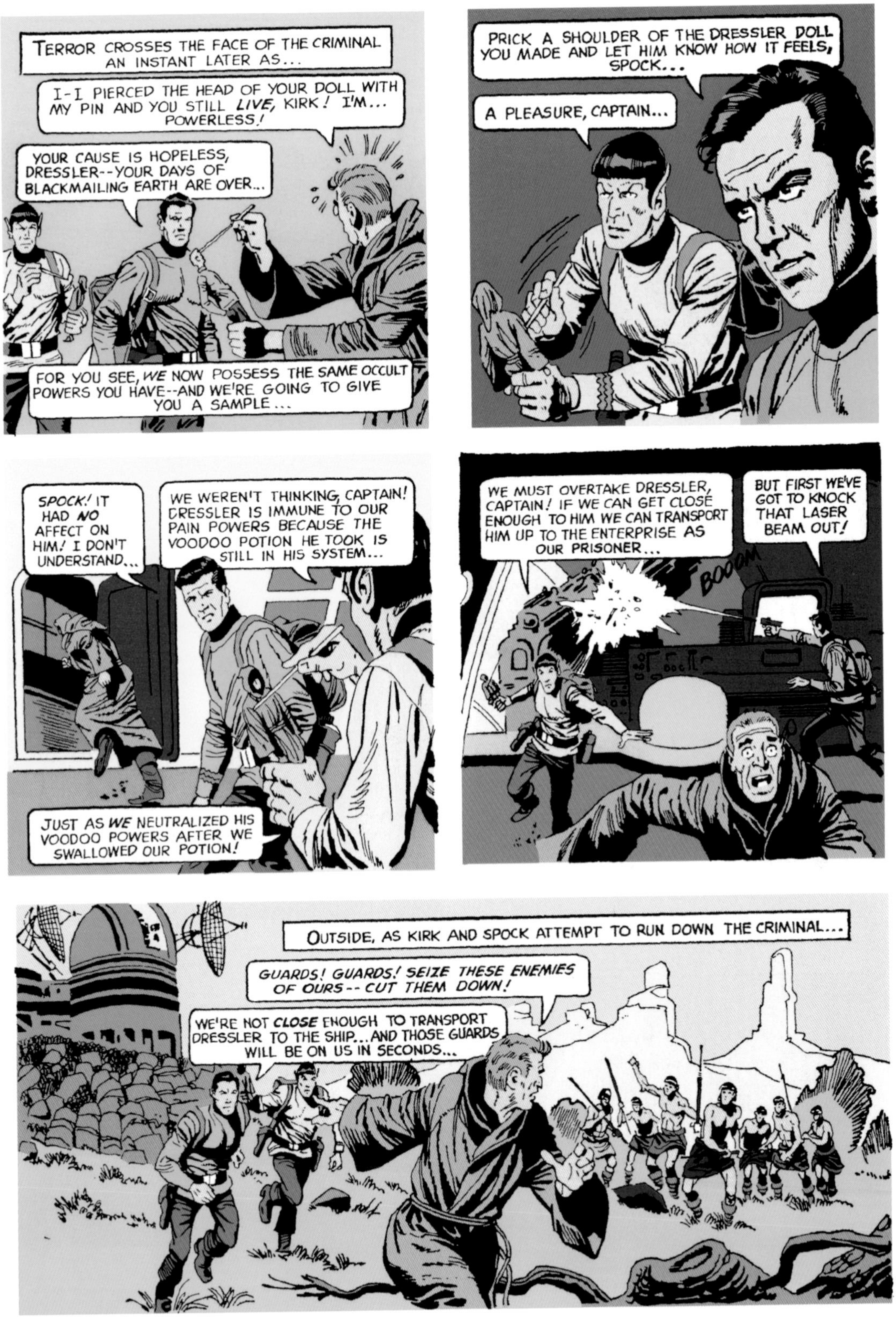
TERROR CROSSES THE FACE OF THE CRIMINAL AN INSTANT LATER AS...
I-I PIERCED THE HEAD OF YOUR DOLL WITH MY PIN AND YOU STILL LIVE, KIRK! I'M... POWERLESS!
YOUR CAUSE IS HOPELESS, DRESSLER--YOUR DAYS OF BLACKMAILING EARTH ARE OVER...
FOR YOU SEE, WE NOW POSSESS THE SAME OCCULT POWERS YOU HAVE--AND WE'RE GOING TO GIVE YOU A SAMPLE...
PRICK A SHOULDER OF THE DRESSLER DOLL YOU MADE AND LET HIM KNOW HOW IT FEELS, SPOCK...
A PLEASURE, CAPTAIN...
SPOCK! IT HAD NO AFFECT ON HIM! I DON'T UNDERSTAND...
WE WEREN'T THINKING, CAPTAIN! DRESSLER IS IMMUNE TO OUR PAIN POWERS BECAUSE THE VOODOO POTION HE TOOK IS STILL IN HIS SYSTEM...
JUST AS WE NEUTRALIZED HIS VOODOO POWERS AFTER WE SWALLOWED OUR POTION!
WE MUST OVERTAKE DRESSLER, CAPTAIN! IF WE CAN GET CLOSE ENOUGH TO HIM WE CAN TRANSPORT HIM UP TO THE ENTERPRISE AS OUR PRISONER...
BUT FIRST WE'VE GOT TO KNOCK THAT LASER BEAM OUT!
BOOOM
OUTSIDE, AS KIRK AND SPOCK ATTEMPT TO RUN DOWN THE CRIMINAL...
GUARDS! GUARDS! SEIZE THESE ENEMIES OF OURS -- CUT THEM DOWN!
WE'RE NOT CLOSE ENOUGH TO TRANSPORT DRESSLER TO THE SHIP... AND THOSE GUARDS WILL BE ON US IN SECONDS...

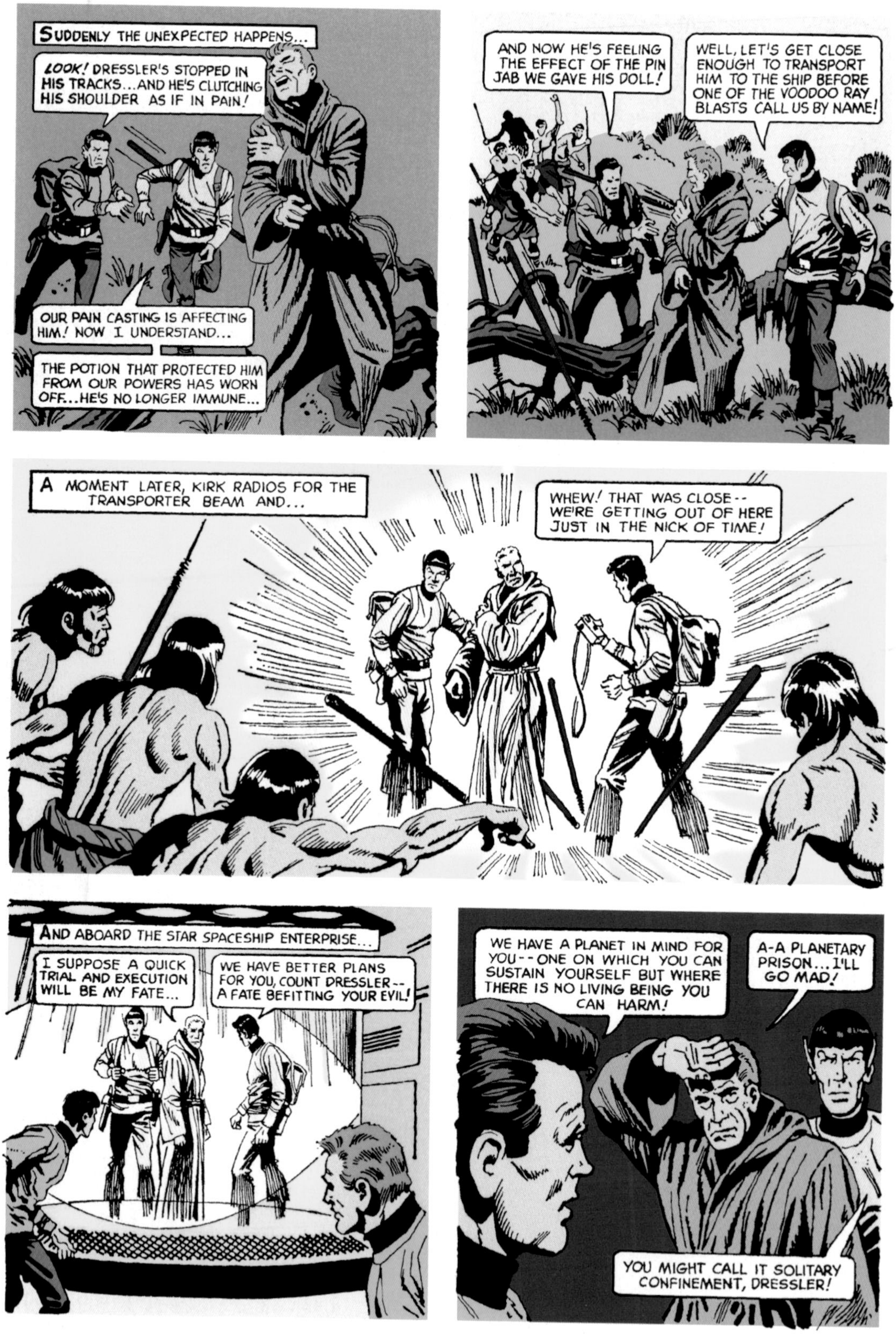
SUDDENLY THE UNEXPECTED HAPPENS...
LOOK! DRESSLER'S STOPPED IN HIS TRACKS...AND HE'S CLUTCHING HIS SHOULDER AS IF IN PAIN!
OUR PAIN CASTING IS AFFECTING HIM! NOW I UNDERSTAND...
THE POTION THAT PROTECTED HIM FROM OUR POWERS HAS WORN OFF...HE'S NO LONGER IMMUNE...
AND NOW HE'S FEELING THE EFFECT OF THE PIN JAB WE GAVE HIS DOLL!
WELL, LET'S GET CLOSE ENOUGH TO TRANSPORT HIM TO THE SHIP BEFORE ONE OF THE VOODOO RAY BLASTS CALL US BY NAME!
A MOMENT LATER, KIRK RADIOS FOR THE TRANSPORTER BEAM AND...
WHEW! THAT WAS CLOSE-- WE'RE GETTING OUT OF HERE JUST IN THE NICK OF TIME!
AND ABOARD THE STAR SPACESHIP ENTERPRISE...
I SUPPOSE A QUICK TRIAL AND EXECUTION WILL BE MY FATE...
WE HAVE BETTER PLANS FOR YOU, COUNT DRESSLER-- A FATE BEFITTING YOUR EVIL!
WE HAVE A PLANET IN MIND FOR YOU--ONE ON WHICH YOU CAN SUSTAIN YOURSELF BUT WHERE THERE IS NO LIVING BEING YOU CAN HARM!
A-A PLANETARY PRISON...I'LL GO MAD!
YOU MIGHT CALL IT SOLITARY CONFINEMENT, DRESSLER!

THE NEXT VOLUME OF THE **STAR TREK** GRAPHIC NOVEL COLLECTION...

STAR TREK: **STARFLEET ACADEMY**

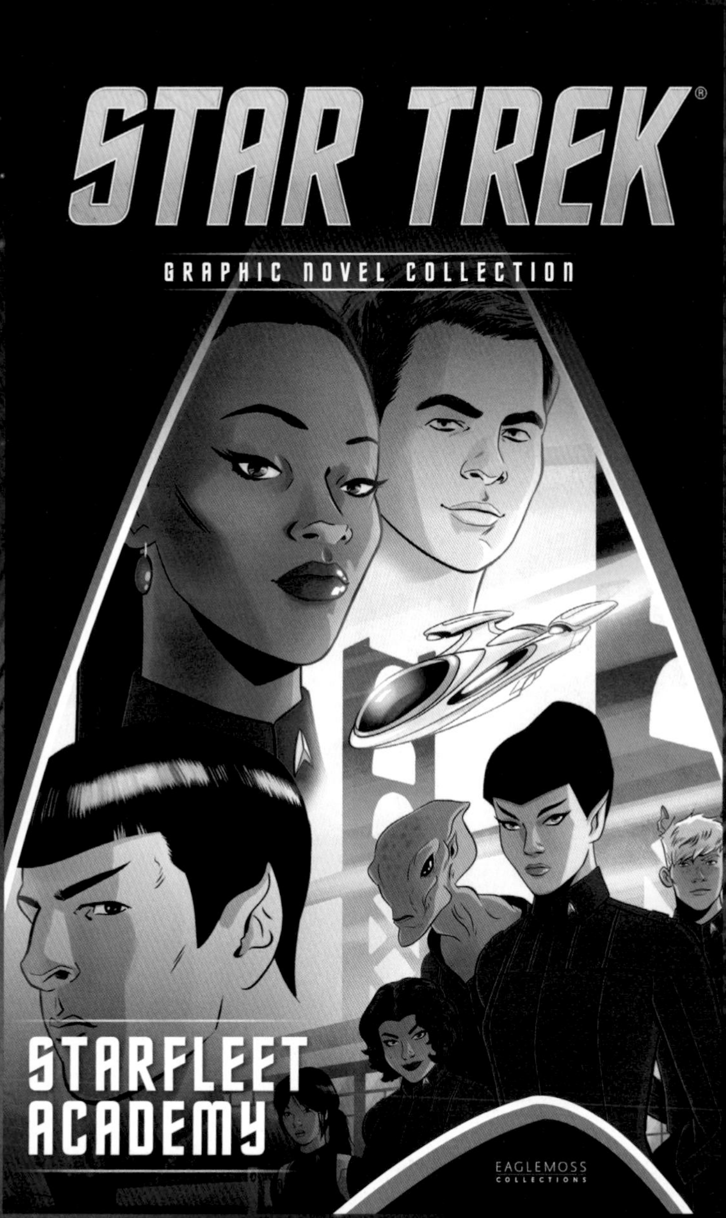
STAR TREK®
GRAPHIC NOVEL COLLECTION
STARFLEET ACADEMY
EAGLEMOSS COLLECTIONS

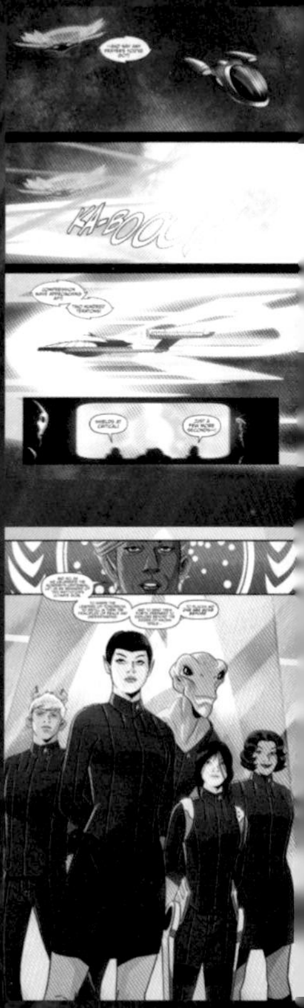

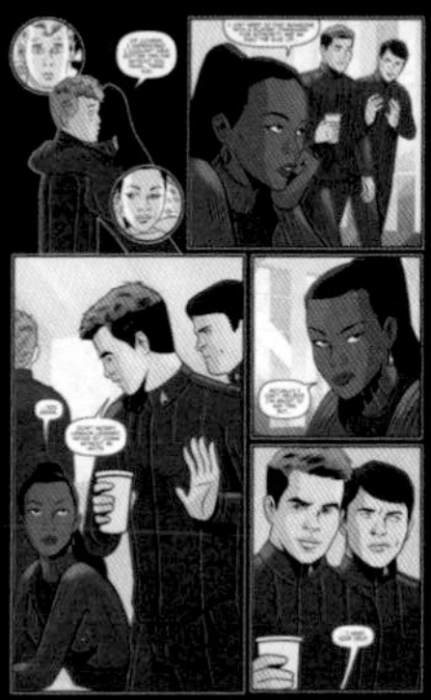

PLUS Issue 8 from The Gold Key Archives, from September 1970: **THE YOUTH TRAP**

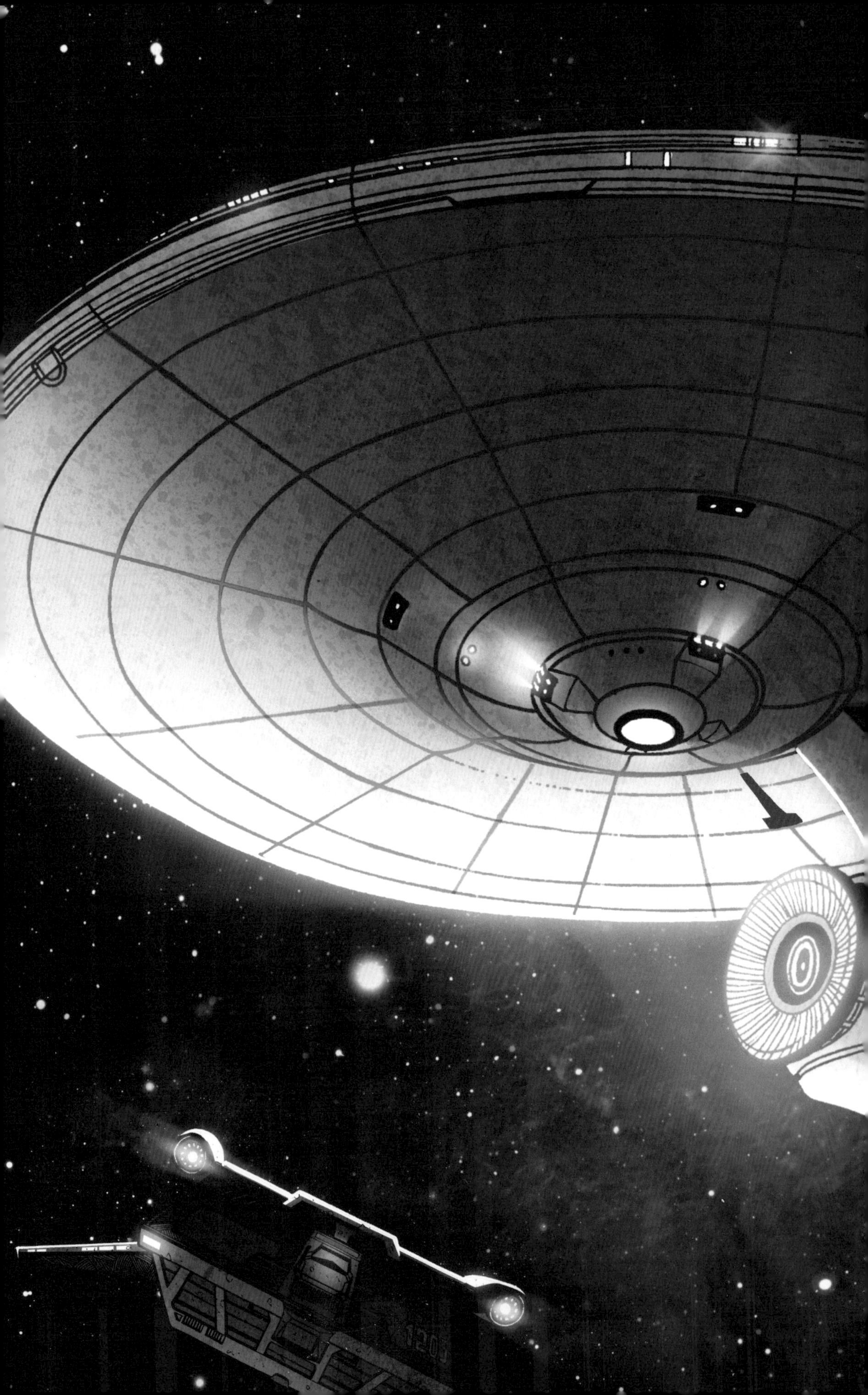